Food Security and Food Sovereignty Challenges in Africa

Edited By

Lere Amusan

Food Security and Food Sovereignty Challenges in Africa

Edited by Lere Amusan

This book first published 2022

Ethics International Press Ltd, UK

British Library Cataloguing in Publication Data

A catalogue record for this book is available from the British Library

Print Book ISBN: 978-1-80441-050-9

eBook ISBN: 978-1-80441-051-6

TABLE OF CONTENTS

Introduction

There is no doubt that Africa is in a crisis of food security. Talking about food sovereignty[1] has become a nightmare for the continent from the time of colonialism because the continent is producing what it does not consume and consumes what Africa can hardly produce, although Africa is considered a potential food basket for the global system. This instability is caused by myriads of factors ranging from the inability of the African government to take action on the climate in terms of investing in technologies that can resolve inherent challenges associated with harsh weather and atmosphere. In addition, the undue influence of the introduction of genetically modified organisms (GMOs), which tends to increase food production at the expense of good health and nutritional stability of consumers. This invariably weakens Africa's food sovereignty. The reality is that most farmers in the continent have been highly influenced by the new media advertisements in favour of GMOs due to the profitability of quantity food-producing out of the inorganic plants and animals. This eventually promotes humanitarian aids with an emphasis on food from developed states since farmers in many of the African states focus on animal feeds and alternatives to fossil fuel crops (Cotula, 2013; FAO, 2012; Love and Bryant, 2017). This is at the cost of food sovereignty that agroecological and regenerative farming is in favour of. Africa supposes to be a food sovereign considering her arable lands, resources, and conducive atmosphere for food and cash crops, but the reverse has been the case due to poor collaborative actions on the climate and profiteering interests of Big Data companies in Africa. This has occasioned recurrent cases of hunger and malnutrition in any part of the continent. However, little did some students and experts in food security realise that

[1] Food security is a situation where there is availability, affordability and accessibility of quantity and quality food for human consumption; it may be from within a state or imported from another state/s. On the other hand, food sovereignty is a state self-sufficient in food production both in quality and quantity without relying on other state/s before feeding its population. Other attributes of it are healthy and culturally appropriate food produced through ecologically sound and sustainable manner. For more understanding of this concept, see Seminar, Sarwoprasodjo, Kinseng, and Santosa, 2018; Tilzey, 2018;

the artificiality in GMOs is partly the leading cause of health challenges such as obesity, hypertension, diabetes, kidney stones and other related health problems (Amusan, 2019a, 2019b; Paarlberg, 2013). This state of ignorance, not only contribute to food insecurity and food fraud but also impedes food sovereignty in Africa. Food insecurity in the sense that, today Africa still suffer more from hunger and mal-nutrition partly because of consumption of food that weakens their immunity on the one hand and low productivity caused by the overreliance of farmers on foreign aids, assistance, and interventions from Multinational Corporations (MNCs), on the other hand (Amusan, 2014; 2017).

Thus, dependency on, and adoption of GMOs in parts of Africa is also partly the reason why food sovereignty is a big challenge. Although Africa can produce food, it lacks control of food productive mechanisms and policies. Most of what is obtainable as food mechanisms and policies are determined mostly by MNCs and their governments, especially, those from the Global North. These MNCs and their home governments are the major decision-making organs of food organisations such as the Food and Agriculture Organisation of the United Nations (FAO), International Fertiliser Development Centre (IFDC), among others. It has conferred them the opportunities to determine and control food mechanisms and policies of other countries, particularly, the developing areas. It limits efforts at promoting food sovereignty in Africa (Foer, 2017). This appalling development questions the saying that the adoption of GMOs in Africa will enhance increased food productivity, security and sovereignty, (Amusan, 2019a; Amusan, 2018; Bond, 2006; Collier, 2008). Unfortunately, the adoption of an inorganic food system by some countries did not address the growing problem of hunger and malnutrition. It led to what Amusan (2019b) described as mercy killing and thanksgiving; and food security with tears in Africa. This policy initiative, rather than achieve its expected ends, worsened the ugly situation of hunger and malnutrition in the continent. It is therefore difficult to achieve zero hunger in line with Sustainable Development Goal 2 when the indigenous peoples have no control of mechanisms and policies of food. The introduction of large-scale farming is not only violating the rights of the indigenous peoples through eviction and monocropping system, but it is also an agent of food fraud ever known in the history of mankind because of the profit ambition of the multinational agribusinesses (Chomsky, 1999; Howard, 2016; Otero, 2018). This development amounts to chronic dependency, which in turn, portrays the tendency of lack of food sovereignty. A good example of this scenario was brought to the fore by Amusan (2017), through research findings that particularly criticised the illegal looting of hoodia plants by countries in the Global North. Hoodia, an organic hunger and thirst suppressant, which could have sustained the San tribe in South Africa, in terms of contributing to their food sovereignty was processed and refined without the knowledge of the local San people who originally own the plant. This is not only the case in Africa as Patrick Bond elucidated in his book, *Looting Africa: The Economics of Exploitation*. Bond identified many plants and animals that are qualified for geographical indications (GIs), prior informed consent (PIC) and access sharing benefits (ASB), but tactically ignored a series of conventions and protocols that protect ecosystems and biodiversity in Africa (Amusan, 2017, 2014; Halabi, 2018; Moran, 2004). This development brings to the fore the need for food sovereignty in Africa, and questions interventions such as technological transfer, foreign aids, GMOs, politics in Africa. These interventions, apart from aggravating tendencies of dependency, capital flights, and myriads of challenges, severely undermines Africa's quest for food sovereignty. It questions the motive behind GMOs and other food security interventions from the West in Africa. This calls for a re-think in the dogmatic acceptance and belief in anything that comes from the Global North to Africa. It equally subjects the tenet of food security and sovereignty to robust intellectual discussions to critically map out a conducive and safer Africanize approach to food security.

Climate change and lack of collaborative actions by African governments are among the major sources of food insecurity and lack of food sovereignty in the continent. The Inter-Governmental Panel on Climate Change (IPCC) report identified that climate change is the leading cause of floods, heatwaves, desertification, violent winds, an outbreak of disease and food insecurity (Amusan, 2017). Food sovereignty is difficult to achieve under harsh weather conditions and lack of adaptation and mitigation strategies are the major cogs in food security discussion. Climate change equally contributes to political insecurity, for instance, the conflict in the Sahel region of Africa as a result of lack of access to productive natural resources of water and arable land for animals being captured by draught and in some cases flooding as a result of the interchangeable *El Nina* and *El Nino* effects in Africa. Vulnerability is another key issue in climate change, it is the extent of predisposition to biological, geophysical and socio-economic systems to the adverse impacts of climatic variability. Farmers in Africa have repeatedly suffered from climatic variability in the forms of erosion, flooding, drought, lack of, or excessive rain among others, these in themselves, are potential sources of food insecurity, which in the long run undermines food sovereignty in Africa. Following the submission of the IPCC (2007), on vulnerability, Brooks expatiate on its effects from two perspectives either as biophysical (ecological) or social, specifically in forms of socio-economic factors such as poor access to food, clean water, poverty, the poor state of technology, patterns of resource distribution, access to insurance against hazards, quality of housing, (Amusan, 2017).

It is also imperative to note that land distribution for commercial agricultural purposes and wealth accumulation hinders the process of food sovereignty in Africa. One of the reasons why Africa is named the food basket of the global system is her massive arable land resources. With this natural wealth, Africa is expected to feed the world and remain food sovereign, but the inordinate chase for wealth and commercialization of lands have made it very difficult for Africa to achieve food security let alone food sovereignty. This view aptly aligns with Carmody (2016) and Amusan (2019a) who argue that politics of allocation of land for commercial agriculture by the political elite class and the relegation of peasant farmers in the distribution of land for food production are some of the hitches in the wheel of Africa's food security.

The inability of Africa to take absolute control of mechanisms and policy for food calls for various approaches to address this problem. Food sovereignty became popular when international trade with a special focus on agriculture becomes a contentious issue from farmers subsidies to dumping politics of food in Africa and other developing areas. Food sovereignty raises two concerns namely: the ability to plan and define policies that will meet citizens' expectations as a priority, the ability to eliminate or reduce global dependency and a need to focus on national and regional needs. It is also important to note that it includes control of policies of food that do not permit dumping practices on other forms of agriculture. For instance, in Africa, attempts have been made to enhance food sovereignty, in the form of national policies and mechanisms that promote food sovereignty, but for the colonial hangover in the continent, this has not been managed effectively (Roger and Emmanuel, 2007).

However, food sovereignty in Africa suffers from few challenges such as lack of cooperation and collective action on climate to boost food production. Similarly, states and regional organisations in Africa that have believed in food sovereignty cannot sustain it. Although, the policy consultation process, may have enables producers' organizations to promote food sovereignty, but the regional and national institutions have not achieved positive outcomes in terms of gaining control of their food mechanisms and policies. These divergent views portray the fact that the concept of food sovereignty remains largely unclear. It fluctuates between the need to control food mechanisms of developing agriculture and states adequately protecting the community's preference. Another challenge is that food sovereignty appears to be more of a concept relevant at the regional scene than the national front, which negates the community control of food productive resources.

It is against this backdrop that this edited book examines the challenges of food security and food sovereignty in Africa. As an edited volume, contributors are from diverse backgrounds such as political science, international relations and diplomacy, public administration, agricultural science and rural extensions, economics and wildlife disciplines. Their various perspectives in looking into the problem bring about holistic approaches in the study of challenges of food security and sovereignty in Africa and proffer various solutions to the issues under discussion. One of the panaceas to food insecurity and lack of control over food productive resources is the need for a developed mechanism and the respective roles of states and donors while considering the autonomous decision-making and leadership aspects of food sovereignty. Also, more thorough debate on the compatibility of food sovereignty with access to food or the right to food. Although some states in Africa suffer from extreme diversification in food, some of them have devised the means of organising themselves into regional economic zones. But pieces of evidence show that these free trade zones do not in themselves promote food security (Roger and Emmanuel, 2007). Rather, other regional organisations from outside the continent are the beneficiary of the free trade agreements within Africa. An example of this is the European Union (EU) through misleading north-south cooperation of the African, Caribbean and Pacific (ACP) and EU unequal exchange relationship (Ighobor, 2014). The same applies to the blurry relationship between America and Africa that culminated in Africa Growth and Opportunity Act (AGOA). A case in point was the imposition of chicken importation on South Africa from America despite relatively developed poultry industry in the country and an understanding of south-south relations of the BRICS that promote chicken business between Brazil and South Africa (Amusan, 2019a). This significant setback the continent quest to promote food sovereignty and security.

Significance of the book

This edited volume advances knowledge in food security and food sovereignty for students of higher learning. This, as mentioned above, will benefit students of development studies, international relations, political science, human geography, sociology, indigenous knowledge systems, economics and agricultural sciences. It will also be useful for food security experts, government, ministries of agriculture, food-producing organizations, policymakers, policy analysts and serve as introductory textbooks to development studies in developing areas by those who are not familiar with Africa's food sovereignty challenges. It is carefully written to enhance understanding of food security and food sovereignty in Africa by known experts, practitioners, and scholars of political science, international relations, agricultural science, economics, public administration, with an interest in food security and climate change. The book will contribute to the body of knowledge when one contextualises the differences and similarities between seemingly the same concepts of food security and food sovereignty. It will deepen understanding of food fraud and MNCs' manipulations of food quality to the detriments of consumers. The book analyses and interprets field data and interrogate relevant literature, which forms the basis for decisions for improving food security and sovereignty in Africa by providing adequate information to advance new knowledge on the issue of international interdependency of unequal exchange and inactions of government against dumping of food through various guise. It will also contribute to a better understanding of the negative implications of GMOs on numerous health challenges across African states. Of relevance to the book is the need to understand why Africa ought to determine and control its food mechanisms and policies for positive outcomes on food sovereignty. Proposing for food sovereignty, where states in Africa control their food production resources and mechanisms will significantly contribute to sustainable development in the reduction of hunger and malnutrition in line with SDGs 1,2 and 3 specifically as well as to reduce the rate of capital flight from Africa. It is hoped that specific collaborative government actions on climate change policies suggestions on how to enhance food security and sovereignty and develop relevant strong institutions to pursue this drive are among the importance of the edited volume. This book will also examine the roles of relevant stakeholders in food security including local Non-Governmental Organisations (NGOs) working with African communities to achieve food sovereignty. This volume is being proposed at a time when Africa is battling with the effects of challenges of Covid-19, climate change, food insecurity and food sovereignty. Scholarly suggestions and measures in this edited book will go a long way in enhancing a better option to achieve food sovereignty and food security in Africa.

The organisation of the book

As indicated in this proposal, this book project is an edited work with seventeen chapters, which starts with the general discussion as a matter of introduction about the book. This is followed by Chapter one by Isa Ishaq Ojibara, which covers food security and climate change in Sub-Sharan Africa. He examines issues that are important to the overall focus of the study to enhance understanding of the conceptual misunderstandings concerning this study and inquiry. It also examines, albeit briefly, the basic understanding of climate change and food security. This chapter submits that despite the low contribution of Africa to the emission of Carbon dioxide (CO_2) globally, it bears the heaviest impacts of climate change with no technology in the form of climate adaptation and mitigation unlike the developed states of the north. The chapter concludes that there is a need for appropriate technology transfer from the north to Africa to address the twin concepts of adaptation and mitigation for sustainable food security.

Moving from this chapter is a discussion by Phemelo Olifile Marumo, who examines food security and sovereignty from a philosophical perspective, the chapter, philosophically reviews food security and sustainable development in Africa. Marumo is of the view that biblically, sustainable development was initiated at the Garden of Eden wherein humanity was mandated to look after the earth and preserve it for the future generation. However, things did not turn as planned and the earth was subjected to other exploitative measures that affected food security and other aspects like environmental changes. Food security is the basis of human life based on the provision of sustainable development of both the environment and humanity. Sustainable development can only be achieved and maintained if the available land and resources are preserved so that they can accommodate the present habitat and still be left for future generations. Thus, it is good for the land to be preserved at all costs. In that way, preservation thereof will in a way provide for the provision of food security. However, due to the present circumstances like earth erosion and lack of earth preservation the substance of food security is threatened and in many cases faces extinction. From the premise, the chapter outline the background surrounding the Earth as the Mother and the supplier of food security, which will be followed by how the earth as the Mother assist in sustainable development. It will further propel to dwell on philosophical review, in which it will give a scenario on the potential damages if a pattern of exploitation of the earth at the expense of health erosion and lack of land preservation perpetuates. Thereafter, the chapter comes with recommendations that could assist the sustainability of food security in South Africa.

Chapter three authored by Lere Amusan and Samuel Chukwudi Agunyai examines food security in Africa without women: a *sine qua non* for food insecurity. The authors of this chapter argued that studies in food security showed that women contribute half of the agricultural labour in food production in rural areas of most African states. They play a critical role in all core areas of food security-availability, accessibility, and utilization. Their expertise in the production and discovery of food with high nutrients has helped to reduce hunger and the number of malnourished people in Africa. But abounding evidence shows that women's critical role in food security is hardly rewarded because of the perceived notion that they are mere agricultural assistants to their male farmer husbands. Added to this, is the fact that they are wrongly perceived to be less productive than the male farmers, and when it comes to the issue of policy formulation and execution, men are traditionally expected to lead, though they may not know what exactly is needed to improve food production that eventually lead to good nutrition. This phenomenon had provoked studies aimed at correcting gender-inequality in agricultural food production in Africa, but information on the effects of exclusion of women in policy formulation and implementation on food insecurity in Africa is scarcely available. The leitmotif of this paper is to examine some cogs in food insecurity with emphasis on lack of access to farm inputs coupled with climate variability and infrastructural amenities deficits to bring about unperturbed transportation of farm products to market. In doing this, the chapter adopts constructivism theory and secondary sources of data as our departing points.

Olajumoke Adeyeye, Monica Orisadare, Ayobami Atijosan and Oluwatoyin Olajide in chapter four further discussion on women in farming and food security. They interrogate gender-inclusive development in rural settings: reframing the issues in the African context. The authors of the chapter argued that gender inequalities remain a common phenomenon hindering transformative changes in many rural communities in Africa, especially in areas of food security and sovereignty. This chapter advances knowledge on how to identify key challenges with gender-based interventions and proposes an analytical framework that can lead to gender-inclusive and transformative changes in rural areas. This framework is based on the multidimensional concept of empowerment, which is seen as a dynamic process rather than an outcome. It focuses on individual agency, resources, institutional environment and other structural and non-state actors at micro and macro levels, which have consequences for agricultural interventions in rural contexts. The authors, averred as a matter of conclusion, that the essence of agricultural intervention programs that seek to bridge the gender gap in rural areas in

Africa must conceive inclusive development from a multidimensional empowerment perspective.

Moving from this is chapter, five, jointly developed by Olawale Rafiu Olaopa and Yusuf Opeyemi Akinwale. The chapter examined the phenomenon of African indigenous knowledge (AIK) and food security in Africa. According to the authors, food is a key instrument of warfare and also a means of influencing and controlling an independent state. Any food insufficient state is vulnerable to danger or threat; lack of protection. The authors are of the view that according to available evidence, the African continent has been spending a significant number of billions of USD yearly on food, beverages, and tobacco importation with more than half of the total sum spent on food importation only. More disheartening is the projection that the spending could escalate by 2025 if the trend continues without any concrete action being taken. This becomes embarrassing and worrisome given the agricultural production potentials of African states in terms of various enviable natural endowments, yet its food insecurity and growing foreign exchange expenditure on food importation is growing. Consequently, policymakers have, due to the detrimental effects of insufficient or dearth of food, started acknowledging the greater potential for agricultural production to enhance the continent's food sufficiency. Much had been done in the area of policy, but the strategy remains ineffective and inefficient as agricultural production and revenues accrued are still very low. This then requires looking elsewhere. This paper, therefore, aims at presenting the policy challenges to boost domestic competitiveness, further develop domestic markets, and unlock investments for agriculture in Africa. Using the qualitative research method, this study found that efforts at unlocking agricultural potential and tackling food insecurity failed to recognise and integrate indigenous people and their resources in the agricultural production development agenda. This study suggested that proper utilization of indigenous knowledge within the framework of sound science, technology, and innovation capacity in the agricultural sector would foster food security in Africa.

Olabimpe Ajoke Olatunji and Lere Amusan in chapter six interrogate healthy food, unhealthy people: developmental challenges of inorganic food on African youths. This chapter argues that globalisation as the hallmark of development or what some may describe as mal-development is here to contend with us for a long time in Africa. The twin issue of food security and food sovereignty continue to generate arguments among students of social sciences. While some are of the view that food and nutrition are important for development, the production of the same is always ignoring the intricacies of food quality and food quantity. In developed environments or states, consumption of fast food is a common thing and Africans in Africa always like to display their social and financial status based on affordability and accessibility of fast foods. The question that this paper intends to address is whether the consumption of fast food that is known to be inorganic due to its production by large scale farmers who specialised in mono-cropping poses health challenges among the youths. This is a result of the introduction of unhealthy hybrid seeds and animals that lead to some health challenges hardly known in Africa. Issues of various types of cancer are plaguing the continent. Multinational pharmaceutical corporations (MPCs) are feeding fat on this to the detriment of the poverty-stricken continent of Africa. We are going to employ Social Cognitive Theory (SCT) as well as the Ecological Theory of development as a departing theoretical framework. In conclusion, we recommend the promotion of organic food and discourage the consumption of genetically modified (GMOs) food with identified crises.

Chapter seven of the edited book developed by Ogunjinmi, Amusan, Oyeleke, Osunsina, Adewumi, and Oduntan interrogates the significance of bushmeat in food security and income sustainability. They opined that bushmeat harvesting and trade play significant roles in the food security and livelihood of inhabitants of developing countries, particularly in Africa. It is an indispensable component of rural diets, contributing to protein, fats, vitamins, micro, and macronutrient intake. This chapter berates governments for not developing a policy that can integrate harvesting and trade in wildlife into national food security programmes, despite the contributions of bushmeat to food security in the continent. the chapter, therefore, advocates for policies on sustainability in off-take and harvest of bushmeat, utilization, and support for domestication through research and extension services need evolvement.

Chapter eight authored by Aluko Opeyemi Idowu discusses food vendor and food vandalism in Africa: A study on Benin, Cameroon, Niger and Senegal. The author is of the view that food is a basic necessity of life. All countries in the world seek to attain food security. Some have attained the goal while a vast majority of countries in the world especially in Africa has not attained this goal. There are several reasons attributed to the state of food insecurity in Africa. A prominent one is food vandalism due to climate change and incessant communal feuds especially between Fulani pastoralists and the farmers. Other notable food vandalism is the deliberate creation of poverty living by the political class through embezzlement and other corrupt practices to continuously use paucity of food as bate during the electioneering period. Therefore, what is the extent of food insecurity in Africa? No doubt, there is a need for more food vendors to neutralise the effects of food vandalism in Africa. These are both local and international food supply chains that are poised to mitigate food problems such as hunger, starvation, and death. Food insecurity in the four African countries (Benin, Cameroon, Niger, and Senegal) is seen as a typical case that needs urgent attention as the number of people that go without food is growing bigger over the years. Afrobarometer panel data is utilized to analyse the extent of food insecurity in Africa.

Chapter nine, jointly developed by Lere Amusan and Olusola Oloba, titled From Economic Community to Economic Union: A post-coronavirus approach to food security in the ECOWAS region interrogates Jacob Viner's model of trade creation and trade diversion in the post-coronavirus (Post-Covid-19) era and a likely movement from economic community to the economic union. In trying to do this, we call for the actualisation of smooth implementation of eco-currency where the movement of factors of production will be in line with the forces of demand and supply, but with adequate compensation of member states that may negatively be affected by the new arrangement; with emphasis on the landlocked and small states. Covid-19 exposed ECOWAS states' food security vulnerability as many states and individuals were struggling to have access to basic food quality. This brings this paper to a need to encourage agroecological food production in the form of regenerative farming that is more sustainable in the era of new regionalism. To achieve this, the involvement of questionable humanitarian food supply by the western states needs total overhauling to pave way for indigenous food promotion that will serve as a multiplier effect on home-grown food security. The need for this is to learn from the negative impact of access to food during Covid-19. Content analysis of existing literature will dominate our discussion; we are to conclude that food sovereignty as against the controversial western notions of food security will be pushed forward for the region to be food secured based on the availability of enough arable land to produce food in ECOWAS states.

Chapter ten by Victor Ojakorotu and Fie D. Dan-Woniowei is titled, "Oil Extraction and the Question of Food Security in Cabinda of Angola." The chapter examines how the discovery and exploitation of oil and other mineral resources have pitted several host communities against their government, and also multinational corporations. It analyses the impact of oil exploitation activities in the Cabinda region of Angola These take various forms such as minoritism, majoritism and religious conflicts in Africa. This chapter concludes that the Angolan government must ensure that concrete regulatory frameworks are enacted to guide the activities of oil multinationals towards preventing sustained oil pollution and agitations in the Cabinda region, as well as willingness to invest the oil revenues accruing to the nation in agriculture to achieve national food security

In chapter eleven, Ogundeji and Ojo, examine the impact of drought on urban agriculture: A case study of urban livestock farmers in Bloemfontein, Free State province. They argue that urban agriculture can reduce poverty and enhance food security amongst the poor, who are vulnerable to the high cost of food in urban areas. This chapter employed descriptive techniques and inferential statistics to explore the impact of drought on urban agriculture among livestock farmers in Bloemfontein. The majority of the participants identified their farms have been affected by drought. In the same vein, more than 90% of the participants were aware of climate change and believed that it was important to address the issue of climate change. Also, 95% of the respondents did not receive early-warning information and 93% were not registered for a drought-relief programme. With appropriate institutional support, much potential exists for building sustainable livelihoods by promoting urban agriculture in Bloemfontein, as well as in other African urban centres. Generally, the result shows that urban farmers are highly vulnerable to drought, with unreliable dependence on NGO interventions and rainwater storage as coping mechanisms. Besides, urban farmers have extremely low access to information and early warning systems. From a policy point of view, urban farming, in general, has not been given much consideration, neither have the farmers received relief support during drought seasons. It is therefore recommended that improvement should be made towards access to grazing and arable land, adequate workshops, and training in various farming activities. Also, the provision of water supply by the municipality, veterinary services, financial and technical support should be made available as a panacea for improved livelihood.

Monica Bhuda, Kutullo Nick Shai, Thabang Motswaledi, and Phemelo Marumo in chapter twelve argue that indigenous knowledge has been the source used during farming in Africa and it has contributed towards food security especially in the Bushbuckridge Municipality in South Africa. In this chapter, Bhuda et al. were of the view that indigenous knowledge has contributed towards food security especially in the Bushbuckridge Municipality in South Africa. The evident example of its contribution was the restoration, grinding, and storage of the wild fruits (marula and prickle pears) which are later used as potential meals for different households. The chapter permeates from the understanding that the process of storing these wild fruits has shown that they have the potential to be reused and contribute to the economic upgrading of the community. The wild fruits which are stored can later be sold and a higher profit when they are out of season. Therefore, the chapter will showcase that potential by referring to the Ethnobotanical survey which falls under the qualitative research methodology. The result thereof will indicate that stored wild fruits can contribute effectively to food security.

Chapter thirteen by Seun Bamidele discusses food insecurity in Sub-Saharan Africa: A Review of Agricultural Transformation Agenda (ATA) in Nigeria and argues that the severe reduction in food production of sub-Saharan Africa, especially among the Nigerian market between the latest years and the ensuing amplify in the range on ravenous people, bear sharpened the consciousness concerning policy-makers or the usual people in imitation of the fragility over the regulation of the global food in Nigeria. This awareness must be translated into effective economic strategies that will prepare the Agricultural system better to respond to long-term production demands while making it more resilient against various confronting risk factors, all in a bid to ensure that the growing national population will be able to produce and have access to adequate food in future. As a result of this, there is a need to address new agendas and challenges that transcend the contemporary decision-making horizons of agricultural producers, consumers, and policy-makers in Nigeria. This chapter, therefore, critically examines food production under the newly introduced Agricultural Transformation Agenda (ATA) in Nigeria with a special focus on Benue state.

In chapter fourteen, TITUS, Utibe Monday and IJUPTIL, Justin, examine food security and Boko Haram insurgency in Nigeria and argue that insurgency has become a threat to Nigeria's peace and security at present because it constitutes the highest contributor to humanitarian crises most especially in the northeast ranging from the rise in human casualties, internally displaced persons, refugees' debacles and food insecurity. This chapter provides an overview of the link between food security and insurgency in Nigeria's northeast. It discusses the effects of conflict (insurgency) on food security, and the political, social, and demographic factors that could exacerbate these effects. The chapter adopts the State Fragility theory as a theoretical framework and methodologically used survey method involving the use of Key informant Interviews (KIIs) for collection and analysis of data on the issues under investigation. The empirical findings indicate that there is a significant relationship between the Boko Haram insurgency and food security crises. By way of recommendation, the paper advocates the need for the Nigerian government to focus more on reducing human casualties, loss of livelihood, food insecurity to nip into the bud threats emanating from the humanitarian crises and Boko Haram insurgency in the region.

Oladiran Akinsola Ayodele discusses incessant oil spills and their implication on food production in the Niger Delta in chapter fifteen. The author submits that an untold hardship has been brought to the inhabitants of the Niger Delta region of Nigeria where crude oil is extracted. The

Oladiran maintains that mangroves swamp, the forests near the coast, have usually given room for plant products, fishes, other aquatic animals in the local communities. He said that however, oil spills have damaged these natural resources and also caused danger to coastal line fish hatcheries and pollute the fish, thereby reducing their commercial value. The inhabitants of the Delta are essentially fishermen and farmers; oil spills have disrupted their sources of livelihood. The settlement of oil on the bank or the shores of the sea kills the living organism; it came in contact with and also settles to the bed of the sea to destroy more organisms, impacting negatively on the food security of the nation. The incessant oil spills resulted in environmental pollution, which has led to a significant reduction in local food production. This has led to a shortage and an excessive rise in the price of food, placing it beyond the reach of the common man. This chapter, therefore, discusses oil spills as the major cause of this state of affairs and makes useful recommendations to alleviating the sufferings of the people. To ameliorate the situation, the Nigerian government has responded by establishing a legal framework to control oil spills to reduce the attendant environmental degradation. Some of these laws, the National Environmental Standards and Regulations Enforcement Agency Act (NESREA), 2007, Environmental Impact Assessment Act, and the Constitution of the Federal Republic of Nigeria, 1999 are discussed. The chapter also examines the influence of international law regimes on the control and compensation for oil spills. It employs a qualitative research method that is library-based. In his submission, the author avers among others recommends strict compliance with environmental laws as well as the implementation of policies of government aimed at reducing the negative effects caused by the extraction of crude oil in the Niger Delta region of Nigeria.

In chapter sixteen, Elijah Babasola Afolabi Agbaje and Olumide Omodunbi examine the Nigerian situation as a case study on the issue of food security through a farm settlement approach. As an agrarian nation with great prospects for full employment and food security, the authors observed that Nigeria, against the late sixties' predictions, become one of the starving nations of the world with mass idling manpower. The increasing impact of gentrification on the lower rungs of the society further reveals the fear that more of the potential productive populace, against all intents of sustainable development, will become more cripplingly idle, starved, and homeless. This chapter deploring both historical, field trip, and survey methods, examine the nexus of negative effects of a generational shift in agro-allied preoccupation and the trajectories of abandoned and wasted opportunities in the nation's traditional farm settlements. Agbaje and Omodunbi interrogate whether resuscitation of assisted-traditional farm settlements as a component of readily available developmental factors could count as a ready means by which problems associated with unemployment and mass underdevelopment can be mitigated in Nigeria.

Chapter authored by Victor Okorie and Lere Amusan contribution to ongoing discourses on how to transit economies from brown to green. Its focus is on farm youths' willingness to act pro-environmentally in the context of sustainable soil management and agronomic practices. The chapter complements recent scholarships, which seemed to have privileged farming practices' characteristics over farmers, in the narratives of sustainable land use. In doing so, the chapter expands a bourgeoning body of literature emphasising individual characteristics and context constraints as critical determinants of farmers' pro-environmental behaviours. Using a multistage sampling procedure, about one hundred and forty self-identified farm youths were interviewed in the study. Perception of negative effects of brown practices; input support pay; imposing taxation on brown practices; the level of environmental awareness; educational status; the perceived degree of input ownership; and perceived ability to make a change had positive and significant relationships with youths' willingness to act pro-environmentally at 0.05 probability level. The chapter argues that farm youths represent a window of opportunity in transiting economies from brown to green production and that investment in a well-planned environmental education and formulation of input support and taxation policies might turn the youths' willingness to act pro-environmentally to actual environmental behaviour.

Target audience and comparison with other books on food security and food sovereignty

The target audience of the edited volume includes academics, researchers, undergraduate and postgraduate students of political science, agricultural science, economics, public administration, African international relations, development studies and political geography students. Additionally, the books will be an invaluable resource for food security practitioners and public policy analysts. Readers of this book can use it for several purposes, including:

1. Acquiring a deeper understanding of the African attempt at food sovereignty, African collaborative actions on climate, the implications of food fraud and dumping in Africa
2. Those who are researching food security, climate change and Sustainable Development Goals (SDGs), especially, goals 2, 3, and 13, and food sustainability in Africa
3. Reference material and case studies for authors, analysts and postgraduate students with interests in food security
4. Understanding the motive behind the introduction of GMOs, destructive technologies, MNCs patent of food and plants in Africa; will also enhance understanding of biopiracy and bioterrorism and their implications developing areas with a special focus on Africa

There is no doubt that many books have been written on food security and food sovereignty in Africa; the area of departure of this edited book is that it is the first comprehensive scholarly book that examines some areas that were not addressed in some of these published books in detail. Issues that may contribute to food sovereignty in Africa, such as formulation of policy to boost more production of bushmeats as an important agent of food security, collaborative actions on climate change, allowing more women to participate in food security enterprise, transiting economies from brown to green production, advocating for Africa's control of mechanisms and policies of food, traditional farm settlement as means of food sustainability receive academic interrogation. Also of import in this book are the issue of efforts of many African governments to eliminate excessive dependency on GMOs and inorganic foods, due to their implications for various health challenges in Africa (Amusan, 2017; Goldberg, 2018; Norwood and Mix, 2019; Paarlberg, 2013; Pollan, 2006). Some of the works that address challenges of food security and food sovereignty in Africa focused more on specific areas. Peter K. Arthur's (2012) *food security and Sovereignty in Africa:*

Issues, policy challenges and opportunities is an interesting article on the plights of Africa's food security and sovereignty, it only focuses on the institutional mechanisms and capacities factors as the major cause of food insecurity and lack of Africa's food sovereignty without looking into the problem holistically. Habib and Ray (2019) examine food sovereignty and the struggle for socio-economic justice in North Africa. Angela's inability to link the socio-economic struggle for food sovereignty in North Africa to food fraud and control of food policies in Africa through platforms such as new media technologies, and Big Tech politics calls for further intellectual discussions addressed in this edited volume. This edited book draws contributors from African scholars who are familiar with the terrains they research on.

Professor Lere Amusan
Department of Political Studies and International Relations,
North West University, South Africa

References

Amusan, Lere. 2019a. Feeding the people, Uplifting the Continent: Nigeria and South Africa in the Struggle for Food Security in Africa. Inaugural Lecture delivered at the North-West University (Mafikeng) on 15 November. DOI: 10.13140/RG.2.2.19636.81282

Amusan, Lere. 2019b. Mercy Killing and Thanksgiving: Food Security with Tears in Africa. being a Paper presented at Faculty Distinguished Lecture Series 1 held on Friday, May 17. DOI:10.13140/RG.2.2.21142.78407.

Amusan, Lere. 2018. Multinational Corporations' (MNCs) Engagement in Africa: Messiahs or Hypocrites? *Journal of African Foreign Affairs*, 5(1), pp.41-62

Amusan, Lere. 2017. "Politics of Biopiracy: An Adventure into Hoodia/Xhoba Patenting in Southern Africa." *African Journal of Traditional, Complementary and Alternative Medicines*,14(1), pp. 103-109.

Amusan Lere, 2014. "The Plights of African Resources Patenting through the Lenses of the World Trade Organisation: An Assessment of South Africa's Rooibos Tea's Labyrinth Journey". *African Journal of Traditional Complement Alternative Medicine*,11(5):41–47

Amusan, Lere and Olutola, Oluwole (2017). Contextualising African Women's Empowerment in Agriculture: Challenges from Climate Change and Mineral Extraction Perspectives. Journal of *International Women's Studies, 18*(4), 117-130. Available at: http://vc.bridgew.edu/jiws/vol18/iss4/9

Cotula, Lorenzo. 2013. *The Great African Land Grab?: Agricultural Investments and the Global Food System.* London and New York: Zed Books.

FAO (Food and Agriculture Organisation of the United Nations). 2012. Greening the Economy with Agriculture. Rome: FAO

Habib, Ayeb and Ray, Bush, 2019 Food Insecurity and Revolution in the Middle East and North Africa: Agrarian Questions in Egypt and Tunisia. London and New York: Anthem Press.

Howard, Philip H. 2021. Concentration and Power in the Food System: Who Controls What We Eat? London: Bloomsbury Academic.

Arthur, Peter K. 2012 "Food security and sovereignty in Africa: issues, policy challenges and opportunities". ACBF occasional papers, no.17. Harare: ACBF

Bond, Patrick. 2006. "Looting Africa: The Economics of Exploitation". London and Pietermaritzburg: Zed Books and University of KwaZulu-Natal Press.

Chomsky, Noam. 1999. Profit over People: Neoliberalism and Global Order. New York: Seven Stories Press.

Collier, Paul. 2008. "The Politics of Hunger: How Illusion and Greed Fan the Food Crisis". Foreign Affairs. 87(6): 67-79

Foer, Franklin. 2017. "World Without Mind: The Existential Threat of Big Tech". New York: Penguin Random House.

Goldberg, Ray A. 2018. Food citizenship: food system advocates in an era of distrust. New York and Oxford: Oxford University Press.

Halabi, Sam F. 2018. Intellectual Property and the New International Economic Order: Oligopoly, Regulation, and Wealth Redistribution in the Global Knowledge Economy. New York and Cambridge: Cambridge University Press.

Ighobor, Kingsley. 2014. "Trade between Two Unequal Partners." Africa Renewal. August. https://www.un.org/africarenewal/magazine/august-2014/trade-between-two-unequal-partners.

IPCC, Working Group II (2007). Glossary of Terms. IPCC Fourth Assessment Report: Climate Change 2007, Working Group II: Impacts, Adaptation and Vulnerability. Retrieved from http://www.ipcc.ch/publications_and_data /ar4/wg2/en/annexessglossary-a-d.html (accessed in September 2021).

Love, John and Bryant, John A. (eds.). 2017. Biofules and Bioenergy. Oxford: John Wiley & Sons.

Moran, Katy. 2004. "Benefit Sharing Under the Convention on Biological Diversity." In, Riley, Mary (ed.). Indigenous Intellectual Property Rights: Legal Obstacles and Innovative Solutions. New York and Oxford: Altamira Press, pp. 153-172.

Norwood, F. Bailey and Mix, Tamara L. 2019. Meet the food radicals. New York and Oxford: Oxford University Press.

Otero, Gerardo. 2018. The Neoliberal Diet Healthy Profits, Unhealthy People. Austin, TX: University of Texas Press.

Paarlberg, Robert. 2013. "Food Politics: What Everyone Needs to Know". Oxford: Oxford University Press.

Pollan, Michael. 2016. Omnivore's dilemma: a natural history of four meals. New York: Penguin Books.

Roger Blein and Emmanuel Jeud 2007. "Food sovereignty in West Africa: From Principles to Reality". Being the First Regional Forum on Food Sovereignty organised by ROPPA (Network of West African Peasant Organisations and Producers) in Niamey – November 2006.

Seminar, Annisa Utami., Sarwoprasodjo, Sarwititi., Kinseng, Rilus., and Santosa, Dwi. 2018. Peasant Understanding of Food Sovereignty: Indonesian Peasants in a Transnational Agrarian Movement. Makara Hubs-Asia. 22(2): 129-142. DOI: 10.7454/hubs.Asia.1250918

Tilzey, Mark. 2018. Political Ecology, Food Regimes, and Food Sovereignty: Crisis, Resistance, and Resilience. Cham, Switzerland: Palgrave Macmillan.

Chapter 1
Food Security and Climate Change in Sub-Saharan Africa

Isa Ishaq Ojibara

Our climate is rapidly changing, and agriculture is most affected by it. Agriculture production in Sub-Saharan Africa countries is expected to be highly affected by the ravaging global warming (Amusan, 2009; Anya, Ofem, Binang & Umoren, 2012). Several humanitarian crises bedevilling the sub-region have been linked to environmental conditions such as extreme and prolonged droughts and flooding exacerbating the risk of rural populace in the region to chronic physical problems (Connolly-Boutin & Smit, 2015). Though global food production is almost at per with the increasing growth in population from the 1960s, sub-Saharan Africa exhibits signs of strain (Kohler, 2012). Thus, the increasing population growth in Sub-Saharan Africa means there is high competition for arable land for agricultural purposes. The severity of extreme weather conditions traced to climate change is an emerging pressure in the region that is experienced for a very long time (Ibid, 2015). Food security and livelihoods have been recognized to be severely affected by climate change (Thompson & Sconnes 2009). Extreme weather in sub-Saharan Africa like droughts and flooding limit farmer's ability to grow crops and rear livestock, farmers and herders will have no choice than to adjust to changes in water regimes to maintain their food production and well-being (Kebede, Hasen & Negatu, 2011). Recent literature on food insecurity has also linked climate change and conflict to be a real problem especially in Sub-Sahara Africa (Martin-Shields & Stojetz, 2018). The incessant herders-farmers' clashes have been proposed to be as a result of climate change.

It is expected that sub-Saharan Africa would be more likely affected by climate change than other regions of the world. The temperature in the region is becoming very high, and the livelihood of a larger share of the people in the region depends heavily on rain-fed agriculture. While comparing with other regions of the world, sub-Saharan Africa is the least cultivated area with irrigated farming. Irrigated farming contributes only to 5% of the total cultivated area of the region, it 37% in Asia and 14% in Latin America (Ringler, Zhu, Cai, Koo, & Wang, 2010). The report by (IPCC) provides evidence with strong scientific proof that suggests the realness of climate change and the threat it poses on the economy, social, and environment. Global warming is unequivocal as is now obvious from research that there is an increase in average global air, temperature, sea level, and widespread melting of snow (Connolly-Boutin & Smit, 2015).

Over the years, Africa has lost her position of being an exporter of food into being a net importer with the highest malnourished people in the world. The high level of importation of food has also contributed to chronic food insecurity that affects almost 28% of the continent population, which is nearly 200 million people; more so, this has also increased the number of people dying from hunger (Clover, 2003).

Climate change: A conceptual Discourse

Climate change can be defined as any change in climate over time whether due to natural variability or as a result of human activity, which alters the composition of the global atmosphere (IPCC, 2007). Thus, the change in the composition of the global atmosphere may be slow, unseen and difficult to notice for a long time, which may be directly or indirectly caused by different activities by a man in addition to natural climate variability over time (Antwi, 2013). The impacts of climate change are already being felt on biodiversity, human systems, and the entire global ecosystem (Kotir, 2010).

Concept of food security: Availability, access, and utilization

The concept of food security has been transformed from its initial definition and meaning, particularly as the rate of food insecurity soars globally. FAO definition of food security is widely regarded as the most complete definition. The organization defines food security as

"When a situation exists that allows all people have physical, social and economic access to sufficient, safe and nutritious food that meets daily nutrition's value and food for an active and healthy life" (World Food Summit 1996).

While it was Amartya Sen (1981) that introduced the concepts of access and entitlements to food (in)security literature, food security was initially defined as mere production of food as was attested to by the World Food Conference in 1974 (Baro and Deubel 2006). However, it is now clear that food production alone cannot guarantee food security, hence, the addition of concepts of availability, access and utilization, and more recently stability.

Food availability, access, and utilization are very crucial pillars of food security. The problem of food insecurity is a multifaceted and interrelated of the three pillars of food security which in most cases can be traced to have economic, social, and political dimensions to food security (Clover, 2003). Connolly-Boutin & Smith (2015) succinctly explain food availability, access and utilization as

> "Food availability means the cultivation and channel of distributions, sales and final consumption of food. While access is to the affordability of food which refers to the amount of money people are ready to pay for a given quality, quantity and type by people, utilization is the nutritional value which is beneficial to the body".

As seen from the above, food availability alone is not a single determinant of food security in any region at any given time. Food can be available in large quantities because of favourable weather, good agricultural policy, effective harvesting method, or food importation/ food aid (Ojo & Adebayo, 2012). However, food availability may not necessarily translate to its accessibility. For instance, a bad transport system has affected the proper distribution of food from farms, mostly rural areas, to urban centres. Again, the insufficient or lack of linkage between agro-processing industries and harvested food may lead to massive food wastage every year. Massive importation of food, particularly by sub-Saharan Africa countries, reduces foreign reserves, causes budgetary imbalance and most imported food items are not good for human consumption (Davies, 2009). The availability of food is considered necessary, but it does not guarantee it access, and access to food is as important as its availability, which in the final analysis is not enough for its utility and stability (Kotir, 2010).

Climate change and food security

Africa climate can be categorized into seven climatic zones: tropical rainforest, tropical wet and dry, tropical dry, mountain, Mediterranean, middle-latitude dry, and humid (ibid, 2010). Climate change affects all the three pillars of food security i.e., availability, access, and utilization. Agriculture is an essential sector to the livelihood, economic growth, and development in most countries of sub-Saharan Africa. Agriculture contributes 20 – 30 percent of Gross Domestic Product and 55 percent of all the export from the continent (World Bank 2007). Agricultural output has been greatly affected by climatic change, negatively impacted standard of living in rural areas, and a reduction of active farmers. (FAO, IFAD, UNICEF, WFP and WHO, 2019).

The rural population contributed to over 70% of the sub-Saharan Africa population, which livelihood and economic sustenance heavily dependent on rain-fed farming and other agricultural activities like fishing and roaring of animals (World Bank, 2007). Irrigation farming is just developing in sub-Saharan Africa and very small while comparing with other regions; it contributes about 4 percentages of cultivated land for sub-Saharan Africa, 39 percentages in South-Asia, and 29 percentages in East-Asia (World Bank 2007). Also, erosion, environmental degradation, increasing food prices, and illness have all been linked to climatic change (GCF, 2016).

In a study carried out by FAO, the organization opined that severe drought caused by the climatic change may affect over 30 million Africans by the end of 2050 (Clover, 2003). Apart from the high susceptibility of Sub-Saharan Africa to climate change, agriculture in the region also face numerous challenges of biophysical, political, socioeconomic, and armed conflict which all lower the region's adaptation capability (IPCC 2007). The reoccurring conflicts between pastoralists and farmers in Nigeria, Ghana, and Kenya are attributed to the struggle for arable land. The drought of Chad Basin and Boko Haram insurgency in the North East of Nigeria led both farmers and pastoralists to move from the affected area (Amusan,

2013). Chad Basin provides a livelihood for farmers, fishermen and pastoralists in North East of Nigeria, Cameroon, Niger, and Chad.

Three methods have been identified to assess the impact of climate change on agriculture in sub-Saharan Africa. These methods include but not limited to crop simulation models, agro-ecological (AEZ) models, and cross-sectional Ricardian models (Kotir, 2010). Since climate change affects biodiversity, soil, and water, it is expected that these would have direct or indirect consequences on food availability, access, utilization, and stability (IASC 2009). In the same vein, climate change has been linked to have an impact on calorie intake in the region. Calorie level is expected to increase between the year 2000- 2050 in Sub-Saharan if there is no record of climate change and its inherent problems (Kotir, 2010), with the incident of climate change, however, it is expected that there would be 21% decline in calories per person in 2050 (IFPRI 2009).

Arable land in sub-Saharan Africa, which is required for cultivation, has been limited by environmental degradation, which in turn affects food production caused by depletion of rivers, pest attacks, high mortality of animals, low soil fertility, increasing the incident of deforestation and decreasing available land for agriculture. The implication of climate change is not limited to food production and availability alone. Climate change implication also extends to food distribution. Flooding has caused numerous destruction to infrastructure like roads, bridges, which increase the price of food in the market and bring economic disequilibrium of food supply and demand (Perez-Escamilla, 2017).

The destruction on infrastructure caused by environmental degradation like flooding and erosions, means food products are struck in the farms, which is majorly located at rural areas, are wasted, thereby results in economic losses to the farmers, rural development, food supply, increasing food price and generally reduce the Gross Domestic Product of the countries in sub- Saharan Africa. Though food (in) security has been linked to rapid change in climatic conditions, however, it is not the singular factor affecting yield and agricultural productivity.

Impacts of climate change on food security in Sub-Saharan Africa

IPCC (2007) reported that temperature in sub-Saharan Africa would be higher than the global average, thereby the region is likely to be hotter than any other region with a reduced rainfall (Ringler, Zhu, Cai, Koo, & Wang, 2010). In their study, Ringler, Zhu, Cai, Koo, & Wang (2010), adopted the Comprehensive Climate Change (CCC) to Analyse the relationship between food (in) security and climate change. The prediction of CCC is generally based on past predictions by incorporation of the 17 GCMs.

Staples	**Without climate change (%)**	**With climate change (%)**
Rice (paddy)	72	107
Wheat	53	82
Maize	71	126
Rice (processed)	34	48

Table 1: *Predicted cost of selected staples by 2030 in SSA*
Sources: (Sasson 2012, p 7).

The table above indicates a direct relationship between climate change and an increase in the cost of food. From the table, it is evident that the price of all the selected staples would increase due to climate change. For paddy rice, the increase in cost without climate change is expected to be 72%; however, with the probability of climate change, the cost is expected to increase by 107%. The cost of wheat is expected to increase by 2030 without incident of climate change by 53% and 82 with climate change by 2030. The cost increase also would have impacts on Maize and processed rice. This confirms Sasson, (2012) argument that 239million people suffered hunger in the region in 2010 due to an increase in food prices. An increase in the cost of basic food means many people would not likely afford the cost, in the region with a high poverty level, and suffer from malnutrition and hunger. Again, drought may likely cause the loss of 60-90million hectares of land by the end of 2060, and this may likely increase people affected by malnutrition to 600million by the end of 2080 (ibid, 2012).

The region has constantly been hit by heavy and severe floods and droughts which affect the ecosystems and agro ecosystems, threatening the lives of millions of people (Sasson, 2012). For instance, the drought in Ethiopia affected more than 75,000 people (ibid, 2012), creating a humanitarian crisis like displacing people into a refugee camp. Even though the region contributes about 5% of the global greenhouse emission, the region is more prone to the threats of climate change than any other region (ibid, 2012). The challenges of reoccurring drought across the region have put the region to the uncertainties of economic inequality (Simmons, 2017). However, it must be noted that the problem of food insecurity is not as a result of or limited to a single causal factor, but a complex web and interconnected phenomena. The other factors may include but not limited to poverty, poor infrastructure, armed conflict, inadequate finance, and poor agricultural policies by government, corruption, and a high rate of diseases like HIV/AIDS, malaria among the vulnerable groups in the region.

Dry, hot, and getting hotter: Impact of drought on food security in the Horn of Africa

The horn of Africa, southern Africa, and Sahel has been consistently affected by drought (Zeng, 2003). The extreme droughts in East Africa have pitched the farmers with herders, thereby reducing the production of agricultural produce at ultima capacity (Kebede, Hasen &Negatu, 2011). The incessant clashes between the pastoralist and farmers have resulted in the increasing number of people affected by hunger in Kenya, Ethiopia, and Somalia (Oxfam, 2017). About 2.9 million Somalis faced severe hunger in the 2016-2017 food crises. According to Oxfam (2017), the food crises occasioned by the drought in 2016-2017 put 6.2 million people on emergency food aid, more than 365,000 acutely malnourished children, and an estimated 3.2 million people need water, with a high rate of cholera outbreak during the period (OCHA, 2017).

The drought crises of 2010-2011 in the Horn of Africa (Ethiopia, Somalia, Burundi, Kenya, and Rwanda) affected over 13 million people, in Somalia, the drought-affected about 4 million Somalis, which required almost $1billion to solve the humanitarian crisis (International Federation of Red

Cross and Red Cresent Societies, 2011). The refugee camp located in Dollo Ado witnessed about 50% of people faced with malnutrition primarily caused by drought (ibid, 2011). Similarly, about 5.6 million people were affected by the recent drought in 2016-2017, culminated in hunger and famine that affected more than 9.5 and an estimated 300,000 children died of malnutrition-related illness in Ethiopia, Burundi, Rwanda, Kenya, and Eritrea (OCHA, 2017).

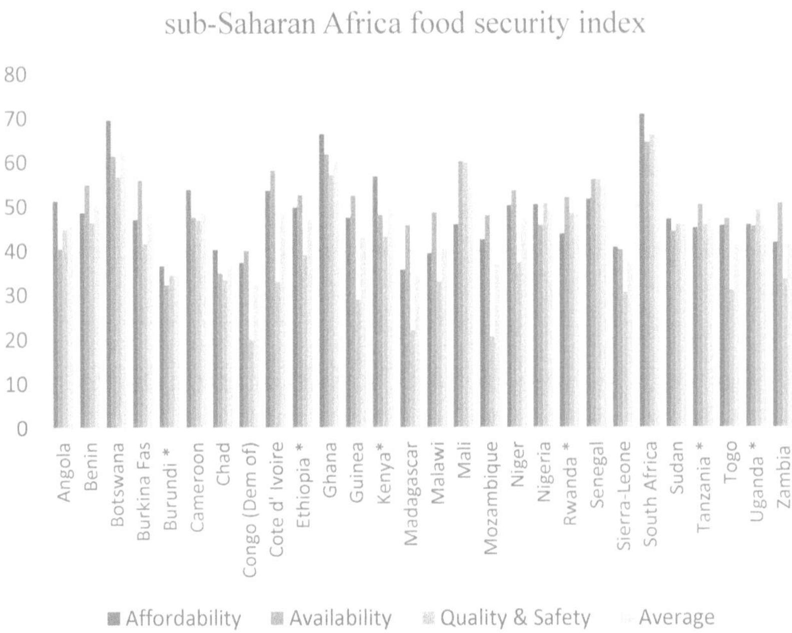

Table 2: *sub- Saharan Food Security Index for 2019*
Sources: Compiled by Author (Data from Global Food Security Index, 2019).

Horn of Africa Countries

Global Food Security Index (GFSI) examines the state of food systems across 113 countries. It was developed by The Economist Intelligence Unit and supported by Corteva Agriscience to measure the level of food security globally using combining the three pillars of food security of availability, affordability, and quality & safety indices. The index ranked each country's performance on each of the pillars, and then aggregates the average score. South Africa tops the overall GFSI for 2019 in sub-Saharan Africa, followed by Botswana, another southern African country. Ghana is third and the best ranked West Africa Countries. Kenya, Ethiopia, Rwanda, Tanzania, Uganda, and Burundi-the horn of Africa, ranked, 8th, 12th, 14th, 15th, 17th, and 28th respectively.

Regionally, the overall GFSI for the horn of Africa, which was regarded as the epicenter of the severe food crisis on the continent showed impressive results. Although Burundi-a country in East Africa is ranked the lowest, the sub-regional index showed improvement. South Africa tops on the three-level affordability, availability and quality & safety. However, Cameroon and Mali showed impressive results on affordability and quality & safety respectively. Globally Singapore, Ireland, United States, Switzerland are top 4, with Finland and Norway sharing the 5th place. Globally, it was revealed in 2019 that 88% of the countries on the index have sufficient food supply for the year under review. Despite the high percentage of food supply globally, GFSI 2019 revealed that 820 million are hungry (The Economist Intelligence Unit, 2019).

Other Africa countries

The challenges posed by climate change to food production are not limited to the horn of Africa in the sub-region alone. Other countries have also witnessed the negative consequence of climate change on their agriculture. The people living around the Faguibine Lake in Mali depends heavily on the water for fishing and irrigation, however, the lake has lost most of its water body to depletion and forced the local people to abandon the cultivations of crops to the rearing of animals (Djoudi, Brochhaus & Locatelli, 2013). Besides, most of the arable land for cultivation in Wenchi, Ghana, have lost their fertility, thereby forcing the farmers to change from planting cash crops such as cocoa, cashew, cotton, etc., to the cultivation of adaptable crops to short-season farming and highly tolerant crops to drought-like yam, cowpea, and maize, which generate lesser income than the cash crops (Adjei-Nsiah, Issaka, Fening, Mapfumo, Anchirina & Giller, 2010). Madagascar was also hit with a strong and severe drought in 2008, which affected over 720,000 people battled starvation and chronic food insecurity (Sasson, 2012). Aside from the increasingly high prices of food in Nigeria, the drought and armed conflict in North East of Nigeria, Chad,

Niger, and Cameroon have increased the susceptibility of the region to chronic food insecurity in the nearest future (Ojo & Adebayo, 2012).

Food and Agriculture Organization listed over nineteen (19) countries in sub-Saharan Africa for which have witnessed a dramatic increase in food prices (Sasson, 2012). The list consists of all the countries in the horn of Africa with chronic drought and famine. In 2008, the journal Science (cited in Sasson, 2012) opined about 30% of maize production would be lost in South Africa from 2012-2030 (ibid, 2012). The rapid soaring food prices have resulted in riots across the sub-region. Protesters were against the 65% increase in food prices in Burkina Faso, same as in Cameroon where the taxi drivers embarked on strike due to increase in the price of fuel changed rapidly to food prices protest with 20 people lost their lives, and arrest of over 100 people (Walt, 2008). Police in Senegal had to adopt drastic measures which include the use of tear gas to disperse protesters of food prices in March 2008 (ibid, 2012).

Vulnerability

Africa accounts for only 3.6% (UN Statistics Common Database 2006, cited in Antwi, 2013, p 10), of global CO2 emissions and the regions have been battling with the increasing rate of deforestation, and accordingly with a decrease in its carbon absorption capacity which may have negative consequences on the development of the continent and global climate change (ibid, 2013). While comparing with other regions, Africa's CO2 emission is very small, but it faces the most imminent danger of climatic change with high risk to the livelihood of the majority of the people.

According to Antwi (2013), agricultural sectors are mostly affected by and faces a higher risk of climate change.

> "It affects agriculture and livelihood by crop losses, animals and fish farming are lost to water scarcity, destruction of productive assets, pastoralist systems, inland & coastal fishing, aquaculture communities, forest-based systems, rural communities especially in coastal, flood plains, dry land, etc., deterioration in nutritional status

for women of reproductive age, children, elderly, ill & socially disabled people" (Antwi, 2013).

The food insecurity in individual household food may affect direct negative impact on the quantity and quality of dietary intake of the general population, hence impacting on maternal nutrition and health, offspring mental growth and development and potentially increasing risk to infectious diseases, as well as the risk of anaemia in women (FAO, IFAD, UNICEF, WFP and WHO, 2019).

Adaptation strategies and action plan

Adaption strategies are some measures that can be taken which are necessary to limit or mitigate the risk of climate change to the environment, water bodies, soil, agriculture, livestock, and the entire ecosystem. Adaption strategies are also to ensure sustainable agriculture practices. In other words, adaptation strategies for climate change are actions or measures deploy by farmers to adapt to changes occasioned by the climatic change. The adaption strategies are to ensure higher productivity or output in the time of climate change. Farmers in the sub-region have recorded high temperature with a decline in rainfall; yet many farmers in the sub-region are still ignorant of adaptation strategies to mitigate the constantly changing climate (Connolly-Boutin and Smith, 2015).

Farmers in the region have identified the increasing shortage of arable land for cultivation, and inadequate financing of the agricultural sector as some of the challenges against adaptation strategies maximize agricultural output. Another challenge to adaptation strategies to climate change is lack of understanding of the problems confronting the sector, the lack of basic knowledge of the challenges pose by climate change has limit the interventions by farmers, policy-makers, and academics (Maxwell, 2000 cited in Clover, 2003: 8).

Over the years, rural farmers have adopted some local methods like crop rotation, land fallow system, and diversification of crops to mitigate against climate change (FAO, IFAD, UNICEF, WFP and WHO, 2019). Forests provide highly nutrition diets which are a direct solution to malnutrition, the presence of forest mitigate the effect of climate change to the ecosystem (Metu, Okeyika, & Maduka, 2016). However, desertification has been on the increase due to deforestation, drought, and rapid urbanization. Others adaptation strategies include early warning systems of consequences of climate change (Antwi, 2013), adaptation of different agricultural systems, rapid infrastructural development like roads, silos, pesticides; improve agricultural policy-making and implementation, good coordination of agro-processing industries and large-scale farms

To prevent Africa's high risk of climate change and its consequences on food security on the continent, different mitigating methods and action plans have been enumerated to national governments, donor agencies, and the international community. To Oxfam, (2017) "The United Nations pleads for $1.9bn appeal must be redeemed to urgently solve malnutrition and provide support for local populace affected, highly industrialized countries must support the call for a reduction in the emission of greenhouse gases and massive afforestation" (Oxfam, 2017). Food aid or transfer can also limit the vulnerability of climatic change in sub-Saharan Africa. It has been found that food aid reduced vulnerability in Ethiopia (Devereux, 2007). Although the major limitation of food aid has been identified to be high transaction cost and if mostly, a short time solution. For instance, Barrett and Maxwell (2005) cited in Devereux, (2007), stressed that the bulk of the money for food aid by the United States in 2000 was spent on logistic expenses. Also in their argument Clay et al. (1998) cited in Devereux, (2007), "claimed financial aid is for effective than food aid".

Despite numerous adaptive action plans by national governments, donors' agencies and international organization, the region capacity to mitigate against climate change is extremely low, which is linked to acute poverty, high-rate illiteracy among Africans farmers, an inadequate insurance scheme for farmers, poor irrigational facilities which left farmers to rely on rain-fed farming. These risks or vulnerabilities are a result of a lack of coordinated policies, information channels, and slow technology change in the sub-region to the present reality sub-region (Ringler, Zhu, Cai, Koo, & Wang, 2010; Kotir, 2010).

Conclusion

This paper examines the impact of climate change on food security in sub-Saharan Africa and the realness of climate change with its far-reaching effect on agriculture. It affects most specifically, the availability, accessibility, affordability, and quality of food security, which are direct sources of livelihood of millions of people in sub-Saharan Africa. Even though Africa contributed to the emission of CO_2 is the lowest in the world, it bears the heaviest impacts of climate change. The incessant drought and flood have contributed to food shortage, poverty, environmental degradation, massive rural-urban migration, conflict, and malnutrition in the sub-region. Different adaptive strategies are needed as a matter of conclusion to mitigate the negative consequences of climate change on food security in sub-Saharan Africa.

References

Adjei-Nsiah, S., Issaka, R., Fening, J., Mapfumo, P., Anchirina, V., Giller, K. (2010) Farmers' perceptions of climate change and variability and existing opportunities for adaptation in Wenchi area of Ghana. *International Journal of Climate Chang Impacts Responses* 2(2), 49–60

Amusan, L. (2013). Nigeria and its Neighbours in the Age of Climate Change: An Assessment of the Lake Chad Basin Area. In Adeoye A. Akinsanya and John A. Ayoade (eds.). *An Introduction to Political Science in Nigeria.* Lanham, Maryland: University Press of America, pp. 261-82.

Amusan, L. (2009). *Africa and Climate Change in the Era of Complex Interdependent Globalised International System.* Working Paper. No. 2. October. *Journal of Alternative Perspectives in the Social Sciences* (JAPSS). Florida, USA. http://www.japss.org. (n.d.).

Antwi, A. (2013). *Climate Change and Food Security: An overview about the issue.* Accra: FES.

Anya, M., Ofem, N. I., Binang, W. B., & Umoren, E. P. (2012). Climate change and food security in Africa. *Asian Journal of Agricultural Research, 6*(2), 52-59.

Clover, J. (2003). Food security in Sub-Saharan Africa. *Africa Security Review, 12*(1), 5-15.

Connolly-Boutin, L., & Smit, B. (2015). Climate change, food security, and livelihoods in sub-Saharan. *Reg Environ Change,* 1-15. doi:DOI 10.1007/s10113-015-0761-x

Devereux, S. (2007, July 30). The impact of droughts and floods on food security and policy options to alleviate negative effects. *AGEC Blue book,* 47-58.

FAO, IFAD, UNICEF, WFP and WHO. (2019). *The State of Food Security and Nutrition in the World 2019: Safeguarding against economic slowdowns and downturns.* Rome: Food and Agriculture Organization .

International Federation of Red Cross and Red Cresent Societies. (2011). *Drought in Horn of Africa: Preventing the next disaster.* Geneva: International Federation of Red Cross and Red Crescent Societies.

Kohler, H.-P. (2012). *Popolation.* Copenhagen : Copenhagen Consensus project.

Kotir, J. H. (2010). Climate change and variability in Sub-Saharan Africa: A review of current and future trends and impacts on agriculture and food security. *Environment Development Sustainability , 13,* 587–605. doi:DOI 10.1007/s10668-010-9278-0

Martin-Shields, C., & Stojetz, W. (2018). *Food security and conflict: Empirical challenges and future opportunities for research and policy making on foof security and conflict.* Food and Agricultural Organization . Rome: FAO Agricultural Development Economics Working Paper 18-04.

Metu, A. G., Okeyika, K. O., & Maduka, O. D. (2016). Achieving Sustainable Food Security in Nigeria: Challenges and way forword. *3rd International Conference on African Development Issues (CU-ICADI 2016)* (pp. 182-186). Remo: Covenant University Press.

Ojo, E., & Adebayo, P. F. (2012). Food security in Nigeria: An overview. *European Journal of Sustainable Development*, 199-222.

Oxfam. (2017). *A climate in crisis: How climate change is making drought and humanitarian disaster worse in East Africa.* Worldwide: Oxfam.

Perez-Escamilla, R. (2017). Food security and the 2015–2030 sustainable development goals: From Human to Planetary Health. *Current Development in Nutrition*, 1-8.

Ringler, C., Zhu, T., Cai, X., Koo, J., & Wang, D. (2010). *Climate change impacts on food security in Sub-Saharan Africa: insights from comprehensive climate change scenarios.* International Food Research Policy Institute, Environment and Production Technology Division. Washington, D.C: international Food Research Institute.

Sasson, A. (2012). Food security for Africa: An urgent global challenge. *Agriculture and Food Security, 1*(2), 1-16.

Simmons, E. (2017). *Reccuring Storms: Food insecurity, political instability and conflict.* Center for Strategic & International Studies. Washington DC: CSIS Global Food Security Project.

The Economist Intelligence Unit. (2019). *Global Food Security Index.* London: The Economist Intelligence Unit Limited.

Thompson, J., & Scoones , I. (2009). Addressing the dynamics of agri-food system: An emerging agenda for social science research. *Environmental Science Policy, 12*(4), 386-397.

Zeng, N. (2003). Drought in the Sahel. *302*(5647), 999–1000. doi:10.1126/science.

Chapter 2
Food Security and Sustainable Development in Africa: A Philosophical Review

Phemelo Olifile Marumo

Introduction

According to Marumo (2016:12), God entrusted humanity with tremendous authority - to rule the earth and be an overseer, but with greater authority comes great responsibility for managing its resources wisely and God will hold humanity accountable for humanity's failure for the stewardship. To achieve this objective, humanity was required to leave in harmony and in a relationship with the earth. In harmonizing this relationship, humanity was to toil the land, eat from the earth, clothe from the earth, and preserve it for future generations. However, as sin prevailed humanity failed on its duties to be kept as the custodian, and consequently humanity was expelled from the Garden. The expulsion of humanity from the Garden thwarted God's plan for the preservation of the earth and sustainable development. From this resultant above, the paper contends that be shared as a creature who is superior to others maintain was duty-bound to ascertain that the earth is preserved and sustained and that could have added to the development of both humanity and generations to come as a sustainable entity. The other important aspect in the conundrum was that substance of the earth meant that food security was prime, and it has to be the basis of development. This is mentioned because humanity cannot survive without food security and food security has to be serviced by humanity in a suitable atmosphere, therefore, both are cahoots in the sustenance of food security.

According to Frans Cronje, Deputy Chief Executive Officer at the South African Institute of Race Relations (SAIRR), South Africa has a total surface area of 122 million hectares. As of March 2011, 31 million hectares or 25 percent of that surface area was in the hands of the State. The remaining 91 million hectares or 75 percent of the surface area was privately-owned. The balance of State and privately-owned land varied greatly between provinces. For example, in the great expanses of the Free State and the Northern Cape private owners held 89 percent and 91 percent of the surface area respectively. In both the Western Cape and Gauteng, 55 percent was held by the State. State-owned land would previously have been regarded as part of the white-owned 87 percent. It follows then that it should now be regarded as black-owned, which means that at least a quarter of the country's surface area is in black hands. Nothing is preventing the State from handing the title to much of that land to black people.

Cronje further adds that since 1995, 2.6 million hectares or the equivalent 2.1 percent of all land has been handed to blacks via land restitution programmes. This figure pushes the amount of land in black hands to at least 27.1 percent. Also, more than R5 billion was paid out to restitution claimants who accepted cash payments instead of having land returned to them. That R5 billion was sufficient to purchase an additional 2.6 million hectares which would have pushed the amount of land in black hands to just 30 percent.

In South Africa, the environmental issue is intertwined considering the fact the poor and the marginalized that were in certain instances being deprived of the ownership of the land. This is evident from the number of cases of land distribution still pending in South Africa as stated by the Land Commission. According to Liesl Peyper of News 24, there are currently 6 607 land claims outstanding in South Africa, Rural Development and Land Reform Minister Gugile Nkwinti told Parliament on Wednesday. He was responding to an oral question from the NFP's Nhlanhla Khubisa, who wanted Nkwinti to give an update on the number of claims settled and those outstanding. According to Nkwinti, his department has settled 804 land claims in the past financial year, against its target of 615, and finalised a further 672 against a target of 454. The department further called on a research unit at the University of KwaZulu-Natal to assist with outstanding land claims.

Based on the above alarming statistics which are inclusive of uncertainty about reaching a solution to address land issue, Moyo (2009:1) can be justified as he unpacks the problems surrounding land debacle by echoing that the greatest threat to security in southern Africa lies in the unequal land ownership patterns in countries where poor people's livelihoods depend on farming. Presently there too many land debates on ownership based on racial lines and that suggest the fallibility of efforts for reconciliation that fails humanely and fairly address economic and political justice concerns. A major problem in addressing land conflict is the radically based ideological distortion that shrouds social, political, and economic debates about land and agriculture in southern Africa. This brings the paper to the African understanding of the land.

The land as Mother Earth

The land has been a centre of controversy, discourses, debates, and tension in Africa due to the understanding and interpretation of the land and its usage. Others regard the land as their source of income and that it can be used profitably for development, others think that it must be shared equally, whilst others maintain that it is sacred. These different worldviews or ideologies bring forth tensions and squabbles around the land issue and its attributes. Adeyemo (1997:63) highlights that the Shona shares with most Africans the belief that the land is sacred because it belongs to the ancestors. It is ancestral land and bears the remains of the ancestors, particularly in the form of graves of chiefs. Shona religion is based on the grave. In the central rituals of *kumutsa midzimu* (rituals in honour of ancestors) the point of entry is the grave. In other rituals, libations are poured on the ground and umbilical cords are buried. It is the abode of the dead. This relationship between humanity and the land is important as it serves as a culture forte of Africans. Thence the Africans saw the Earth as the Mother.

Different names and traits have been assigned to Mother Earth, It would seem, about Daquah (1968 and Boaten (1998:42) that responding positively to the dictates of nature African regarded the earth (*Asase*) as 'mother' (*Asase Yaa/E/ua*), the provider and sustainer of life. Humanity, therefore offered prayers before cultivating and after that through celebrations called 'harvest festivals' such as Howowo (Ga), *Ohum (Abuakwa),* and *Odirwa (Akuapel)* to commemorate the generosity of Mother Earth. To allow the earth to continuously play its mothership role and to enhance biodiversity, Africans developed a body of laws and regulations known as taboos to regulate their relationship with Mother Earth.

The chapter maintains that Mother Nature is not an object of manipulation by industrialist economic forces because African worldview enables communities to take control of their destiny.

Land and food security

Most of our food is grown on the land, so there has always been a close link between the delivery of food security and land use. United Nations Academic Impact Report (2016) states that before the use of industrial fertilisers, improved crop cultivars and modern livestock breeds the relationship between food and land through producing more food largely meant converting more land into agricultural. This meant the ecosystem services were affected because the forest and natural ecosystems were there one which was cultivated. This was not the case in the African philosophy thought of the land-use.

The above can be endorsed to what Boogaard (2019:274) argues that the agriculture in Africa has been a focus on economic growth, external inputs from multinationals like pesticide, improved seed varieties, and artificial fertilizer. This practice has in a way marginalised how Africans understand and implemented food security. The expert advice from the multinational companies on agriculture was not accommodative of the African worldview on the use of land (Amusan & Setlalentoa, 2017). Hence this led to misunderstanding and the sustainability of the land by Africans. This has downgraded the way Africans saw the land as Mother Earth and something that gives life and protection. The understanding that was steamrolled from a western worldview rendered the understanding of African food security useless.

Formerly, the African philosophy saw the land as the giver of food and protection. This notion promoted respect for the land because it was obvious that without the land food scarcity will be eminent and people will die of hunger. The respect from which the land acclaimed or received was the sign of its importance and how it can promote sustainable development through its contribution to fertility and growth. To sustain Mother Earth, the Africans have methods, pointing example will how the Diola tribe in Guinea-Bissau rice harvest declined due to declining rainfall, desertification, and wild spread soil erosion and they used a sustainable way of preserving rice and the earth. According to Davidson (2012:370), the Diloa people realized that the sustenance of rice depends on Mother Earth, even if climate changes contribute to a low crop. Thence each household started to produce only enough rice to last for three months, and even when this supply is exhausted, most Guinean Diola spends the rest of the year scraping together what they can on a day-to-day basis to buy a kilogram of imported rice. In this way the Diola people could rest the land for future cultivation and hope for optimum crops.

Land and sustainable development

According to Saygin (2017: 4) maintains that scarcity of land resources demands that different strategy must be implemented to get the land to optimum use especially in developing countries, due to pressure, which the resource place on the land, making it largely unavailable. These strategies should be effective in protecting soil, water, and water resources from extinct and land degradation in a fragile ecosystem that is facing enormous pressure. This is can only be achievable when sustainable resource management is successful and anchored appropriate land-use measures. For example, according to Awuah-Nyameke (2012:86), some measures are what the Akan tribe sees as a taboo when defecating near a river, or plough near it. They believe that those acts expose the river to direct rays of the sun and that can result in the evaporation of the water in the river. To curb evaporation of water and the river running dry some deeds are prohibited near the river. Thus the perennial flow of the water in the river is ensured. These measures seemed to have contributed positively and effectively towards earth preservation in the Akan tribe paradigm. Thus development is sustained.

Furthermore, according to Awuah-Nyameke (2012), the Akan society attaches to Bosompo (the sea goddess) who controls the day. Every Tuesday has a traditional religious implication because no one is allowed to fish on that day. Besides, fishing on Tuesday can offend the sea goddess; therefore, it is a taboo to fish on Tuesday. This practice also is seen as a measure of cooling the sea and resting the sea because the livelihood of the Akan tribe is based on fishing. If they fish non-stop they will end up with no fish at all, hence the resting of the sea and development will cease.

References

Adeyemo, T., (1997) S*alvation in African tradition,* Nairobi, Kenya Evangel Publishing House.

Amusan, L. and Setlalentoa, M. (2017). An Assessment of Socio-Cultural Aspect of Large Scale Food Production Policies and Politics in Africa. *Transylvanian Review,* XXV(17), pp. 4347-4356.

Awuah-Nyameke, S., (2012) 'Religion and Development: African Traditional Religion perspective', *Journal Religious Studies and Theology,* 31(1); 75-90.

Boaten, B.B., 'Traditional Conservation Practices; Ghan Example', *Research Review EW* 14(1); 42-51.

Boogaard, B.K., (2019) 'The relevance of connecting sustainable agricultural development with African philosophy', *South African Journal of Philosophy,* 38(3); 273-286.

Cronje, R., (2012) Land Ownership and Land reform in South Africa viewed in sangonet, www.ngopulse.org/article/land-ownership-and-land-reform-south-africa

Danquah, I.B., *The Akan Doctrine of God,* London, Frank Cass & Co. Ltd.

Davidson, J., (2012) 'We Work Hard: customary imperatives of the Diola work regime in the context of environmental and economic change', *African Studies Review,* 52(2); 119-141.

Marumo. P.O., (2013) Christianity and African Traditional Religion in dialogue; An Ecological Future for Africa, Ph.D. thesis, Northwest University, Mafikeng, South Africa.

Moyo, F.L., (2009) Women embodied spiritually to the Mother Earth and sexual education in Malawi; A theological search for women's sexual empowerment in the era of HIV/AIDS, UKN. Thesis- Ph.D.

Saygin, S.D., (2017) 'Strategies to Enhance Sustainability of Land Resources in Arid Regions',

http://dx.doi.org/10.5772/intechopen.72492

United Nations Academic Impact (UNAI), (2016) The Intimate Relationship between Food Security and Land ... viewed in https://academicimpact .un.org/.../intimate-relationship-between-food-security-and-land

Chapter 3
Food Security in Africa Without Women: a *Sine Qua* for Food Insecurity

Lere Amusan and Samuel Chukwudi Agunyai

Introduction

Food availability, accessibility, and utilization are critical components of food security that women all over the world are actively involved in. They play a key role in quantity production of food, processing, distribution, marketing, seed processing, nurturing of vegetation, and reproduction of plants and animals; all of these contribute significantly to food security. For a very long time in Africa, policies on food security have repeatedly favoured male farmers than their female counterparts; this is partly because of the general belief that agricultural activities (such as land cultivation, planting, weeding, transporting of harvested crops, cash crops and harvesting and policy framework on seedlings, etc.,) are dominated by men. But evidence (Camilla, 2009; UNDP, 2010; FAO, 2011; ADB, 2013) are abounding to show that women play a significant role in ensuring availability, accessibility, and food use; yet, they have low representation and voice in decision making concerning their daily agricultural activities. It is a misplaced priority when women who actively involved in food production, distribution, and nutrition are excluded from policy formulation and implementation concerning food security.

This by implication could not only widen the gender productivity gap but could lead to food insecurity. Gender inequality or the gender-productive gap in agricultural production is a big threat to world hunger and food security. For instance, Njuki, Parkins, Kaler, and Ahmed (2016) submit that one in four people or 23.2% of the Sub-Sahara African population are affected by hunger. To end hunger in Africa, gender-inequality in food security must be addressed. This is because African women play a key role in the critical areas of food security. Food security is the ease with which people; in all cases get safe and adequate food to sustain a strong and lively life (World Food Summit, 1996). Thus, its core areas include availability in terms of adequacy and quantity continually, accessibility in terms of having resources or the means to acquire food for nutritious diet and utilization in terms of the appropriate use of food. The role of women in these core areas cannot be overemphasized in Africa. They are majorly engaged in the production of food in large quantities, its transportation to the market to make it accessible to the people, and provide adequate advice on the use of food than the male farmers.

This is largely consistent with FAO's (2011) report which specifically states that more female farmers are involved in the production of food, processing, distribution, and marketing. This had partly reduced the number of hungry people and promotes food security in Africa. But Africa could have achieved much more in food security and eradication of hunger if women farmers are targets of agricultural policies. Agricultural policies, specifically the ones on food security have favoured more male farmers than female farmers in Africa.

Yet, there is robust evidence in the literature that shows that policies that empower female farmers have contributed largely to agricultural productivity. For instance, FAO (2011a) predicted that if female farmers easily get lands for farming and credit as their male counterparts, agricultural production could rise from 2.5% to 4% and numbers of malnourished people could reduce by less than 20%. This report laid more credence to findings in Mukasa and Salami (2016) that productivity gains of 2.8%, 8.1%, and 10.3% were derived respectively from an intervention aimed at closing the gender productivity gap in Nigeria, Tanzania and Uganda. Despite projections and realities about women's key role in agricultural production, they still face unbearable conditions. And policies that could address these conditions and constraints have been hijacked by men farmers who majorly specialize in cash crops.

Food security is beyond planting or farming to earn income, it is about food production, its distribution, and effective utilization in terms of nutrition. Men farmers are hardly found in these core areas of food security, where women play an active role. Yet, they were not targets of most agricultural policies. This is partly because most agricultural policies in Africa are formulated without their inputs and such policies neglect prevailing conditions confronting African women farmers. Africa runs a patriarch dominated societies, where women's voices are hardly heard including in the agricultural sector where they play an active role. Consequently, this had adversely undermined not only food production in Africa, but had aggravated numbers of malnourished people in the continent and made them vulnerable to food insecurity. Dankelman (2010) and FAO (2011a) reported that women's inability to access land for food production, credit, extension services, technologies had rendered women vulnerable to food insecurity.

Also, FAO (2011) specifically reported that despite women's key role in global production of food, less than 20% of the land and 5% of agricultural extension services are accrued to them worldwide. Added to this report, was that of World Bank (2015) which specifically reveals how (9 in 10 countries) it studied, have a minimum of one law hindering the economic prospects of women, including low access to credit. All of these ugly conditions, no doubt, contribute to food insecurity in Africa. The foregoing nonetheless, information on effects of agricultural policy formulation and implementation, skewed to disfavour women in terms of lack of access to farm inputs, climate variability, and infrastructural facilities on food insecurity is scarcely available.

Understanding the implication of women exclusion from policy decisions on food security in Africa will guide the design of appropriate policy aimed at promoting access of women to credit, land, technologies, and closing the gender-inequality production gap in Africa. Our understanding of the contexts that removal of all barriers (social-cultural, religion, natural, men hegemony, policy-induced barriers) confronting women farmers is critical to achieving food security in Africa. Drawing on the constructivism theory, the paper seeks to examine the effects of women's low voice/participation in agricultural policy formulation and implementation on food insecurity; determine the effect of women's lack of access to farm inputs, climate variability and infrastructural deficits on food insecurity. These were the view to deepen knowledge on the nexus between food security without women and food insecurity in Africa. To ensure a logical approach to achieving these objectives, they are discussed under several headings. The conceptual review of food security and constructivism theory is discussed in the next section. In the subsequent sections we examine food security, policy and women farmers in Africa, effects/cogs of food security without women on food insecurity in Africa, redressing the gender imbalance in food security and lastly conclusion.

Conceptual and theoretical analyses of food security

The increasing complications of hunger, population growth, gender-imbalance in food production, poor nutrition, underutilization of food, and variability of climate change within most countries of the world over the years have created, among others, intellectual excitement and attention about food security. Consequently, it has gained increasing attention partly because food is the essence of life for all living beings, states, or countries. Its relevance to sustainable state security and development is not lost on many researchers across the globe. This, in itself, has necessitated the need to understand food security in both theoretical and practical sense. It is defined as the ability of everybody to get easy access to food, at all times, in the exact quantity and quality to boost their strength and make them sustainably active and strong considering its proper use. It represents the production of food in good quantity and quality (nutrient), its accessibility, and proper use by everyone at all times to maintain a healthy strong life. Food security covers production/availability, accessibility (the wherewithal), and utilization/adequacy (good nutrient). The 1975 UN defines it as an adequate production of food at global and national levels. This definition takes a conventional look at food security as pointedly noted by Clover (2003). It is beyond the mere production of food, which centres on availability, its accessibility, and utilization in terms of adequacy and stability are major determinants to ascertain if food is secured or not.

Similarly, UNEP (2002) reports that food security has three main components namely: availability, access, and optimal uptake of nourishment. But Indzembi (2013) classified it into four segments namely availability, accessibility, stability, and utilization. Availability of food means quantity and quality supply of food, it must be readily available in terms of effective production, adequate stock of food, engaging in trading it at both national and international markets. Food accessibility bothers on the ability of the people in terms of resources-money, infrastructure, transportation among others, to get hold of, demand, or consume nutritious food that could sustain their healthy life. However, food should be adequate and effectively utilized by people to get full nutrients from it. That is, food must be of high quality. This is closely related to that of Indzembi (2013) who submits that food utilization is an appropriate quality of food. The stability of food refers to, according to the Food Security and Nutrition (2013) non-volatility of equilibrium of demand and food supply.

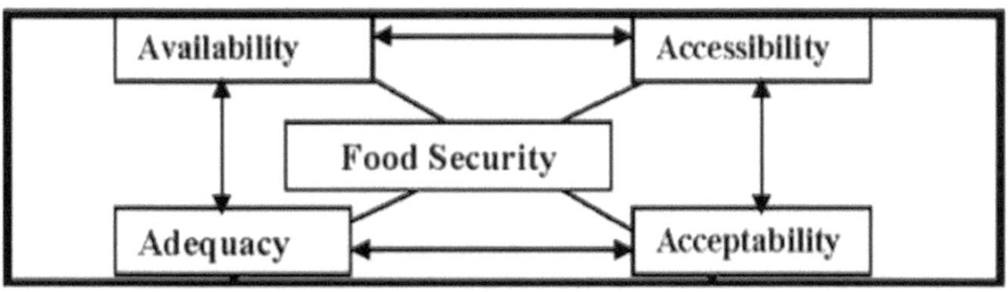

Components of Food Security
Adapted from the works of Boon (UNESCO-EOLSS Sample Chapters)

However, there is robust evidence in the literature to show that each of these segments is plagued with numerous challenges that have provoked tendencies of food insecurity in Africa. Food insecurity is the non-availability of food at the right time to all people, lack of wherewithal to make a demand, or get nutritious food and inappropriate use or inadequacy of food. A country or continent without a secured food is prone to hunger and malnutrition. Clover (2003) sees it as the inability of livelihoods at the household level to get easy access to sufficient food.

Africa remains the most largely affected continent by hunger and malnutrition, although hunger and malnutrition are a global phenomenon that ravages not only African countries but many countries of the world. The foregoing, notwithstanding is aptly documented in FAO (2011) report which specifically reveals that there was a dramatic increase in the numbers of people experiencing hunger globally between 1990-2007 and it grew worse with economic and financial crises of 2008-2009. Specifically, the IFPRI (2011) reports that (GHI) of 122 countries for 1990-2011 shows that

GHI for Sub-Saharan Africa fell by 18% while that of South Asia and East and North Africa stood at 25% and 39% respectively. This shows that Sub-Saharan Africa is worse hit by hunger, as it was confirmed in the findings of the UNESC (2012) that shows that five of the six countries ravaged by hunger were Sub-Saharan African countries.

Added to this, is a large number of malnourished people in Africa because sources of food in some African states are far below global hygienic, sanitation, and nutrient standard. For instance, FAO (2017) reports that the numbers of undernourished people in SSA rose from 220 to 224 million, representing 25% of 815 million people undernourished globally in 2016. From this report, it is obvious that a quarter of the world's undernourished people live in Sub-Saharan Africa, making it the region with the highest cases of malnourished people in the world. Several factors such as variability of climate change, global or local hike in prices of agricultural produce, poor agricultural infrastructural facilities, gender-imbalance, and one-sided (male farmers) dominated agricultural policies, weak institutions among others could have accounted for food insecurity crisis in Africa. Low cost of commodities, harsh climatic conditions such as the El Nino that resulted in low harvest and loss of livestock were contributory factors, FAO (2017) causing low food productivity in Sub-Saharan Africa. The report specifically linked the challenge of food security in South Africa and Nigeria to conflict, drought or flood and low commodity prices and global economic hardship.

Sub-region	Number of undernourished (millions)		Change so far (%)
	1990-92	2014-16	
Eastern Africa	103.9	124.2	19.6
Middle Africa	24.2	58.9	143.7
Southern Africa	3.1	3.2	2.3
Western Africa	44.6	31.5	-29.4
SS-Africa	**175.7**	**217.8**	**23.9**

Percentage Distribution of Malnourished people in Sub-Saharan Africa: 1990-1992, 2014-2016
Source: FAO (2017)

The number of undernourished people is continually increasing in Sub-Saharan Africa. It is worse in East Africa and Central Africa than Southern and Western Africa as depicted in the table above. The remarkable reduction in numbers of undernourished people in Western Africa could be linked to timely government interventions and collaboration with other developed agricultural nations. For instance, many governments of the West African states implemented the Comprehensive Africa Agriculture Development Programme (CAADP). This program covers all the critical areas of food security. FAO (2015) specifically reports that progress in the reduction of undernourished people in Western Africa is linked to efforts of West Africa regional organizations such as ECOWAS and WAEMU in the building of strong regional institutions and human capacities for agricultural development with a special focus of food security and mitigation of risk at the sub-region.

Constructivism underpinning of food security

Constructivism holds the view that shared ideas, mutual agreement, knowledge, and human consciousness is the basis of political action, decision, or policy. It is of the view that collectively held or inter-subjective ideas and understanding are a determinant of social life. It argued that equality and consideration of other people's constraints and abilities in decision or policymaking will not only bring out the joy in a society, but it could promote sustainable development as against inequality that provokes rifts, suspicion, and insecurity. Similarly, Amusan (2018) contends sees constructivism as equality and sympathy for others, which in turn brings out the joy in society rather than inequality that breeds hatred, resentment, and insecurity. Constructivism is against individualism, selfishness, and the imposition of ideas or the passing of decision or policy on people without their contributions or share ideas or knowledge. It embraces collectivity and the tendency of collective construction of program or decision binding on people in the society. Brue and Grant (2007) hold the view that constructivism is devoid of selfishness that binds people together in a functional workable society. Guzzani (2000) sees it as a metatheoretical commitment on three critical tenets: as a social construction of knowledge, epistemological claim, construction of social reality, ontological claim, and reality and knowledge are mutually constitutive, reflexive claim. But generally, Jung (2019) constructivism operates on three assumptions: first, that idea is the basis of human interaction and not material benefits; secondly, the idea is the inter-subjective belief as a shared collective understanding, thirdly, that belief constructs the actors' identities and interests.

Thus women farmers in Africa are key actors in the agricultural sector yet their ideas and knowledge are mostly not considered during policy formulation and implementation. Odney (2013) notes that despite the inclusion of women's land rights in the constitution of some African states, in reality, little is achieved concerning equal access and controls over land due to weak execution of enabling laws, thus women are rarely seen making a decision. Unlike the tenets of constructivism, because male farmers are in key positions in the agricultural sector, they repeatedly skewed policies on food security to their benefits than their female counterparts. Equality and sympathy for others proffered by Amusan (n.d.) as tenets of constructivism, that promotes the joy of society are never put into consideration by those who design agricultural policies in Africa. The exclusion of women farmers who are key players in food security from the policymaking processes and execution is the bane of lingering cases of food insecurity in Africa. The actions and practices of framers of food security policies are all against the tenets of constructivism. The theory stipulates that rather than material gains, the idea of every key actor should be the basis of decisions or interactions. And that the idea is the inter-subjective belief shared collectively by all participating members (in this case, farmers: male and female). While the belief of members constructs their collective interests.

In Africa, the interests of women farmers such as access to land, credit, and training in extension services, technologies for farming, seedlings, and strong agricultural institutions among others are not collectively constructed and considered. It is of the view and tenets of constructivism that collectively held decision or policy will advance sustainable development and progress of a society than the imposition of few or a certain group of people decides on all actors or members. Drawing from forgoing submission, food security in Africa may continue to lag or drag if women are not participating in the policymaking process and execution. Food security without women involvement in policy decisions will amount to food insecurity in Africa. Several signs of progress could be achieved if African women farmers are involved in policy decisions about food security. It could close the gender-productivity gap, address constraints like poor access to land, credit, extension services, technologies, socio-cultural, economic and religious barriers, climate variability among others that affect women in Africa. Since women play a key role in food production, their involvement in policy-making processes could help reduced constraints limiting the productivity of female farmers in Africa.

Women, food security and policy in Africa: A critical discourse

It is no more new news that most agricultural activities take place in the rural area. The rural area is agrarian in nature and production in this area is mainly on a small household basis, that is, subsistence farming. This assertion is similar to that of Odney (2013) who avers that rural life and farming are the mainstays of countries in Africa. This accounts for why huge numbers of African population reside in this area and depend largely on household agricultural activities, for income earnings and consumption

(Odney 2013). It is on record (Devender and Krishna 2011; FAO 2011; Nahusenay and Tesfaye 2015) that women actively perform half of the labour required for agricultural production in the region.

This, however, makes them a key player in food security in most African states. For instance, food production in good quantity and quality requires labour that cannot only be provided by male farmers, but also by female farmers who are highly experienced in small scale farming. Rural women display a full passion for farming starting from planting to harvesting crops (Amusan & Saka, 2018; Nahusenay, 2017). Comparatively, women seem to be more available for agricultural labour and production than men who are easily forced out of rural areas by climate variability, job opportunities, and economic hardships. This is because women are more attached to their children, family, and domestic duties than men (Amusan & Ngoh, 2016). This makes them readily available for agricultural labour and food production in rural areas.

The foregoing shows that women are central to food security in Africa and globally. This submission had earlier been documented in the report and findings of the United Nations (2015), FAO (2009), and Amusan and Saka (2018). Specifically, UN (2015) reveals that women are responsible for more than half of global food production. FAO's report shows that women perform half of the agricultural labour in rural areas and contribute even more in many countries. Amusan and Saka (2018) on the other hand, found that the role of women is central to development. In addition to this, the efforts of women in food availability, accessibility, and utilization are well documented. For instance, they produce, process, distribute, market, utilized, and accessed food with the money they make from agricultural labour, though; they are mostly not paid as family farmers. This aptly confirms findings in Njuki et.al (2016) which reveals that despite women's critical efforts in core areas of food security, their labour is largely undervalued and laden with numerous constraints. Similarly, Karbeer (2012) discovered that the labour of women in family agricultural activities and care services like a child, sick and elderly care, fetching of water, fuelwood, cleaning, purchasing, and preparing of food are hardly paid for.

Yet, rural female farmers are likely to spend more than the men on food in terms of providing their family and children with nutritious food, its distribution to household members, determinants of food adequacy, pay children school fees and care services. All of these improve the household's food security. But when it comes to taking vital decisions or formulating policies concerning food security, they are relegated to the background or neglected. ILO (2009) in its report notes that female farmers are not only neglected by policymakers, but they are also not recognized as productive farmers, despite their critical roles in all the core areas of food security. This, however, is consistent with findings in Mondal (2013) which reveals that women are hardly involved in the decision-making process. This is confirmed in the report of the International Centre for Research on Women (2008) that reveals that women are not yet a mainstay of agricultural development and programs, despite their huge role in food security. This is partly because decision-makers still see women as home assistants or producers in farm households and not as farmers and economic agents, added to these, is the fact that development community lacks accurate data on women roles in agricultural production to devise and promulgate appropriate policies that can cover women constraints in food security (ICRW 2008). It is important to note that appropriate enabling laws and policies can help eradicate challenges confronting women in food security; this is because gender-equality and equal access to agricultural incentives and resources will safeguard food security in Africa. For instance, International Development Law Organization (2016) reports that policies, laws, and legal systems can play a crucial role in the removal of barriers plaguing women's ability to own land for agricultural activity and productive resources.

From the foregoing analyses, it can be inferred that many of the African states still have large numbers of hungry and malnourished people, partly because, women, as key actors in the agricultural sector are left out of the policymaking process and execution, thus, most of their needs and constraints are often not covered by the available policies. Consequently widening the gender-productivity gap and leading to the tendency of food insecurity. Gender-based discrimination is one of the most significant obstacles to the realization of food security for everyone (FAO 2004). This fear was however dispelled by the UNDP (2012) which reveals that giving women greater voice in decision-making at all levels will increase food security.

Food insecurity in Africa: X-raying the cogs and constraints facing women

Agriculture is central to women's livelihood in Africa; this is partly because, by nature, they are calmer, caring, and more domestic. For Amusan and Olutola (2017) the general image of women in Africa is that of domestic workers. All of these qualities make them fit for agricultural activities that promote food security, especially in rural areas. But despite their critical role in food security in Africa, they are faced with a myriad of cogs undermining their active participation in food production, accessibility, and utilization. These cogs range from the variability of climate change, lack of equal access to farm inputs (land, seedlings, fertilizers, technologies), lack of access to credit, extension services, poor agricultural infrastructural facilities-vehicles, accessible roads among others. Buttressing this view, was the UNDP's (2012) report which confirms that women face obstacles such as lack of financial credit, assets and farm inputs, and infrastructural deficit which further aggravate women's vulnerability to food insecurity and reduces their overall agricultural productivity. Also, women find it very difficult to adapt to climate stress, because of their inability to access credit, lack of access to land, social capital, and technology, and in some severe cases, they are socially, culturally and economically discriminated against using stringent law (UNDP 2012). Thus, food insecurity is grossly affected by the following cogs in Africa.

Limited access to farm inputs

Land, seedlings, fertilizer, water among other farm inputs are required for food production. And most women in Africa lack access to land and the few ones that have access to it do not have access to seedlings, fertilizer, and clean water for planting. This submission had earlier been affirmed by Nahusenay (2017) who reveals that Ethiopian women farmers are excluded from deciding what crops to plant; purchase and sale of livestock, farm inputs, land plots, etc. The major decisions are usually made by husbands and in rare cases shared by both (Nahusenay 2017). This is mainly because of the assumption that women are only in the farm to assist their husbands, most policymakers and government interventions that aim the improvement of food security, often undermine the role of women in food production. This invariably provokes the tendency of food insecurity in Africa. For instance, Odney (2013) found that gender-inequality over access and control of land and natural resources is an obstacle to the sustainable management of natural resources and development. Women's landlessness, according to Odney (2013) has consequences for the sustainable socio-economic development of Africa. Similarly, World Bank (2016) reports that gender-inequality over access and control of land and productive assets undermine and inhibit food security at local, national, and international levels.

Climate variability

Climate stress in terms of the unmitigated flood, drought, erosion, and sudden drylands are potential triggers of food insecurity in Africa. Climate change affects women than men, partly because they lack the resources in terms of finance, social capital, and technology to combat climate stress, thus making them highly prone to food insecurity. Added to this, was the findings in the World Bank (2010) report, which categorically reveals that 25 out of 35 economies in SSA have stringent laws that restrict women's quick response to climate change. The effects of climate stress on food insecurity had provoked numerous studies (UNDP 2011; FAO 2007; IPCC 2007a, 2007b) which concluded that unmitigated climate change is potentially detrimental to food security in Sub-Saharan Africa.

Comparatively, women are affected by climate change than the men, this is because, cultural norms and tradition permit men to leave their household and family, in search of job opportunities, leaving their wife behind to bear the risk of climate stress alone. This adversely affects the wellbeing of women farmers in Africa. Climatic stresses on agricultural production make women particularly vulnerable to food insecurity (UNDP 2012). Similarly, UNEP (2008) reports that food security is grossly affected by drought or unreliable rainfall, food security can be particularly challenging (UNEP 2008)

Infrastructural facilities deficits

Food security would certainly thrive with the availability of agricultural infrastructural facilities like a storehouse for safe keep of harvests, farming tools like a plough, harvesting caterpillars, irrigation works, market, communication, tools and tractors, transportation system and good road networks that could enhance unperturbed transportation of farm produce to the market. African women farmers generally don't have access to credit and resources that can provide these basic infrastructural facilities. There is a huge deficit in the procurement of these facilities partly because women lack the wherewithal to procure these facilities. And policies that could have helped them procure infrastructural facilities rarely consider women as beneficiaries.

Specifically, UNEP (2008) in its report reveals that the deficit in infrastructure (roads, transportation, communication, and market) affects food security in Africa. In addition to this, lack of procurement of appropriate technologies (ICTs, tools, and tractors for harvesting and general lack of knowledge in the use of new technologies) could undermine food security in Africa (UNEP 2008). Similarly, ILO (2009) reveals that poor water, sanitation, and energy infrastructure in many developing countries adds to their time and labor burdens for water and fuelwood collection (ILO 2009).

Lack of access to the market

The movement of farm produce to the market requires not only a good transport system but a good road network. Effective distribution of food, a critical element of food security largely depends on the availability of good transport and road network system. Women play an active role in ensuring that food produced gets to the market. But studies (Nahusenay 2017; UNEP 2008; World Bank 2008) have shown that the bad road network and transportation systems have contributed to food insecurity in Africa. On several occasions, farm produce does not get to the market, while those that manage to get to the market, spend long hours and days on traffic jam due to bad roads and transport system. Most of the time, women bear the brunt of poor transportation and bad road network system, during food distribution. For instance, UNEP (2008) notes that, the lack of access to the market could lead to inconsistent supply of food and food insecurity.

Lack of access to credit and financial resources

Unlike male farmers' counterparts, women lack access to credit facilities to farm. This is largely due to the belief that women are only on the farm to assist their husbands, thus making most financial institutions reject their request for a loan facility. Besides, most women do not have the collateral security to borrow loans from financial institutions, thus affecting their productivity and food security in SSA. They, according to Nahusenay (2017) rarely have access to the resources that would make their work more productive and ease their heavy workload. Women's travails over access to credit were particularly more revealing when ILO (2009) reports that they have less than 10 percent access to agricultural credit offered to small-scale farmers.

Human capital /training and extension services deficits

Generally, poor training in extension services and poor education in farming limits human capital development in agriculture. Farmers whether males or females need adequate agricultural training and education to improve their productivity. Scientific evidence (ILO 2009; Okali 2011; UNDP 2015) showed that comparatively, female farmers are less educated, poorly trained, and have minimal access to extension services. Similarly, Amusan and Olutola (2017) opined that women are highly poor and uneducated in Africa, while ILO (2009) reported that women only have access to a meager 7% of agricultural extension services. Women's inability to receive a quality education in farming had contributed to the lingering cases of food insecurity in Africa.

Exclusionary policy framework

African women farmers are rarely consulted and considered during decision making. In Africa, policymaking in the agricultural sector is male-dominated; it is skewed to disfavor women. This is attributed to reasons why women farmers have low access to credit; land, skilled training, facilities, and extension services, there are few enabling laws or policies that target women farmers as beneficiaries. Even when there are policies, such policies are formulated and implemented to target men farmers than women farmers because women are not considered as productive farmers in Africa. The ones that target women as beneficiaries, men farmers, often use their positions to restrict women's access to agricultural incentives. This inevitably provokes the tendency of food insecurity in Africa. This submission contributes adequately to exiting bodies of evidence or knowledge (Kabeer 2000; Rao 2008; ILO 2009; WB/FAO/IFAD 2009; Odney 2013; FAO 2011; Nahusenay 2017) on non-inclusion of women in the agricultural policymaking process in Africa.

A critical look at the cogs affecting women farmers in Africa shows that food security without women farmers will certainly heighten cases of hunger, malnutrition, and low agricultural productivity, inaccessibility, and inappropriate use of food. All of these factors are potential sources of food insecurity in Africa. Food insecurity had persistently ravaged Africa because of the systematic and technical exclusion of highly experienced, dedicated, and caring key players (women) in rural agricultural farming. Food security in Africa is linked to agricultural activities of farmers in rural areas. And women's critical role in food production is key to food security in Africa.

Food insecurity in Africa: Redressing the gender imbalance

It is the argument and finding of this paper that one of the strategies that could be adopted by African states to tackle food insecurity is the removal of all barriers limiting women farmers' agricultural productivity. Food availability, accessibility, and utilization would be more improved when more women have unbridled access to agricultural incentives like male farmers. African states and leaders should look inward and carry out a comprehensive re-analysis and evaluation of existing agricultural policies on food security to cover and target more women farmers in terms of improving their access to agricultural incentives.

Also, African political leaders should reinforce their political will to effectively implement international agreed decisions on declarations and conventions on equality of rights. Effective implementation of international conventions on the removal of all barriers and discrimination against women in Africa will go long way in eradicating constraints facing women farmers and in turn contribute to an increase in food production, thus, reducing hunger and malnutrition in Africa.

Theoretically, agricultural decision-making organs or bodies can be organizationally expanded to allow more active involvement of women in decision making. This could make them have a voice in policy formulation and implementation of food security. In addition to this, the policy will be more comprehensive rather than being one-sided. The quest for a provision that guarantees the active participation of women in policy formulation and implementation could trigger competition (the need to be more productive) between male and female farmers in rural areas. But competition over high productivity in food production will reduce food insecurity in Africa. Also, a clause or provision that includes women in the policy-making process and implementation could be perceived as the empowerment of mediocre, because of the widely held assumption and view about women's low level of education, especially in the rural areas. It is important to note that, the idea for women advocacy at the decision-making level is to promote healthy competition between male and female farmers. To this end, such provision should be extended to rural areas. In this way, even in some African states where women suffer from socio-cultural and religious restrictions, the advocacy for more women in the decision making could end such practices. Furthermore, it will correct the notion that women are not mere agricultural assistants to men.

We need to state that while the suggestion for the inclusion of more women in the decision-making process remains achievable, promoting gender equity in agricultural food production requires a systematic approach. Besides, African states and leaders should pay more attention to legislation and education, which promotes women's equal access to agricultural incentives (land, credit, skilled training, extension services, technologies, inputs among others) in Africa. The importance of having more women at the helm of affairs or decision making is to reduce food insecurity in Africa.

Conclusion

Findings in this study show that low participation or complete exclusion of women from agricultural policy decisions on food security has hurt food production, availability, accessibility, and utilization in Africa (see Odney 2013, ILO 2009; FAO 2011). It is also evidently clear that food security without women is potentially a source of food insecurity in Africa. Women, especially the ones in rural areas are the engine and power that moves food security in Africa. The little progress achieved in terms of reduced hunger and malnutrition, high productivity of food, its accessibility, and utilization in Africa, was because women, despite their numerous constraints (landlessness, lack of access to credit, farm inputs, skilled training, technologies, communication, socio-cultural and religious barriers) still play an active role in agricultural production. It is, therefore, the contention of this paper, that there is significant nexus between women's critical role in agricultural labour and food security in Africa, excluding them from policies on food security would continually make them vulnerable to food insecurity and this is not healthy for Africa.

References

ADB, (2013). Gender Equality and Food Security: Women's Empowerment as a Tool against Hunger. Available: http://www.adb.org/publications/genderequality-and-food-security-women's-empowerment-tool-against-hunger.

Amusan, L. (2018). Motion without Movement: Poverty Reduction through embedded Liberalism in the Post-Apartheid South Africa. Rauhut, V and Hatti, N. (eds), Poverty, Politics and the Poverty of Politics, pp. 213-238. Delhi: B.R. Publishing Corporation.

Amusan, L. and Ngoh, MS. (2016). Women as agents of development: an assessment of Modimola Village in the North West Province of South Africa through the Expanded Public Works Programme (EPWP). Gender & Behaviour, 14(2), pp. 7238-7245.

Amusan L., and Olutola, O. (2017). Contextualizing African Women's Empowerment in Agriculture: Challenges from Climate Change and Mineral Extraction Perspectives. Journal of International Women Studies, 18(4): 117-130. Available at: http://vc.bridgew.edu/jiws/vol18/iss4/9

Amusan, L., and Saka L. (2018). Women: Towards a conceptual framework. In Ojakorutu V., and Olaopa O.R., (eds), Perspective on Women in Socio-Political Development in Africa, pp.19-44. Academic Press: London- Washington.

Brue, S. L, and Grant, R. R (2007). The Evolution of Economic Thought. Mason, OH: Thomson South-Western.

Camilla, T. (2009). Climate Change in Africa, Zed Books, London.

Clover J. (2003). Food Security in Sub-Saharan Africa. African Security Review 12(1).

Devender D and Krishna RC. (2011) "Socio-Economic Conditions of Agricultural Labour in Andhra Pradesh: A case study in Karimnagar District". International Journal of Business Economics and Management Research 2.3 (2011): 115-134.

Dankelman, I. (2010) Gender and Climate Change: An Introduction, London: Earthscan

FAO. (2009). Guide to Conducting a Right to Food Assessment. Available: http://www.fao.org/fileadmin/templates/righttofood/documents/RTF_publications/EN/3_toolbox_Assessment_guide.pdf.

FAO. (2011a). The State of Food Insecurity in the World (How does international price volatility affect domestic economies and food security?) Rome: FAO.

FAO. (2011b). The State of Food and Agriculture. Rome: FAO.

FAO. (2015). The State of Food and Agriculture. Available: http://www.fao.org/3/a-i4910e.pdf; Cerise, S., Do Discriminatory Social Institutions Matter for Food Security? (2012), OECD, available: http://www.oecd.org/dev/development-gender/49756756.pdf.

FAO. (2015). Regional overview of food insecurity: African food security prospects brighter than ever. Accra, FAO.

FAO. (2017). Regional Overview of Food Security and Nutrition: The Challenges of Building Resilience to Shocks and Stresses. Accra.

Guzzini, S. (2000). A Reconstruction of Constructivism in International Relations. European Journal of International Relations, 6, 147-182.

Food Security and Nutrition (2013) Food Security and Nutrition Information System in Cambodia. Accessed July 4, 2019, at http://www.foodsecurity .gov.kh/wifsan.

Guzzini, S. (2000). A reconstruction of constructivism in international relations. European Journal of International Relations, 6, 147-182.

ICRW (2008). Women, Food Security, and Agriculture in a Global Market Place. Washington, D.C. US.

IDLO (2016). Women, Food, Land: Exploring Rule of Law Linkages, using Law to Strengthen Food Security and Land Right for Women. Rome, Italy

ILO. (2009). Global Employment Trends for Women. Geneva: ILO.

Indzembi, F. C. (2013). New Challenges to Food Security in Sub-Saharan Africa. A Research Thesis submitted to the graduate degree program in Global and International Studies and the Graduate Faculty of the University of Kansas in partial fulfilment of the requirements for the degree of Master of Arts.

Intergovernmental Panel on Climate Change IPCC (2007) Climate Change 2007: Synthesis Report of the Fourth Assessment Report of the Intergovernmental Panel on Climate Change, Geneva: Intergovernmental Panel on Climate Change.

Jung, H. (2019). The Evolution of Social Constructivism in Political Science: Past to Present, SAGE Open, 9(1): 1-10. DOI: 10.1177/2158244019832703.

Kabeer, N. (2012) Women's Economic Empowerment and Inclusive Growth: Labour Markets and Inclusive Development, Discussion Paper Vol. 29, No. 12, London: School of Oriental and African Studies and Centre for Development Policy and Research.

Mondal M. (2013). "The Role of Rural Women in Agriculture Sector of Sagar Island, West Bengal, India". International Journal of Engineering and Science 2.2 (2013): 81-86.

Mukasa, A. and Salami, A. (2016) 'Gender equality in agriculture: What are the benefits for Sub-Saharan Africa?' Chief Economist Complex | AEB 7, no.3.

Nahusenay A and Tesfaye T. (2015) "Roles of Rural Women in Livelihood and Sustainable Food Security in Ethiopia: A case study from Delanta Dawunt District, North Wello Zone". International Journal of Nutrition and Food Sciences 4.3 (2015): 343-355.

Nahusenay, A. (2017). The Roles of Rural Women on Agricultural Labor Conscriptions in Ethiopia: The Case of Delanta District, South Wello Zone. EC Nutrition 6.4 (2017): 144-155.

Njuki, J., Parkins, J. R., Kaler, A., & Ahmed, S. (2016). Gender, Agriculture, and Food Security: Where are we? In Njuki, J., Parkins, J.R., & Kaler, A. (eds), Transforming Gender and Food Security in Global South, pp.1-18, Routledge, Taylor and Francis Group: London and New York.

Odney, M. (2013). Improving Access to Land and strengthening Women's land rights in Africa. A paper presented at the Annual World Bank Conference on Land and Property, The World Bank - Washington DC, April 8-11.

Okali, C. (2011). Achieving Transformative Change for Rural Women's Empowerment. An Expert paper presented at Expert Group Meeting: Enabling rural women's economic empowerment: institutions, opportunities and participation, 20-23 September 2011, Accra, Ghana.

Rosario, T. C. (2016). The Case of Korean Investments in the Greater Mekong Sub-region. ASPJ Africa and Francophonie. 7(2): 57-76.

United Nations, (2015) Transforming our World: The 2030 Agenda for Sustainable Development. A/RES/70/1, available: https://sustainabledevelopment.un.org/content/documents/21252030%20Agenda%20for%20Sustainable%20Development%20web.pdf.

UNDP (2010). Gender, Climate Change and Community-Based Adaptation, New York.

UNDP (2011). Human Development Report, New York.

UNDP (2012) Africa Human Development Report 2012: towards a food secure future, New York: UNDP, www.undp.org/content/dam/undp/library/corporate/HDR/Africa%20HDR/UNDP-Africa%20HDR-2012-EN.pdf.

United Nations Economic and Social Council (2012). Status of Food Security in Africa. Eighth Session of the Committee on Food Security and Sustainable Development andRegional Implementation Meeting for the Twentieth Session of the Commission on Sustainable Development, 19-21, November 2012, Ethiopia.

UNEP (2002), Africa Environment Outlook: Past, Present and Future Perspectives, UNEP, Nairobi, pp. 422.

UNEP (2008). Organic Agriculture and Food Security in Africa. United Nations, New York and Geneva.

World Bank (2008). Gender in Agriculture Sourcebook. Agriculture and Rural Development, Washington, DC: The International Bank for Reconstruction and Development.

World Bank/IFAD/FAO (2009) Gender and Agriculture Sourcebook: Investing in Women as Drivers of Agricultural Growth, Washington, DC: World Bank.

World Bank (2010). Sub-Saharan Africa Managing Land in a Changing Climate: An Operational Perspective for Sub-Saharan Africa.

World Bank (2015). Ethiopia Poverty Assessment 2014: Overview. Poverty Global Practice. Africa Region. Washington, DC.

Chapter 4
Gender-Inclusive Development in Rural Settings: Reframing the Issues in African Context

Olajumoke Adeyeye, Monica A. Orisadare, Ayobami B. Atijosan and Oluwatoyin O.C. Olajide

Introduction

Worldwide, gender has been considered as a development issue because men, women, boys and girls are participants as well as beneficiaries of development efforts (Moser, 2012). This is because the world population of about 7.5 billion is almost evenly distributed between the male and female sex. Hence, marginalizing or excluding substantial proportion of the world population, either in contribution to or benefiting from development efforts would make futile all efforts targeted at attaining sustainable development (Sen and Grown, 1987). This is because women and men have different needs and concerns (RAI, 2018; World Bank, 2009) and they experience the impact of social, physical and cultural factors in different ways (Lips 2016). There is therefore the need to consider gender issues when planning and implementing development programmes and strategies; this would ensure that men, women, boys and girls participate and benefit equally (Moser, 2012).

Central to the concept of gender is gender relations which is the relations of power between women and men (Abrams and Harvery, 2017; Amusan and Saka, 2018). These are revealed not only in the division of labour and resources between women and men, but also in ideas and representations – the ascribing to women and men of different abilities, attitudes, desires, personality traits, behaviour patterns, and so on (Agarwal, 1997). Gender relations determine household security, well-being of the family, and agricultural production and many other aspects of rural life (Doss, 2001; Das and Mishra, 2018).In sub-Saharan Africa (SSA), especially in the rural areas, patriarchy is still dominant, guiding the way of life and behaviour of the people (Izugbara, 2005; Lecouteres and Wuyts, 2017). Gender norms, stereotypes and beliefs with bias against women are put in place to control and confine them (Godsil et al., 2016). In most circumstances, these biased stereotypes, norms and beliefs influence several inter-related social, economic and cultural factors making women to become subjugated into a subordinate role. In designing the different approaches for achieving inclusive development, most efforts have been based on the unitary model which assumes development as single proxy indicators such as income or consumption. Although income could be a good measure in identifying the poor, however, this approach would be limited to a one-dimensional measure of poverty (Amusan, 2018). This is because poverty can also be defined through social marginalization and exclusion, different manifestation of malnutrition, poor living conditions, lack of access to basic services, resources and employment opportunities (De La O Campos et al., 2018). It is therefore important to consider a multidimensional approach which can provide greater insight into the degree of exclusion and social marginalization so as to design effective strategies which would foster context-based gender-inclusive development in SSA.

For Africa to experience inclusive agriculture and rural development, it is important to consider gender-inclusive development in agriculture and rural development to foster sustainable growth and development. This is because gender gaps exist in agriculture and rural development which serves as hindrance to achieving sustainable food security and poverty alleviation in rural communities. Such gaps include constraint in access, ownership and control over decisions on agricultural resources and unequal intra-household power relations, as well as bias social and cultural norms in ownership and rights to pertinent agricultural resources such as land. These constitute a great hindrance in the pathway to empowerment of rural dwellers especially women.

Based on the foregoing, this paper therefore argues that for intervention programmes to produce transformative outcomes, multidimensional empowerment has to form the core. In addition, efforts should change from implementing foreign solutions to changing structures, institutions and other non-state actors that negatively influence the success of agricultural interventions in rural contexts. It is on these bases that we propose this analytical framework.

Key issues in gender discourse on rural settings

Poor conceptualization of empowerment

Within the context of gender and rural development, several approaches have been developed and adopted to explain and correct inequalities between men and women within the households and in the society in general. Since the 1960s, development experts have advocated for different approaches to guide the integration of issues of gender and women concerns in development (Parpart and Barriteau, 2000). Some of the prominent approaches are Welfare Approach; Women in Development (WID) Approach; Women and Development (WAD) Approach; Gender and Development (GAD) Approach; and the Empowerment Approach. However, some of these approaches have been faulted. For instance, the Welfare approach emphasized the roles of women as wives and mothers and the belief that macroeconomic strategies for growth would automatically trickle down to women through men especially their husbands. The WID and the WAD approaches advocate for equal participation of women in education, employment and other spheres of society; however, they failed to question the underlying causes and nature of women's subordination and oppression (Cornwall and Rivas, 2015). The GAD perspective holds advantage over the WID and WAD because it leads to the design of intervention and affirmative action strategies which ensure that women are better integrated into ongoing development efforts. Of importance to this study is the empowerment approach which emerged as a result of the criticism of the previous development approaches (Lutrell et al., 2009). According to Razavi and Miller (1995), the empowerment approach is premised on the notion of equity; hence, it takes a view of anti-poverty and efficiency approaches in its strategies.

Several authors have found it difficult to arrive at a uniform, cross-cutting definition of empowerment, leading to a varying and loosely definitions shaped by individual experiences, personality, specific context and culture (Page and Czuba, 1999; Alkire et al., 2013). Despite this, there seems to be the convergence around the theme of the ability to possess power or give authority to the powerless in a particular situation. While empowerment can be said to be context-dependent; however, a fundamental belief is that empowerment is not just an outcome but a process of progression from a disempowered state to an empowered one. It is therefore more than simply marginal increase in incomes; rather, it requires a transformation of power relations (Kabeer, 2005). Hence, if power cannot change or expand in relationships, empowerment cannot happen (Page and Czuba, 1999).

Based on the foregoing, it is important to situate this study within the context of empowerment as not just an outcome but also as a process. Hence, definitions such as those of Kabeer (1999), Alsop et al., (2006) and Narayan (2002) readily help to contextualize this study. The definition of Alsop et al., (2006) has two important aspects. First is the aspect related to Amartya Sen's (1985) concept of agency. The second part relates to institutional environment which gives people the ability to exert agency successfully (Ibrahim and Alkire, 2007). Similarly, Kabeer (1999) definition of empowerment encompassed three dimensions: resources (defined to include not only access but also future claims to material, human, and social resources), agency (including processes of decision making, negotiation, and even deception and manipulation), and achievements (well-being outcomes). Narayan (2002) definition emphasized four main elements: access to information, inclusion and participation, accountability, and local organizational capacity. This points to the fact that focus on individual choice can limit the definition of empowerment, especially in cultural contexts wherein community and mutuality are valued.

Based on the different definitions, we argue that the underlying issues guiding empowerment can be summarized as follows:

- Expansion of individual's or group's capacity and capabilities (agency) to make choices particularly in contexts in which this ability had been denied to them;
- Enabling environment defined by access to opportunities and resources that can aid the process of making choices; and

- Ability to transform the choices people make into desired actions and outcomes.

Lack of clarity in the design and implementation of development programmes

For development programmes to achieve its laudable objectives, it needs to be participatory, that is, carry along the beneficiaries in the process. This is usually stated in the strategies and methods of implementing these. However, in most instances the objectives are not achieved despite the time spent in planning, and the huge resources and investments made. A possible reason is regarding the intended targets as mere beneficiaries rather than active participants in decision-making processes on agricultural intervention programmes. In other words, they are meant to benefit from the outcome of the projects rather than taking active parts in the conceptualization, design, implementation and evaluation. The failure of the rice threshing project in Northern Nigeria is a typical example(UNIFEM 1993).While the objective is to assist rural women in processing rice more effectively through the use of bicycle-mounted threshers, it was reported that the innovation was rejected by women. This is because the exposure of thighs during operation was deemed culturally inappropriate. Similarly, women's low adoption of Money Maker Hip Pump in Central Kenya and manual pumps in Zimbabwe was due to the fact that the women 'felt exposed' when operating the above-ground models of manual pumps, among other reasons (Njuki, et al, 2014).Therefore, programmes that seek to introduce new technologies need to take into account the socio-cultural and religious factors influencing gender considerations in the design and implementation. This was attested to by Doss (2001) who noted the enormous diversity and complexity between different African villages, not to talk of countries, in designing technology for African female farmers.

In the context of gender and rural households, according to Cozzens and Sutz (2012), inclusiveness of innovations can be assessed from two angles: process and outcome. However, the 6-ladder of inclusive innovation framework developed by Heeks et al (2013) provide a ready tool to analyse the level of inclusion of intended targets in development programmes and policies. This defines inclusiveness in six stages: intention, consumption, impact, process, structure and post-structure. Intention signifies the motivation behind the project. Does it address the needs or wants or problems of the intended targets? Consumption is determined by the level of adoption of the innovations while impact signifies the level of impact of the project on the beneficiaries. This is measured by impact on the well-being, assets, or capabilities of the intended targets. Process measures the level of involvement of the intended targets in the project. Who defines the objectives of the project? At what level are the intended targets involved? Involvement can further be sub-divided using Arnstein's (1969) ladder of participation as being informed, being consulted, collaborating, being empowered, or controlling. The last two: structure and post-structure assess the inclusiveness of the institutional environment where the innovation is developed. More importantly, the structure through which these projects are conceived and implemented should be inclusive. This means that the underlying institutions, organisations and relations that make up an innovation system are inclusive. This requires significant structural reform of structures and institutions through which these projects and programmes are implemented. Without this, policies and projects aimed at inclusion in rural areas will only achieve temporary or superficial inclusion.

Misconstrued definition and contextualization of social exclusion

Sen's social exclusion framework can also be used to provide an interesting dimension to assessing gender inclusiveness of intervention projects in Africa. The framework assessed exclusion from two contexts: instrumental versus constitutive exclusion and active versus passive exclusion(Sen, 2000).Being excluded can sometimes be in itself a deprivation and this can be of intrinsic importance on its own (constitutive exclusion). This can however lead to negative consequences for the individual (instrument exclusion). Both constitutive and instrument exclusions are capability deprivations because they disallow individuals from being and doing what they value. Examples abound in the context of rural areas. Inability to have access to credit for agricultural activities may be constitutive because it is a form of capability deprivation; however, it can lead to worse consequences – poverty (instrumental exclusion). Another example is the non-education of girls in rural areas. This not only denies them their human right (constitutive) but also disempowers them from having a voice in several issues affecting them such as marriage, birth control, employment opportunities, among others. Excluding women from participation in leadership activities in rural communities, not only excludes them from social activities (constitutive) but also disallows them from having a voice on decisions that affect them in the communities such as citing of rural projects like bore hole, health facilities etc. These decisions are made by men, driven by men's priorities to serve men's objectives. Understanding the context of social exclusion therefore allows for development of projects and policies that tackle the roots of disempowerment. Missing out on this may lead to wrong interpretation of root causes of disempowerment and poverty but also wrong implementation of laudable projects. Empowering women and girls for instance should focus more on incentivizing education of young girls in addition to other initiatives rather than giving farming implements and credit to women who lack the capability to control decisions on these resources.

Social exclusions can also be tackled from the view of poor policies and biased norms and beliefs aimed at women in rural areas (active exclusion) as well as their unintended consequences (passive exclusion). Programmes and policies that focus on inclusion in rural areas should therefore seek to distinguish between the active fostering of an exclusion—whether done by the government or by another wilful agent—and a passive development of an exclusion that may result from a set of circumstances without such volitional immediacy (Bhalla and Lapeyre, 2016). Norms and beliefs that vest political participation in rural areas exclusively on men sometimes have negative effects on issues that border on women and children in the community. These same norms limit the participation of men in domestic and reproductive activities in rural areas (Ferrant et al., 2014). These have unintended consequences on women's participation in income generating activities. The heavy domestic workload limits the kind of employment women can take, restrict their mobility, and income-generating capacity. This also has effects on decisions on household expenditures and other major expenditures, and so the cycle continues!

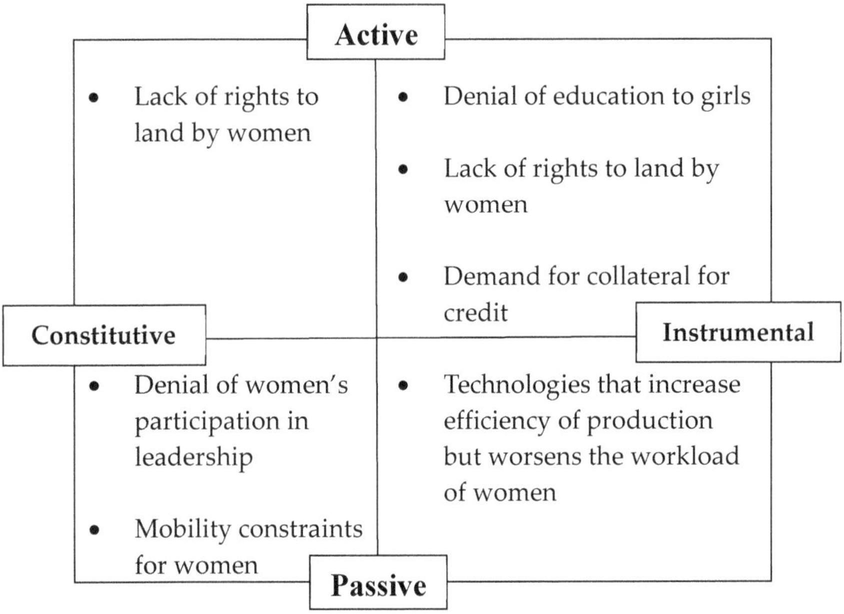

Figure 1: *Social Exclusion*
Adapted from Sen (2000)

Neglect of non-economic activities in computation of System of National Accounts/GDP

Poverty is regarded as a multidimensional concept that cuts across different areas of life and livelihoods of rural dwellers; hence, the different features of deprivations in the quality of life must be evaluated in order to get a broad view of the concept of poverty (Alkire et al., 2013). Similarly, feminist economists posit that focus on income and assets as the only means for women's empowerment can water-down the significance of challenges that women face (Bain et. al., 2020). Therefore, the wellbeing of women is a function of not only income or consumption but also revolves around their capacity to make choices in other spheres of life including time (Bardasi and Wodon, 2009). Time approach to poverty measure presents an effective measure since it allows for individual-based measurement which is easier to measure than income or consumption. It is defined as a state of deprivation where people do not have enough time for rest due to high demanding work time (Bardasi and Wodon 2009). Time use issues have strong gender dimensions in Africa because of its significant implications on women's overall potential and actual contribution to society. For African women, they work long hours on domestic chores and are involved in the collection of water and wood aside from their participation on the farm and market activities. Women's greater role in the household's unpaid domestic work for their families' maintenance and subsistence also results in higher levels of stress from juggling multiple tasks at once (Hillesland, 2016). On the contrary, being less burdened by domestic work and having greater control over one's own time would afford women the needed time to improve their skills in agricultural production (human capital dimension) and also engage in social activities and occupy leadership positions. Hence, this makes it important to consider reproductive-related activities in national system of accounting (Samantroy, 2015).

A recent study in the context of Southwest Nigeria indicates a wide gender gap in time poverty; about 48 percent of rural women are time poor compared to about 15 percent of men (Adeyeye et al, 2019). Time poverty is determined through a threshold of 10.5 hours in which an individual is regarded as inadequate if the person works more than 10.5 hours a day while work activities in this context covers economic and domestic activities. Specifically, women's work-related activities as a proportion of total daily activities constitute about 43% compared to about 33% for men. In addition, women's work is more diverse with about 91% focusing on farming, own business (largely trading), cooking and domestic work while farming only occupied about 70% of men's work activities (Adeyeye et al, 2019).Assessing time use on daily activities as well as time available for leisure from gender perspectives are important concerns that need to be examined in devising strategies and polices targeted at empowering and improving the well-being of rural smallholders in developing countries like Nigeria. This is fundamental to achieving policy objectives aimed at driving the SDGs especially goals 3 and, 5 and 7.

Key elements of gender-inclusive, empowerment approach for rural development in Africa

Inclusive developmental multidimensional empowerment

Empowerment is the quality of life measured not in terms of rising income or educational attainment alone, rather it must be inclusive of other personal, relational and structural concepts which could enable individual to exercise their rights and enjoy a meaningful life.

Empowerment, as understood and promoted in the context of development and poverty reduction, is a multidimensional and interdependent process involving social, political, economic and legal changes that will enable the marginalized to participate meaningfully in shaping their own futures (Cornwall et al. 2008). Empowerment as a complex and dynamic concept cannot be capture with only one indicator. In agriculture, empowerment occurs when a woman has adequate achievements across different conditions pertinent to her productivity. Therefore, for agriculture and rural development projects to be inclusive, it must move beyond the one-dimensional measures that limit women's empowerment to single indicators like income, consumption, educational attainment. Adopting the multidimensional measure of empowerment will provide a great insight into how empowerment draws from and affects different aspects. Examples of multidimensional approaches that have been developed for measuring empowerment include the Women's Empowerment in Agriculture Index (WEAI) and the Oxfam Women's Empowerment Index. The WEAI is a multidimensional empowerment framework which measures the empowerment, agency and inclusion of women in the agricultural sector (Alkire et al. 2013). The index measures empowerment directly at the individual level across five domains (5DE) pertinent to agriculture. These are: decisions about agricultural production; access to and control over productive resources; control over the use of income; leadership in the community and time allocation. The WEAI was developed in 2012 as a tool to monitor women's empowerment within the US Government Feed the Future Initiative. However, it has also been used extensively by a variety of organizations to assess the state of empowerment and gender parity in agriculture, track changes in women's empowerment, and identify key areas in which empowerment needs to be strengthened (Malapit et al. 2015). The WEAI has two components – the five domains of empowerment (5DE) and the Gender Parity Index (GPI). While the 5DE reflects the percentage of women who are empowered in five domains, the GPI reflects the percentage of women who are empowered or whose empowerment score meets or exceeds that of the men in their households. The WEAI thus provides an aggregate index that shows the degree to which women are empowered in their households and communities (Alkire et al. 2013).

Oxfam Women's Empowerment Index (WEI) provides a context-specific composite index for the measurement of women's empowerment. The framework recognizes three levels at which change can take place: personal, relational and environmental. Changes at the personal level occurs within the person and it refers to changes in how a woman sees herself, how she considers her role in society and that of other women, how she sees her economic role, and her confidence in deciding and taking actions that concern herself and other women. Changes at the relational level occur in the relationships and power relations within the woman's surrounding network. This addresses changes both within the household and within the community, and encompasses markets, local authorities and decision makers. Changes at the environmental level occur in the broader context which can be informal or formal changes. Informal changes include changes in social norms and attitudes and the beliefs of wider society while formal changes occur in the political and legislative framework (Lombardini et al., 2017).

In addition, to achieve inclusive development, programming and projects should be encompassing. An example is the Care USA Pathways (Women in Agriculture) Program. The program focuses on improving poor smallholder women farmer's productivity and profitability by empowering women to more fully engage in equitable agriculture systems. Funded by the Bill and Melinda Gates Foundation, Pathways is designed to improve the food security and livelihood resilience of poor smallholder women farmers and their families. The programme adopts the Farmer Field and Business School (FFBS) which is a hands-on, learning by doing approach which is built on the traditional Farmer Field School (FFS) approach, which places emphasis on hands-on management skills based on adult learning principles. The FFBS is encompassing because it includes other areas pertinent to smallholders lives and productivity. Thus, it involves the inclusion of community approaches to visioning and planning, sustainable agriculture, market engagement, nutrition, gender, and performance monitoring.

Focus on micro level interventions and measurements

Often, women's empowerment and gender inequality are typically measured at the aggregate country level. This prevents disaggregation based on heterogeneities between regions, socioeconomic status, marital status, age, or ethnicities. Indicators such as those used for tracking MDG3 (ratios of girls to boys in primary, secondary, and tertiary education; the share of women in wage employment in the non-agricultural sector; and the proportion of seats held by women in national parliament), are presented at the aggregate macro level thus, may not provide direct measures of empowerment as experienced by individuals. Other prominent macro-level indicators such as the Gender Empowerment Measure (GEM), the Gender-related Development Index (GDI), Gender Inequality Index (GII), developed by the UNDP and the OECD Social Institutions and Gender Index (SIGI) are also computed at the aggregate level. However, as pointed out by Alkire et al., (2013), empowerment is first of all intrinsically experienced by individuals. Furthermore, empowerment is first personal, with individual's unique definition of what it means to be empowered based on his or her life experiences, personality, and aspirations. Hence, indicators for measuring empowerment must prioritize experiences at the micro-level. This would enable development practitioners to understand how project or programme has contributed to men or women's empowerment.

Focus on transformative activities emphasizing changes in structural, relational and institutional factors.

To bring about transformative change in agriculture and rural development, government, development agencies and practitioners need to focus on developing and implementing strategies that would identify the underlying factors hindering gender-equitable development. To achieve this, provision must be included in development programmes to identify and tackle relational, structural and institutional issues in forms of norms, beliefs, roles, relations, policies and legal issues hindering gender-inclusive rural development. For example, on the recognition of the negative impact of workload on women's participation in development programme, the CARE USA Pathways (Women in Agriculture) program in Tanzania as part of its program included a gender module 'Daily Activities'. This module highlights the different productive and reproductive activities carried out by men and women in the 24 hours daily activities. This help in bringing to limelight the excess workload of women with attending influence on the men to share some domestic activities so that women can also have more time to participate more in productive activities.

Engaging men as key players for transformative change

There is a tendency in literature to confuse gender with women issues. The focus of many gender equality programmes and projects in rural areas are tilted towards women empowerment. This is easy to explain and rationalize as the limitations, challenges and barriers facing women in rural areas are well documented. Women and girls are one of the most vulnerable and disadvantaged groups where they lack the voice in decision-making on issues that concern them. This is worse in developing areas, especially in rural communities where decision-making is guided largely by norms and beliefs accentuated by patriarchy. This is particularly important in agriculture because, in many cases, even where women produce crops or livestock, it is the men who market and subsequently keep the income (Abdelali-Martin and Dey de Pryck, 2014). In case of access to land, evidence pointing to wide gender disparity in land ownership especially in developing countries, with women being the most disadvantaged (World Bank, 2009; FAO, 2011). This is manifested in discrimination against women on issues of inheritance of land. Single women can inherit from their parents, brothers, or sisters; but often not from their husbands – because married women do not have ownership and inheritance rights under customary law (Adepoju, 1997). Among the Yorubas in Southwest Nigeria for example, concept of co-ownership of property by couples is non-existent. The presumption being that all major properties, including land, belongs to the husband; and women are regarded as part of the property of the husband and therefore cannot inherit properties from the husband (Familusi, 2012; Aluko, 2015; Olagbegi-Oloba, 2015). However, women can be inherited by brothers of the deceased (Familusi, 2012). The situation is further worsened because most projects and interventions aimed at eradicating gender inequalities in rural areas have failed due to deep-seated social norms driven by patriarchy. Worse still, government policies and programmes enacted by government have failed in tackling the challenges in rural areas. Olagbegi-Oloba (2015) posited that legislations, case laws and international conventions on human rights which Nigeria is signatory to and gives women equal access to own, hold and transfer of properties as men, are rendered ineffective by customary laws practiced in rural communities. The argument therefore in most development parlance is that for gender equality to be attained in rural settings, development programmes and initiatives have to focus on women issues.

Despite this compelling evidence, this paper argues that for development initiatives to attain inclusiveness, it is important for empowerment programmes to be presented as a win-win model, rather than a zero-sum model which depicts empowerment of women as taking power from the more powerful, the men, thereby resulting in the loss of power by men (de Haan, 2017). However, a shift in development circle is to emphasize that men have more to gain, in all contexts, whether in the household or community, if women are empowered like them. Gender equality should not be interpreted as competition between men and women for resources but a fair and equitable access and distribution of these based on needs, uniqueness and peculiarities of each sex. This strategy may offer another and even better approach that formal laws and policies which are weak and difficult to implement in rural areas due to entrenched norms. For instance, the CARE Pathways program earlier cited utilizes the concept of male role models to attack prevalent and entrenched norms like *bushoke* in rural Tanzania. This is a derogatory term used to label a man who participates in household and domestic chores. The challenge of development policies and programmes therefore will be to engage, incentivize and project male role models and champions. In addition, there is the need to inculcate gender issues in educational curriculum of pupils at the early education level. This is to raise a critical mass of male gender justice champions which can effectively curtail the negative effects and practice of patriarchy and neo-patriarchy in rural areas.

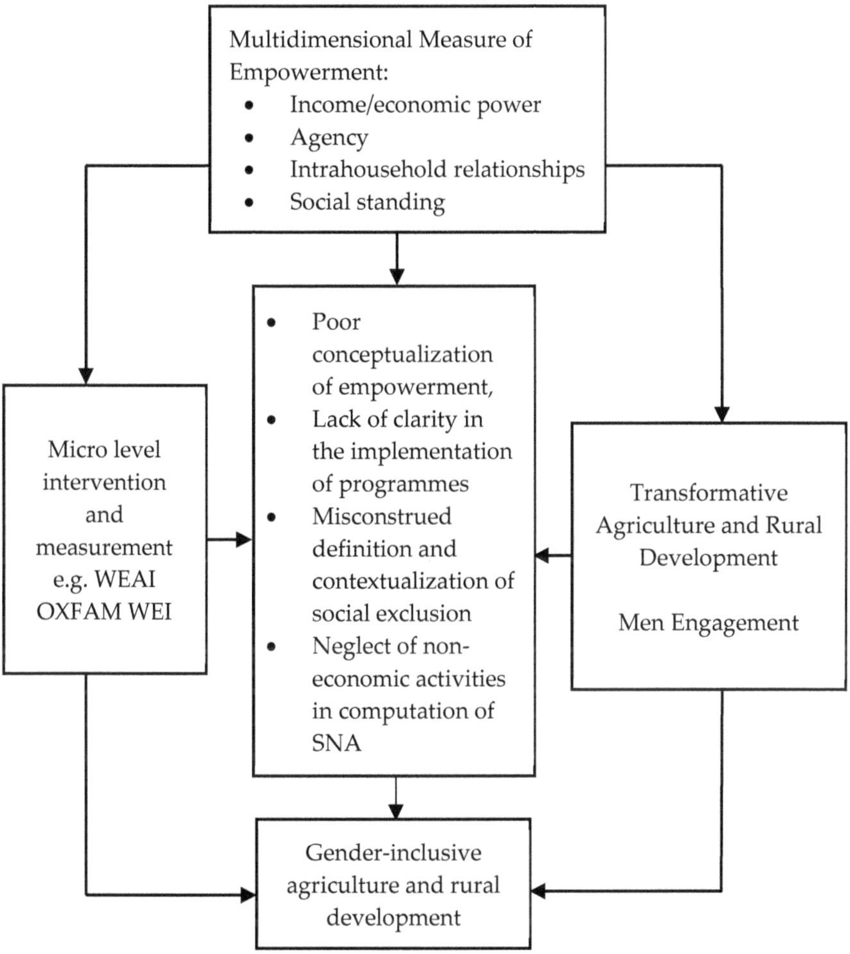

Figure 2: *Gender-inclusive framework for agriculture and rural development*
Source: Authors

Conclusion

This chapter presents an analytical framework for reframing the discourse on gender-inclusive development issues in rural settings in Africa. This arises from the failure of several developmental intervention programmes, especially in agriculture, to achieve the desired objectives in rural areas. This is because agriculture which constitutes the bedrock of rural development is gendered and evidence abounds of the importance roles that rural women play in meeting the challenges of agricultural production and development in sub-Saharan Africa. However, gender gaps and constraints exist in agriculture and rural development which hinders the ability of these women to fully participate in and benefit from agriculture and rural development programmes.

Key gender issues identified in agriculture and rural development include poor conceptualization of empowerment, lack of clarity in the implementation of programmes and projects, misconstrued definition and contextualization of social exclusion and the neglect of non-economic activities in computation of System of National Accounts/GDP. Therefore, for rural development programmes to be gender-inclusive, this paper proposes four key elements of gender-inclusive rural development framework in Africa. These include adopting the multidimensional measure of empowerment; focus on micro level measure of empowerment; and shift of policy to transformative changes that tackles norms and beliefs and other non-state actors. The framework also recommends a win-win model of empowerment where men are engaged as active participants in fostering gender inclusive programmes. This is because gender issues operate within a bigger and dominant environment in rural areas; hence, addressing multidimensional empowerment without simultaneous tackling the structural and non-state actors influencing gender in rural setting will make the achievement of agricultural intervention programmes a mirage.

References

Abdelali Martini M. & Dey de Pryck, J. (2015). Does the feminisation of agricultural labour empower women? Insights from female labour contractors & workers in Northwest Syria. *Journal of International Development* 27(7): 898-916.

Abrams, L., & Harvey, E. (2017). Introduction: gender and gender relations in German history. In *Gender Relations German History* (pp. 1-38). Routledge.

Adepoju, A. (ed) 1997. Family, Population and Development in Africa. London: Zed Books.

Adeyeye, O., Ogunleye, A. S., Akinola, A. A., Reed, H., Didier, A., Wineman, A., & Abdoulaye, T. (2019). Women's Empowerment and Technical Efficiency: What Role for Technology Adoption in Nigeria? Paper presented at the 2019 Agricultural & Applied Economics Association Annual Meeting, Atlanta, GA. July 21-23 (No. 2224-2019-2723).

Agarwal, B. (1997). Bargaining and Gender Relations: Within and Beyond the Household. *Feminist economics* 3(1): 1-51.

Alkire, S., Meinzen-Dick, R., Peterman, A., Quisumbing, A., Seymour. G.., and Vaz, A. (2013). The Women's Empowerment In Agriculture Index. *World Development*, 52: 71–91.

Alsop, R., Bertelsen, M.F. and Holland, J. (2006). Empowerment in Practice: From Analysis to Implementation. Washington DC: The World Bank

Aluko, Y. A. (2015). Patriarchy and Property Rights among Yoruba Women in Nigeria. *Feminist Economics*, 21(3), 56-81.

Amusan, L. (2018). Motion without Movement: Poverty Reduction through Embedded Liberalism in the Post-Apartheid South Africa. In Daniel Rauhut and Neelambar Hatti (eds.), *Poverty, Politics and the Poverty of Politics*, Delhi: B.R. Publishing Corporation, pp. 213-238.

Amusan, L. and Saka, L. (2018). Women: Towards a Conceptual Framework. In Victor Ojakorotu and Olawale R. Olaopa (eds.), *Perspectives on Women in Socio-Political Development in Africa*, London and Washington: Academica Press, pp. 19-44.

Arnstein, S. R. (1969). A ladder of citizen participation. *Journal of the American Institute of planners*, 35(4), 216-224.

Bain, C., Ransom, E., & Halimatusa'diyah, I. (2020). Dairy Livestock Interventions for Food Security in Uganda: What are the Implications for Women's Empowerment? Rural Sociology.

Bardasi, E., & Wodon, Q. (2009). Working long hours and having no choice: time poverty in Guinea. *Feminist Economics*, 16(3):45-78.

Bhalla, A. S., & Lapeyre, F. (2016). Poverty and exclusion in a global world. springer.

Cornwall, A., Gideon, J., & Wilson, K. (2008). Introduction: Reclaiming feminism: *Gender and neoliberalism*. IDS bulletin, 39(6), 1-9.

Cornwall, A., and Rivas, A. M. (2015). From 'gender equality and 'women's empowerment to global justice: reclaiming a transformative agenda for gender and development. *Third World Quarterly*, 36(2), 396-415.

Cozzens, S., & Sutz, J. (2012). Innovation in informal settings: a research agenda. IDRC, Ottawa, Canada, 1-53.

Das, K. S., & Mishra, D. K. (2018). Woman and work in rural Assam: pattern and determinants. *Journal of Social and Economic Development*, 20(2), 213-239.

de Haan, A. (2017). The Win-Win Case for Women's Economic Empowerment and Growth: Review of the Literature. GrOW Working Paper 2017-03, Growth and Economic Opportunities for Women Program, International Development Research Centre, Ottawa.

Dela, O., Campos, A. P., Villani, C., Davis, ,B., & Takagi, M. 2018. Ending extreme poverty in rural areas: Sustaining livelihoods to leave no one behind. Rome, FAO (available at http://www.fao.org/3/CA1908EN/ca1908en.pdf).

Doss, C. R. 2001. Designing Agricultural Technology for African Women Farmers: Lessons from 25 years of experience. *World development*,29(12): 2075-2092.

Familusi, O. O. 2012. African Culture and the Status of Women: The Yoruba Example. *The Journal of Pan African Studies* 5(1): 299-312.

Ferrant, G., Pesando, L. M., & Nowacka, K. (2014). Unpaid Care Work: The missing link in the analysis of gender gaps in labour outcomes. Boulogne Billancourt: OECD Development Center.

Food and Agriculture Organisation (FAO) (2011). The State of Food and Agriculture: Women in Agriculture Closing the Gender Gap. Rome: FAO

Godsil, R. D., Tropp, L. R., Goff, P. A., & MacFarlane, J. (2016). The effects of gender roles, implicit bias, and stereotype threat on the lives of women and girls. *The Science of Equality*, 2(1), 1-88.

Heeks R., Amalia M., Kintu R., and Shah N. (2013). I4ID: Definition, Conceptualisation and Future Research Priorities. Development Informatics, Working Paper Series, Paper No. 53, Centre for Development Informatics, Institute for Development Policy and Management, SEED, University of Manchester

Hillesland, M. 2016. Causal Mapping of The Gender Integration Framework. US Government Feed the Future Initiative

Ibrahim, S. and Alkire, S. 2007. Agency and empowerment: A proposal for internationally comparable indicators. *Oxford development studies*,35(4): 379-403.

Izugbara, C. O. (2005). The socio-cultural context of adolescents' notions of sex and sexuality in rural south-eastern Nigeria. *Sexualities*, 8(5), 600-617.

Kabeer N. 2005. Gender Equality and Women's Empowerment: A Critical Analysis of the Third Millennium Development Goal. *Gender and Development* 13(1): 13-24

Kabeer, N. 1999. Resources, agency, achievements: Reflections on the Measurement of Women's Empowerment. *Development and change*,30(3): 435-464.

Lecoutere, E., & Wuyts, E. (2017). Confronting the wall of patriarchy: does participatory intrahousehold decision-making empower women in agricultural households? Working papers/University of Antwerp. Institute of Development Policy and Management; Université d'Anvers. Institut de politique et de gestion du development.-Antwerp.

Lips, H. M. (2016). A new psychology of women: Gender, culture, and ethnicity. Waveland Press.

Lombardini, S., Bowman, K., & Garwood, R. (2017). A 'How To' Guide To Measuring Women's Empowerment: Sharing experience from Oxfam's impact evaluations. Oxfam GB.

Lutrell, C., Quiroz, S., Scrutton, C. and Bird, K. (2009). Understanding and Operationalising Empowerment. London: *Overseas Development Institute.* pp. 1-16

Malapit H., Kovarik C., Sproule K., Meinzen-Dick R. and Quisumbing A. 2015. Instructional Guide on the Abbreviated Women's Empowerment in Agriculture Index (A-WEAI), IFPRI.

Moser, C. (2012). Gender planning and development: Theory, practice and training. Routledge

Narayan D. (2002). Empowerment and Poverty Reduction: A Source Book. Washington DC: The World Bank

Njuki, J., Waithanji, E., Sakwa, B., Kariuki, J., Mukewa, E., & Ngige, J. (2014). Can market-based approaches to technology development and dissemination benefit women smallholder farmers? A qualitative assessment of gender dynamics in the ownership, purchase, and use of irrigation pumps in Kenya and Tanzania (Vol. 1357). Intl Food Policy Res Inst.

Olagbegi-Oloba, V. B. (2015) Women's Right to Land Ownership in Nigeria: A Critical Examination. ABUAD Journal of Public and International Law (AJPIL), 1(1): 1-13.

Page, N. and Czuba, C. E. (1999). Empowerment: What Is It? Journal of extension 37(5): 1-5

Parpart, J. L. and Barriteau, E. (2000). Theoretical Perspectives on Gender and Development. IDRC.

Rai, S. M. (2018). Institutional mechanisms for the advancement of women: mainstreaming gender, democratizing the state? Manchester University Press.

Razavi, S. and Miller, C. (1995). From WID to GAD: Conceptual Shifts In The Women And Development Discourse (Vol. 1). Geneva: United Nations Research Institute for Social Development.

Samantroy, (2015). Reconciling work and family life: A study of women's time use patterns, unpaid work and workplace policies. NLI Research Study Series No. 113/2015

Sen A. (1985). Well-being, agency and freedom: The Dewey Lectures 1984. The Journal of Philosophy 82(4): 169-221.

Sen, A. (2000). Social exclusion: Concept, application, and scrutiny. Social Development Papers No. 1. Asian Development Bank

Sen, G., and Grown, C. (1987). Development alternatives with women for a new era. London: Earthscan.

UNIFEM (United Nations Development Fund for Women). (1993). Cereal Processing: FoodCycle Technology Source Book. New York: Practical Action.

Van der Merwe (2017). Developing an Analysis Framework to Evaluate Inclusive Innovation System Performance. Master's thesis, Stellenbosch University, South Africa.

World Bank 2009. Gender in Agriculture Sourcebook. World Bank: Washington, DC.

Chapter 5
African Indigenous Knowledge (AIK) and Food Security in Africa

Olawale Rafiu Olaopa and
Yusuf Opeyemi Akinwale

Introduction

The amount and quality of food and the degree of its accessibility to all and sundry should be simple in any society desirous of terminating starvation and underfeeding. It is also a sine qua non for guaranteeing a better and industrious labour force. Not minding the fact that agricultural sector provides employment for a significant proportion of African population and responsible for more than half of the continent's GDP, Africa is still the most threatened region in the globe as far as food production and security are concerned (Roser and Ritchie, 2013, FAO, 2019). This, as shown in figure 1 below, is exemplified by the greater proportion of the region's population suffering from undernourishment.

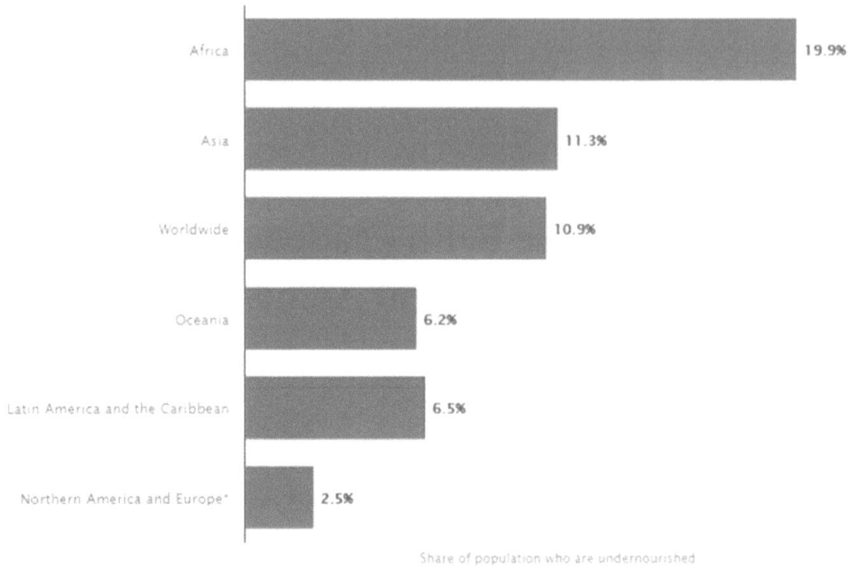

Figure 1: *Percentage of people undernourished worldwide in the period 2018 by region*
Source: Statista (2020)

The proportion of undernourishment of different regions within Africa is also shown in Figure 2. While Eastern and Middle Africa are above the continent's average undernourishment percentage with 30.8% and 26.5% of their population are undernourished, others are below the continent's average though the West Africa region is increasing rapidly in the recent time. Meanwhile, Southern Africa and Northern Africa occupy the least of undernourished people in Africa with approximately 8.0% and 7.1% of undernourished people respectively.

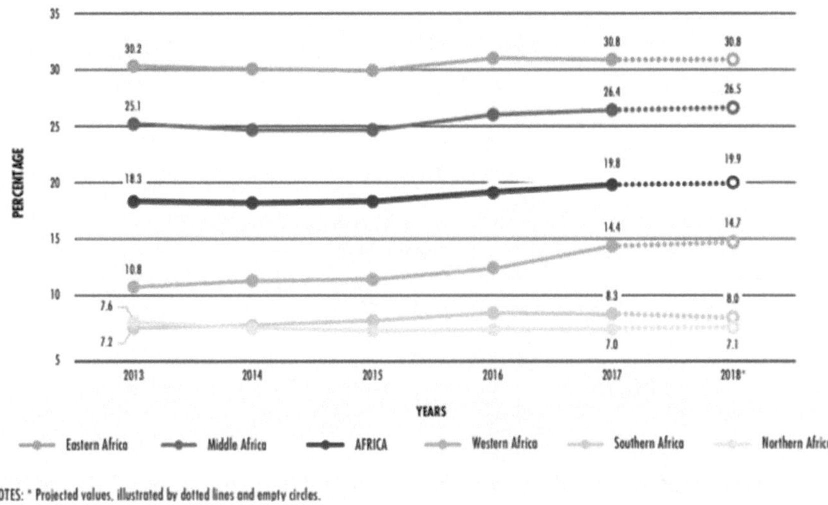

Figure 2: *Percentage of undernourished people in African regions between 2013 and 2018*
Source: FAO (2019)

One of the serious challenges facing developing economies of the world is essentially food insecurity, a state of absence of access to adequate quantity of hygienic, and nourishing food that can enhance people's wellbeing (Mozumdar, 2012; Muzari, 2016 FAO, IFAD, UNICEF, WFP and WHO. 2017, 2019). These economies are inexplicably vulnerable to resource and commodity price fluctuations. The situation is worsened by poor agriculture infrastructure, governance, and weak institutions all of which account for little productivity and a heavy reliance on food importation.

1n 2018, less than 10 percent of the world population were classified as having double challenges of the deficient amount of food (energy) and undernourishment or starvation, a condition of severe food insecurity (Our World in Data, 2020). Africa's share (25.7%) of this is highest, almost one-third of the population are severely food unsecured. This is depicted in Figure 3 below.

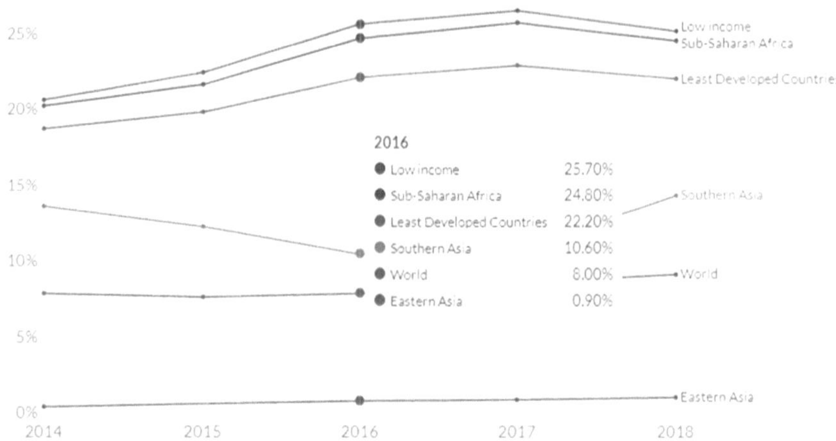

Figure 2: *Percentage of people suffering from severe food insecurity between 2014 and 2018*
Source: Our World in Data (2020)

Across the globe, around 697 million were argued to be severely food insecure in 2018. Out of this population, almost half lived in Africa (Our World in Data, 2020; Roser and Ritchie, 2013) as depicted in figure 4 below.

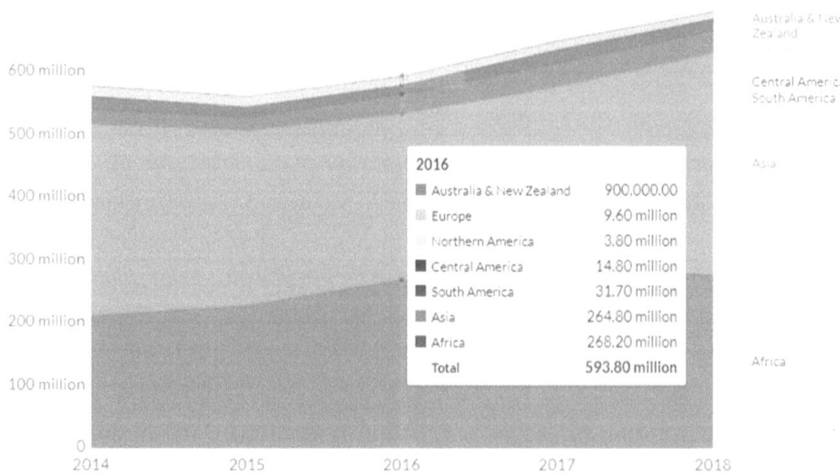

Figure 4: *Number of people suffering from food insecurity between 2014 and 2018 by region*
Source: Our World in Data (2020)

A lot of reasons have been adduced for low agricultural productivity and hence food insecurity across Africa (Masood, Ellahi and Batool, 2012;

Asenso-Okyere, 2012; Alejandro, 2015; Africa Link, 2016). This ranges from the feminization of agricultural occupation which has resulted into discrimination against women in terms of land ownership and which sternly limits their opportunities to another related benefit including equal access to inputs, participation in decision making, education, finance, and markets (Tshatsinde, 1990; Amin, Ali, Ahmad and Zafar, 2009; Thagwana, 2009; Labintan, 2010; SOFA Team and Doss, 2011; Amusan and Ngoh, 2016; Amusan, 2018; Ugwu, 2019). This inequality has been confirmed to have a great impact on farm yields (FAO, 2011) and consequently on the net food import bill that keeps rising.

There have been increasing potentials of Africa's agricultural production given its resources endowment, especially the continent's unexploited arable land. However, increased food demand and changing consumption habits are significantly affecting food imports, which are predicted to be on the increase by 2025 except it is counterbalanced by increased African production. The fact that the export of primary agricultural production is still very high in Africa unlike other regions provides a prospect for agriculture an opportunity for wealth creation and employment generation, particularly in the developing economies. Given the importance of food and nutrition, promoting agricultural practices of the indigenous people has the potential to increase productivity and increase food security.

Although, African Development Bank (AfDB) for instance, has provided some strategies for sustainable agricultural transformation in Africa especially to rekindle the potential of low-income countries by repositioning their thinking towards handling the sector with more serious concern to enhance industrialization (Africa Link, 2016; Adesina, 2018; AfDB, 2019). This notwithstanding, unlocking agricultural potential and tackling food insecurity will require a bottom-up approach that involves the integration of the indigenous people and their resources in agricultural production and development. It is on this note that this paper presents the integration of indigenous knowledge as a policy framework to boost domestic agricultural production and international competitiveness in Africa.

Reasons for improving agricultural sector for self-sufficiency and food security

In the pursuit of a better life for its citizens, almost all the countries in the world have set some development goals for target by 2030. As argued and outlined by the United Nations, all countries have committed to the 17 live-changing goals, also referred to as the Sustainable Development Goals (SDGs). Some of the goals are related to poverty reduction and food security. Although these goals are interconnected, the concern of this paper is specifically on goal 2, zero hunger. Notwithstanding, the discussion will be relatedly done.

The attainment of goals I, reducing poverty, and 2, banishing hunger of the SDGs calls for special attention to be directed to the agricultural sector. This was fuelled by the ever-increasing prices of food in the global market. This has led to various attempts to transform and improve the sector through various policies. This is against the understanding that raising agricultural productivity improves food production as domestic farmers and foreign farmers firms will be encouraged to produce more (Muzari, 2016) and at the same time encourage the intensification of efforts by the international community to improve food manufacturing capacity in the Sub-Sahara Africa (Makino, 2012) thereby guarantee food security in the continent. This is against the fact that the agricultural sector is all-encompassing in nature. It includes livestock, fisheries, crops, and forestry which remain the main source of food. The effective performance of the sector, therefore, has a high propensity to reduce poverty and guarantee food security. This view is corroborated by that of UNDP (2012) that the rural poor in Africa depend on agriculture for their means of livelihood. In terms of the relationship among poverty, food insecurity, and agricultural productivity, Thirtle et al (2003) argued that a consistent decline in poverty and food insecurity was noticed as agricultural production increases. Sachs (2005) supported this argument when the study shows that there is a direct relationship between cereal yields production in developing countries and their average annual growth of GDP. In the same argumentative plane, FAO (2004) posited that increases in productivity have a strong correlation with increased food availability among the families in the rural economy. If properly harnessed, increased productivity from agricultural development can help facilitate the poverty reduction process and reduce food insecurity.

This is noticeable in rural areas where poverty is prevalent. An increase in farm productivity has the prospect to facilitate increased growth in income, reduction of poverty, and fast-tracking food security (UNDP, 2012). Therefore, for the continent to attain food security, it must ensure an increase in agricultural productivity (Mozumdar, 2012; Muzari, 2016).

Despite the above relationship, the contribution of the farming sector in sub-Sahara Africa is disheartening. The sector is characterized by low productivity due to many challenges (FAO, 2005; Chauvin et al, 2012). Consequently, a lot of measures have been provided to solve the challenges. These include raising spending in farming-related activities, motivate the younger ones to engage in commercial farming, joining appropriate organizations, enriching the amount and value of farm yield, maintaining the availability of agricultural merchandises, closing the gap between research and development, devise approaches for engaging and financially motivating female folks among other incentives (Guardian Editorial Board, 2017).

Indigenous knowledge and resources as a new paradigm for accelerating sustainable food security.

No doubt, Africa has benefitted from the various policies implemented to improve agricultural yields and production (Pernechele, Balié, and Ghins, 2018), and invariably outstanding progress in its economic performance (Adesina, 2019). This has to some extent impacted positively on the continent's image (Chakrabarty, 2019). However, high growth has not resulted in a considerable reduction in food shortage. The rate of hunger continues to increase in most, if not all, of the regions, though except Eastern Africa in 2017 when compared with the previous year, 2016 as depicted in table 1 below. This notwithstanding, several countries in East Africa such as Ethiopia and Djibouti are at the present facing dearth of food supply arising from persistent lack of rainfall. In others, an increase in hunger as a result of famines and prolonged conflicts as in South Sudan and Somalia and North-Eastern Nigeria (Chakrabarty, 2019).

	2005	2010	2012	2014	2016	2017
Northern Africa	6.2	5.0	8.3	8.1	8.5	8.5
Sub-Sahara Africa	24.3	21.7	21.0	20.7	22.3	23.2
Eastern Africa	34.3	31.3	30.9	30.2	31.6	31.4
Central Africa	32.4	27.8	26.0	24.2	25.7	26.1
Southern Africa	6.5	7.1	6.9	7.4	8.2	8.4
Western Africa	12.3	10.4	10.4	10.7	12.8	15.1
Africa	**21.2**	**19.1**	**18.6**	**18.3**	**19.7**	**20.4**

Table 1: *Prevalence of undernourishment (%) in Africa, 2005-17*
Source: Food and Agriculture Organisation (2018)

The extent to which agricultural productivity can determine the level of hunger and guarantee food availability and sustainable food security is depicted by Global Agricultural Productivity (GAP) Index which is used to trace productivity trends. The 2018 edition GAP revealed that the increase in the global agricultural productivity growth was less than the rate at which the demand for food, feed, fiber, and fuel was increasing. As shown by the GAP index in Figure 5 below, the Global Harvest Initiative (GHI) calculated that increase in global agricultural productivity (as measured by Total Food Production, TFP) must double agricultural output through productivity growth by 2050 to ensure and guarantee the attainment of SDG 2 and sustainable food security. However, the average annual TFP growth rate in developing countries characterized by low-income is particularly appalling and the trend, it allows to continue will have a devastating effect on their economies. The implication is that they will have to strain their budget to import more food to meet the consumption demand of their citizens.

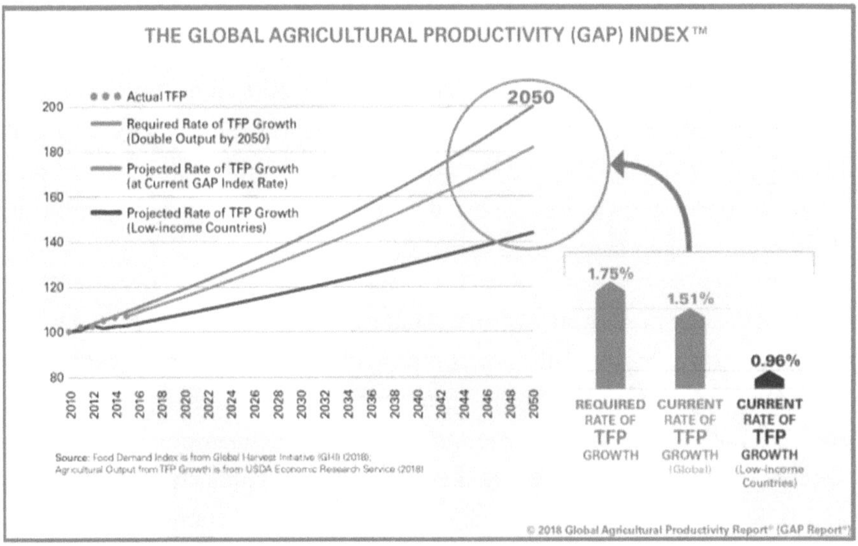

Figure 5: *The 2018 Global Agricultural Productivity Index*

In summary, insufficient food remains a very big obstacle for African growth. Advanced progression improved foreign export earnings, and extant policies can only relieve the economies in the short run. They are not sufficient to assist the continent accomplish the food sufficiency agenda. In turn, what is critically required is a considerable plan to exploit the continent's indigenous knowledge to intensely boost farm yields for reduced famine, low foreign spending, and mitigate problems imposed by the environment.

Without hesitation, the continent has prospects for agricultural production and employment opportunities for the rural poor. It is endowed with more than half of the world's virgin or uncultivated arable land; the same applies to the blue economy (Amusan, Mphambukeli & Okorie, 2019). The rapid increase in net food imports due to increased food demand and changing consumption patterns is likely to be on the increase in the next five years through 2050 (FAO, 2009; Sharma, Nguyen and Grote, 2018). However, this could be counterbalanced by increased African production. Given the importance of food and nutrition, promoting the agricultural sector for increased productivity requires a paradigm shift to utilizing indigenous knowledge and resources in the efforts to surmount those challenges to increase agricultural yields and production in Africa. Many factors are affecting agricultural production among which are climate change, land degradation, poor soil fruitfulness, the land tenure system, poor education, poor valuable inputs, old agricultural practices, and natural disaster. The knowledge of the indigenous people in this respect can be harnessed and leveraged. This will not only ensure effective rural communities' and citizens' participation but guarantee the success of the agricultural development agenda and food security.

Climate change poses a significant challenge to agricultural activity. Heavy and prevalent rainfalls with its accompanying floods, and temperature, for instance, have a great impact on agricultural output across the world. The report by Kyei-Mensah, Kyerematen, and Adu-Acheampong (2019) also shows and corroborates the effects of environmental changes on-farm yield. IK has assisted various indigenous peoples and communities across the world to familiarise, adjust, and continue to endure the dynamics of social and environmental changes (Domfeh, 2007; Olaopa, Eegunranti, and Ojakorotu, 2017). They have creatively developed some knowledge framework which they use to effectively provide solutions to problems arising from climate change. The local communities in Africa had age-long well-built and enduring that is relevant and socially accepted for understanding, observing, and predicting weather and climate. This is facilitated through their recognized and reputable indicators which are transferred from generation to generation. This knowledge consequently enhances their understanding of contemporary technical knowledge and skills for environmental management (Olaopa, Eegunranti, and Ojakorotu, 2017; Olaopa, 2019a, b). For example, in Swaziland, indigenous knowledge is applied and used in disaster management especially in predicting flood occurrence through the sign shown from the height of birds' nests near rivers. The study of the position of the sun and the cry of a specific bird on trees near rivers is used to envisage the onset of the rainy season for farming (Domfeh, 2007) while the presence of certain plant species indicates a low water table (Singh, 2011).

In the Central African region, the Natives rely on and trust the knowledge of old ones in the interpretation of natural signs and symbols to predict any occurrence and take proactive solutions (Eyong, 2007). Specifically, in Northwestern Cameroon for example, it is argued that too much and the infrequent cry of dogs, crow of fowls at mid-day and rare move of ants and flies together are signs and symbols of a looming overspill of a nearby river across its banks and the likely destruction of farm activities and productivity (Eyong, 2007). This premonition offers them the opportunity to search for a solution ahead of the occurrences. A typical example of a situation where serious disasters, including poor harvest, famine, drought, and other outbreaks have been predicted and preventive measures made before they occurred in the Mount Cameroon's eruptions (Eyong, 2007). In these circumstances, indigenous knowledge has been effective, modest, and more economical compared to modern technologies.

It has been argued that the use of fertilizers has assisted in achieving a greater increase in agricultural productivity (Olson, 1983). However, most of the modern fertilizers hurt soil fertility in the long run because of their chemical composition. Pests and diseases are other major impediments to an increase in crop production. Modern pesticides could also adversely affect soil fertility and productivity. Indigenous knowledge of the indigenous people in the area of agricultural practices has greatly assisted them to alleviate these problems (Adigun, 2014).

No doubt, frail farm know-how significantly affects the output. In developing countries, the claim is that productivity is low because farmers typically use the old traditional ways of cultivation. However, this seems to be a misconception. Indigenous people have had a significant breakthrough as far as science, engineering and technology are concerned. Simple technology has been deployed to advance their well-being. Before the discovery and introduction of modern technology, indigenous communities have discovered appropriate technologies that made them adapt to the dictates of their environment and advance their entrepreneurial opportunities and potentials. Some of these indigenous technologies that ensure and guarantee food security include bee-keeping, growing weeds, varieties of the local crop, and animal pests' repellents in line with the dynamics of their local climatic conditions.

In Nigeria, the destruction of farm products, including food crops, is prevented from being destroyed by animals like cattle by planting some plants around the farm boundary and its surroundings. Such animal repellent plants include Jatropha plants (Lapalapa) and Senna alata plant (wild water yam). The smells of these plants are naturally hated by animals with a passion. The Castor plant (Egunsi) in itself is very poisonous that no animal will dare to eat it.

In Sudan for instance, drawing on local technical knowledge enhances impeccable and acceptable undertaken of soil survey and mapping better and faster than through a formal scientific approach. In terms of correlation and relationships that underline scientific enterprise, indigenous people have been able to draw inferences form different circumstances and their consequences. For instance, their indigenous knowledge has offered them the opportunity to draw a correlation between the likelihood of prolonged dry season and vulture's incubation during the period of anticipated rainfall. Through observations, farmers can forecast precisely through the position of their shadow in the tropic region. Besides, the knowledge avails them information about soil types (Domfeh, 2007).

One of the factors affecting productivity in agriculture is the assumed low level of knowledge and understanding of food and fibre systems by the local farmers. It is believed that this limits their ability to produce, explore, and share primary information about agricultural practices, hence low productivity (Masood, Ellahi and Batool, 2012). In Africa, traditional agriculture is characterized by planting arrangements predicated on the farming skill, information, and practices that are articulated in the native dialect (). This practice changes alongside changes in the environment and it is driven by local inventions and discoveries (Warren, 1989). More so, traditional agriculture is environmentally friendly with a strong crop production system that guarantees enhanced production security. With traditional agriculture, crop security, a sine qua non to subsistence farmers, is certain and facilitated by the development of a multifaceted system comprising a variety of crops, spacious plantings, different genetic resources, among other practices that are adapted to local conditions and risks (Domfeh, 2007). All these practices have assisted in solving the problem of land degradation (Mudita, 1999) and maintain some level of environmental sustainability (Ramdhani and Santosa, 2012) since this is one of the most important environmental problems confronting agricultural practices and food production in Africa.

This need to develop a framework to protect the environment through local knowledge and its integration with scientific have been recognized in various international conventions such as the 1992 UN Conference on Environment and Development (UNCED). This is against the propensity of the practice to ensure and guarantee food security if they are harnessed and integrated with modern agricultural practices. Traditional agricultural practice in Ghana and elsewhere, for example, has proven the efficacy of the use of plant products for insect control decades before the advent of synthetic pesticides (Appiah-Opoku 1999; Dougoud, Toepfer, Bateman and Jenner, 2019). Apart from the fact that these are natural products, they are biodegradable, they limited disease infection and lower risk of shrub damage compare with modern chemicals. The World Bank acknowledged the enviable contributions of women farmers in Columbia and Rwanda. Their cherished indigenous knowledge about bean cultivation assisted in the process of adaptation of modern cultivation techniques (World Bank, 1998). These provide significant prospects and knowledge to be harnessed in the pursuit of sustainable food security agenda.

Of equal importance is the problem posed by agricultural productivity and food sufficiency by the land tenure system. Strong relationship exits concerning appropriate land policies and food security (ECA, 2004). The land is communally owned in the typical African societies and allows farming to be practiced by all members of the families, and the land is passed from generation to generation. This makes it difficult for any member to individually dispose of the land in which all members are entitled. However, colonialism distorted this arrangement which is the bane of most of the land tenure problems that are being witnessed now in Africa (Amusan & Oloba, 2019; ECA, 2004). This is exemplified by poor land tenure policies that do not consider African cultural traditions and beliefs concerning land ownership and control (Masood et al, 2012). The aftermath is crises that eventually lead to underutilization and low yield.

Conclusion and recommendations

Africa needs to improve its food production and determine the most efficient strategy to do this. Agriculture is the main sector of the economy which provides opportunities facilitating food sufficiency and reduced poverty which is the major challenge in the rural areas (Oloba and Amusan, 2019). Involving the rural communities and harnessing their indigenous knowledge, resources and practices have a high propensity in solving most, if not all, of the different causes of low agricultural productivity and food insecurity.

To effectively accomplish this requires evidence-based policy to determine and take stock of existing indigenous knowledge and resources in agricultural practices and invest in research and development (R&D) to further improve on them in a manner compatible with modern practices. A lot of issues are involved which includes the identification and/or establishment of a relevant institution for indigenous knowledge mapping.

Besides, the agriculture revolution should be anchored within the framework of Science, Technology, and Innovation (STI) for better results. Since citizens' involvement in agricultural transformation for food security is being canvassed and that every STI policy provides a promising platform for STI operational performance with any development agenda and transformation that is citizen-cantered, people's participation is encouraged and improved since their indigenous knowledge and practices are recognized.

More so, the policy will assist in the process of making available a strong STI capability and capacity needed to evolve a food secured economy (See Amusan and Ajibola, 2019). More importantly, it will ease the means of attaining the knowledge and skill to harness indigenous knowledge and practice of agriculture alongside modern techniques for agricultural development, food security, and poverty reduction. This will be strengthened by effective agricultural education that is tailored towards awareness about farming practices, management, and techniques. Once these are dedicatedly pursued, it will boost African domestic competitiveness, further develop domestic markets, generate employment, reduced the continent's poverty level, and unlock investments for agriculture in Africa.

There is no doubt that African IKS is facing extinction due to many challenges ranging from the oral or verbal means of its transmission, the low literacy level of the custodian of AIK resulting to ineffective communication of the beliefs and practices, refusal to utilize the knowledge because it is seen as unreliable and not empirical, the problem of biopiracy due to the effect of globalization among others (Goolam, 2013), this, therefore, calls for the urgent need for its protection, documentation, deliberate learning, a reformation where required and then extensively circulated to facilitate development.

References

Adigun, T. A (2014) Application of Competitive Intelligence in Indigenous Knowledge: The Role of the Library Professionals in Nigeria. Journal of Research in Education and Society, Vol.5 No. 2, August

Adesina, A (2018) Reversing Africa's cocoa paradox: Why Easter celebration signals a call to action. African development Bank Group, March 30.

Adesina, A (2019) Foreword to the African Economic Outlook 2019

Africa Link (2016) Reason for Low Agricultural Productivity across Africa Identified. September 10. Available at: http://www.africalink.ch/index.php/en/news/top-stories/139486-reason-for-low-agricultural-productivity-across-africa-identified

African Development Bank (2019) Feed Africa. Communication and External Relations Department. African Development Bank. Abidjan, Côte d'Ivoire, www.afdb.org

Africa: Prospects for the Transformation of the Agricultural Sector. UNDP, Regional Bureau for Africa.

Alejandro, N. P (2015) The Challenge of increasing agricultural productivity in Africa south of the Sahara. International Food Policy Research Institute (IFPRI). July 17.

Amin, H., Ali, T., Ahmad, M and Zafar, I (2009) Participation Level of Rural Women in Agricultural Activities. Pak. J. Agri. Sci., Vol. 46(4), 2009 ISSN (Print) 0552-9034, ISSN (Online) 2076-0906 http://www.pakjas.com.pk

Amusan, L (2018) Globalisation of Land and Food Security Challenges in Africa. *African Renaissance,* special issue, December, pp.81-97.

Amusan, L. and Ajibola, K. S (2019) Human Resource and Food Insecurity in Africa: Adventure in Africa Solution for African Problems. *Journal of Gender, Information and Development in Africa (JGIDA),* special issue, March, pp.63-82.

Amusan, L., Mphambukeli, T. and Okorie, V. O. (2019). Blue Economy, Brics and the Challenges of Food Security in the Western Indian Ocean. *Journal of Reviews on Global Economics,* 8, 1567-1575. DOI: https://doi.org/10.6000/1929-7092.2019.08.140

Amusan, L. and Ngoh, M. S. (2016) Women as Agents of Development: An Assessment of Modimola Village in the NorthWest Province of South Africa through the Expanded Works Programme (EPWP). *Gender and Behaviour,* pp. 7238-7245.

Amusan, L and Oloba, O. (2019). Achieving the Sustainable Development Goals (SDGs) One and Two through Goal 14 in the West African States. *African Renaissance,* 16(Special Issue 2, August), pp. 91-102.

Appiah-Opoku, S. (1999). "Indigenous Economic Institutions and Ecological Knowledge: A Ghanaian Case Study." The Environment, 19: 217-227

Asenso-Okyere, K (2012) Food Security - Productivity boost. Feb. 15 Available at: https://www.dandc.eu/en/article/africas-agricultural-productivity-must-rise

Chakrabarty, M (2019) Africa is rising but so is hunger. Observer Research Foundation (ORF), May 27. Available at: https://www.orfonline.org/expert-speak/africa-rising-but-hunger-51311/ (Accessed 9 May 2020)

Chauvin, N. P., Mulangu, F. and Porto, G. (2012) Food Production and Consumption Trends in Sub-Sahara Africa: Prospects for the Transformation of the Agricultural Sector. UNDP, Regional Bureau for Africa.

Chauvin, N.P., Mulangu, F. and Porto, G. (2012). Food

Domfeh, K.A. (2007) "Indigenous Knowledge Systems and the Need for Policy and Institutional Reforms". Tribes and Tribals, Special Volume No. 1: 41-52.

Dougoud, J., Toepfer, S., Bateman, M. and Jenner, W. H (2019) Efficacy of homemade botanical insecticides based on traditional knowledge. A review. Agronomy for Sustainable Development, 39: 37 https://doi.org/10.1007/s13593-019-0583-1.

Guardian Editorial Board (2017) $35 billion food importation into Africa. The Guardian, August 17. Available at: https://guardian.ng/opinion/35-billion-food-importation-into-africa/ (Accessed on 9 May 2020)

Eyong, C. T. (2007). Indigenous knowledge and sustainable development in Africa: Case study on Central Africa. Indigenous Knowledge Systems and Development: Relevance for Africa, 121–139. (Accessed on 22 February 2016)

Food and Agricultural Organisation (FAO) (2004) The State of Food insecurity in the world. Rome: FAO

Food and Agricultural Organisation (FAO) (2005) Food Security and Agricultural Development in Sub-Sahara Africa: Building a case for more public support. Policy Brief No. 1. Rome: FAO

Food and Agricultural Organisation (FAO) (2009) Global Agriculture towards 2050; FAO: Rome, Italy, 2009

Food and Agricultural Organisation (FAO) (2011) The State of Food and Agriculture 2010-2011: Women in Agriculture -Closing the gender gap for development. Rome, FAO

Food and Agriculture Organization of the United Nations (FAO), the International Fund for Agricultural Development (IFAD), the World Food Programme (WFP), and the World Health Organization (WHO) (2015). The State of Food Insecurity in the World 2015 Meeting the 2015 international hunger targets: taking stock of uneven progress. Rome, FAO ISBN 978-92-5-108785-5.

Food and Agriculture Organization of the United Nations (FAO), the International Fund for Agricultural Development (IFAD), the United Nations Children's Fund (UNICEF), the World Food Programme (WFP), and the World Health Organization (WHO) (2017). The State of Food Security and Nutrition in the

World 2017. Building resilience for peace and food security. Rome, FAO. Available online.

Food and Agriculture Organization of the United Nations (FAO), the International Fund for Agricultural Development (IFAD), the United Nations Children's Fund (UNICEF), the World Food Programme (WFP), and the World Health Organization (WHO) (2019). The State of Food Security and Nutrition in the World 2019. Safeguarding against economic slowdowns and downturns. Rome, FAO. ISBN 978-92-5-131570-5

Goolam, M (2013) Indigenous Knowledge must be harvested for development. Paper presented at the British Council's Going Global 2013 conference in Dubai from 4-6 March as part of a debate on importing knowledge systems to solve local problems.

Kyei-Mensah, C, Kyerematen, R and Adu-Acheampong, S (2019) Impact of Rainfall Variability on Crop Production within the Worobong Ecological Area of Fanteakwa District, Ghana. Hindawi Advances in Agriculture Volume 2019, Article ID 7930127, 7 pages https://doi.org/10.1155/2019/7930127

Labintan, A (2010) Women Farmer's and Agriculture Growth: Challenge and Perspective for Africa face the economic crisis. Poster presented at the Joint 3rd African Association of Agricultural Economists (AAAE) and 48th Agricultural Economists Association of South Africa (AEASA) Conference, Cape Town, South Africa, September 19-23, 2010

Makino, K. (2012) Boosting Sustainable agricultural growth in Sub-Sahara Africa (Chapter 2 of the book, For inclusive and Dynamic Development in Sub-Sahara Africa)

Masood, A., Ellahi, N and Batool, Z (2012) Causes of Low Agricultural Output and Impact on Socio-economic Status of Farmers: A Case Study of Rural Potohar in Pakistan. International Journal of Basic and Applied Science, Vol. 01, No. 02, pp. 343-351 Oct.

Mozumdar, L (2012) Agricultural Productivity and Food Security in the Developing World. Bangladesh J. Agric. Econs. XXXV, 1&2(2012) 53-69

Mudita, I. (1999). The Readiness of Solving Land Degradation on Eastern Indonesia: The East Nusa Tenggara Case.

Muzari, W (2016) Agricultural Productivity and Food Security in Sub-Sahara Africa. International Journal of Science and Research (IJSR), Vol 5 No. 1, pp1769-1776 ISSN (Online) 2319-7064.

Olaopa, Olawale. R, Eegunranti, Benjamin A and Ojakorotu, Victor (2017) Indigenous Knowledge (IK), Millennium and Sustainable Development Goals (MDGs & SDGs) and Sustainable Development In Africa: Opportunities, Challenges And Policy Recommendations In M.N Amutabi (ed) (2017) Beyond Agency, Voice and Space in Africa's Development. Centre for Democracy,

Research and Development (CEDRED), Nairobi, Kenya. ISBN 978-9966-1933-2-2, chap. 22, pp.270 – 280.

Olaopa OR (2019a) Achieving Effective Water Management and Access within Africa's Socio-Political and Cultural Complexities: Issues and Policy Directions/Options. In: Mujtaba IM, Majozi T, Amosa MK. (eds) Water Management: Social and Technological Perspectives. CRC Press, Taylor and Francis Group, pp 21-37 (New York)

Olaopa, Olawale. R (2019b) The Challenges of Governance and Institutional Structure for Sustainable Water and Food Security: Lesson for BRICS States. African Renaissance (AR) ISSN: 1744-2532 (Print) ISSN: 2516-5305 (Online) Indexed at: EBSCO, ProQuest, J-Gate and Sabinet. Also indexed and accredited by IBSS and SCOPUS. Special Issue, August. pp 71-90.

Oloba, O. and Amusan, L (2019) Assessing the impact of Neglect of Agriculture on Food Security: A Case Study of Ekiti State, Southwestern Nigeria. African Renaissance, special issue, March, pp.41-59

Olson, R. (1983). The Use of Fertilizer and Soil Amendments. Jhon Wiley and Sons, Washington, DC, 203-226.

Our World in Data (2020). Share of Population with severe food insecurity for the period between 2014 and 2018. Available at https://ourworldindata.org/search?q=share+of+population+with+severe+food+insecurity. (Accessed on 30th June 2020)

Pernechele, V., Balié, J. and Ghins, L. (2018) Agricultural policy incentives in sub-Saharan Africa in the last decade (2005–2016) – Monitoring and Analysing Food and Agricultural Policies (MAFAP) synthesis study, FAO Agricultural Development Economics Technical Study 3. Rome, FAO. 77 pp.

Production and Consumption Trends in Sub-Saharan

Ramdhani, M. A., and Santosa, E. (2012). Key Success Factors for Organic Farming Development. International Journal of Basic and Applied Science, 1(1), July, 7-13

Roser, M and Ritchie, H (2013) - "Hunger and Undernourishment". *Published online at OurWorldInData.org*. Retrieved from: 'https:// ourworldindata.org/hunger-and-undernourishment' (Online Resource)

Sachs, J. (2005) The end of poverty: How can we make it happen in our lifetime. London, UK. Penguin Press, 396 pp.

Santosa, E. (2012). Rice Organic Farming is a Programme for Strengthening Food Security in Sustainable Rural Development. International Journal of Basic and Applied Science, 1(1), 1-6.

Sharma, R., Nguyen, T. T and Grote, U (2018) Changing Consumption Patterns—Drivers and the Environmental Impact. Sustainability, 10, 4190; doi: 10.3390/su10114190.

Singh, D (2011) The wave that casts people: the value of indigenous knowledge for disaster risk reduction. Available from http://www.unisdr.org/archive/21236. (Accessed 6 July 2020)

SOFA Team and Doss, C (2011) The Role of Women in Agriculture. ESA Working Paper No. 11-02. Agricultural Development Economics Division. The Food and Agriculture Organization of the United Nations www.fao.org/economic/esa

Statista (2020). Percentage of people undernourished worldwide for the period 2018 by region. Available at: https://www.statista.com/statistics/273291/number-of-people-with-malnutrition-worldwide/. (Accessed on 30th June 2020)

Thagwana, M. S. (2009) Trends in Women's Participation in Agriculture at Tshiombo Irrigation Scheme, Limpopo Province. A mini-thesis submitted in partial fulfilment of the requirements for the degree of Master of Philosophy in Land and Agrarian Studies University of Western Cape Institute for Poverty, Land and Agrarian Studies, November.

Thirtle, C., Lin, L., and Piesse, J. (2003) The impact of research led agricultural productivity growth on poverty reduction in Africa, Asia and Latin America. World Development, Vol. 31 No.12, pp. 1959-75.

Tshatsinde, M A (1990) Factors Leading to Low Productivity among Rural Women in Agricultural Production, Agrekon, 29:4, 359-362, DOI: 10.1080/03031853.1990.9525124 Available online at: https://doi.org/10.1080/03031853.1990.9525124

Ugwu, P. C (2019) Women in Agriculture: Challenges Facing Women in African Farming. ResearchGate, March. Available at: file:///C:/Users/Olawale/Downloads/WOMENINAGRICULTURECHALLENGESFACINGWOMENIN AFRICANFARMING.pdf (Accessed on 10 May 2020)

UNDP (2012) Sustainable agricultural productivity for Food, Income and Employment. Chapter 4 of Africa Human Development Report 2012. United Nations Development Programme.

United Nations. Economic Commission for Africa (2004-12). Land tenure systems and their impacts on food security and sustainable development in Africa. Addis Ababa: © UN. ECA, http://hdl.handle.net/10855/593" (Accessed on 12 June 2020)

Warren, Dennis Michael (1989) The Impact of Nineteenth Century Social Science in Establishing Negative Values and Attitudes towards Indigenous Knowledge Systems. In Indigenous Knowledge Systems: Implications for Agriculture and International Development, D. Michael Warren, L. Jan Slikkerveer, and S. Oguntunji Titilola, eds. Pp. 171-183. Studies in Technology and Social Change, No. 11. Ames: Technology and Social Change Program, Iowa State University.

World Bank (1998) on Indigenous Knowledge for Development: A Framework for Action. Knowledge and Learning Center, Africa Region. World Bank.

Chapter 6
Healthy Food, Unhealthy People: Developmental Challenges of Inorganic Food on African Youths

Olabimpe Ajoke Olatunji and Lere Amusan

Introduction

Human development is a complex phenomenon, which involves a pattern of change beginning right from the conception of foetus in the womb to the time the baby is born. This continues unto childhood, adolescence, adulthood, and even unto death. Thus, development continues throughout the human lifespan. There are several processes that are involved as humans grow and develop; one of such important processes is biological, which comprises changes in an individual's physical nature. The effect of diet and nutrition on an individual is an important aspect of the biological processes of human development (Otero, 2018; Paarlberg, 2013). Diet and nutrition is so important because it can determine a lot about the nature of human development such as the development of the brain, height, weight, health, and many other aspects of human development (Okorie, Maphambukeli & Amusan, 2019).

Food in the body is essential for human growth, health, and maintenance while humans eat, we do not just eat but good nutrition should be considered in the process of eating. Particularly in the young age group, enough nutrients are most desired for a healthy body and brain development because this is good not only for the immediate formation of healthy behaviour pattern but for later development of healthy living. The link between human development and food security is well established in the research literature (Amusan & Olawuyi, 2019; Muro & Burchi 2012; Pollan, 2009; 2016). Food security in this wise is the availability of food at all times in quantity and quality for a productive life and healthy living across the life span (Cavalcanti, 2005:152). Social Scientists have correlated the diet of youths and have suggested a variety of psychological, behavioural and social factors associated with healthy eating. Some of these factors include family and friends influence (Salvy, Howard, Read & Mele, 2009), peers support (Steeves, Jones-Smith, Hopkins & Gittelsohn, 2016), individual motivation, and abilities (Burg, 2008). Other factors include barriers to healthy eating such as availability of essential food (Amore, Buchthal, & Banna, 2019), life satisfaction (Schnettler, Lobos, Miranda-Zapata, Denegri, Ares & Hueche, 2017) and dietary trend (Bielawska, Tomczyk & Labuz-Roszak, 2019).

In spite of extensive evidence supporting the positive effects of healthy eating among the emerging adult group, inadequacy exists in both the quality and quantity of their food intake. The onset of adolescence stage (between ages 9 and 18 or 21 years, Santrock, 2013) in human development is a critical juncture for the onset of behaviours that are relevant to health; Thus, the early formation of a healthy behaviour pattern such as a preference for certain kinds of food not only have immediate health benefits but shapes growth and development as the individual advances in age. This could eventually help to delay or prevent some illnesses into adulthood or old age. A healthy diet shows a higher intake of energy from organic fruits, vegetables, and milk with a lower intake in fat, oil, sugar, and sweet groups of food. Many of the contemporary youth live on fast food meals which contain a lot of fat and less of fruits and vegetables; this invariably increases the rate of obesity among them especially in the female youth and tendencies for ill health in later years. This is more common in an era where food fraud is the order of the day as applies both in developed and developing countries (Nestle, 2010). In a longitudinal study by researchers from the School of Public Health, University of Minnesota (2009), it was discovered that frequent intake of fast food (three or more times a week) promotes obesity while in another study, it was found that eating regular family meals which are organically based during early adolescence was linked to healthy eating habits five years later.

It is the intention of this paper to look into how the youth could negotiate the maze of inorganic food that is cheaper, but poisonous to the body system. In trying to do this, we are going to examine the psychological implications of unhealthy food in African Youths. To unravel this, this paper adopts the eclectic view of Social Cognitive theory and Ecology theory. The authors are unmindful of other relevant theories such as constructivism, critical and liberal theories that could be employed, but our comfortability in the two theories to be adopted will shed more light in this paper.

The theoretical framework

Social Cognitive Theory demonstrates how people grow, and develop through learning, imitation, and observation. The theory explains how human behaviour, feelings and thoughts are shaped by observing other people's behaviour. The process of observing others form an important part of life-span development (Bandura 1986) proposes that people cognitively represent the behaviours of others and many times they eventually adopt or replicate such behaviours. The individuals that are observed are known as models while in modern societies, such models could be parents, a family member, an influential person in the society, friends within a peer group, and several others whom they find attractive in a way or other. The behaviour of these models is encoded cognitively having paid attention to such and they later imitate such behaviour.

The model of Social Cognitive Theory comprises three elements namely, the person /cognition, the environment, and the behaviour. The developmental period of the later adolescence (Age 15 to 22 years) and emerging adulthood (Age 18 – 29 years) is unique in the sense that it is a period where the search for autonomy and independence increases. This is the age bracket that the content of this paper will refer to as a youth. Environmental factors, such as friends, type of parents, school experience, socio-cultural factors, and availability of the type of food will influence the behaviour and the type of food to be consumed.

The ecological theory developed by Bronfenbrenner (1979) will also be used to explain the concept of these age brackets and such influences on their choice of eating healthily or not. Ecology theory explains that human development is influenced by five basic systems from the environment. These systems are identified as a microsystem, mesosystem, exosystem, macrosystem, and the chronosystem. According to this theory, the microsystem is the system in which individual lives, and as such, the person has direct contact and gain experiences with the social agents involved in the daily activities that a person is involved in. Such agents in the microsystem include the person's family, neighbourhood, school, and peers. The individual in these various contexts is an active participator and a constructor of these settings. The mesosystem is a combination and interactions of the microsystems coming together to influence the person involved. Examples may include the connections between family experiences and school experiences or peer experiences to family experiences. For example, children who are exposed to good nutrition at home may have friends in the school whose parents pack them with snacks for lunch; this invariably makes such children to be exposed to such food junk and to develop an interest in them. In the exosystem, the person does not have a direct and active participatory role in the system, unlike the first two environmental systems where the person is inactive participation. For example, the socio-economic status of the family can be a product of the exosystem which the parents or the children have little or no control over. The socio-economic status of the family will go a long way in the determination of the kinds of food that is provided by the family. This might likely affect the habit that is formed around food by the family members especially the children. The culture of the place where a person lives is the major determinant of the macrosystem. Culture defines the behaviour patterns, belief system, and all other elements of a person as they move from one generation to the other. Some of the elements of culture are dressing, greeting style, type of songs, marriage rites, food types, and many others. Some African cultures believe in some types of local food and herbs that boost energy or increases intellect over others not minding the scientific implications and health benefits of such food on human body. The chronosystem involves major environmental events or socio-historical happenings for life and its effects on the person. For example, divorce is a major influence on every aspect of a child's development, the effect of which determines a lot in the life of individuals across all the periods of development in the life of that child.

The eclectic view of these two theories in the explanation of the concepts of youth and their nutrition patterns is such that both could describe dietary behaviour and most other habits of children into adolescence and beyond as being products of the physical, social and human environment. While social Cognitive theories emphasise learning and observation from the environment, Ecological theorists on the other hand emphasise the social contexts beyond the family such as religion, peer influence as influential in children's development.

Unhealthy people amid plenty

Many researchers have indicated in their studies that unhealthy nutrition can pose serious developmental (both long term and short term) health problems in individuals. Some of these problems pose a lot of challenges and could be emotional, physical, or even cognitive. One of the great influences of nurture (environmental factor) on human development is nutrition. Nutrition has a great influence on all aspects of human growth and development. This is because food remains a constant essential aspect of healthy growth and development right from the womb and throughout life. Thus, inadequacies in the area of food combination result in impairment in the general development of humans. Many factors can be identified as reasons for youths in Africa eating unhealthily. Poor nutrition and unhealthy eating habits tend to increase as age advances thus eating experiences of the youth is a consequence of their eating behaviour from childhood. Little wonder why children's dietary patterns are shaped and related by the interplay of parental or family values, culture, economic status of parents, the social media influence, physical and social environment (e.g., school level), and some other factors. Youth are usually not conscious of the effect and implication of diet on them because they are usually more preoccupied with other aspects of their lives e.g., social and emotional lives though we might say that because of the strong influence of their economic power, that is, their financial strength, they are usually not working or even earning less than adults to the extent of purchasing better products. Also, the youthful exuberance of having poor understanding of these junk foods is also a great factor that contributes to their choice of food.

The parental or family values play a significant role in the interplay in the choice of food of children and this goes a long way in the determination of their later lifestyles. The family choice plays an important influence in shaping the eating habit of their children. Parents all over, are the primary givers of the basic amenities of a child for survival to the world including food, shelter, clothing, and socialisation to the family values and culture of the society. Many factors are responsible for the choice of food that is provided by the parents especially the mother who is most directly involved in the purchase and preparation of food to the members of the family. The type and the nature of job of the mother, the family structure, the cultural orientation of the parents and the orientation parents have towards good nutrition go a long way in the choice of food parents provide for their children. For example, a mother that resumes work in the early hours of the day and comes back late in the night may not have enough time to adequately provide good food for the family, she probably does more by providing ready-to-eat food in form of snacks or purchase more of fast food for the children to compensate for the long hours spend at work. The family structure can in a way determine the type of nutrition the children are exposed to. For example, a family where the father is not present may make the woman buy and prepare just anything for the children or where there are too many children in the home as in a polygamous setting, the family might not be rich enough to eat a well balanced diet but only what is available and affordable for the family. Every culture has a consistent type of food that is unique to her, this may dictate the type of food that is available to a family, and this will shape the family type of food. The knowledge and belief parents hold about healthy eating and nutrition will determine to a large extent, the kind of food that is provided to the family.

Many scientific findings have supported the fact that youths are influenced by their online social circles on their eating habits and behaviour. The habit of modelling a star or an important personality that one sees constantly on social media, the constant exposure of some kind of adverts of a type of food or snacks on the social media, the number of hours youth dedicated to the world of social media could prevent them from preparing and making quality food for themselves and the family. Too much involvement in social media may suppress the brain from feeling hunger pangs, to this extent they eat less or little and when they eat, they go for ready-made-food that is available.

The negative consequences of the eating pattern of youth which involve eating food too much of sodium, sugar and oil can result into physical health challenges ranging from mild to serious ones such as headache, dental problems, acne, depression, heart problems, and diseases, obesity through weight gains and many emotional problems.

Psychological implications of unhealthy food

Unhealthy foods are referred to as the classes of food that add little or no nutritional value to the body. These are majorly organic food that is genetically modified and may also involve such classes of food that are classified as junks. Junk foods contain foods that have plenty in salt, sugar, or fat and oil. It includes such fast foods which are usually ready – to- eat food. These foods include bakery foods, ice-cream, soft drinks, snacks, and a few others. It appears that the more junk food or organic food one consumes, the less likely one has taken the essential nutrients that the body needs. The egocentricism (self-consciousness) which is a characteristic feature of adolescence stage is also a period whereby the onset of the preoccupation with their body image develops. The consciousness of how their body looks like starts at this period and progresses into early adulthood. Thus, youths are generally linked with much behaviour that presents poor health and early death in adults. Conversely, the early formation of healthy patterns begins at this period such as a preference for healthy foods. As these youth progress in age, they start to develop a pattern of food lifestyles such as skipping breakfast, not eating regular meals, not eating with family, taking snacks during the day, eating a class of food excessively to a point of exceeding a normal weight and many other habits which progresses as they grow and develop in age. Fast foods are usually produced to make one crave for more, this addictive nature that goes with fast foods makes the brain to want to crave for more, and eventually one eats more of them.

Brain chemical activities are affected by food with a high content of sugar and fat; continues dependent on such food makes the brain always ask for the same in the form of addiction. This is in line with a Mice Model that was conducted in the University of Montreal where mice that are fed with junk food displayed withdrawal symptoms when food was changed. This is also common among human beings when the food system that was known for sometimes is replaced with another. This may cause stress and inability to deal with the same, which predispose vulnerability to depression and continual 'cravings' for these junk foods to maintain emotional homeostasis. Besides, the excess consumption of junk foods as being known to send wrong and mixed signals to the brain to the extent that the processing of hunger signals and the type of food eaten is not given the correct interpretation to the brain. This, most times leads to overeating of these processed and fried foods to the extent that this leads to addiction to such foods.

In recent research (Miranda, Morici, Zanoni & Bekinschtein, 2019), scholars are of the view that activities of the brain peptide, Brain-Derived Neurotrophic Factor (BDNF) BDNF are affected by high sugar and fat food content and are responsible for memory formation and learning activities. Thus, healthy people that ate junk food for a short while performed poorly on cognitive tests that and thus deteriorate memory. This implies that poor diet and nutrition usually alter certain chemical reactions in the part of the brain responsible for memory, attention, and mood. Another major discovery of the effect of junk food such as fatty foods and sweets is that it can increase the production of insulin in the body. Insulin is usually produced in the pancreas, and it helps in the transportation of glucose and a part of the production of insulin is found in the brain where it helps in transmitting signals between nerve cells and helping to form memories. Where there is too much of insulin production in the body system, the response of the brain stops to the essential hormone and may become resistant to the high insulin. This in turn may impair and also resist the brain's ability to think, retain, recall, and to create memory thus increasing dementia.

Conclusion and Recommendations

Nutrition is a major determinant of good health across all ages in humans. Young people need to be food secured to help boost their vitality, help the brain and body to function well to promote both physical and mental health. The dietary patterns of youths are shaped by the interplay of their environmental microsystems to their macrosystems. These include the family affinities, to the peer group influence, to the culture and values of the land, the economic status of both family and the society, the social media environments, the physical environments and major life events around all are influential in forming a healthy habit of food around an individual. The food that is usually termed unhealthy is those that are genetically modified, those foods that contain too much salt, sugar, or fats and, it also includes fried or cooked foods classified as junk or fast-food and ready-to-make foods that produce high cholesterol in the body. An unhealthy diet has a negative consequence on the human body. Apart from the fact that it is a pattern that might have been developed before or at the adolescence stage, it is also a pattern that affects later health patterns even into adulthood and beyond. Taking much of these classes of food is detrimental to the physical, emotional, and mental health. The increase in eating disorder experienced in the contemporary world of youth are as a result of the various dietary lifestyles that they are involved in some of which may include, a pattern of not eating breakfast, not eating regular meals and relying on snacks as the main source of food during the day, eating consistently and following a binge to a point of exceeding the appropriate age weight, or not eating at all in the pursuit of thinness. Many of the illnesses and diseases that often surfaced at mid-life into old age (such as cardiovascular disorders, diabetes, and chronic diseases) are linked to poor health habits developed right from the youthful age and are usually the cause of early death in the adult years.

Apart from the physical detrimental health hazards that poor nutrition poses to the body, mental health aspects of these youths are not spared in the process of unhealthy eating habits, eating unhealthy food are known to cause serious damage to the brain which may suppress the brain activity, alter some chemical changes in the brain activities making it more dependent on such foods and could even cause a meltdown of the brain functions in such that memory, speed, and learning may be slowed down. In the same vein, the emotional health hazards of not eating right can alter the mood of individuals, it is very important to avoid stress because when the body is stressed there is the tendency in human to involuntarily prefer junk foods as a result of the stress hormone called cortisol that is produced during stress which increases the sugar content in the blood.

The health pattern of Adolescence, emerging and young adults can be improved upon by reducing certain health –impairing lifestyles which are usually brought about as a result of cues flying from the environment during the developmental processes of individuals. Such cues are products of environmental elements whose influence impinge on individuals. These can be behaviours picked from 'models' in the environment that are cognitively represented by individuals. These models can be parents, family members, or a celebrity whom one lives with or have social contact with on social media. It is recommended that youth should be engaging in health-improving lifestyles such as including a proportionate serve of fruits, vegetables, proteins, grains, and dairy on daily meals and occasional eating of sugary, fatty, and salty food only in a small amount. They should be interested in educating themselves on food that is appropriate for them and those that are harmful, they must learn to create time for cooking their meals, shop for healthy combinations of organic food items from a farmer's market and enjoy eating healthy food with their family and friends without social media distractions. They should learn to manage stress and be mindful of their food intake and health. Regular exercise is essential for the health of these younger generations to burn unnecessarily fat, improve blood circulation in the body, increases energy, and improves mood. Staying off drugs and alcohol are also beneficial to healthy living among the youth.

Maintaining overall good health will naturally lead to healthy weight management and improves psychological well-being. Also, parents and family members who are strong influencers of children's food choices because of the control they exercise on children as the primary givers before the influence of peers and others come in are advised to take more interest in the choice of food that is available to the family to promote healthy lifestyles of the children. Eating experience right from childhood provides sustenance in which the child begins to mimic the eating choices and behaviours modelled by family members, this pattern continues with the child into adolescence and youth age unless a developmental milestone in the life of the individual is hijacked by a defective environmental factor which causes a deflection of the parental choices on nutrition. The role of the society (macrosystem) which comprises of the religious society, the school system and Government agencies to recognise and promote food system for the growth and development of the younger generations thus consciously promoting food security system and providing a healthy eating environment in all their policies so as to influence what, where and how much food that is consumed by the youths to reduce obesity and an unhealthy eating pandemic of African youth. Accessibility to healthy food must be emphasized and improved upon to make these classes of food affordable and to raise awareness about how important these foods are through television, advertisements, social media, and all sorts.

This study concludes that youth should be made to understand how to eat healthy food and to develop good habits around food. This involves eating organic food in quantity and quality from varieties of food that are available and eating less or total avoidance of genetically modified food.

References

Allen, A. (2010). "Ethics and Post-structuralism." In Bell, Duncan (Ed.), *Ethics and World Politics*. New York: Oxford University Press, pp. 54-72.

Amusan, L. 2019. Mercy Killing and Thanksgiving: Food Security with Tears in Africa. Being a Paper Presented at Faculty Distinguished Lecture Series 1 Held on Friday, May 17, 2019. Faculty of Social Sciences, Federal University, Oye-Ekiti, Nigeria. DOI:10.13140/RG.2.2.21142.78407.

Amusan, L and Olawuyi, S. O. (2019). "Between Food Quality and Quantity for all in Africa: What they Refuse to tell us about GMO." *Gender & Behaviour*, 17(1), pp. 12284-12298.

Cavalcanti, H. B. (2005). "Food Security." In Dodds, Felix and Pippard, Tim (Eds.), *Human and Environmental Security: An Agenda for Change.* London: Earthscan, pp. 152-165.

Chignell, A. (2018). "Religious Dietary Practices and Secular Food Ethics; or, How to Hope that Your Food Choices make a Difference even when you Reasonably Believe that they Don't." In Barnhill, Anne., Budolfson, Mark., and Doggett, Tyler. (Eds.), *The Oxford Handbook of Food Ethics.* New York: Oxford University Press, pp. 287-312.

Miranda, M., Morici, J. F., Zanoni, M. B., and Bekinschtein, Pedro. (2019). "Brain-Derived Neurothrophic Factor: A Key Molecule for Memory in the Healthy and the Pathological Brain." *Front Cell Neurosci. 13: 363.* doi: 10.3389/fncel.2019.00363.

Nestle, M. (2010 *Safe Food: The Politics of Food Safety*. Berkeley and Los Angeles, California: University of California Press.

Okori, V. O., Maphambukeli, T. N. and Amusan, L. (2019) Exploring the Political Economy of Water and Food Security Nexus in BRICS. *Africa Insight.* 48(4), pp. 21-38.

Otero, G. (2018). *The Neoliberal Diet: healthy Profits, Unhealthy People.* Austin, TX: University of Texas Press.

Pollan, M. (2016). *Omnivore's Dilemma: A Natural History of Four Meals.* New York: Penguins Books.

Pollan, M. (2009). *In Defense of Food: An Eater's Manifesto.* New York: Penguin Books.

Chapter 7
Significance of Bushmeat in Food Security and Income Sustainability

Ogunjinmi, A.A., Amusan, L., Oyeleke, O.O., Osunsina, I.O.O., Adewumi, A.A., and Oduntan, O.O.

Introduction

Feeding an ever-increasing population is one of the greatest challenges facing the human race (Hoffman & Cawthorn, 2012). According to FAO et al. (2018), there is strong evidence of a rise in hunger throughout the world. Estimates indicate an increase in the number of people affected by undernourishment or chronic food deprivation from around 804 million in 2016 to nearly 821 million in 2017 (FAO *et al.*, 2018), an indication that vast global population of humans is not food secured.

Food security is access to enough food at all times for active and healthy life (Swamy & Pinedo-Vasquez, 2014). FAO (1996) also describes food security as "when all people, at all times, have physical and economic access to sufficient, safe and nutritious food to meet their dietary needs and food preferences for an active and healthy life". Economic and social justice of any nation could not be said to have been enshrined without the fulfilment of food security, as such, adequate production, quality, and availability are essential to the achievement of food sufficiency. ACAPS (2018) posited that the security of food remains a major concern in countries such as Nigeria. African Centre for Economic Transformation (ACET, 2015) also opined that despite the improvement in overall nutrition and protein consumption in the past two decades in Africa, sufficient protein consumption remains an issue of concern, especially among the poor. Protein deficiency-induced malnutrition remains a challenge for many people across West Africa (ACET, 2015). According to FAO *et al.* (2015), although there has been a reduction in the proportion of malnourished Nigerians from 19.3% in 1990 to 8.5% in 2010 the number of undernourished increased from roughly 10 million to almost 13 million from 2010 to 2012. For sub-Saharan African and less developed nations, food intake requirements are estimated to be below international standard and past efforts at increasing and improving agricultural output through agricultural production programs have not brought the desired impacts (Otaha, 2013). Protein deficiency poses a significant threat with increasing population, low income, and the gap between food production and consumption (Brown *et al.,* 2007).

The importance of natural biodiversity to human survival cannot be overemphasized despite increasing agricultural productivity and plantation forestry as it provides the materials needed for human survival such as food, micro-nutrients, medicines, fuel, and raw materials for construction and farming inputs (ABCG, 2004). Wildlife products are valuable commodities, and wild meat is considered to be of premium value owing to its high value per unit weight compared with other forest products (Williamson, 2002). Wildlife according to Ziegler (2010) has been hunted for food for centuries, and people have traditionally hunted games for subsistence use or barter. Trading in wildlife is vital to meeting the needs of a significant proportion of the world's population with products derived from tens of thousands of species of plants and animals traded and used of, among other things, medicine, food, fuel, building materials, clothing, and ornamentation (Traffic, 2012). Many rural livelihoods in developing countries depend heavily on wildlife resources both plants and animals (Roe *et al.,* 2002). Bushmeat is one of those forest products which have been demonstrated to have major significance for rural communities, particularly in the humid and sub-humid tropics (Ziegler, 2010). Cawthorn and Hoffman (2015) opined that bushmeat is a key contributor to the food security of millions of people in the developing world, most notably in Africa, Latin America, and Asia.

Bushmeat: An important wildlife resource

Generally, bushmeat refers to non-domesticated terrestrial mammals, birds, reptiles, and amphibians harvested for food, medicines, and other purposes. Fauna and Flora International (2018) defines wild meat or bushmeat as wild animals hunted or harvested in tropical and sub-tropical countries for food, including mammals, amphibians, insects, reptiles, and birds, but excluding fish or aquatic molluscs. The CBD Bushmeat Liaison Group defines bushmeat (or wild meat) hunting as the harvesting of wild animals in the tropical and sub-tropical forests for food and non-food purposes, including medicinal use (UNEP *et al.*, 2011). The primary reason for hunting and trapping mammals according to Ripple *et al.* (2016) is to acquire meat for human consumption, medicinal products, ornamental use, and pet trade. The consumption of bushmeat is nothing new according to Federal Food Safety and Veterinary Office, FSVO, Undated), however, the amount of meat as well, as the global distribution of bushmeat, has increased drastically, due to factors such as population growth, more efficient hunting through more sophisticated weapons and the accessibility of formerly isolated/remote forest areas (FSVO, Undated).

Wild meat or meat from wild animals has been playing a significant role in the life and survival of forest-dwelling rural populations arguably from the period of hunter-gatherer agricultural practices to this modern and technological development age. The use of bushmeat constitutes a major form of consumptive utilisation of wildlife and it is widely practised in West and Central African countries including Nigeria, Ghana, Liberia, Sierra Leone, Guinea, Congo, Central African Republic, and a host of others. The exploitation of wild animals for food has increased in recent years among the forest dwellers and the staggering quantity of bushmeat was being consumed annually (Wildlife Conservation Research Unit, 2019). Although humans have been hunting wildlife in tropical forests for 100,000 years or more, consumption of wild animals is escalating in many parts of sub-Saharan Africa and across humid tropics over the past decades (Milner-Gulland *et al.*, 2003, Fa, 2016). Aside from consumption, it also an important livelihood option, particularly, during the off-farming season.

A high economic value is attached to the subsistence use of and the commercial trade in wild meat, making it an important source of livelihood for both rural and urban communities trading bushmeat (Olupot *et al.*, 2009). According to Swamy and Pinedo-Vasquez (2014), millions of tropical forests inhabitants' livelihoods depend on bushmeat. In Nigeria, many families in rural areas are supported from by bushmeat related employment for their many men and women (Federal Government of Nigeria, 2015). Bushmeat also serves as a reliable safety net during times of economic recession and hardship, thus an important contributory factor for preventing people from falling into poverty as well as poverty alleviation.

Wild animal types hunted and traded as bushmeat

In the tropics and subtropics, wild animals hunted as bushmeat varies, depending on the animals indigenous to each region. It covers various categories such as ungulates, primates, rodents, reptiles, and birds. However, according to SCBD (2011), while invertebrates and birds are undoubtedly locally significant dietary items, the larger vertebrates constitute the majority of the terrestrial wild animal biomass consumed by humans. COP (2017) observed from various studies on hunting, that vertebrates contribute almost all of the wild meat consumed and traded. By class, mammals are the most common, followed by birds, reptiles, and amphibians. According to Petrozzi *et al.* (2016), mammals dominate the trade in wildlife. In the late 1990s, it was estimated that over 5 million tons of wild mammal meat were annually consumed in Neotropical (0.15 million tons) and Afrotropical (4.9 million tons) moist forests (Fa and Peres, 2001, Nasi *et al.*, 2011)). According to Fa *et al.* (2005), ungulates and rodents comprise 73% and 12% of the total biomass harvested respectively and account for around 42% and 39% of the recorded carcasses in African moist forests. In Nigeria for example, Eniang *et al.* (2008) reported 21 species of wild animals with different parts sold as bushmeat in the Oban region of Cross River State while Bassey *et al.* (2010) showed that at least 30 different species of wild animals were traded as bushmeat. Bitty *et al.* (2014) reported that bushmeat was frequently sold in local restaurants. Table 3 shows the animal types used and traded as bushmeat, which include vulnerable, threatened, and endangered species.

Class	Animal Type
Mammals	
	Grasscutter
	Giant rat
	Mongoose
	Porcupine
	Pangolin
	Bush dog
	Bush cat
	Monkey
	Hyrax
	Duiker
	Civet
	Bushbuck
	Roan antelope
	Buffalo
	Sitatunga
	Elephant
	Hippopotamus
	Bush pig
	Red river hog
	Squirrel
	Hare
	Bats
	Otter
	Potto
	Genet
	Drill
	Chimpanzee
	Guenons
	Colobus
	Chevrotain
	Baboon
	Gorilla
	Mona monkey
	Mangabeys
	Patas monkey

Table 1: *Wild animals commonly hunted and traded as bushmeat and their conservation status*

Reptiles	
	Python
	Tortoise
	Monitor lizard
	Turtles
	Crocodile
	Gabon viper
	Red-necked cobra
	Puff adder
Molluscs	
	Snail
Birds	
	Francolin
	Guinea fowl

Table 1 continued: *Wild animals commonly hunted and traded as bushmeat and their conservation status*

Bushmeat and sustainable protein supply

Animal protein from bushmeat consumption

Many countries in the developing world including Nigeria are experiencing inadequate protein supply and consumption. Adekunmi *et al.* (2017) suggested the consumption of products of animals in diets as a major solution to close the protein gap. In the view of the Sustainable Development Solutions Network (2013), modest increases in consumption of animal source foods can contribute substantially to ensuring dietary adequacy, preventing undernourishment, and improving nutritional deficiencies in most low-income countries. However, in most sub-Saharan African countries, including Nigeria, FAO (2009) reported that the level of consumption of protein from animal sources is low.

Wild meat is a major contributor to the consumption of animal protein, which is based on taste, status, availability, and cultural significance. In countries with abundant wildlife such as Democratic Republic of Congo and the Central African Republic, consumers typically eat bushmeat as it is the cheapest or most available form of meat, although not necessarily the most preferred (van Vliet *et al.*, 2010, Fargeot, 2010 cited in van Vliet *et al.*,

2010). Even in urban centres where consumers of bushmeat have the choice of several sources of protein, they opt for bushmeat for a variety of reasons including taste or cost (van Vliet *et al.*, 2010) and consumption of wild meat has risen (Barnet, 2000), despite being considered insignificant in the past studies (Rushton *et al.*, 2005). Among rural and urban people, bushmeat serves as an important source of protein in the diets (van Vliet *et al.*, 2011). The percentage contribution of bushmeat to the overall protein intake of rural households in Central Africa is between 30 to 80% (Godoy *et al.*, 2009). In a study conducted in some communities around the Oban Sector of Cross River National Park Nigeria, Adedoyin *et al.* (2017) reported that as much as 86% of inhabitants of Ifumkpa, Ekuri, Esang, Aking/Osomba, and Ekang communities consumed bushmeat. Wild meat consumption by rural people has been estimated at around 63kg per capital per annum in the Amazon, and 51kg per capital per annum in the Congo Basin (Nasi *et al.*, 2011). Recent data indicate that 23,000 tonnes of bushmeat are harvested annually in Sarawak (Bennet, 2002), 67,000-164,000 tonnes in the Brazilian Amazon (Robinson and Redford, 1991, Peres, 2000), and 1 million-3.4 million tonnes in Central Africa (Wilkie and Carpenter, 1999, Fa, 2001).

Nutritional value of bushmeat

The species used as bushmeat provide an equivalent or even greater quality of food than domestic meats with less fat and more protein (Nasi *et al.*, 2008). Available evidence demonstrates that bushmeat is a significant source of fats, micro and macronutrients which are important to human health (van Vliet *et al.*, 2017) and most wild animals utilised as bushmeat are low in fat and equal or better than domestic animals in protein content and greater in vitamin content (Malaisse and Parent, 1982, Ntiamao_Baidu, 1997). Malik *et al.* (2011) showed that the meat of African giant land snail is higher in crude protein than meat from domestic animals.

In a study conducted in Amazon, Sarti *et al.* (2015) observed that 32% of the household caloric intake was made up of bushmeat, 72% of protein consumption, and 77% of iron with households presenting higher nutritional status, that is, lower intake of carbohydrates (-10%), and higher intake of proteins (+46%), iron (+151%), and zinc (+23%) than household not consuming bushmeat. Golden *et al.* (2011) showed that children that consume a higher quantity of wildlife had greater haemoglobin concentrations. Malaisse and Parent (1981) provided the energy and mineral content of some rodents used as a food resource (Table 1). Tewe and Ajayi (1978) Ajayi (1979), Ajayi, and Tewe (1979) and Malaisse and Parent (1981) compared the proximate composition of wild meats and some domestic animals (Table 2). The values for energy and mineral content of the selected species and the proximate composition of meat from wild animals showed that wild meat is of high nutritional value.

Species		**Energy**	**Ca**	**P**	**Fe**
	KJ	Cals	Mg	Mg	Mg
Paraxerus cepapi	497	119	230	250	5
Aethomys kaiseri	455	109	400	270	15
Cricetomys gambianus	936	224	400	360	10
Dasysmys sp.	526	126	280	225	10
Lophuromys flavopunctatus	601	144	300	170	7
Praomvs.sp.	618	148	270	300	10
Saccostomus campestris	723	173	550	350	15
Thamnomys. sp.	418	100	280	225	10
Pelomys fallax	459	110	210	270	8
Hystrix africae-australis	937	233	150	310	5
Thryonomys swinderianuss	1132	271	320	380	20
Cryptomys hottentotus	668	160	150	220	15

Table 2: *Comparative analysis of Energy and mineral content of some rodents used as food resource*

Source: Malaisse and Parent, 1982.

Adapted from Ntiamao-Baidu, 1997.

Species	Moisture	Protein	Fat	Ash
Rodentia				
Paraxerus cepapi	74.3	21.0	3.2	1.5
Aethomys kaiseri	73.1	19.1	3.0	2.0
Cricetomys gambianus	49.1	42.6	4.7	2.6
Dasysmys sp	71.7	21.0	4.0	2.0
Lophuromys flavopunctatus	66.7	27.5	2.9	2.6
Praomvs.sp.	70.0	19.8	7.0	2.0
Saccostomus campestris	68.4	19.0	10.2	2.2
Thamnomys. sp.	70.7	16.3	3.4	2.0
Pelomys fallax	75.1	19.9	2.8	1.8
Hystrix africae-austrialis	48.0	45.8	41	1.7
Thryonomys swinderianuss	52.0	28.0	16.8	2.9
Cryptomys hottentotus	69.2	16.6	9.9	1.8
Carnivora				
Long-snouted mongoose *Herpestes naso*	72.7	18.8	1.9	3.3
Forest Genet *Genetta pardina*	31.8	55.4	9.3	6.0
Suidae				
Red river hog *Potamochoerus aethiopicus*	70.1	23.8	1.6	1.1
Artiodactyla				
Royal antelope Neotragus pygmaeus	74.5	23.4	0.9	1.2
Crown duiker Cephalophus sp	74.6	20.8	3.4	1.2
Grey duiker Siyvicapra grimmia	59.5	33.4	2.0	4.0
Bushbuck Tragelaphus scriptus	47.6	50.9	12.2	3.7
Domestic animals				
Ox (beef)	73.8	19.6	12.0	1.0
Sheep (mutton)	78.5	17.2	2.9	1.0
Pig (pork)	64.8	19.4	13.4	0.8

Table 3: *Proximate composition of meat of some wild animal species compared with selected domestic animals*

Source: Tewe and Ajayi,1978, Ajayi,1979, Ajayi and Tewe,1979, Malaisse and Parent, 1981.

Adapted from Ntiamao-Baidu, 1997.

Bushmeat trade and sustainable income

In places where bushmeat is abundant, trading in bushmeat has become common and has developed into the informal sector which makes a significant contribution to household economies (Refisch & Kone, 2004, Bitty *et al.,* 2014) and constitutes an essential contributory source to livelihood in both rural and urban setting (Wilkie& Carpenter, 1999, Nasi *et al.,* 2011, van Vliet *et al.,* 2011, 2015). Trading in bushmeat offers greater advantages than other farm-based agricultural products. Brown and Williams (2003) highlighted the advantages of bushmeat trade as low risk and flexible, with minimal capital costs, and thus particularly attractive to the poor. Others include excellent storage qualities, easily transportable, and a high value /weight ratio and thus fit in with the realities of rural life in the tropics (Brown & Williams, 2003).

Bushmeat trade is increasing at an exponential and unsustainable rate with a concomitant higher population of hunters and traders with a profit-oriented motive (Eniang *et al.,* 2008). Bushmeat forms an indispensable income source for both rural and urban household and plays an important livelihood activity for hunters, wholesalers, and restaurant owners. In Western and Central Africa, hunting for bushmeat has transformed into an expansive enterprise with the sole reason for income generation (Wright & Priston, 2010). CBD (2011) stated that people engaging in trading bushmeat along highways, in open markets, through hawking, or in restaurants, and shop halls derive significant income along the supply chains. According to Schulte-Herbruggen (2011), even, many households that engage in other means of income generation activities persist in the exploitation of already reduced wildlife populations. The bushmeat trade is a vital income source to millions of people, particularly for the poor in rural areas (Bakarr *et al.,* 2002, Bennet, 2002, Davis, 2002, Mainka & Trivedi, 2002, Milner-Gulland *et al.,* 2003, Nasi *et al.*, 2008, Sarti *et al.,* 2015). A large number of households in rural areas obtain appreciable part of their disposable income from trading in wildlife products (Roe *et al.,* 2002).

The value of the contribution of bushmeat to the economic sustainability of rural and urban areas is difficult to estimate. This is because according to van Gils (2016), trading is very demanding to trace. After all, it occurs informally and illegally. Despite this, estimates have been reported from various studies. For example, in South East Gabon, Starkey (2004) reported that bushmeat trade contributes 15-72% of total household income, a very important income source for 33% of the respondents in Lebialem, Cameroon (Wright & Priston, 2010), 24% in North Myannar (Rao *et al.*, 2010). Bushmeat sector is estimated to account for the overall monetary benefit for 15 million people per year in Cameroon (Lescuyer & Nasi, 2015).

Profitability analysis of bushmeat marketing in Ondo, Osun and Ogun States in Southwest Nigeria by Oniya (2017) shows that an average bushmeat marketer earned a gross income of ₦48,762.16 monthly and that bushmeat trade is profitable with a return on investment of 1.56%. Bassey *et al.* (2010) estimated the value of bushmeat traded in eight border communities of South-East Nigeria amounted to ₦9, 765,600 – approximately $65,000 per month. Soaga *et al.* (2014) also observed an average annual profit of ₦453, 004 in Abeokuta, Nigeria, and indicated that bushmeat trade was profitable. Davies (2002) estimates showed that domestic trade in bushmeat range from US$42 to US$205 million across countries in West and Central Africa. The economic value of bushmeat trade equals 1-1.5% of the GDP of the country in West and Central Africa (Caspary, 2001, Davies, 2002). When income shortages are highest, bushmeat sales increase, stalling income poverty (ACET, 2014). Bushmeat trade contributes to the income and poverty alleviation of marketers (Oniya, 2017). Furthermore, investment in farming of wildlife for bushmeat and trade has also been shown to be profitable. Aiyeloja and Ogunjinmi (2013) reported that farming wild animals were above the poverty line, worthwhile, and profitable, it is a veritable employment source for a large number of people, particularly in rural and urban fringes.

Domestication: Meeting protein requirement and income sustainability

Domestication is the taming and breeding of wild animals in captivity for the production of meat and other purposes. Breeding according to Smythe (1991 cited in Mason, 1984) involves "selection away from some of the characteristics of the wild type". Due to the pressure on wild populations of animals used as bushmeat and other purposes, domestication has been advocated as having the potential to reduce pressure on the wild stock and ensure sustainable production and use of wild animals. Wild animals suggested as having potential for domestication and farming include crocodile, ostrich, grasscutter, a giant rat, snail, quail, bush fowl, porcupine, bushbuck, duikers, and other antelopes. Intensive and comprehensive domestication programs and research on grasscutter (Mensah, 1991, Ntiamao-Baidu, 1980, Asibey, 1974, Ajayi, 1971), giant rat (Ajayi *et al.*, 1978, Ajayi, 1975, 1971), snails (Agbelusi and Ejidike, 1992, Elmsie, 1982, Ajayi *et al.*, 1978, Ajayi, 1971), bush fowl (Aro and Akinmoladun, 2015) and other species of wild animals have been carried out with varying degrees of success. Of the 148 big wild terrestrial herbivores in the world, only 14 have been successfully domesticated (Diamond, 1997). Many livestock farmers are now diversifying into farming wild animal species as Micro-livestock including snails, cane rats, and guinea fowl (Ogunjinmi *et al.*, 2013).

For wild animals to be selected for domestication, certain key biological characteristics such as diet (i.e., the efficiency of turning vegetative matter into meat) growth rate (the ability to grow quickly), ability to breed in captivity, relatively easy disposition, tendency not to panic, and well-defined dominance hierarchy with ability to have a leader imprinted on their group (Diamond, 1997) must be possessed by the wild animals under consideration for domestication.

Bushmeat consumption risk and wildlife sustainability

Bushmeat and zoonotic diseases risk

Zoonotic disease infections are among the most common on earth, accounting for more than 60% of all human infectious diseases (Ekong *et al.*, 2012). Most emerging zoonotic diseases are of viral origin and transmitted by vectors (Taylor *et al.*, 2001), which for the most part are wildlife (Woolhouse and Cowtage-Sequeria, 2005, Cleaveland *et al.*, 2007). Bushmeat hunting and butchering are part of a broader spectrum of activities in sub-Saharan Africa that bring people and animals into direct and potentially risky contacts (Maurice *et al.*, 2017). Tendency of exposure to the risks from zoonotic diseases from a wide range of bushmeat related activities such as hunting, processing, and contacts with insects or insect bites is very high in occurrence (Kruse *et al.*, 2004). Multiple studies report a high risk for zoonotic transmission of blood-borne pathogens like retroviruses through contact with non-human primates, and this risk seems to be particularly high in Tropical Africa (Mossoun *et al.*, 2017).

Trapping, transportation, trading, handling, and consumption of bushmeat exposes humans to a variety of risks from viral, parasitic, and other disease organisms emanating from wild animals including Ebola, yellow fever, and HIV (Animal Welfare Institute, undated). According to Smith *et al.* (2012), approximately 75% of newly emerging diseases are zoonotic and most of these diseases originate from wild animals. Infectious diseases such as Ebola, SARs, Anthrax, and HIV-AIDS are likely to have been transmitted to humans while processing and consuming bushmeat and these could be transmitted to domesticated animal species (avian influenza, swine flu) (Smith *et al.*, 2012). The highest risk of disease transmission occurs during the butchering of animals, e.g., skinning, opening of the body cavity, removal of organs, and cutting of meat (Kurpiers *et al.*, 2016). Some zoonotic pathogens that have emerged in the Cameroon-Congo Basin region from 1970-2005 and their wild reservoir are in Table 4.

Pathogen or disease	**Reservoir species**	**Risk behaviour**	**Reference**
Arboviruses (dengue, yellow fever)	Various	Human presence in region for habitation, work or leisure	Morse, 1993, Krippner and Laer, 2002, Vicens *et al.*, 1993
Ebola	Unknown	Hunting wildlife, necropsy	Klenk, 1999
Monkeypox	Squirrels and others		Jezek *et al.*, 1986
HIV-1 and -2	Chimpanzee, Sooty mangabe	Hunting, butchering non-human primates	Hahn *et al.*, 2000
Anthrax	Ungulates	Butchering or eating carcases	
Herpes B virus	Range of non-human primates	Keeping pests	Ostrowski *et al.*, 1998
Salmonellosis	Range of non-human primates	Keeping pets	Fox 1975
Cutaneous leishmaniasis		Logging/road building, ecotourism, research	
Loa		Logging/road building, ecotourism, research	
Simian foamy viruses	Gorilla, mandarin, De Brazza's guenon, other unknown species	Hunting non-human primates	Wolfe *et al.*, 2004
Chromomycosis		Wood collection	

Table 4: *Some zoonotic pathogens that have emerged in the Cameroon-Congo Basin region, 1970-2005*

Source: Adapted from Wolfe et al., 2005.

Bushmeat and extinction risk

Despite the contribution of bushmeat to food security and livelihood sustainability, meeting bushmeat demand has put untold pressure on the sustainability of the wild stock. With the exponential population growth and commercialisation of wildlife hunting sector, the sustainability of wildlife populations has been negatively impacted, and with the dwindling population of wildlife, hunting at subsistence level, which hitherto sustainable, is no longer the practice, leading to unsustainable offtake. According to Robinson and Bennett (2000), Milner-Gulland and Bennett (2003), Ripple *et al.* (2016), and Gray *et al.* (2018), the sustainability of hunting are questionable in many locations and empirical evidence reveals persistent directives and local extinctions of numerous species across Africa, Asia, and Latin America, particularly where hunting is supplying urban markets. Ripple *et al.* (2019) analysed how human activities are impacting conservation status of megafauna within six classes: mammals, ray-finned fish, cartilaginous fish, amphibians, birds, and reptiles and found that 70% of megafauna species with sufficient information are decreasing and 59% are threatened with extinction and that direct harvesting of mega fauna for human consumption of meat or body parts is the largest individual threat to each of the classes examined and a threat for 98% of threatened species with threat data available. The largest vertebrates are mostly threatened by direct killing by humans (Ripple *et al.*, 2017).

Bushmeat hunting and consumption are not sustainable. There is compelling evidence that the scale of current hunting is a serious threat to many forest species and ecosystems (UNEP *et al.*, 2011). Many species of wildlife have been extirpated through persistence and widespread hunting pressure, particularly in West and Central African regions (Milner-Gulland *et al.*, 2003). It has been suggested that the take-off of wild animals from nature in Africa is six times higher than sustainable use would be (Bartnett, 2000). Trading in bushmeat has been identified as among the greatest threats to the maintenance of biodiversity, second only to habitat destruction (Hoyt, 2004). In the global study conducted by The Intergovernmental Science-Policy Platform on Biodiversity and Ecosystem Services (IPBES, 2018), poaching and illegal wildlife trade are one of the indirect drivers of biodiversity loss and the loss of nature's contributions to people while according to Brashares *et al.* (2004), the multibillion-dollar trade in bushmeat is among the most immediate threats to the persistence of tropical vertebrates.

Conclusion

Bushmeat contributes significantly to food security in West and Central African countries. It is an important component of diets providing protein, fats, micro and micronutrients, and vitamins. The bushmeat trade is also critical to livelihood and income sustainability through employment and cash income from sales of bushmeat and other products from wild animals. Evidence indicates that income from hunting and trading in bushmeat is critical to preventing income-related poverty among the rural poor particularly those whose livelihood depends on bushmeat trade. Despite the important roles of bushmeat as food security and livelihood options, and the dwindling population of wild animals on which these are premised, policies relating to sustainable harvest and trade have not been the focus of countries with the high impact of bushmeat harvest and trade. Policies on sustainability in off-take and harvest of bushmeat, utilization, and support for domestication through research and extension services must be evolved.

References

ACAPS (2018). ACAPS thematic report 2018. Famine in Ethiopia, Nigeria, Somalia, South Sudan and Yemen.

ABCG. 2004. African Biodiversity Collaborative Group and Bushmeat Crisis Task Force meeting notes from: Food Security and Conservation in Africa: Addressing hunger and farming issues to conserve wildlife. African Biodiversity Collaborative Group.

Adedoyin, S., Jimoh, S. & Omifolaji, J. (2017). Bushmeat utilisation in Oban Sector of Cross River National Park: A biodiversity palaver. InfotechOpen, Chapter 3, p.35-49, In Global Exposition of Wildlife Management.

Adekunmi, A.O., Ayinde, J.O., & Ajala, A.O. (2017). An assessment of animal protein consumption patterns among rural dwellers in Osun State, Nigeria. *Ife Journal of Agriculture,* 29(1): 84-94.

African Centre for Economic Transformation, ACET (2014); Bushmeat and the future of protein in West Africa. *West Africa Trends,* 9: 1-16.

Agbelusi, E.A. & Ejidike, B.N. (1992). " Utilization of the African giant land snail *Archachatina marginata* in the humid area of Nigeria " *Tropical Agriculture,* 69(1): 88-92.

Aiyeloja, A.A. & Ogunjinmi, A.A. (2013). Economic aspects of grasscutter farming in Southwest Nigeria: Implications for sustainable adoption and conservation. *International Journal of Scientific and Engineering Research,* 4(10): 17-23.

Ajayi, S.S. (1971). Wildlife as a source of protein in Nigeria: some priorities for development. *The Nigerian Field,* 36 (3): 115-127.

Ajayi, S.S. (1975). *Domestication of the African Giant Rat* (Cricetomys-gambianus, *Waterhouse*). Publ. Dept for Res. Management, University of Ibadan, Ibadan, Nigeria: vi + 44 pp.

Ajayi, S.S., Tewe, O.O. & Faturoti, E.O. (1978). Behavioural changes in the African giant rat (*Cricetomys gambianus* Waterhouse) under domestication. *E. Afr. Wildl. J.,* 16: 137-143.

Ajayi, S.S. (1979). Utilisation of forest wildlife in West Africa. Misc/79/26, Food and Agriculture Organisation, Rome, 79 pp.

Ajayi, S.S. & Tewe, O. (1979). Performance of the African giant rat (*Cricetomys gambianus,*

Waterhouse) on commercial rations and varying dietary protein levels. *J. Lab. Animals,* 12: 109-112.

Animal Welfare Institute (Undated). Bushmeat. Bushmeat Brochure, AWI, Washington, D.C.

Aro, S.O. & Akinmoladun, O.F. (2015). Preliminary investigations on the domestication and adaptive breeding of African Bush Fowl (*Francolinus bicalcaratus*). *Livestock Research for Rural Development,* 27(5) 2015.

Asibey, E.O.A. (1974). Wildlife as a source of protein in Africa South of the Sahara. *Biological Conservation*, 6 (l): 32-39.

Bakarr, M. I., Ampadu-Agyei, O., Adomako, E. & Ham, R. (2002). Bushmeat utilisation, human livelihoods and conservation of large mammals in west Africa. pp. 45-53. *In*: Mainka, S.A. & Trivedi, M. (eds.) *Links between Biodiversity Conservation, Livelihoods and Food Security: the Sustainable Use of Wild Species for Meat*. Gland, IUCN.

Barnett, R. (2000). Food for Thought: The Utilisation of Wild Meat in Eastern and Southern Africa. TRAFFIC East/Southern Africa, Nairobi.

Bassey, E., Nkonyu, L. & Dunn, A. (2010). A reconnaissance survey of the bushmeat trade in eight border communities of South-East Nigeria, September – October 2009. Arcus Foundation and Wildlife Conservation Society, 21pp.

Barnett, R. (2000) Food for thought: The Utilization of Wild Meat in Eastern and Southern Africa. TRAFFIC/WWF/IUCN, Nairobi, Kenya

Bennett, E.L. (2002) Is there a link between wild meat and food security? *Conserv. Biol.* 16, 590–592

Bitty, E.A., Kadjo, B., Benne, J-C.K. and Kouassi, P.K. (2014). Bushmeat survey: an indicator of wildlife disappearance in Soubre Region, Cote d'lvoire. *Livestock Research for Rural Development*, 26(3):

Brashares, J.S., Arcese, P., Sam, M.K., Coppolillo, P.B., Sinclair, A.R.E. & Balmford, A. (2004). Bushmeat Hunting, Wildlife Declines, and Fish Supply in West Africa. *Science*, 306: 1180-1183

Brown, D. & Williams, A. (2003). The case for bushmeat as a components of development policy: issues and challenges. *International Forestry Review*, 5(2): 148-155.

Brown, D., Fa, J.E. & Gordon, L. (2007). Assessment of recent bushmeat research and recommendations to Her Majesty's Government. Final Report. Department for Environment, Food and Rural Affairs, 91pp

Caspary, H.U. (2001). Regional dynamics of hunting and bushmeat utilization in west Africa- An overview. pp.11-16. *In*: M. I. Bakarr, G. A. B.de Fonseca, R. A. Mittermeier, A. B. Rylands & K. W. Painemilla (eds.) *Hunting and Bushmeat Utilization in the African Rain Forest. Perspectives Toward a Blueprint for Conservation Action*. Washington DC, Conservation International.

Cawthorn, D.-M., & Hoffman, L.C. (2015). The bushmeat and food security nexus: A global account of the contributions, conundrums and ethical collisions, *Food Research International* (2015), http://dx.doi.org/10.1016/j.foodres.2015.03.025

Cleaveland, S., Haydon, D.T., & Taylor, L. (2007) Overviews of pathogen emergence: which pathogens emerge, when and why? In: Childs JE, Mackenzie JS, Richt JA (eds) Wildlife and emerging zoonotic diseases: the biology, circumstances and consequences of cross-species transmission. Springer, Berlin, pp 85–111

COP (2017). Addressing unsustainable use of terrestrial and avian wild meat. In 12th Meeting of the Conference of the Parties, Manilla, Philippines, 23-28 October 2017. UNEP/CMS/COP12/Doc.24.2.3

Davies, G. (2002): Bush Meat and International Development. *Conserv. Biol.*,16(3): 125-132.

Diamond, J. 1997. Guns, Germs and Steel. A short history of everybody for the last 13,000 years. Vintage, London, UK.

Ekong, P.S., Juryit, R., Mwapu, N., Dika, N.M., & Nguku, P. (2012). Monica Musenero Prevalence and risk factors for zoonotic helminth infection among humans and animals - Jos, Nigeria, 2005-2009. *PanAfrican Medical Journal*, 12(6): http://www.panafrican-med-journal.com/ content/article/12/6/full/

Elmslie, L.J. (1982). Snails and snail farming. *World Animal Review*, 41: 20-26.

Eniang, E.A., Eninag, M.E. & Akpan, C.E. (2008). Bushmeat trading in the Oban Hills Region of South-Eastern Nigeria: Implications for sustainable livelihoods and conservation. Ethiopian Journal of Environmental Studies and Management, 1(1): 70-83

Fa, J.E., and Peres, C.A. (2001). Game vertebrate extraction in African and Neotropical forests: an intercontinental comparison. Pages 203–241 in J. D. Reynolds, G. M. Mace, J. G. Robinson, and K. H. Redford, editors. Conservation of exploited species. Cambridge University Press, Cambridge, United Kingdom.

Fa, J. E., Ryan, S. F., & Bell, D. J. (2005). Hunting vulnerability, ecological characteristics and harvest rates of bushmeat species in afrotropical forests. *Biological Conservation*, 121, 167–176.

Fa, J.E. (2016). Importance of antelope bushmeat consumption in African wet and moist tropical forests. In: Bro-Jørgensen, J., Mallon, D.P. (eds.) Antelope Conservation: From Diagnosis to Action. CIFOR, 78-91

Fauna and Flora International (2018). Exploring bushmeat consumption behaviours among Phnom Penh Citizens. Fauna and Flora International, 72pp.

Fargeot, C. (2010). Bushmeat consumption in Central African Republic. XXIII IUFRO Congress, 23rd–28th of August 2010, Seoul, South Korea

Federal Government of Nigeria (2015). Nigeria: Fifth National Biodiversity Report. Federal Ministry of Environment, Abuja. 89pp

Food and Agriculture Organization (1996). Rome Declaration on world food security and World Food Summit plan of action. Rome, Italy: FAO.

Food and Agriculture Organization (2009), Fisheries: the state of World Fisheries and Agriculture (SOFIA), 2009 PART I: World review of fisheries and agriculture; Fish consumption p. 58-65

FAO, IFAD and WFP. (2015). *The State of Food Insecurity in the World 2015. Meeting the 2015 international hunger targets: taking stock of uneven progress.* Rome, FAO.

FAO, IFAD, UNICEF, WFP & WHO. (2018). *The State of Food Security and Nutrition in the World 2018. Building climate resilience for food security and nutrition.* Rome, FAO.

Fox, J.G. (1975). Transmissible drug resistance in Shigella and Salmonella isolated from pet monkeys and their owners. *J Med Primatol.* 1975;4:165–71.

FSVO (undated). Bushmeat: Information and identification guide. Federal Department of Home Affairs, Federal Food and Safety and Veterinary Office and Tengwood Organisation. 31 pp.

Golden, C.D., Fernald, L.C.H., Brashares, J.S., Rasolofoniaina, B.J.R. & Kremen, C. (2011). Benefits of wildlife consumption to child nutrition in a biodiversity hotspot. *Proceedings of the National Academy of Sciences of the United States of America,* 108:19653–56.

Gray, T. N., Hughes, A. C., Laurance, W. F., Long, B., Lynam, A. J., O'Kelly, H., Ripple, W. J., Seng, T., Scotson, L., & Wilkinson, N. M. (2018). The wildlife snaring crisis: An insidious and pervasive threat to biodiversity in Southeast Asia. *Biodiversity and Conservation,* 27(4): 1031–1037.

Hahn, B.H., Shaw, G.M., de Cock, K.M., Sharp, P,M. (2000). AIDS as a zoonosis: scientific and public health implications. *Science,* 287:607–14.

Hoffman, L.C. & Cawthorn, D.-M. (2012). What is the role and contribution of meat from wildlife in providing high quality protein for consumption? *Animal Frontiers,* 2(4):40-53.

Hoyt, R. (2004). Wild Meat Harvest and Trade in Liberia: managing biodiversity, economic and social impacts. ODI Wildlife Policy Briefing, Number 6, April 2004. ODI

IPBES (2018): Summary for policymakers of the regional assessment report on biodiversity and ecosystem services for Africa of the Intergovernmental Science-Policy Platform on Biodiversity and Ecosystem Services. E. Archer, L. E. Dziba, K. J. Mulongoy, M. A. Maoela,M. Walters, R. Biggs, M-C. Cormier-Salem, F. DeClerck, M. C. Diaw, A. E. Dunham, P. Failler, C. Gordon, K. A. Harhash, R. Kasisi, F. Kizito, W. D. Nyingi, N. Oguge, B. Osman-Elasha, L. C. Stringer, L. Tito de Morais, A. Assogbadjo, B. N. Egoh, M. W. Halmy, K. Heubach, A. Mensah, L. Pereira and N. Sitas (eds.). IPBES secretariat, Bonn, Germany. 49 pp

Jezek, Z., Arita, I., Mutombo, M., Dunn, C., Nakano, J.H., & Szczeniowski, M. (1986). Four generations of probable person-to-person transmission of human monkeypox. *Am J Epidemiol.* 123:1004–12.

Klenk H-D. (1999). Marburg and Ebola viruses. Current topics in microbiology and immunology. Berlin: Springer.

Krippner, R., & von Laer, G. (2002). First confirmed dengue-1 fever cases reported from Cameroon. *J Travel Med.* 9:273–4.

Kruse, H., Kirkemo, A., & Handeland, K. (2004). Wildlife as Source of Zoonotic Infections. *Emerg Infect Dis,* 10(12), 2067-2072

Kurpiers, L.A., Schulte-Herbrüggen, B., Ejotre, I., & Reeder, D.A.M. (2016). Bushmeat and Emerging Infectious Diseases: Lessons from Africa. In: F.M. Angelici (ed.), *Problematic Wildlife.* Springer International Publishing, Switzerland. Chapter 24, pp. 507-551.

Lescuyer, G. & Nasi, R. (2015). Financial and economic value of bushmeat in rural and urban

livelihoods in Cameroon: Elements for a public policy. *XIV World Forestry Congress, Durban, South Africa, 7-11 September 2015.*

Mainka, S.A. & Trivedi, M. (2002). *Links between Biodiversity Conservation, Livelihoods and Food Security: the Sustainable Use of Wild Species for Meat.* IUCN, Gland.

Malik, A.A., Aremu, A., Bayode, G.B.& Ibrahim, B.A. (2011). A nutritional and organoleptic assessment of the meat of the giant African land snail (*Archachatina maginata* swaison) compared to the meat of other livestock. *Livestock Research for Rural Development,* 23 (3) 2011

Maurice, M.E., Manyi, E.S., & Munge, E.L. (2017). Primate Bushmeat Consumption: A Source of Zoonotic Disease Risk in Tombel Area, Southwest Region, Cameroon. *International Journal of Environmental Sciences and Natural Resources,* 5(2): 1-7.

Mensah, G.A. (1991). Wildlife farming: grasscutter rearing Thryonomys Swinderianus In, Proceedings of the 10th World Forestry Congress, pp 301-309.

Milner-Gulland, E.J., Bennett, E., Abernethy, K., Bakarr, M., Bodmer, R., Brashares, J., Cowlishaw, G., Elkan, P., Eves, H., Fa, J., Peres, C., Roberts, C., Robinson, J., Rowcliffe, M. & Wilkie, D. (2003). Wild meat: the bigger picture. *Trends in Ecology and Evolution,* 18 (7): 351-357.

Morse, S.S. (1993). Examining the origins of emerging viruses. In: Morse, S.S., editor. Emerging viruses. New York: Oxford University Press; pp. 10–28.

Mossoun, A., Calvignac-Spencer, S., Anoh, A.E., Pauly, M.S., Driscoll, D.A., Michel, A.O., Nazaire, L.G., Pfister, S., Sabwe, P., Thiesen, U., Vogler, B.R., Wiersma, L., Muyembe-Tamfum, J-J., Karhemere, S., Akoua-Koffi, C., Couacy-Hymann, E., Fruth, B., Wittig, R.M., Leendertz, F.H., Schubert, G. (2017). Bushmeat hunting and zoonotic transmission of simian T-lymphotropic virus 1 in tropical West and Central Africa. *J Virol* 91:e02479-16. https://doi.org/10.1128/JVI.02479-16.

Nasi, R., Brown, D., Wilkie, D., Bennett, E., Tutin, C., van Tol, G. & Christophersen, T. 2008: *Conservation and use of wildlife-based resources: the bushmeat crisis.* Technical Series 33. Montreal/Bogor, Secretariat of the Convention on Biological Diversity/Center for International Forestry Research (CIFOR).

Nasi, R., Taber, A. & van Vliet, N. (2011). Empty forests, empty stomachs? Bushmeat and livelihoods in the Congo and Amazon Basins. *International Forestry Review,* 13(3):355–68.

Ntiamoa-Baidu, Y., 1980. The ixodid parasites of the grasscutter Thryonomys swinderianus Temminck in Ghana. Unpublished PhD Thesis, Edinburgh University, 285 pp

Ntiamoa-Baidu, Y. (1997). Wildlife and food security in Africa. FAO conservation guide 33. Italy, Rome: FAO.

Ogunjinmi, A.A., Oyeleke, O.O., Orimaye, J.A., and Ogunjinmi, K.O. (2013). Livestock farmers' adoption and willingness to farm wildlife species in Akure, Ondo State, Nigeria. *Applied Tropical Agriculture*, 18(2): 46-51.

Olupot, W., McNeilage, A.J., and Plumptre, A.J. (2009) An analysis of socio-economics of bushmeat hunting at major hunting sites in Uganda. Wildlife Conservation Society, 108pp.

Ostrowski, S.R., Leslie, M.J., Parrott, T., Abelt, S., & Piercy, P.E. (1998). B-virus from pet macaque monkeys: an emerging threat in the United States? *Emerg Infect Dis.* 4:117–21.

Otaha, I.J. (2013). Food insecurity in Nigeria: way forward. *African Research Review,* 7(4): 26-35.

Petrozzi, F., Amori, G., Franco, D., Gaubert, P., Pacini, N., Eniang, E.A., Akani, G.C., Politano, E. and Luiselli, L. (2016). Ecology of the bushmeat trade in West and Central Africa. *Tropical Ecology,* 57(3): 545-557.

Rao M., Htun, S., Zaw, T., & Myint ,T. (2010). Hunting, Livelihoods and Declining Wildlife in the Hponkanrazi Wildlife Sanctuary, North Myanmar. *Environmental Management*, 46:143–153

Refisch, J. & Koné, I. (2004). Market Hunting in the Taï Region, Côte d'Ivoire and Implications for Monkey Populations. *International Journal of Primatology,* 26 (3): 621-629

Ripple, W.J., Abernethy, K., Betts, M.G., Chapron, G., & Dirzo, R. et al., (2016). Bushmeat hunting and extinction risk to the world's mammals. *Royal Society Open Science,* 3: 160498. http://dx.doi.org/10.1098/rsos.160498

Ripple, W.J., Wolf, C., Newsomea, T.M., Hoffmanne, M., Wirsingd, A.J. & McCaule, D.J. (2017). Extinction risk is most acute for the world's largest and smallest vertebrates. *PNAS,* 114 (40): 10678-10683

Ripple, W.J., Wolf, C., Newsome, T.M., Betts, M.G., Ceballos, G., Courchamp, F., Hayward, M.W., Van Valkenburgh, E., Wallach, A.D., & Worm, B. (2019). Are we eating the world's megafauna to extinction? Conservation Letters, 12:e12627. https://doi.org/10.1111/conl.12627

Robinson, J.G. & Redford, K.H. (1991) Neo-Tropical Wildlife Use and Conservation, Chicago University Press

Robinson, J.G. & Bennett, E. L. (2000). Hunting for Sustainability in Tropical Forests Columbia Univ. Press, New York.

Roe, D., Mulliken, T., Milledge, S., Mremi, J., Mosha, S. & Grieg-Gran, M. (2002). Making a killing or making a living? Wildlife trade, trade controls and livelihoods. Biodiversity and Livelihoods Issues 6. Earthprint , IIED, and Traffic

Rushton, J., Viscarra, R., Viscarra, C., Basset, F., Baptista, R., & Brown, D. (2005). How important is bushmeat consumption in South America: Now and in the future. Wildlife policy briefing no. 11. London, UK: Overseas Development Institute.

Sarti, F. M., C. Adams, C. Morsello, N. Van Vliet, T. Schor, B. Yagüe, L. Tellez, M. Quiceno-Mesa, and D. Cruz. (2015). Beyond protein intake: bushmeat as source of micronutrients in the Amazon. *Ecology and Society* 20(4):22. http://dx.doi.org/10.5751/ES-07934-200422

Schulte-Herbruggen, B. (2011). The importance of bushmeat in the livelihoods of cocoa farmers living in a wildlife depleted farm-forest landscape, SW Ghana. PhD Thesis, University College, London.

Secretariat of the Convention on Biological Diversity (2011) Livelihood alternatives for the unsustainable use of bushmeat. Report prepared for the CBD Bushmeat Liaison Group. Technical Series No. 60, Montreal, SCBD, 46 pp.

Smith, K.M., Anthony, S.J., Switzer, W.M., Epstein, J.H., Seimon, T., Jia, H., Sanchez, M.D. *et al.* (2012). Zoonotic viruses associated with illegally imported wildlife products. *PLoS One* 7:71–79

Smythe, N. (1991). Steps toward Domesticating the Paca (Agouti = Cuniculus paca) and Prospects for the Future. In Robinson, J.G. and Redford, K.H. (editors) Neotropical Wildlife Use and Conservation. University of Chicago Press pp 202-216

Soaga, J.A., Shotuyo, A.L.A., Oduntan, O.O. & Fatoki, J.G. (2014). Economic analysis of bushmeat trade in Abeokuta, Ogun State. *Journal of Agricultural Science and Environment,* 14: 97-108

Starkey, M. (2004). Commerce and subsistence: the hunting, sale and consumption of bushmeat in Gabon. Fitzwilliam College. Cambridge University, Cambridge, United Kingdom.

Sustainable Development Solutions Network (2013). Solutions for sustainable agriculture and food systems. Technical Report for the Post -2015 Development Agenda. Thematic Group on Sustainable Agriculture and Food Systems of the Sustainable Development Solutions Network.

Swamy, V. & Pinedo-Vasquez, M. (2014). Bushmeat harvest in tropical forests: knowledge base, gaps and research priorities. CIFOR Occasional Paper 114.

Traffic Bulletin (2012) Introduction. Traffic Bulletin 24.

Taylor, L.H., Latham, S.M., & Woolhouse, M.E.J. (2001). Risk factors for human disease emergence. *Philos Trans R Soc Lond B Biol Sci.* 356:983–9.

UNEP/CBD/SBSTTA (2011). Livelihood alternatives for the unsustainable use of bushmeat. UNEP/CBD/SBSTTA/15/INF/7 September 2011, 44pp.

van Gills, E. (2016). Changes in livelihood practices and dependence on bushmeat. Comparative case study of rural villages in Gabon. MSc Thesis, Wageningen University, The Netherlands.

van Vliet, N., Milner-Gulland, E., Bousquet, F., Saqalli, M. & Nasi, R. (2010). Effect of small-scale heterogeneity of prey and hunter distributions on the sustainability of bushmeat hunting. *Conservation Biology*, 24: 1327–1337

van Vliet, N., Nasi, R., & Taber, A. (2011). From the forest to the stomach: bushmeat consumption from rural to urban settings in Central Africa. In *Non-timber forest products in the global context* (pp. 129-145). Springer Berlin Heidelberg.

Van Vliet, N., Quiceno, M. P., Cruz, D., Neves de Aquino, L. J., Yagüe, B., Schor, T., Hernandez, S. & Nasi, R. (2015). Bushmeat networks link the forest to urban areas in the trifrontier region between Brazil, Colombia, and Peru. Ecology and Society 20(3): 21. http://dx.doi.org/10.5751/ES-07782-200321

Van Vliet, N., Moreno, J., Gomez, J., Zhou, W., Fa, J.E., Golden, C., Alves, R.R.N. & Nasi, R. 2017. Bushmeat and human health: Assessing the evidence in tropical and subtropical forests. *Ethnobiology and Conservation*, 6(3): 1-45.

Vicens, R., Robert, V., Pignon, D., Zeller, H., Ghipponi, P.M., & Digoutte, J.P. (1993). Epidemic of yellow fever in North Cameroon in 1990–1st isolation of yellow fever virus in Cameroon. *Bull World Health Organ*, 71:173–6.

Wildlife Conservation Research Unit (2019). Bushmeat consumption in tropical forests. Retrieved on 19/05/2019 from https://www.wildcru.org/research/reas-5/

Williamson, D. (2002). Wild meat, food security and forest conservation. In: Mainka, S.A. and Trivedi, M. eds. *Links between biodiversity conservation, livelihoods and food security: the sustainable use of wild species for meat.* Pp. 19-22, Switzerland and Cambridge, UK: IUCN, Gland

Wilkie, D.S. & Carpenter, J.F. (1999) Bushmeat hunting in the Congo Basin: an assessment of impacts and options for mitigation. *Biodiv. Conserv.*, 8, 927–955.

Wolfe, N.D., Switzer, W.M., Folks, T.M., Burkes, D.S., Heneine, W. (2004). Simian retroviral infections in human beings–reply. *Lancet*, 364: 139–40.

Wolfe, N.D., Daszak, P., Kilpatrick, A.M. & Burke, D.S. (2005). Bushmeat Hunting, Deforestation, and Prediction of Zoonotic Disease Emergence. *Emerging Infectious Diseases*, 11(12): 1822-1827

Woolhouse, M.E., & Gowtage-Sequeria, S. (2005). Host range and emerging and re-emerging pathogens. *Emerg Infect Dis*. 11(12):1842-1847.

Wright, J.H. & Priston, N.E.C. (2010). Hunting and trapping in Lebialem division, Cameroon: bushmeat harvesting practices and human reliance. *Endangered Species Research*, 11: 1-12.

Ziegler, S. (2010). Application of food balance sheets to assess the scale of the bushmeat trade in Central Africa. *Traffic Bulletin*, 22(3): 105-116.

Chapter 8
Food Vendor and Food Vandalism in Africa: A Study On Benin, Cameroon, Niger and Senegal

Opeyemi Idowu Aluko

Introduction

Food security is a major issue in world politics. Any country that is not able to feed its citizen is heading for disasters. Therefore, food accessibility, availability, affordability, and sustainability are important all over the world. Several disasters had occurred across the world due to food shortage and unavailability. Several countries in conflict or wartime are grossly susceptible to food insecurity, malnutrition, food-related diseases, and death due to starvation. The United Nation in several policies such as the millennium development goals and the sustainable development goals among others. These entire quests are to prevent food disasters in various countries in the world. Special food aid, new food vendors, and food supplements are given especially to the vulnerable groups in the society such as the children, women, and elderly people. Africa is the worst hit with food crises (Amusan, 2018). This is due to climate change, poor planning, and poor storage of food, bad governance, crude agricultural prowess, and incessant conflict among religious or ethnic groups. Horrific food insecurity repercussions had been witnessed such as the starving of children in the Horn of Africa countries such as Somalia, Ethiopia, some parts of Kenya, among others. Others are found in West Africa such as Mali, Benin, Niger, Cameroon, Senegal, Ghana, and Nigeria among others. It is novel to say that Africa is blessed with agrarian potentials but the realities confronting the continent cast shadows on the food security breakthrough of the continent.

It suffices to say that many families in Africa go to bed without food and wake up with the reality of no food (Wegenast and Beck, 2020; Walker,

NDao, and BeLue, 2020). This does not mean that there is no food within such a community but the accessibility to nutritious food is a mirage. Such food affordability is luxuries for many families to talk less about sustaining nutrition. The available foods are mainly carbohydrate concentrates which had health and mental adverse effects. To curtail these adverse effects, there are needs for proper food vendor service provisions across the communities to ensure food supply which will enhance the mental, psychological and physical health and wellbeing of the entire country.

Food vendors are both governmental and non-governmental agencies that are saddled with food and food supplement distribution among the people in the community. The governmental agencies include; agricultural and food chain agencies across countries and other international groups that ensure food and financial bailouts to countries in food crises such as the Food and Agriculture Organization (FAO), International Monetary Fund (IMF) and the World Bank among others. Other food vendors in the local settings are peasant agricultural product traders that sell at retail prices to the people directly. This could be in terms of raw foodstuff or the finished cooked food.

In many nooks and crannies of cities in Africa, there are retail food vendors that sell foodstuff to the citizens directly in piece meal quantity. These groups ensure food availability at an affordable rate and quantity. Other food vendor groups dispense cooked food in designated places (Feyaerts, Van den Broeck, and Maertens, 2020). They readily make food available to the citizen by ensuring the sustainability of food supply at a rate within the capacity of the people and affordable to them. These groups to a large extent had reduced the scourge of paucity of nutritious food in African communities. However, can we say that the food vendors had resolved the problems of food security in Africa? Have they been able to make affordable food for every member of the family? To a large extent, they have not been able to do this because of the food vandalism menace that prevails in many African societies. Food vandalism is a situation whereby agents of food shortage or scarcity prevail and that are responsible for food wastage resulting in food insecurity. They are phenomenon that are seldom beyond human control that result in food wastage, shortage, insecure, and dangerous. These include; food poising as a result of preservative chemicals or warfare, climate change and herdsmen, and farmers' conflict among others.

This study analyses the account of food insecurity in Africa despite the resources available in each country of the continent to combat the menace. Therefore, the guiding question is; over the past year, how often, if ever, have you or anyone in your family: Gone without enough food to eat? Afrobarometer panel data from 1999 till 2018 is utilised. In essence, to what extent have food insecurity ravage African countries? The method of accessing data was face to face interviews with a random selection sample of 2400 people in each country. The selected countries include; the Benin Republic, Cameroon, Niger, and Senegal. The choice of the selection is due to the typical cases of food security problems in those countries and under reportage in the academic literature.

The study uses the Social Conflict Theory (SCT) and Neo-Malthusianism Theory to analyse the reason why food vendors have not been able to resolve the crises of food crises in Africa and as well to advance the discussion on population growth and food production crises. Conclusions are drawn on the premise that food security can be attained whenever there are good governance and rational followers who can lay claim on the government for their rights.

Conceptual framework

Food insecurity is a situation that exists when people lack secure access to sufficient amounts of safe and nutritious food for normal growth and development and active and healthy life. It may be caused by the unavailability of food, insufficient purchasing power, inappropriate distribution, or inadequate use of food at the household level. Food insecurity, poor conditions of health and sanitation, and inappropriate care and feeding practices are the major causes of poor nutritional status. Food insecurity may be chronic, seasonal, or transitory. Food security, on the other hand, is a situation that exists when all people, at all times, have physical, social and economic access to sufficient, safe and nutritious food that meets their dietary needs and food preferences for active and healthy life (Amusan, 2018; Alemaw et al, 2020). Based on this definition, four food security dimensions can be identified: food availability, economic and physical access to food, food utilization, and stability over time.

The Social Conflict Theory (SCT) and Neo-Malthusianism Theory as used in this study revealed that food crises are limited to a class of people in society. These are the poor that uses poor farm implements, they have poor food harvest, economic power, and access to food supplements and health facilities. Instead of the state to adhere to the principles of good governance by ensuring more food vendors in the community the growing population results into a struggle for survival and security which leads to menace food vandalism. SCT provides the theoretical explanation for social class competition among state actors and non-state actors in their attempts to protect their selfish interests. This class struggle leads to the acquisition of weapons and ammunition for self-preservation thus leading to social conflicts and threats to national security and sustainable economic development. Marx and Engel (1848) asserted: The history of all hitherto existing society is the history of class struggles. Freeman and slave, patrician and plebeian, lord and serf, guild-master and journeyman, that is, the oppressor and the oppressed all stood in constant opposition to one another.

The continuous struggle over political authority and economic resources between the rich and the poor, producers and consumers, the ruling party and opposition parties, majority ethnic groups, and minority groups among others justifies the existence of a social conflict in human society. The primary motive for the social conflict is the survival and preservation of their lives from starvation. Food security is a major reason for social class conflicts. The rich want to acquire more food in surplus while the poor in the community rely on the mercies of the rich for land ownership, adequate food production, and general economic survival. SCT theory further asserts that social structures such as political institution, economic organs, legal institutions, and traditional authorities among others are created in every society through a conflict between groups with conflicting ideological interests and diverse means of control over state resources. Individuals and resources, in turn, are influenced by these structures and by the 'unequal distribution of power and resources in the society' (Knapp, 1994). This implies that threats to security especially survival and food are motivated by the struggle among rival social classes or groups in their quest for group economic interests, relevance, and political dominance. Therefore, in a society where there is an exploitation of one class or group by another one over food security and general economic wellbeing may results in armed struggle and full-scale warfare if these dysfunctional relations are not redressed.

In addressing this social conflict to ensure food security for all classes, the population, and food production ration is essential. Therefore, the Malthusian theory as postulated by Thomas Malthus is used to see the extent of the problem and how to overcome it. The Malthusian theory focuses on the relationship between population growth and food required for basic subsistence. He reasoned that the amount of food produced per capita in any continent; Europe Africa, Asia among others was declining in relation to the population. This is a trend he predicted to portend devastating consequences for human beings; he warned against pestilence, famine, contagious disease, congestion, infanticide, and war among others. In modern times, the theory was reconstructed as Neo-Malthusian theory to fit into a model of a threat to national security often caused by conflict among state actors and non-state actors over ownership and control of natural resources.

The general argument of the neo-Malthisians theory is that the available natural resources and food relative to human beings are limited (Gleditsch and Theisen, 2006). The expanding population growth, increasing consumption of scarce resources, and the harmful extraction of available scarce resources combine to deplete these resources quantitatively and qualitatively. The resulting scarcities of food historically often trigger cut-throat competition among diverse actors, which eventually leads to social conflict that threatens national security.

This implies that the rising population combined with scarce natural resources especially food threatens national security as a result of cut-throat competition and survival of the fittest race among interest groups in society. These diverse social groups employed available legal and illegal means to gain food security by control over scare natural resources. The phenomenon of a growing population without corresponding growth in food production leads to the menace of food vandalism.

Food vendor and food vandalism in Africa

Africa remains the region with the highest prevalence of undernourishment with about one in four people out of about 1 billion estimated to be undernourished. While sub-Saharan Africa has the highest prevalence of undernourishment, there has been some improvement over the last two decades the prevalence of under-nourishment declining from 32.7 percent to 24.8 percent. However, food insecurity remains a major challenge to good governance, growth, and development in the continent. The primary cause of food insecurity in Africa and developing countries, in general, is the inability of people to gain access to food due to widespread poverty and unemployment, which also inhibits purchasing power and prevents assured access to food supplies. Also, global food prices have risen dramatically in the last few years and are forecast to rise further or become more volatile (FAO, 2011). Food price volatility has exerted considerable pressure on global food security, and many Africans depend on the market for their food supply and vulnerable to high food prices. Related to high food prices is a high cost of farm input which limits yield and production levels that as well lead to sub-optimal input utilization. For instance, fertilizer consumption in Sub-Sahara Africa is one of the lowest in Africa (FAO, 2012).

Furthermore, the inherent characteristics of climate affect food security significantly in unpredictable ways such as the detrimental effect on pests, crop diseases, crop production, animal husbandry, and humans. Climate change conditions affect both the physical and economic availability of food items. Their impacts on income-earning opportunities can affect: the ability to buy food from food vendors, the availability of certain food products from either local or international food vendors. Food vandalism as a result of climate change changes the demand for seasonal agricultural labour, consequent upon changes in production practices; this will in turn affect income-generating capacity. A major good governance issue among farmers in Africa is the limited access to credit facilities. Certain credit facilities are assessable by some class of farmers than the other in Africa which further entrenched class struggle and food vandalism (Ogunniyi et al, 2020). Less than 10 percent of irrigable land is being irrigated which further enforces the neo-Malthusian theory of poor food vendor over the population growth. More so, the global economy is knowledge-driven and food system efficiency is dependent heavily and directly on agricultural technological innovations and innovations in relevant sectors. Africa's adult literacy level is less than seventy percent thereby causing a deficiency in the use of technology in solving food vandalism and insecurity.

In Africa, the rural poor who are the active stakeholders in food availability account for about forty percent and are mainly involved in subsistence farming. This crude farming system is under severe violent attacks (Abosede, 2020). These attacks include the Fulani-farmer's conflict over the right to grasses, crops, and farmland. The conflict had destroyed crops worth billions of dollars in a space of ten years in Africa. Several lives of the farmers and other innocent community members were wasted in the feud across Africa (Ado, Savadogo, and Abdoul-Azize, 2019; Schleifer and Sun, 2020). This food vandalism phenomenon, therefore, results in acute food insecurity in many African countries. Farmers are forced to abandon their crop farms to take refuge in internally displaced peoples' camps across Africa.

An international food vendor, the Food and Agricultural Organization (FAO) warned that many African countries will be faced with severe famine due to the reoccurring crises resulting in the destruction of crops and farmlands by terrorist groups. The resultant effects of terrorist groups such as the Islamic State group, Al-Shabab, Al-Qaeda, and Boko Haram will not only affect the food productions in the epicentre countries but there will be a domino effect on the entire continent. Therefore, there is a need for food vendors such as governmental and nongovernmental international agencies to supply food and food supplements to such areas.

Poor food storage and food transportation is a cogent food vandalism mode in Africa. Food produced in seasonal form is mostly available in accessible quantity and quality in the harvest season. More than twenty percent of the food produced is wasted due to poor storage technologies. The quality of the little quantity stored over a while deteriorates. Food vandalism is also propelled with a bad transportation scheme for the various forms of foodstuffs. A large chunk of perishable foods is wasted in the process of transportation from rural areas to the urban markets. Consequently, prices of foodstuffs skyrocket particularly in the urban part of the country limiting affordability and accessibility and sustainability of food.

Finally, in Africa, the apparent inconsistency in the government's specific intervention policies on Agriculture and implementation strategies further compounds the problem of food security. Agricultural policies had resulted into more haphazard food vendors and promote food vandalism because they are yet to adequately address the following areas; (i) Poor access to credit, technical inputs, machines and farm implements by farmers (ii) Poor infrastructures such as rural roads, water supply, irrigation facilities storage facilities and market infrastructure (iii) Poor budget allocation to agricultural sector (iv) Degradation of agricultural natural resources especially soil and water bodies. (v) Uncontrolled grazing, nomadic Pastoralism, and livestock migration, and (h) Poaching and settlement within protected areas and bush fires.

The following tables (I-III) and figures (I-VI) revealed the food (in) security prowess of four African states (Benin Republic, Cameroon, Niger, and Senegal). The leading question is; over the past year, how often, if ever, have you or anyone in your family: Gone without enough food to eat?

Country: Benin	**Total**	**R3 2005-2006**	**R4 2008-2009**	**R5 2011-2012**	**R6 2014-2015**	**R7 2017 -2018**
Never	45.3%	52.7%	32.5%	50.8%	45.0%	45.5%
Just once or twice	12.1%	11.9%	17.1%	11.8%	9.8%	10.0%
Several times	25.6%	17.6%	32.9%	24.2%	26.9%	26.3%
Many times	14.3%	15.2%	14.9%	10.0%	16.6%	14.7%
Always	2.7%	2.4%	2.5%	3.2%	1.6%	3.6%

Table I: *Benin Republic. Gone without enough food to eat over the years (2005-2018)*
Source: Afrobarometer Data 2020

Over the past years 2005-2018, data on hunger and food security in the Benin Republic revealed that above fifty percent (50%) of the people have gone without enough food to eat. The panel data revealed that the scourge of food insecurity is relatively stable with a record of people go without enough food to eat stood below sixty percent (60%). In 2005-2006 the record of people gone without enough food to eat was forty-seven percent (47%), in 2008-2009 the altitude rouse to a record high of sixty-seven percent (67%) of the people gone without enough food to eat. This change is attributed to climate change. In 2011-2012, the record of people gone without enough food to eat dropped to forty-nine percent (49%). This reduction is attributed to measures of both local and international food vendors that supply food materials and supplements to the communities. However, there is a slight rise to fifty five percent (55%) of people gone without enough food to eat in 2014-2015 as a result of government administrative bureaucracy in the administering of food and farm supplies (Olaye et al, 2019; Béné, Riba and Wilson, 2020). This level was maintained in the 2017-2018 record of people who have gone without enough food to eat. This shows a level of stability in curtailing the scourge of food vandalism and insecurity in the Benin Republic.

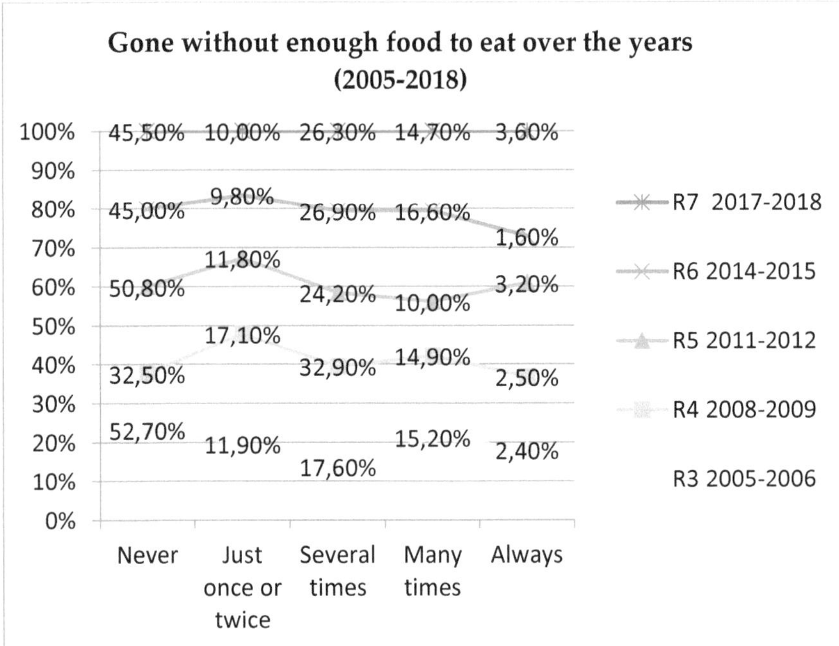

Figure I: *Benin Republic. Gone without enough food to eat over the years (2005-2018)*
Source: Afrobarometer Data 2020

The summary data on hunger and food security in the Benin Republic revealed that a total of forty five percent (45%) of the population have never gone without enough food to eat. However, a large percent of fifty five percent (55%) remarked that they have gone without food in several dimensions over the years. A total of twelve percent (12%) opined that they had gone without enough food to eat just once or twice, forty percent (40%) a combination of several times and many times category opined that they had gone without enough food to eat several or many times while eight percent (8%) said they always go without enough food to eat. The level of food insecurity in the Benin Republic is at high ebb and the services of food vendors are imminent.

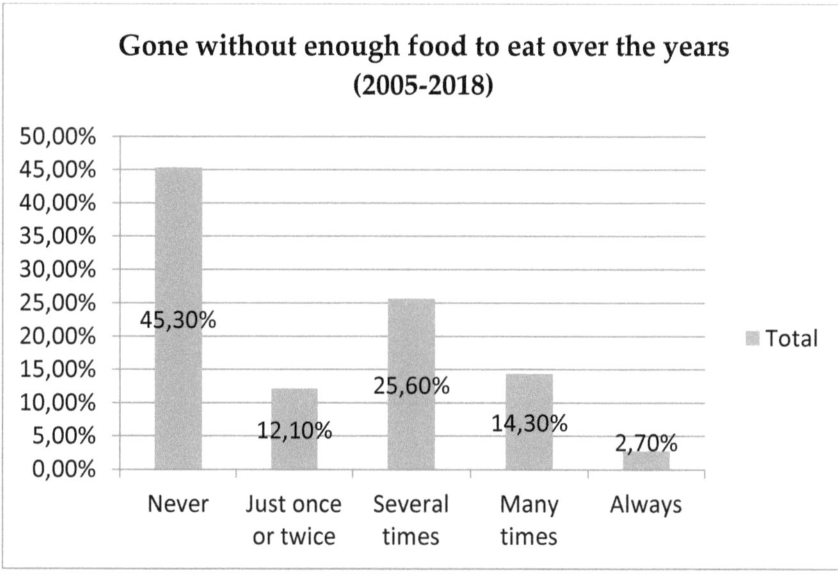

Figure II: *Benin Republic. Gone without enough food to eat over the years (2005-2018)*
Source: Afrobarometer Data 2020

Country: Cameroon	**Total**	**R5 2011-2012**	**R6 2014-2015**	**R7 2017-2018**
Never	42.8%	44.4%	45.6%	38.6%
Just once or twice	12.0%	9.3%	15.4%	11.4%
Several times	24.8%	24.3%	23.4%	26.8%
Many times	16.7%	18.3%	13.7%	18.2%
Always	3.2%	3.1%	1.5%	4.9%
Don't know	0.4%	0.6%	0.4%	0.3%

Table 11: *Cameroon: Gone without enough food to eat over the years (2011-2018)*
Source: Afrobarometer Data 2020

Over the past years 2011-2018, data on hunger and food security in Cameroon revealed that above fifty-five percent (55%) of the people have gone without enough food to eat. The panel data revealed that the scourge of food insecurity is getting worse by the year with a record of people go without enough food to eat stood above fifty-five percent (55%). In 2011-2012 the record of people who have gone without enough food to eat was fifty-six percent (56%), in 2014-2015 the altitude was about fifty-four percent (54%) of the people gone without enough food to eat. This change is attributed to local and international food vendors that supply food materials and supplements to the communities (Tambi, Atemnkeng, and Bime, 2017; Kc et al, 2018). In 2017-2018, the records of people who have gone without enough food to eat rouse shapely to about sixty one percent (61%). This high altitude is attributed to measures of climate change and severe communal feuds between the Fulani and the farmers. This shows a level of instability in curtailing the scourge of food vandalism and insecurity in Cameroon.

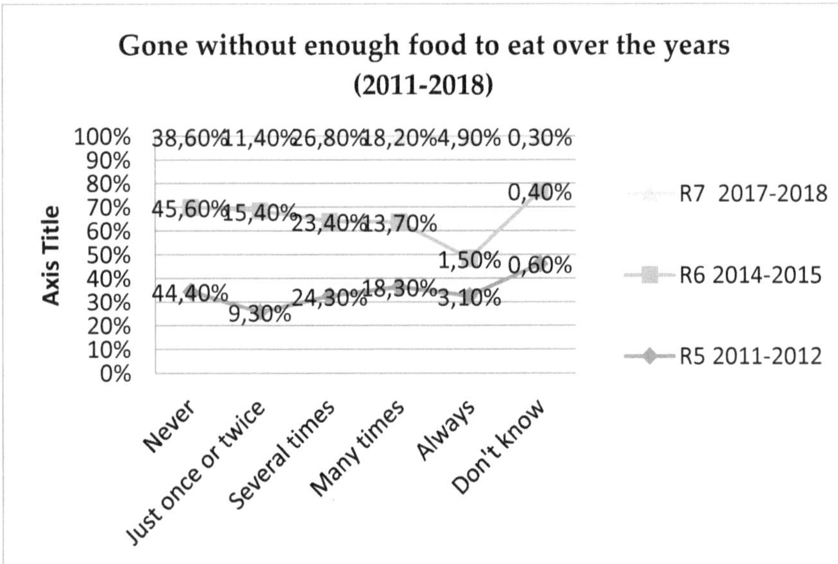

Figure III: *Cameroon: Gone without enough food to eat over the years (Total)*
Source: Afrobarometer Data 2020

The summary data on hunger and food security in Cameroon revealed that a total of forty-three percent (43%) of the population have never gone without enough food to eat. However, a large percent of fifty-seven percent (57%) remarked that they have gone without food in several dimensions over the years. A total of twelve percent (12%) opined that they had gone without enough food to eat just once or twice, forty-two percent (42%) a combination of several times and many times category opined that they had gone without enough food to eat several or many times while about three percent (3%) said they always go without enough food to eat. The level of food insecurity in Cameroon is at high ebb and the services of food vendors are imminent.

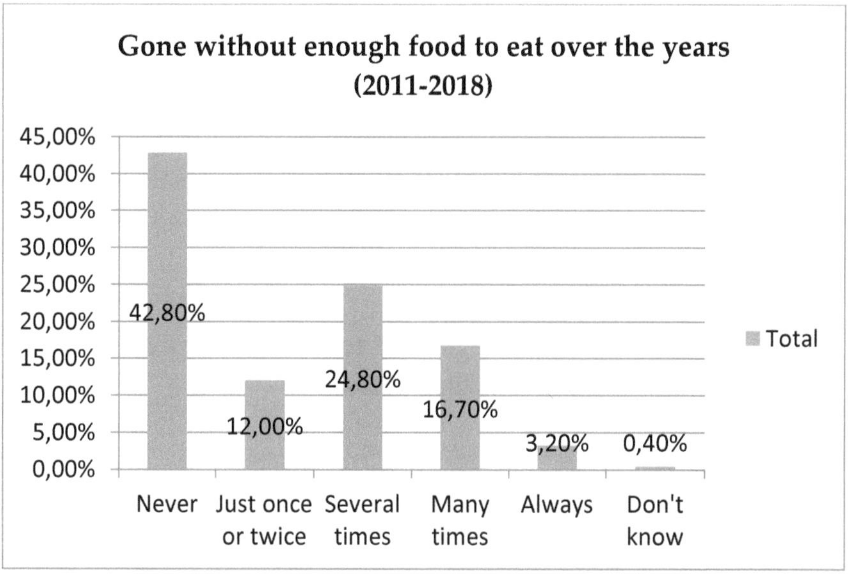

Figure IV: *Cameroon: Gone without enough food to eat over the years (2011-2018)*
Source: Afrobarometer Data 2020

Country – Niger	TOTAL	**R5 2011-2012**	**R6 2014-2015**	**R7 2017-2018**
Never	33.8%	32.9%	42.0%	26.6%
Just once or twice	7.0%	6.3%	6.7%	7.9%
Several times	25.9%	25.2%	26.6%	25.9%
Many times	25.8%	24.6%	18.7%	34.1%
Always	7.4%	10.9%	5.9%	5.5%

Table 111: *NIGER: Gone without enough food to eat over the years (2011-2018)*
Source: Afrobarometer Data 2020

Over the past years 2011-2018, data on hunger and food security in Niger republic revealed that there is acute hunger in the country. About sixty-six percent (66%) of the people have gone without enough food to eat. The panel data revealed that the scourge of food insecurity is getting worse by the year with a record of people gone without enough food to eat stood above sixty-six percent (66%). In 2011-2012 the record of people gone without enough food to eat was sixty-seven percent (67%), in 2014-2015 there was a slight improvement however, the record of the people gone without enough food to eat was about fifty-eight percent (58%). This change is attributed to local and international food vendors that supply food materials and supplements to the communities (Béné, Riba and Wilson, 2020). In 2017-2018, the record of people gone without enough food to eat became acute and was about sixty-three percent (63%). This high altitude is attributed to measures of climate change and severe communal feuds between the Fulani and the farmers. This reveals that there is a level of instability in curtailing the scourge of food vandalism and insecurity in the Niger.

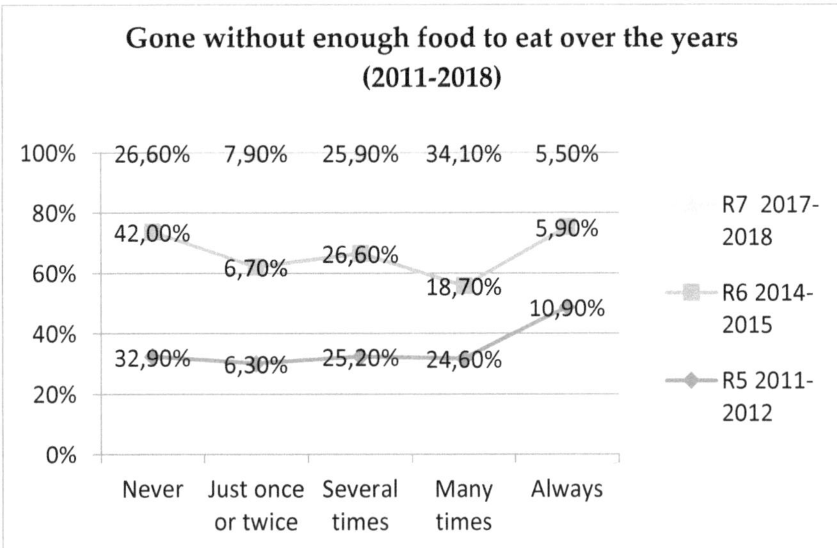

Figure V. *Niger: Gone without enough food to eat over the years (2011-2018)*
Source: Afrobarometer Data 2020

The summary data on hunger and food security in Niger revealed that a total of thirty-three percent (33%) of the population have never gone without enough food to eat. However, a large percent of sixty-seven percent (67%) remarked that they have gone without food in several dimensions over the years. A total of seven percent (7%) opined that they had gone without enough food to eat just once or twice, fifty-two percent (52%) a combination of several times and many times category opined that they had gone without enough food to eat several or many times while about eight percent (8%) said they always go without enough food to eat. The level of food insecurity in Niger is at high ebb and the services of food vendors are imminent.

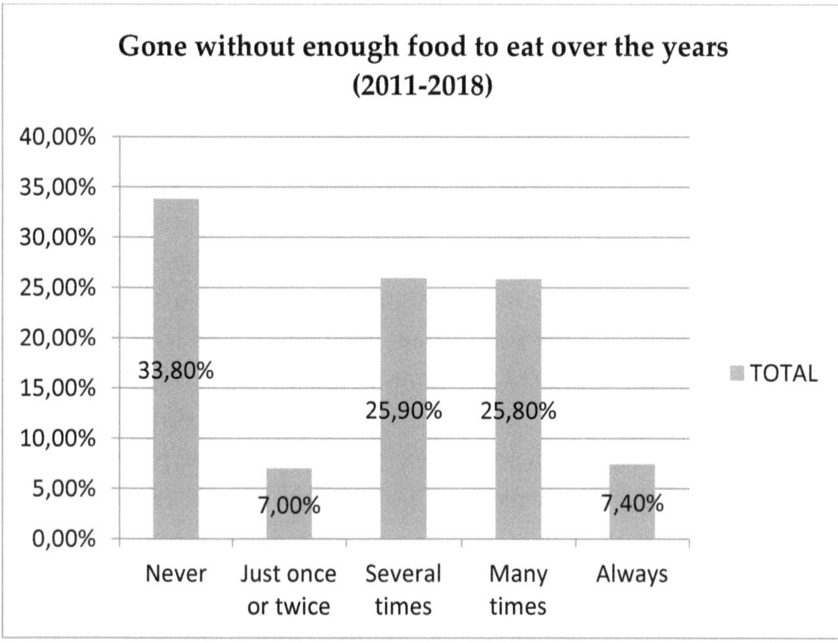

Figure VI. *Niger: Gone without enough food to eat over the years (Total)*
Source: Afrobarometer Data 2020

Country: Senegal	**Total**	**R2 2002 /2003**	**R3 2005/ 2006**	**R4 2008/ 2009**	**R5 2011/ 2012**	**R6 2014/ 2015**	**R7 2017/ 2018**
Never	53.0%	58.1%	55.9%	42.2%	46.5%	56.6%	58.7%
Just once or twice	6.5%	8.2%	4.3%	6.5%	5.0%	5.6%	9.2%
Several times	20.4%	20.6%	17.1%	20.1%	24.8%	19.5%	20.4%
Many times	15.4%	11.8%	13.3%	21.4%	20.7%	15.5%	9.4%
Always	4.6%	1.0%	8.8%	9.5%	3.1%	2.7%	2.1%

Table IV: Senegal Gone without enough food to eat over the years (2011-2018)
Source: Afrobarometer Data 2020

Over the past years 2002-2018, data on hunger and food security in Senegal revealed that there is relative food security in the country. About forty-seven percent (47%) of the people have gone without enough food to eat. The panel data revealed that the scourge of food insecurity is getting ameliorated by the year with a record of people gone without enough food to eat stood below forty-five percent (45%). In 2002-2003 the record of people gone without enough food to eat was forty-two percent (42%), in 2005-2006 there was a slight increase, however, the record of the people gone without enough food to eat was about forty-four percent (44%). In 2008-2009 there was a further increase in food insecurity; however, the record of the people gone without enough food to eat was a record high of about fifty-eight percent (58%). This high altitude is attributed to measures of climate change and severe communal feuds between the Fulani and the farmers. In 2011-2012 there was a slight improvement in food security; however, the record of the people gone without enough food to eat was about fifty-three percent (53%). Also, in 2014-2015 there was a consistent significant improvement in food security; however, the record of the people gone without enough food to eat was about forty three percent (43%). Moreover, in 2017-2018, the record of people gone without enough food to eat became significantly reduced and was about forty-one percent (41%). This change is attributed to local and international food vendors that supply food materials and supplements to the communities (Akpaki et al, 2020; Savy et al, 2020). This reveals that the level of instability in curtailing the scourge of food vandalism and insecurity in Senegal is reducing and food security is achievable with more consistent effort in improving food vendor and general economic development.

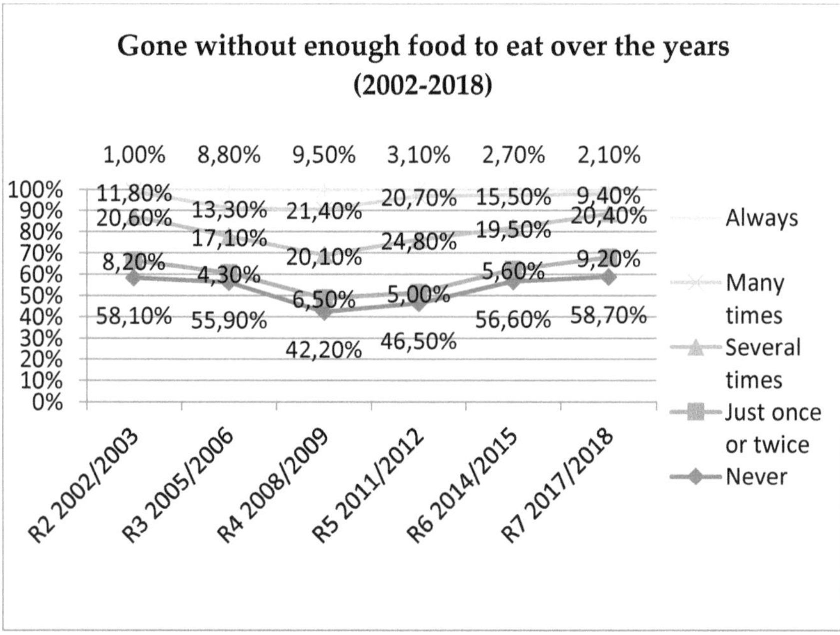

Figure V: *Senegal Gone without enough food to eat over the years (2002-2018)*
Source: Afrobarometer Data 2020

The summary data on hunger and food security in Senegal revealed that a total of fifty-three percent (53%) of the population have never gone without enough food to eat. Therefore, a minimal percent of forty-seven percent (47%) remarked that they have gone without food in several dimensions over the years. A total of seven percent (7%) opined that they had gone without enough food to eat just once or twice, thirty-six percent (36%) a combination of several times and many times category opined that they had gone without enough food to eat several or many times while about five percent (5%) said they always go without enough food to eat. Therefore, the level of food insecurity in Senegal is at a minimal level and the services of food vendors are imminent.

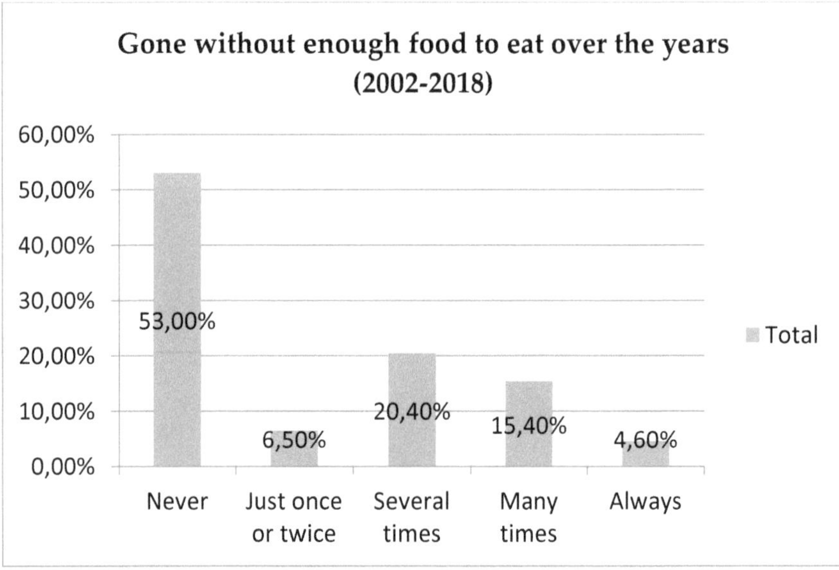

Figure VI: *Senegal Gone without enough food to eat over the years (Total)*
Source: Afrobarometer Data 2020

Conclusion

Food security is a major part of national security and development. Several countries in the sub- Sahara Africa are suffering from malnutrition, hunger, among others. The survey of four countries in Africa; Niger, Cameron, Benin, and Senegal revealed that Africa is far from achieving food security. This problem is further compounded by climate change which reduces the availability of water to the farmland and increases the scourge of drought. Also, food becomes insecure due to actions attributed to food vandalism. These include; the feud between farming communities and pastoralists and other land-related communal conflicts. The work of food vendors at the local level, national level, and the international level cannot be overemphasized. The local food vendors in Africa have sustained to a good extent food available to the locale according to their economic capabilities. The national and international food vendors had contributed to the sustenance of the farming communities by acquiring farm inputs, food supplements, and basic training that can boost food production, preservation, and distribution in Africa.

However, the number of people who go without enough food to eat over the years in Africa has been on the increase. This had prompted effects on the political-economic and social lives in Africa. Food insecurity had become a tool in Africa that had deepened the level of class consciousness between the rich and the poor. Subsequently, due to the huge level of poverty in the societies, political leaders in Africa are using food distributions as a tool to control the masses during political events such as election campaigning. This dimension of food vendor had made food security to become a perpetual challenge in Africa. Therefore, for this menace to be corrected and resolved in Africa; there must be economic empowerment of the masses in Africa through the creation of jobs and improvement of basic infrastructure in the society. The economic gap created by political office holders through embezzlement and all forms of corruption in the society must be curtailed. There must be an equitable distribution of wealth in Africa and an appropriate tax system. This will make accessibility to food easy, availability of food a reality, affordability of food effortless, and sustainability of food certain.

The reoccurring problems of food vandalism through communal crises, Fulani- farmers feud, and other acts of vandalism that affect farming and farm products must be resolved in such a way that that the reoccurrence must be prevented. The international community should as well monitor the distribution of their food vendor assistance to affected communities in Africa. This will prevent diversion of food to private firms who in return will hoard the commodity and sell at an exorbitant price instead of free distribution to the affected community. This act will eventually lead to the persistency of food insecurity and other related vices such as malnutrition, starvation, hunger, and death.

References

Abosede, S. (2020). Water, Food Security, and Trade in Sub-Saharan Africa. In *Handbook of Research on Globalized Agricultural Trade and New Challenges for Food Security* (pp. 384-399). IGI Global.

Ado, A. M., Savadogo, P., & Abdoul-Azize, H. T. (2019). Livelihood strategies and household resilience to food insecurity: insight from a farming community in Aguie district of Niger. *Agriculture and Human Values*, 36(4), 747-761.

Afrobarometer (2020) *Over the past year, how often, if ever, have you or anyone in your family: Gone without enough food to eat? Benin Republic, Cameroon, Niger and Senegal* Afrobarometer online data analysis www.afrobarometer.org/online-analysis accessed on 26/3/2020

Akpaki, K., Galibois, I., Sall, M., & Blaney, S. (2020). Assessing the Food Availability and Food Insecurity Situation among Communities of Matam Region, Senegal. *Ecology of Food and Nutrition*, 1-20.

Alemaw, B. F., Podisi, B. K., Mwale, S., & Simalenga, T. E. (2020). Climate Change Adaptation Research and Policy for Agriculture in Southern Africa (CCARPASA)—Evidence from Rainfed Systems. In *Climate Variability and Change in Africa* (pp. 183-189). Springer, Cham.

Amusan, L. (2018). Globalisation of land and food security challenges in Africa. *African Renaissance*, 15(Special Issue 1), 83-99.

Béné, C., Riba, A., & Wilson, D. (2020). Impacts of resilience interventions–Evidence from a quasi-experimental assessment in Niger. *International Journal of Disaster Risk Reduction*, 43, 101390.

Feyaerts, H., Van den Broeck, G., & Maertens, M. (2020). Global and local food value chains in Africa: A review. *Agricultural Economics*, 51(1), 143-157.

Food and Agricultural Organization (2011), *Nigeria Food Security Report 2011*, Rome: FAO.

Food and Agricultural Organization (2012), *Food Security Statistics- Nigeria; FAOSTAT*, Rome: FAO.

Kc, K. B., Legwegoh, A. F., Therien, A., Fraser, E. D., & Antwi-Agyei, P. (2018). Food price, food security and dietary diversity: A comparative study of urban Cameroon and Ghana. *Journal of International Development*, 30(1), 42-60.

Knapp, P. (1994). One World –Many Worlds: Contemporary *Sociological Theory* (2nd Ed.). HarperCollins College Div, pp. 228–246.

Marx, K. and Engels, F. (1848) *The Communist Manifesto*, introduction by Martin Malia (New York: Penguin group, 1998).

Ogunniyi, A. I., Mavrotas, G., Olagunju, K. O., Fadare, O., & Adedoyin, R. (2020). Governance quality, remittances and their implications for food and nutrition security in Sub-Saharan Africa. *World Development*, 127, 104752.

Olaye, A. R. B., Adedeji, P. A., Zokpodo, K. L., & Moreira, J. (2019). Towards sustainable rice processing: a case of Republic of Benin. *International Journal of Innovation and Sustainable Development*, 13(3-4), 333-347.

Savy, M., Fortin, S., Kameli, Y., Renault, S., Couderc, C., Gamli, A., ... & Martin-Prevel, Y. (2020). Impact of a food voucher program in alleviating household food insecurity in two cities in Senegal during a food price crisis. *Food Security*, 1-14.

Schleifer, P., & Sun, Y. (2020). Reviewing the impact of sustainability certification on food security in developing countries. *Global Food Security*, 24, 100337.

Tambi, M. D., Atemnkeng, J. T., & Bime, M. J. (2017). Women in agricultural production and food security in rural Cameroon. *International Journal of Agricultural Policy and Research*, 5(3), 70-79.

Walker, R. E., NDao, F., & BeLue, R. (2020). Exploring the Concept of Food Insecurity and Family Hunger in Senegal, West Africa. *International quarterly of community health education*, 40(2), 99-104.

Wegenast, T., & Beck, J. (2020). Mining, rural livelihoods and food security: A disaggregated analysis of sub-Saharan Africa. *World Development*, 130, 104921.

Chapter 9
From Economic Community to Economic Union: A Post-Coronavirus Approach to Food Security in the ECOWAS Region

Lere Amusan and Olusola Oloba

Introduction

An enabling and secure environment for food safety has a great potential for food security and economic development. The contributions of food security to economic development cannot be overemphasized. Essentially, quality food is a quality life. Economic models have often been adopted over the years to examine and evaluate food security and development. However, the experience towards food security especially among African countries has not been better off before the coronavirus (Covid-19) pandemic; in fact, the Covid-19 pandemic has exposed the food security vulnerability for most African countries. Ensuring food security for long-term time horizons has been an issue to most policymakers, researchers, and government in the 21st century. Food security exists when all people, at all times, have physical and economic access to sufficient, safe and nutritious food to meet their dietary needs and food preferences for active and healthy life (World Food Summit, 1996). Understanding and the ease of peculiar factors; such as trade restriction, access to market, and landlocked for the sustainability of food security and their interactions is needed to guide policymakers and government deciding on today's policies for future advantage and better life (Amusan & Agunyai, 2021).

Magalhaes (2014) had identified political instability and inconsistent structural policies as the major forces increasing the prevalence of food insecurity. This provides need for government intervention to formulate appropriate policies that will alienate the complex and dynamic nature of food insecurity facing most African countries having known that food security is an integral part of the Sustainable Development Goals (SDGs).

Despite the resource endowment of Africa, most of the countries in the region are characterized by low development indicators. There are about 1.5 billion people that are poor among developing countries (people living below $1.25 per day). However, 75% of these people are from Sub-Saharan Africa (SSA) (Food and Agricultural Organisation, FAO 2016; Osabohien, Osabuohien and Urhie 2018).

Also, the World Health Organization's (WHO) Estimates of the Global Burden of Foodborne Diseases has alerted African decision-makers and regulators to the importance of food safety and the urgency for prioritizing action to diminish the burden of disease. The report estimated that, in Africa, such food safety hazards were responsible for approximately 137,000 deaths and about 91 million cases of acute foodborne illnesses on an annual basis, the highest estimates worldwide. Diarrheal disease agents were responsible for nearly 70 percent of foodborne diseases in lower-income sub-regions of the continent. Among the continents worldwide, this represented the greatest global disease burden, with 2500 disability-adjusted life years (DALYs) per 100,000 population individuals in Africa. The report concluded that "the large disease burden from food highlights the importance of food safety, particularly in Africa" (WHO, 2015). The global pandemics of 2019 through 2020 have called policymakers and government to address policy thrust that will sustain food security among countries in the region. At the regional level, C19 exposed ECOWAS states' food security vulnerability as many states and individuals were struggling to have access to basic food quality.

The need to encourage agro-ecological food production at the regional level that will regenerate farming that is more sustainable for food security becomes essential in the era of unreliable, inconsistent, and inaccurate climatic and polluted environmental conditions. Extant literature has established that increased vulnerability of farmers contributed to low production (Osabohien, Matthew, Gershon, Ogunbiyi & Nwosu 2019; Ejemeyovwi, Osabuohien & Osabohien 2018; Osuma, Ikpefan, Osabohien, Ndigwe & Nkwodimmah 2018). Besides, weak soil fertilizer has been the major factor responsible for the low production of agricultural output. The average fertilizer use in SSA is still very low at 9 kg/hectare, compared to 125 kg/hectare in other parts of the world (Amit, 2006). These are indicators that enhance the prevalence of food insecurity within the region of Africa. Also, access to the market for agricultural produce becomes an issue among countries in the region. Political instability, porous border, lack of infrastructural facilities, and unfavourable policies towards agriculture output has been the attributes of countries in ECOWAS hence, having food insecurity become inevitable.

The problem of food insecurity is likely to be exacerbated in densely populated, poor infrastructural development, poor market access, and poverty-stricken areas of Africa where the arable land frontier has been exhausted, and where farm sizes are small and declining due to increased population pressures. An environment characterized by such a setting relies on land markets to gain access to food security (Teklu and Lemi, 2004; Benin and Pender, 2008; Ghebru and Holden, 2008; Deininger and Mpuga, 2009; Jin and Jayne, 2013). However, many of countries in Africa have inherited highly arbitrary and spurious borders that vastly inhibit the efforts to have access to the market, improve food security, and reduce hunger. Prevalence of hunger and undernourishment are chronic issues for many of the people of the West Africa region. Although there is little disagreement on the magnitude and importance of food insecurity in this region, its causes and control are subject to considerable debate and research. Little progress has been achieved in reducing the prevalence of undernourishment and the number of underweight children in West Africa, particularly since 2005 (FAO, IFAD, & WFP, 2015).

The creation and diversion of sustainable agriculture is the key to improved food security and agricultural productivity. While import dependency has made the ECOWAS region vulnerable to food security and supply shocks that originate from external factors, external relationships and access to the market have helped reduce food insecurity for the region (Wailes & Chavez, 2015). For country-specific studies, literature provided that during the 2007-2008 global food crisis, international rice export prices spiked by nearly 300% and several key rice exporters imposed export bans. As a result, ECOWAS, national leaders, international research and donor agencies, and non-governmental organizations have addressed food security concerns by increasing rice productivity, liberalizing trade, and developing regional food reserves. Wailes, Durand-Morat and Diagne

(2016) assessed the regional and national approaches to improving food security for the rice consumption in West Africa; they found that West Africa accounts for nearly 25% of global rice imports. The elimination of rice imports reduces global rice prices. Results suggest the need for achieving self-sufficiency in West Africa becomes paramount since they contribute a significant proportion at the global level. However, if self-sufficiency makes domestic rice uncompetitive with imported rice, then West African consumers will demand a significant price discount for domestic rice, thus reducing benefits to producers and consumers.

However, regardless of attempts made to achieve food security in Africa, without eliminating the gap in the nearness to the market among countries, food insecurity will become inevitable. Proximity to the market is an integral part of self-sufficiency and food security. The closer the access to the market, the more likely its transaction costs can be reduced especially through the forces of demand and supply. A wide study has established the contributions of access to the market. Access to market harnessed income to farmers, Hiroyuki, and Nagarajan (2012). The shortage of food is due to lack of access to the market, Darshini (2012). Improving market access for farmers can have a profound impact on their food security (Jordan and Jayne, 2013). The question that still lingers is on how to create an accessible market for West African farmers to increase productivity and improved food security. The issue is critically important since an efficient market system can play an important role in supplying yield- enhancing modern inputs at reasonable prices and in assuring remunerative prices for farmer's production which are potential for food security. Africans' livelihoods depend heavily on agriculture, with approximately 70% of the population living in rural areas and working in agriculture-related sectors. Agriculture, which comprises approximately 25% of Africa's GDP, accounts for the majority of Africa's exports (FAOSTAT, 2015). While consumption of main staple crops is on the rise within the ECOWAS region, but the production has been unable to keep pace with consumption especially among major crop production. Population growth and income growth combined push crop consumption growth ahead of productivity growth. This is an indication that an improvement in the productivity of agricultural output will bring about sustainable food security and economic development.

Overview of ECOWAS region

The ECOWAS region had a combined estimated population of over 349 million with economies consisting of a combined GDP of around USD 716.7 billion with an average per capita GDP of USD 2130.4 across 15 independent countries. The total trade of the region on average stood at USD 208.1 billion where exports were projected at approximately USD137.3 billion while imports total about USD 80.4 billion. Among the countries within the region of ECOWAS, Nigeria trade has the highest score accounted for about 76 percent of total trade (Ghana, 9.2%; Côte d'Ivoire, 8.64%). ECOWAS countries intra-trade statistics lag compared to other countries of the world and economic region.

The region's developmental issues are complex and intricate. There are significantly large differences between urban and rural areas. ECOWAS is grappling with perennial poverty challenges. On average, the poverty rate is approximately 75% in Sub-Saharan Africa, (Brookings, 2019; World Bank Report, 2016; Food and Agricultural Organisation, FAO 2016; Osabohien, Osabuohien and Urhie 2018). Also, ECOWAS countries dominate the world's poorest economies. Nigeria has since overtaken India to become the poverty capital of the world. The region is grappling to sustain its food production due to drought challenges which are increasing in both frequency and severity, with some analysts largely attributing this to climate change, (AFDB, 2014), failure of market access Darshini (2012) and also the Chinese coronavirus. While there are some regions that are obtaining surpluses in agricultural food production, ECOWAS has poor distribution channels largely due to poor transport infrastructure, porous border, and trade restriction, inefficient institutions that promote redistribution and trade facilitation, as well as information asymmetry. Taking into account the fact that the geopolitical space of Africa is larger than its European and Asian counterparts, poor infrastructure, high tariff, and non-tariff barriers and weak trade facilitation procedures only add to the low production and high transaction costs of an already poor continent.

Overview of precursor papers

Beginning in 1990, West Africa has made good progress in alleviating caloric undernourishment in Sub-Saharan Africa, with the total prevalence of under-nourishment (PoU) in West Africa projected to decrease from 24.2% to 9.6% by 2016 (FAO, IFAD, & WFP, 2015). Though, the improvements have not been uniform across the region. In Burkina Faso, Guinea-Bissau, Liberia, Senegal, and Sierra Leone, PoU level is projected to remain above 20% in 2016. Table 1.0 shows a 37% increase in total per capita calories for West African countries between 1981 and 2011. The availability of food staples - grains, roots, and tubers accounted for 80% of the growth, with rice possessing the largest share of any food.

Growth in rice consumption in West Africa since 2000 has been possible due to domestic supply, which has increased by 88%. Table 2.0 shows a 42% increase in area harvested and an average annual increase of 3.5% in crop yields per hectare. Despite the increase in production, rice imports have more than doubled, thus making the region vulnerable to the volatile world rice market (Wailes, 2005). The range of the import dependency ratio varies widely within the region, from 1% for Mali up to a high of 79% for Benin. The volatile rice market has led to a strong interest in more investment in domestic rice production, the development of a regional emergency food reserve, and the harmonization of trade policies. While ensuring adequate supplies of basic staples such as rice will not fulfil all the nutritional requirements in West Africa, however, it is a necessary step toward reducing the undernourishment of the population (Lopriore & Muehlhoff, 2003). This is not without access to market and trade unrestricted among member countries as the impact of the self-sufficiency approach envisioned to help West Africa achieve greater food security.

As the world population increases, demand for food, fibre and other agriculture-based products have risen and there is pressure on agriculture to meet the increasing demand. Yet less than half of the world's land is suitable for agricultural production (IDS, 2009, F.A.O, 2003). Some of the main challenges to increasing production include soil degradation, land fragmentation and climate change. Increasing agriculture productivity is therefore important and necessary because of its contribution to food security and poverty reduction among the ECOWAS region. There is increased awareness of the need for sustainable intensification throughout Africa. This has been enhanced by the realization of the need to preserve the natural environment to continue to benefit from the various ecological services it offers.

The years, focus has been on expanding area of cropped land to meet the increasing food demand though not without limitation. In considerations of these limitations to expanding cultivated land, other strategies to increase production became necessary. One of the approaches that literature has addresses was agriculture intensification. Agriculture intensification relies on increasing production per unit of input used (land, labour, seed) (FAO, 2004). Intensification occurs when there is increased productivity or improved efficiency of inputs (FAO, 2004). While agriculture intensification is important to improve farming livelihoods (Warren, 2002), it has different and varying impacts on land, biodiversity, and other natural resources on which agriculture production is dependent. Agricultural development agendas are increasingly shaped due to various surges in food insecurity and low socioeconomic outcomes of most countries in Africa.

The regional and national approaches to improving food security have been assessed in West Africa using the Arkansas Global Rice Model and the RICEFLOW frameworks; the danger towards the pursuit of self-sufficiency was examined. The Coalition for African Rice Development and the Africa Rice Centre has assisted 23 nations in developing national strategies. The study evaluates the strategies of 15 nations for rice land expansion and intensification to increase yields for regional self-sufficiency. Findings show that West Africa accounts for nearly 25% of global rice imports. The elimination of rice imports reduces global rice prices. Results show that achieving self-sufficiency in West Africa is inefficient at the global level. However, if self-sufficiency makes domestic rice uncompetitive with imported rice, then West African consumers will demand a significant price discount for domestic rice, thus reducing benefits to producers and consumers. Although beyond the scope of the finding, a coordinated policy sequencing approach toward enhancing productivity and quality of rice production as well as increasing investment in infrastructure, institutions, and emergency food reserves should be studied more thoroughly to achieve food and nutritional security for West Africa.

Studies have also argued for the role of innovative technologies and international organization on sustainable agriculture and food security (Miller and Tolley, 1989; Durosomo, 1993; Alene and Coulibaly, 2009; Adenle, Sowe, Parayil and Aginam, 2012; Tigabu and Gebeyehu, 2018; Alarcon and Bodouroglou, 2019). Agricultural development agendas in Sub-Saharan Africa are increasingly shaped by a focus on advanced technologies, including Green Revolution hybrid- and genetically modified (GM) crops, but the evidence that these technologies work for smallholder farmers is limited. Agro-ecological approaches, including organic agriculture, largely remain an addendum to agricultural policy agendas. Prioritizing smallholders' needs in agricultural development strategies is crucial in a region in which smallholders make up an estimated 80% of all farms and produce most of the region's food.

The estimation of the agro-ecological food production system in an economic union, on the basis of the Jacob Viner model cannot be overemphasized especially to achieve sustainable food security among the countries at a regional level of Africa. It was an approach of increased production and self-sufficiency market as a means to address food insecurity in West Africa. Economic integration of West African countries is a fundamental goal of ECOWAS. Implementation of the Common External Tariff (CEF) is one of the primary instruments for harmonizing ECOWAS member states to improve food security for the region and free interplay of forces of demand and supply of agro-ecological food production.

The view towards trade creation and diversion was first examined by the Viner (1950) where he argued that free trade agreements are not always welfare enhancing. Using a mathematical model in a partial equilibrium framework, Jacob Viner was able to establish that FTAs lead to trade creation and diversion effects. The former refers to a scenario in which trade shifts from inefficient producers to efficient suppliers who are part of the new trade agreement, while the latter refers to a situation in which member countries shift their trade from efficient non-member countries to inefficient member countries, who simply because they are now part of the new agreement, their products would have become cheaper because tariffs are no longer being applied to their products. Thus, trade creation is viewed as welfare-enhancing whilst trade diversion is welfare reducing.

According to Viner (1950), the process of trade creation and diversion occurs simultaneously, since several member countries will be trading concurrently with different member and non-member countries. Thus, there is a need to empirically establish the net welfare effects to conclude whether or not a particular trade agreement is beneficial. This was because, in his short run theoretical model, results were inconclusive since it would be difficult to determine before the agreement whether trade creation would outweigh trade diversion. In addition, FTA between developed and developing countries leverage on the loopholes in the agreement to engage in unfair trade practices.

An agro ecological food production system would sustain food security especially among West African countries that are characterized by arable farming land though this will be better achieved by the influence of common external tariff since the regional market integration is one of the elements for food security policy thrust. Over the years, the policy frames and thrust to achieve food security in ECOWAS countries have been implemented. Countries in West Africa have long recognized the potential benefits of trade integration. The Economic Community of West African States (ECOWAS) accord1, signed in 1975 and revised in 1993, is one approach towards achieving regional integration and economic development. ECOWAS is designed to evolve into a customs union in which countries harmonize policies, allow for the free movement of factors of production, and adopt a common external tariff (CET) relative to the rest of the world. The implementation of the CET was initially set to start in 2004 but suffered several delays and to date, it is not fully implemented yet. The CET is organized into five different tariff bands of 0, 5, 10, 20, and 35 percent to accommodate the large variations in protection granted across products traded in the region.

Year	1981	1991	2001	2011
Rice	264	304	324	391
Wheat	105	73	120	160
Maize	102	232	177	251
Millet	212	260	251	198
Sorghum	206	240	238	220
Other Cereals	12	8	8	7
Cassava	181	269	274	262
Other root and tubers	112	174	235	281
Sugar	90	71	97	97
Pulses	47	62	80	89
Oil crops	68	43	80	90
Vegetables oils	231	261	282	262
Fruits and Vegetables	115	118	131	134
Meat	49	45	48	54
Other	172	142	162	192
TOTAL	1966	2302	2507	2688

Table 1.0: *Growth in per capita consumption of West African countries*
Source: FAOSTAT (2015).

Variable	Units/Year	2000	2013	Percentage Change
Area Harvested	1,000 ha	4,457	6,326	42%
Yield	mt/ha	0.99	1.31	33%
Production	1,000 mt	4,408	8,293	88%
Per Capita Use	kg	34	50	47%
Total Consumption	1,000 mt	7,901	16,370	107%
Imports	1,000 mt	3,802	8,050	112%
Net Imports	1,000 mt	3,802	7,910	108%
Ending Stocks	1,000 mt	1,078	1,604	49%

Table 2.0: *ECOWAS rice production, consumption, and trade*
Source: United States Department of Agriculture, Foreign Agricultural Service [USDA/FAS] (2015).

Stylized facts

Since the 21st century, a typical country in the West Africa region on average engaged in food trade about 37.6% of merchandise export. This suggests that on average, a country in the ECOWAS region was operating at about 62.4% below the maximum potential trade level. Though, this result is preferable to compare with the import capacity; about 23.7% of merchandise import is being traded with ECOWAS countries. Put differently, there was a possibility that on average ECOWAS countries could increase its trade with other regions of the world by 62.4% without having to incur extra cost in making the merchandise commodities available. As indicated among 11 West African countries, the best-performing country in the merchandize trade was exporting at 97.8% of merchandize export while the least performing country exported 0.02% of merchandize export. This is a good indication for the need to examine the cause of variation among ECOWAS countries and the contributions of a trade agreement within the region.

From Figure 1.0 and 2.0, an investigation on the trend of food trade level among countries in the West Africa over 19years reveals that there is a step-like rise in the merchandise food trade over the years in the 11 countries. In essence, merchandise food export has been increasing relatively between 2000 and 2006 until 2007 and 2008. This sudden decline in food export between 2007 and 2008 could be attributable to the global food crisis. This suggests strong bonds among international communities for trade since the activities of other countries of the world have a significant impact on each other. This is an indication that the world is a global village where shocks across regions could determine, direct, and dictate the tune of an economy. Following the food price crisis of 2007 and 2008, the ECOWAS nations developed regional and national rice development strategies (NRDS) to increase domestic production (Africa Rice Center [Africa Rice], 2011). Strategies such as investment in institutions and infrastructure are expected to facilitate the expansion of rice production areas, particularly irrigated lowlands. Other strategies include the development of production technologies (e.g., certified seed systems) and cultural practices that improve low crop yields. In 2017, export trade rose to about 50% of merchandise export with a 75% growth rate between 2000 and 2017.

In West Africa, access to market and less restrictive trade among ECOWAS union will improve and enhance human development as can be seen especially in Cape-Verde where its food export and human development are both increasing simultaneously compared to other selected countries in West Africa. This country has the highest food export among the selected countries in the western region despite the low contribution of her natural resources endowment. The response of Cape-Verde food importation suggests the need for the exchange of food among member states. In essence, access to market, infrastructural development and the less restrictive border where trade balance of agricultural produce will be achieved are pointers which ECOWAS policymakers should look at to have sustainable food security.

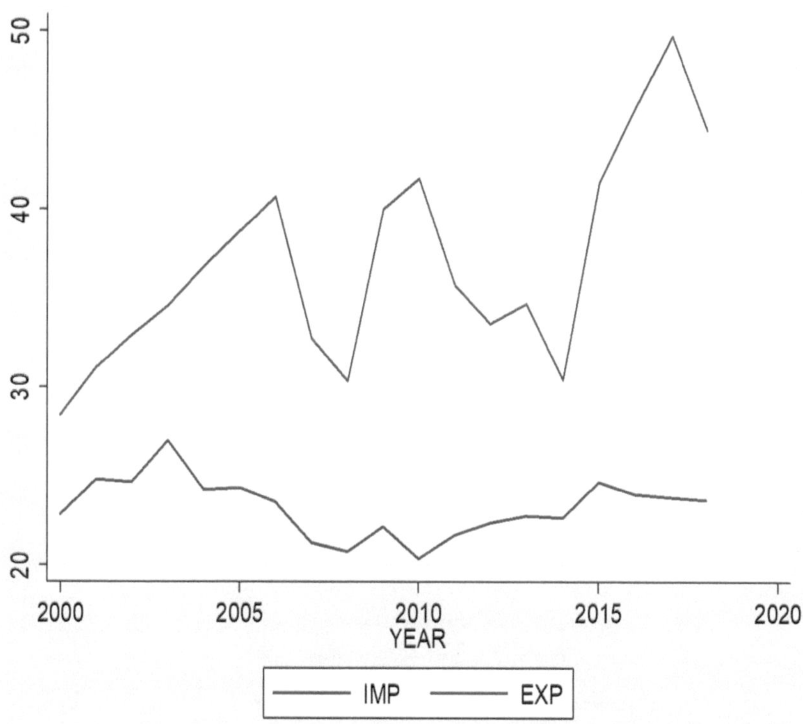

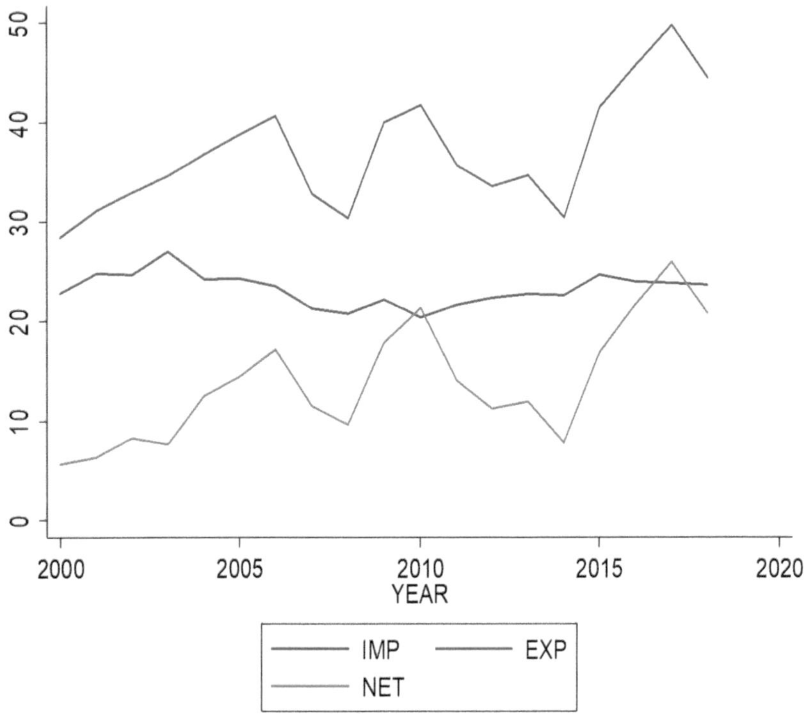

50
40
30
20
10
0
2000
2005
2010
2015
2020
YEAR
IMP
EXP
NET

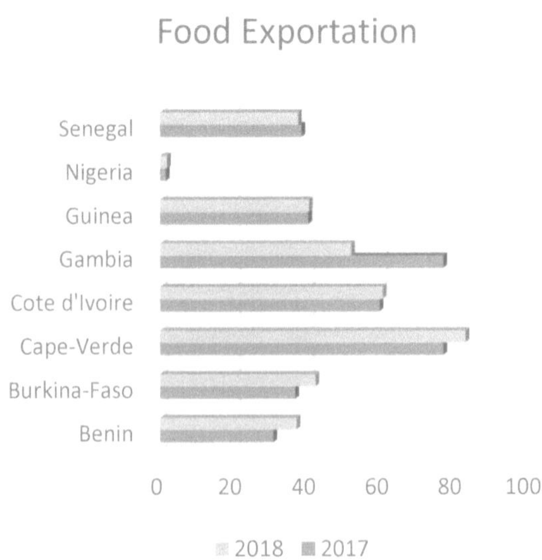

Food Exportation
Senegal
Nigeria
Guinea
Gambia
Cote d'Ivoire
Cape-Verde
Burkina-Faso
Benin
0
20
40
60
80
100
2018
2017

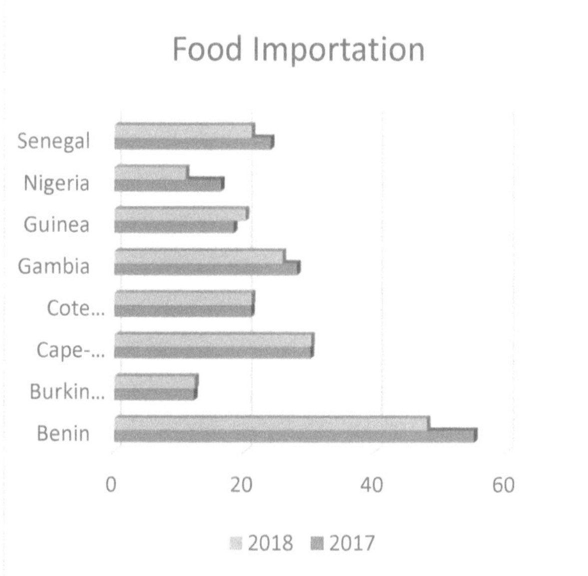
Food Importation
Senegal
Nigeria
Guinea
Gambia
Cote...
Cape-...
Burkin...
Benin
0
20
40
60
2018
2017

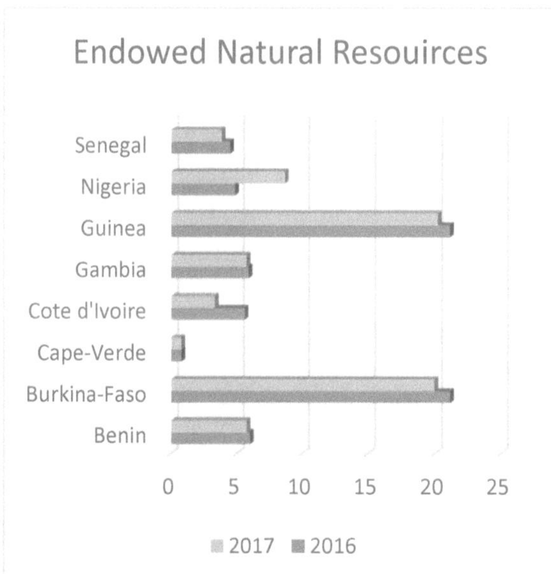
Endowed Natural Resouirces
Senegal
Nigeria
Guinea
Gambia
Cote d'Ivoire
Cape-Verde
Burkina-Faso
Benin
0
5
10
15
20
25
2017
2016

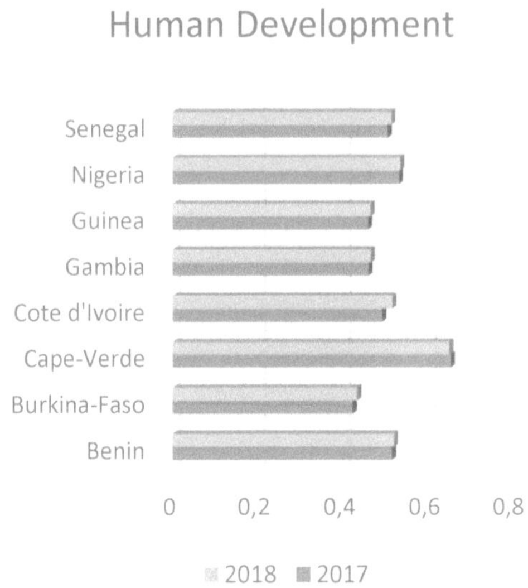

Food sovereignty and food security

Studies across different countries at a distinct period have revealed that to achieve food security, arable land covered will increase. About 40% of Earth's terrestrial surface is already being used for agriculture; many cultivated areas are high-input, intensified landscapes to which pesticides, fertilizers, and irrigation are being applied with a severe impact on biodiversity and other aspects of the natural environment. Yet, the number of chronically food-insecure people remains high at over 795million worldwide (World Food Summit, 1996; Chappell and LaValle, 2011; Beuchelt and Virchow, 2012; FAO, 2015). Food sovereignty has emerged as an alternative approach for achieving food security at the local level while also protecting biodiversity and the environment, and deliver broader social values, via non-industrial farming methods. According to Amusan (2019), and Beuchelt and Virchow (2012), food sovereignty is the right of peoples to healthy and culturally appropriate food produced through ecologically sound and sustainable methods, and their right to define their food and agriculture systems. Besides, Hess (2008) sees food sovereignty as a form of localism, whereby sovereignty is regained over the economy.

Improving food security is frequently expressed as the goal of governments, multilateral and national development agencies, non-governmental organizations, and even transnational corporations. Although this goal might on the surface appear to be a very normative objective, food security can nevertheless carry a lot of ideological baggage. The tensions associated with the use of food security help reveal why food sovereignty emerged and began to be championed as a more expansive vision of food entitlements that is bound up in struggles for radical changes in how agro-food systems are organized. This local movement is currently scaling up from a series of locally embedded projects supported by a broader movement, into a national and international strategy for sustainable food security. The MASIPAG network in the Philippines is replicating projects, (Heckelman and Wittman, 2015; Suh, 2015), and several governments are amplifying the scale of projects by integrating food sovereignty into their legislation of food security strategies. Examples include Venezuela, Bolivia, Ecuador, Nicaragua, Senegal, Mali (Godek, 2015), and the Dominican Republic (Alonso-Fradejas et al., 2015); similar proposals are being discussed in Peru and El Salvador (Godek, 2015). The need for food sovereignty in the ECOWAS region is important especially with the aspect that reflects unequal effective demand rather than absolute scarcity.

Notably, there is a cut in the rates of undernutrition from 23% to 13% among countries of the West African Sahel (calculated from data in FAO et al., 2015). Despite this notable progress, food insecurity remains a serious problem for low-income families in these countries. The prevalence of stunting (an indicator of long-term malnutrition) among children ranges from 29% in Senegal to 55% in Niger (FAO, 2013). Low-income households in Sahelian West Africa face multiple shocks that risk compressing their already-low food consumption levels. Two shocks, in particular, impose significant pressure on vulnerable household's food security.

- Reductions in staple-food production due to drought, flooding, insect attacks, and plant diseases. Given thin markets for many of the region's basic rain-fed staples (millet, sorghum, and maize) and negligible imports of these products into the region, production shocks can lead to strong price spikes, limiting the poor's access to food.

- World price shocks, especially for rice, the main imported staple food in the region. During the 2008 world price spike, the FOB price of the benchmark Thai 5% broken milled rice nearly tripled from the US $316/mt in April 2007 to $907/mt in April 2008 (World Bank, 2016), leading to severe pressure on the Sahel region, which relies on rice imports for nearly 60% of its total rice consumption and close to 10% of its total cereal consumption).

These shocks confirm that poor households bear the brunt of such consumption risks, particularly in closed markets, where trade barriers restrict imports, and the poor find themselves in a bidding war with richer consumers for limited food supplies. In the absence of trade, a drought that reduces domestic rain-fed cereal production would compress already low-calorie consumption of the rural poor, four times as much as other household groups. Conversely, a spike in world rice prices would hit the urban poor hardest, reducing their calorie consumption. Also, literature has highlighted the important shock-absorbing potential of commodity substitution across staple food groups as well as the importance of intra-regional trade with coastal countries in moderating food consumption pressure in the Sahel. This is an indication that policy responses will need to focus on two basic mechanisms that can help to moderate this pressure –trade and consumer substitution among staple foods. Immediately south of the Sahel, coastal West African countries enjoy higher rainfall, dual rainy seasons, more stable staple food production based on root crops (cassava and yams) as well as frequent double.

The economic contributions of agro-ecological food production

Given the necessary indicators, the contribution of agriculture has highly influenced the economic development of the African region, about 65% of employment in Africa is engaged by agricultural activities yet, effort to accelerate the productivity and efficiency in agriculture have been inhibited by arbitrarily political borders. Haggblade (2013) examined the regional requirements for achieving food security. By partitioning agro-ecological zones and natural market sheds, current borders serve as barriers, hampering agricultural technology transfer, hindering agricultural trade and dampening incentives for farmers and agribusinesses to invest in Africa's many regional bread-basket zones. Feasible solutions revolve around neutralising these deleterious effects among economic union through regional scientific networks and corridor development programmes.

Most of the leading economy of ECOWAS country have been identified among the low human development except Ghana (0.592) and Cape-Verde (0.654) which were in the Medium Human Development Group, (FAO, 2019; UNDP, 2019). Diversity in rural and urban farming among countries can constitute part of the drivers for a low level of economic development. The need to increase demand for agricultural products through trade agreements can help the majority of countries in the ECOWAS region to improve the level of economic development. Nwokedi, Iloh and Oghomitse (2019) noted that developed countries leverage on the loopholes in the Agreement to engage in unfair trade practices against developing countries. Also, they show that some neoliberal policies inherent in the Agreement undermine developing countries' attempts at maximizing the benefits of international trade in agriculture to improve their food security status. These policies further limit the capacity of West African states to leverage on the liberalization policy to export to developed countries' markets. However, the wave of globalization that swept across the world at the turn of the 21st century impacted heavily on the nature and character of global trade which agriculture product also needs to achieve food sustainability.

Conclusion

ECOWAS food security is hard hit by the global food crisis and coronavirus pandemic, leaving the region in disarray and near economic comatose. The current hit (C-19) is the largest on the food security after the global food crises of 2008. of course, the porous border and trade restriction effects are stronger within the reality of agrological production and food creation in which each country within the region has little or no domestic insulin to immunize the system against external shocks.

In the first instance, the heavy dependence on importation of food encourages government to raise economic union among the member state in which food trade will be made possible against major global supply. This created serious interaction with less trade restrictions, enhance the effective market system, and equipped any country with agricultural deficiency. Increasing regional food trade is the most powerful tool to offset supply shocks.

The onus of food security revitalization among economic union lies partly on the researchers to provide policy antidote, a fundamental reason for this study. It is evidenced; the crisis has two sides of a coin; the short-run and long-run effects. Present food scarcity experience is a short-run reaction to the coronavirus pandemic, which has strong explanatory power for the behaviour of food insecurity. Therefore, C-19 pandemic shocks transmit strong effects on the poverty level within a period of the pandemic. Secondly, the study suggests stronger access to the market with less restrictive trade among member countries. A solution to the long-run problems depends on how the short-run crises are managed. Any realistic process must follow a holistic approach for a gain of access to the market to be impactful. This is because access to market among ECOWAS country have a long-lasting impact. It should be noted that, if less restriction trade is allowed among members, human participation in trade activities will increase for both men and women and reduce social vices among idle hands, which will result in a rise of human development and improves food security.

Reference

Adenle, A.A., Sulayman, K. S., Govindan, P., and Obijiofor, A. (2012) "Analysis of open-source biotechnology in developing countries: An emerging framework for sustainable agriculture." Technology in Society 34(3): 256-269.

AfDB, O. E. C. D. "UNDP. (2014)." African economic outlook (2014).

Alarcón, D and Christina, B (2011) "Agricultural innovation for food security and environmental sustainability in the context of the recent economic crisis: Why a gender perspective." World Economic and Social Survey.

Alene, A. D., and Ousmane, C. (2009) "The impact of agricultural research on productivity and poverty in sub-Saharan Africa." Food Policy 34(2): 198-209.

Amusan, L. (2019). Mercy Killing and Thanksgiving: Food Security with Tears in Africa. Faculty Distinguished Lecture Series 1, Faculty of Social Sciences, Federal University Oye-Ekiti, Nigeria. DOI:10.13140/RG.2.2.21142.78407.

Amusan, L. and Agunyai, S.C. (2021). The COVID-19 pandemic and the crisis of lockdowns in Nigeria: The household food security perspective. Africa's Public Service Delivery & Performance Review, 9(1). DOI: https://doi.org/10.4102/apsdpr.v9i1.484

Beuchelt, T. D., and Detlef, V. (2012) "Food sovereignty or the human right to adequate food: which concept serves better as international development policy for global hunger and poverty reduction?" Agriculture and Human Values 29, no. 2 (2012): 259-273.

Center, Africa Rice (2011) "Boosting Africa's Rice Sector: A research for development strategy 20112020." Cotonou, Benin.

Chamberlin, J., and Thomas S. J. (2013) "Unpacking the meaning of 'market access': evidence from rural Kenya." World development 41: 245-264.

Chappell, M. J, and Liliana, A. L. (2011) "Food security and biodiversity: can we have both? An agroecological analysis." Agriculture and Human Values 28(1): 326.

Deininger, K., and Paul, M. (2005) "Does greater accountability improve the quality of public service delivery? Evidence from Uganda." World development 33(1): 171-191.

Durosomo, B. (2011) "Technology adoption and Sub-Saharan African agriculture: the sustainable development option." *Agriculture and Human Values* 10(4): 58-70.

FAO, Faostat (2015) "Agriculture database." 2015-12-10] http://faostat3 fao.org.

FAO, IFAD, and UNICEF. "WFP." (2015). The state of food insecurity in the world: 46.

FAO, FHI360. (2016) "Minimum dietary diversity for women: a guide for measurement." Rome: FAO82.

FAO (1996) World food summit: Rome declaration on world food security and World Food summit plan of action. FAO.

Godek, Wendy. (2015) "Challenges for food sovereignty policy making: The case of Nicaragua's Law693." *Third World Quarterly* 36(3): 526-543.

Haggblade, S (2013) "Unscrambling Africa: Regional requirements for achieving food security." *Development Policy Review* 31(2): 149-176.

Heckelman, A. A., and Hannah, W. (2015) "Food sovereignty: A framework for assessing agrarian responses to climate change in the Philippines." *Austrian Journal of South-East Asian Studies* 8(1) : 87-94.

Holden, S. T., K., and Deininger, H. G. (2008) Impact of Land Certification on Land Related Conflicts. Working Paper, Norwegian University of Life Sciences, Ås.

IFAD, WFP. "FAO (2013)." The State of Food Insecurity in the World: The multiple dimensions of food security.

Jacob, V. (1950) "The customs union issue." Carnegie Endowment for International Peace (1950).

Jin, S., and Thomas, S. J. (2013) "Land rental markets in Kenya: implications for efficiency, equity, household income, and poverty." *Land Economics* 89(2): 246-271.

Lopriore, C., and Ellen, M. (2003) "Food security and nutrition trends in West Africa, Challenges and the way forward." FAO, Rome, Italy.

Magalhães, P. C. (2014) "Government effectiveness and support for democracy." *European Journal of Political Research* 53(1): 77-97.

Mahadevia, D. (2012). Decent work in Ahmedabad: An integrated approach. ILO.

Miller, T., and George, T. (1989) "Technology adoption and agricultural price policy." *American journal of agricultural economics* 71(4): 847-857.

Osabohien, Romanus, E. O, and Ese, U (2018) "Food security, institutional framework and technology: Examining the nexus in Nigeria using ARDL approach." *Current Nutrition & Food Science* 14(2): 154-163.

Osabohien, Romanus, Oluwatoyin Matthew, Obindah Gershon, Toun Ogunbiyi, and Ebere Nwosu. (2019) "Agriculture development, employment generation and poverty reduction in West Africa." *The Open Agriculture Journal* 13(1).

Osabohien, Romanus, Eze Osuagwu, Evans Osabuohien, Uche Eseosa Ekhator-Mobayode, Matthew Oluwatoyin, and Obindah Gershon (2019) "Households Access to Agricultural Credit and Agricultural Production in Nigeria: A PSM Model.".

Takeshima, H., and Latha, N (2012) "Local market participation, on-farm diversity and farmer welfare."

Teklu, Tesfaye, and Adugna Lemi. (2004). "Factors affecting entry and intensity in informal rental land markets in Southern Ethiopian highlands." *Agricultural Economics* 30(2): 117-128.

Tigabu, D. G., and M. F. Gebeyehu (2018). Agricultural extension service and technology adoption for food and nutrition security: Evidence from Ethiopia. FARA Research Report 3 (4): 30.

UNDP, UN. (2019)"Stockholm Environment Institute. Manual for preparation of emissions inventory for use in modelling of transboundary air pollution. UNDP, UN, New York.".

Wailes, Eric J. (2005) "Rice: Global trade, protectionist policies, and the impact of trade liberalization." *Global agricultural trade and developing countries*: 177-194.

Wailes, E. J., and E. C. Chavez (2015) "International rice outlook, baseline projections, 2014À2024.Staff Paper 01. University of Arkansas, Fayetteville, AR.".

Wailes, E. J., Alvaro, Durand-Morat, and Mandiaye, D. (2015) "Regional and national rice development strategies for food security in West Africa." Food security in an uncertain world (Frontiers of Economics and Globalization, Volume 15). Emerald Group Publishing Limited (2015): 255-268.

World Bank (2008) World Development Report 2016, Agriculture for Development, Washington DC

World Health Organization (2003) "Food and Agriculture Organization (FAO). (2003)." Diet nutrition and the prevention of chronic diseases. WHO, Geneva: 4-101.

World Health Organization (2019) Preventing disease through healthy environments: exposure to highly hazardous pesticides: a major public health concern. No. WHO/CED/PHE/EPE/19.4. 6. World Health Organization.

World Health Organization (2015) Global status report on road safety 2015. World Health Organization, 2015.

Chapter 10
Oil Extraction and the Question of Food Security in Cabinda of Angola

Victor Ojakorotu and
Fie D. Dan-Woniowei

Introduction

Oil extraction has been reported as the major human activity of all known sources of pollution (World Wildlife Fund (WWF) International, 2015 cited in. Dan-Woniowei & Okeke-Ogbuafor, 2019). Hence, the oil industry in Angola like its counterparts especially, in Sub-Saharan Africa accounts for serious environmental concerns, which not only bother on the health of local communities, but also on their livelihoods (Baumuller, Donnelly, Vines, and Weimer, 2011: 1). It follows that oil extraction has brought about several environmental challenges that make life more difficult for fisher folks and farmers in the Cabinda to be food unsecured in Angola. What it means is that sustained pollution through oil extraction in the region has rendered farmers incapable to cultivate food/cash crops at a sustainable level, nor fisher folks to boast of adequate catch as the arable lands and seas constantly suffer the effects of pollution (Baumuller *et al.* 2011; Rodriguez, Rodriguez, Gutierrez & Major, 2014). In addition, it implies that the goal of national food security cannot be attained in Angola.

National food security is a situation in which all citizens in a country, at all times, have physical, social, and economic access to sufficient, safe, and nutritious food that meets their preferences and dietary needs for active and healthy life (Committee on World Food Security, 2017). In Cabinda where pollution is ceaseless due to oil extraction activities, the local people who live on subsistence agriculture (fishing and farming) will be severely impaired. Available evidence shows that oil pollution degrades the soil (Reeds, 2003), and affect crops and fish production, as well as weakens agricultural prosperity (Akpokodje & Salau, 2015). More importantly, oil extraction emits obnoxious gases that are proven to risk the health of Angolans (Reeds, 2003). Such health conditions could largely affect the productive capacity of the most active population engaged in subsistent agriculture in Cabinda. Available records show that oil pollution has to a large extent increased the mortality rate of the citizens of Angola; the life expectancy of the citizens being the lowest in the continent, ranging from 48.8 years for women to 49.9 years for men (UNDP, 2010).

Another worrisome situation is the way and manner oil is being exploited in the Cabinda of Angola. It has contributed to the alienation and deprivation of the indigenous people of Cabinda. The people are being deprived of the oil wealth generated from their region. It is on record that the oil wells in Cabinda provide more than sixty percent of the oil accruing to Angola. The region is contributing immensely to the Gross National Product (GNP) of Angola but has remained largely underdeveloped. For instance, in the early and late 1990s, it was recorded that 80 percent of the revenue that accruable to the Angolan government was from oil extraction. Available records show that oil accounted for about 90 percent of the country's total export across a long period of time, and making it the key sustenance of its economy (Le Billon, 2007:6). Suffice to state that the Cabindans and other citizens of Angola had little or no benefit from the oil wealth when oil extraction has dispossessed them of their means of livelihood (Rodigruez *et al.*, 2014: 429-430; Lyle, 2005:705). The oil revenues were neither used to invest in the hailing subsistence agriculture sector of the economy to benefit local farmers to boost food security in the country. Baumuller *et al.* (2011:) has argued that a greater part of the oil revenues of Angola was spent on internal security and defense, imports, fuel subsidies, water and electricity, and enrichment of regime families in Luanda, leaving the agriculture sector to account for only eight percent. Thus, it is the interest of this study to examine how oil extraction in the Cabinda province has raised questions relating to food security in Angola.

The Cabinda of Angola

The Province is located in the Northwest of Angola. It is alienated from the rest of Angola by a strip of land belonging to the Democratic Republic of Congo. Cabinda is bordered on the North by Congo-Brazzaville, to the east by the Democratic Republic of Congo, and the West by the Atlantic Ocean. Physically, the people of Cabinda are more or less secluded from the rest of the Angolans (Minorities at Risk Project, 2006). Cabinda is rich in mineral and agricultural resources, which include phosphate, potassium, crude oil, and timber (Martin, 1977:56). The Bakongo ethnic group is the majority group that occupies the Cabinda province. It makes up about 13 percent of the total population of Angola. The Bakongo ethnic group hosts the oil wealth of the country and is popularly known for establishing businesses, religious syncretism, and political movements (Minority Rights Group International, 2020). However, it is interesting to note that the political movements are fallouts of several agitations aimed at achieving self-determination and/or, the abolishment of all forms of oil extraction related problems in the Province. It is also important to state that the agitations/movements met stiff resistance from the Angolan government and accordingly, suppressed heavily. Notwithstanding, the idea has continued to explain why the Cabindas have kept faith with their struggles; for it is cantered on exerting full control of their destiny, as well as placing much emphasis on upholding basic human rights (Carley, 1995:8).

The Movement for the Liberation of the Enclave of Cabinda (MLEC) was the first nationalist group founded by Ranque Franque in Congo-Brazzaville in 1960 to advocate for the independence of Cabinda. Not too long after its adoption, the MLEC witnessed a crack leading to the formation of the Action Committee for the National Union of Cabinda (CAUNC) which was headed by Nzita Tiago. Unlike the MLEC, the CAUNC clamored for the full integration of the Cabinda into Congo-Leopoldville (Martin 1977:58). There was also the Mayombe Alliance, which was referred to as ALLIAMA. From all expectations, the proliferation of separatist groups did not in any way address the plight of the Cabindas, and this necessitated the need for a united front. Hence, a unity conference was held at Pointe-Noire in 1963, and three groups – MLEC, CAUNC, and ALLIAMA (a separatist group known as the Mayombe Alliance), all advocating for the independence of Cabinda met to establish a new party - Front for the Liberation of the Enclave of Cabinda (FLEC) (Martin, 1977:58, Reeds, 2009:46). The idea of the new party is centred on the premise that a united platform would at best serve their collective interest. However, many of the agitations and activities of the

FLEC were short-lived, and this ushered in a new phase in the struggle. In the early 1990s, a movement campaigning for the independence of the Bakongo ethnic group and the province of Cabinda began. Movement para Auto-Determinacao de Bakongo (MAKO) has since dissolved with other disintegrated separatist groups embedded in FLEC (Minority Rights Group International 2020). Undoubtedly, the Cabindas who have become victims of social exclusion and political marginalization are unrelentingly clamoured for their own identity and loyalty which is considered distinct and supersedes what Angola offers (Carley, 1995:6). Their demand for self-determination is one that transcends far beyond the creation of a new state, rather a political entity which would avail them the opportunity not only to take full charge of their political destiny, but also to ensure the protection of their basic fundamental human rights (Carley, 1995:8). The indigenous people of Cabinda refer to Articles 1(2) and 55 of the United Nations Charter as grounds to buttress their calls for self-determination.

Beyond the quest for separation, the Cabindas are also confronted with the problem of resource ownership and control. Though the Angola government reserves the right to deal directly with the oil multinationals whose activities are predominantly domiciled in the Cabinda region, the indigenous people continued to leave in abject poverty and gross underdevelopment. The seeming inability of the Angola government to enact and enforce regulatory laws to check the excesses of the oil multinationals possess a threat to the Cabindas. It is not surprising that the Ministry of Petroleum and the state-owned oil company Sonangol who govern the politico-business landscape of the oil industry in Angola have remained incapacitated (Baumuller *et al.*, 2011: 32), and this has not only worsened the plight of the indigenous people but also strain the relationship between the citizens and the central government in the country.

A direct consequence of such apparent incapacity to hold oil multinationals accountable has increased the level of impunity at which the oil multinationals relate with the host communities in the Cabinda region. Thus, issues such as oil spillage and pollution, which have received both international and local concerns, have been left unattended to. This in turn adversely affects the mainstay of the economy - farming and fishing in the

Cabinda region. In most cases, farmers would either have to make do with the limited harvest or migrate to other non-polluted lands, and this comes with a cost to human life. Fishing is equally affected by the widespread pollution of oil and other toxic chemicals into the Ocean. Rather than implementing the environmental laws as it impacts on the Angolans, the government officials collaborate with the oil multinationals to amass oil wealth so much so that the richest Angolan citizens are government officials (McMillan, 2005:1, cited in Rodigruez, *et al.*, 2014:429).

More problematic is the continuous exclusion of the Cabindas in successive negotiations with the oil multinationals. The direct involvement of the Angolan government in interaction with the extractive industry has witnessed a series of compromise at the expense of the indigenous host communities. The key problem that arises is that there is the inability of successive Angolan governments to ensure that oil multinationals adhere strictly to the laws regulating the extraction of oil and clean up exercises. The mechanisms to ensure the clean-up of the environment of the local communities have not been effectively implemented, and the government negotiations with oil companies in the region are not made public (Rodigruez, *et al.*, 2014:429). In essence, the way and manner the Angolan government and the oil multinationals have operated over time continue to explain why the Cabindas have persistently clamoured for self-government and the deplorable situation they are confronted with.

The question of food security in Cabinda

It has been earlier stated that national food security means that all citizens in a country, at all times, have physical, social, and economic access to sufficient, safe, and nutritious food that meets their preferences and dietary needs for active and healthy life (Committee on World Food Security, 2017: 6). The question is that are the people of Cabinda food secured in a region of sustained oil pollution. Undoubtedly, the peopled cannot be food secured in a region that oil pollution accounts for severe damage to the main sources (land and water bodies) that would have enabled them to achieve food security. Pollution affects the ecological resources and services that the communities depend on for survival (Dan-Woniowei, 2020; Akpokodje & Salau, 2015). Mostly, oil spills from extractive industries drastically reduce the peoples' productive capacity and grossly limit them of access to at all times, sufficient, safe, and nutritious food, and income for other needs as the case in the Niger Delta of Nigeria where one can identify similarities in their socio-economic plights (Amusan, 2014).

It diversely affects the soil surface with almost no remedy. Series of unregulated gas flaring and sustained oil spillage have adversely damaged arable soils and fishing waters. A situation which has forced the majority of the women from the Cabinda communities, whose mainstay were subsistence farming and fishing, to seek alternatives with severe consequences (Reed 2009:11). The degradation of the environment due to sustained oil pollution has greatly impaired farming and fishing activities. The majority of the indigenous people face the perpetual risk of being displaced from their original habitat, and then added the task of keeping their homes; many of the women in Cabinda community become increasingly stressed. It has also brought about changes in the consumption pattern of the wider Angolan population. For example, available records show that ceaseless oil pollution has reduced the consumption of fish among Angolans, who consume about 16 kg of fish per person in a year in comparison to other African countries (Baumuller *et al.*, 2011: 20).

Another aspect of the food security question that relates to oil extraction is that it disrupts the way of life of the people. Farming and fishing are the two main indigenous means of livelihood in Cabinda. Sustained oil pollution from oil multinational corporations has greatly altered the culture of the indigenous Cabinda people. Fishing and farming provide the food and income for the subsistence of households in the Cabinda. Suffice to state that the bulk of the oil produced in Angola comes from offshore. It implies that fishing will be most affected because all the known stages of oil extraction at sea cause environmental pollution. Pollution at sea poisons water bodies and makes life difficult for marine life to survive (Shantz, 2006:23). It also enables fishes to migrate far into safer areas on high seas. It means that fisher folks in Cabinda had to go the extra mile for fishing activities. It also means that additional trips and resources are required with more risks at sea if they have to catch enough fish for food and income to satisfy other necessities of life. Suffice to state that the activities of oil companies cause a lot of damage to the environment including the destruction of underwater habitats and coral reefs among other spots where fishes bred (Baumuller *et al.*, 2011:20-21). The deplorable conditions are generating concerns both within and outside Angola, especially, on issues relating to compensations from Chevron/Texaco for the gross damage done to local communities (Shantz, 2006:23).

More critical of the problem of the oil spill at sea is that it can spread fast adjoining water bodies, and even onshore, causing severe damage to the soil environment (Des Clers 2007: 26). This damage which spreads to the onshore adversely affects the quality of harvest as well as the reduction in nutrients of crops produced, and reduces the income expected from farmers and fishermen in Cabinda, and the entire of Angola. Furthermore, the released components such as nitrogen oxide, sulphur, carbon, phenol cyanide, chromium, and biological oxygen due to oil spillage have the capacity of polluting the arable lands just at the point of their contacts (Brown & Tar 2015: 275 -276). Undoubtedly, the aforementioned chemicals have been identified as a potential threat to fishing and farming activities in Angola and across Africa. As a result, the indigenous people of Cabinda face untold hardship, hunger, and impoverishment.

More worrisome also, is that the Angolan government and the oil multinational corporations seem aware of these challenges of the fisher folks in the region yet, the oil wealth could hardly be used to alleviate their plight. The oil wealth has been a distraction to the Angolan government from investing in the Agriculture sector. Recent statistics have suggested that Angola is rated the second-largest oil-producing country in Sub-Saharan Africa, and has the potential of taking the lead in the future (Le Billion 2007:105). Aside from the abundance of oil, the country is equally endowed with diamond and agricultural resources such as maize, banana, sisal, sugarcane, coffee, palm oil (Tomas 2011:2). Yet, a large section of the population still lives in abject poverty (Le Billion 2007: 105).

Notwithstanding, the Angolan government had made some efforts to improve food production in the country, there had been no sufficient success recorded, and this could be attributed to the staggering nature of the post-conflict recovering in the country (Melo, Cesar, da Silva, Henriques, Domingos and Costa, 2016). The province of Cabinda had witnessed several secession struggles, and in the end, the majority of the citizens in the local communities who had hitherto suffered deprivation and exclusion from oil extraction could hardly benefit from the post-conflict resettlement efforts (Lyle, 2005; Ojakorotu, Kamidza & Eesuola, 2018).

Undoubtedly, the challenges posed by oil spillage have reached an alarming rate due to either government connivance with the oil multinationals to the interest of the oil giants executive directors and shareholders or bad leadership due to lack of relevant technology to monitor the activities of oil companies as the case in Nigeria (Amusan, 2010). Hence, the government must ensure that oil extraction in the Cabinda region is carried out in line with both international and local regulatory frameworks. There are greater needs for the government to demonstrate more enthusiasm in addressing the core challenges faced by the citizenry, and in particular the provision of basic amenities. The government must also invest heavily in agriculture, and this must be complemented by effective policies so as to ensure the country achieves its potentials in the agricultural sector.

Conclusion

It has been argued that sustained oil pollution from years of oil extraction in the Cabinda of Angola has greatly impaired subsistence farming and fishing, the two main occupations and mainstay of the indigenous people of the region. There is hardly, any capacity on the part of the Angolan government to regulating the heinous activities of the oil companies, especially, to stopping the ceaseless pollution in the region. As a result, national food security cannot be achieved. Worst still, the government and the oil multinationals in some way aware of the predicament of the local communities, yet the Angolan government is not willing to invest the oil revenues accruing from the region to improve fishing and farming in ensuring food security in the Cabinda of Angola. In order for Angola to be food secure, the government must address the question of oil pollution from the extractive industries in the Cabinda region, and empower the indigenous people to adequately invest in agriculture. In addition, it must be complemented by effective policies to ensure the country achieve food security.

References

Akpokodje, J. & Salau, S. (2015). Oil pollution and agricultural production in the Niger Delta of Nigeria. *Journal of Environmental Economics*, 6(6):68-75.

Amusan, L. (2014). Evaluating the Gender Content of the Amnesty Programme in the Niger Delta of Nigeria: Any Concern for the Socio-economic Development of Women? *Gender & Behaviour*, 12(3): 5924-5935.

Amusan, L. (2009). The Political Economy of Fossil Fuel in Nigeria. In Ojakorotu, V. (ed.), *Contending Issues in the Niger Delta Crisis of Nigeria*. Houston, TX: JAPSS Press, Inc

Batistich, M. (1995). The right to self-determination and international law. *Auckland University Law Review*, 7:1013-1037.

Baumuller, H., Donnelly, E., Vines, A., & Weimer, M. (2011). *The effects of oil companies' activities on the environment, health and development in Sub-Saharan Africa. Belgium: European Parliament.*

Brown, I. & Tari, E. (2015). An evaluation of the effects of petroleum exploration and production activities on the social environment in Ogoni land, Nigeria. *International Journal of Scientific & Technology Research*, 4(4):273-282.

Carley, P. (1995). *Self-determination: sovereignty, territorial integrity and the right to secession*. Washington DC: United States Institute of Peace.

Castellino, J. (2008). Territorial integrity and the "right" to self-determination: an examination of the conceptual tools. *Brooklyn Journal of International Law*, 33(2):503-568.

Dan-Woniowei, F. D. (2020). An advocacy for marine protected areas initiative for conservation of ecological resources and survival of coastal communities in Nigeria. *Journal of Political Science and International Relations*, 3(3): 56-60.

Dan-Woniowei, F. D. & Okeke-Ogbuafor, N. (2019). Emerging global offshore oil and gas industry in Nigeria: the paradox of legal regimes and survival of coastal communities in the Niger Delta, 83-102 In. Ani, K. J. (ed.), *Environmental conflicts and Peace Building in Africa*: A Festschrift for Victor Ojakorotu, Academica Press, Washington-London.

Des Clers, S. (2007). Mitigating the impacts of oil exploration and production on coastal and wetlands livelihoods in West/Central Africa. *Sustainable Fisheries Livelihood Programme*. http://www.fao.org/fishery/docs/DOCUMENT/sflp/SFLP_publications/English/oil_fish.pdf Date of Access 01 Sep. 2020.

Hammond, J. L. (2011). The resource curse and oil revenues in Angola and Venezuela. *Science & Society*, 75(3):348-378.

Hannum, H. (1998). The right of self-determination in the twenty-first century. *Washington and Lee Law Review*, 55(3):773-780.

Le Billon, P. (2007). Drilling in deep water: oil, business and war in Angola. In Mary Kaldor, Terry Lynn Karl and Yahia Said (Eds). *Oil wars.* London [u.a]: Pluto Press. 100-129.

Lyle, B. (2005). Blood for oil: secession, self-determination and superpower silence in Cabinda. *Washington University Global Studies Law Review*, 4(3):701-718.

Martin, P. M. (1977). The Cabinda connection: an historical perspective. *African Affairs*, 76(302):47-59.

Marxsen, C. (2015). *Territorial integrity in international law – its concepts and implications for Crimea.* https://www.zaoerv.de/75_2015/75_20151_a_7_26.pdf Date of Access 16 Sep. 2020.

Melo, A., Cesar, J., da Silva, L., Henriques, A., Domingos, M. & Costa, S. (2016). *Agriculture innovation partnerships in Angola: successful stories.* Capacity Development for Agricultural Innovation Systems. https://iictcooperacao .files.wordpress.com/2016/12/ext-abstract-cdais-angola.pdf Date of Access 02 Sep. 2020.

Minorities at Risk Project. 2006. *Assessment for Cabinda in Angola.* http://www.mar.umd.edu/assessment.asp?groupId=54003 Date of Access 14 Sep. 2020.

Minority Rights Group International. (2020). *Angola.* https://minorityrights .org/country/angola/ Date of Access 14 Sep. 2020.

Ojakorotu, V., Kamidza, R. & Eesuola, O. S. (2018). Oil wealth paradox and its implication for sustainable development in Angola and Nigeria. *Journal of African Foreign Affairs*, 5(1):85-106.

Reed, K. (2003). Oil boom in Angola: in a poor land, an exploration of the trickle-down effect. https://www.berkeley.edu/news/students/2003/angola/10.shtml Date of Access 17 Sep. 2020.

Rodigruez, J., Rodigruez, F., Gutierrez, C. C., & Major, S. A. (2014). Oil, poverty and environment in Angola. *Boletin de la Asociacion de Geografos Espanoles*, 64:427-432.

Saka, L. & Sani, M. A. (2012). Resource rent and governance crisis in Gulf of Guinea oil states: the case of Angola. *The Social Sciences*, 7(2):321-331.

Shantz, J. (2006). Cabinda: Africa's forgotten war. Undercurrents, *Journal of Critical Environmental Studies*, 15:23-24.

Tomas, J.A.S. (2013). Agriculture as a tool for development in Angola. *African Journal of Agricultural Research*, 8 (50):6642 – 6650.

Vines, A. & Weimer, M. (2009). Angola: Thirty years of Dos Santos. *Review of African Political Economy*, 36(120):287-294.

WWF International Living Blue Planet Report (2015). *Species, habitats and human well- being.* Institute of Zoology, Zoological Society of London (ZSL), 1-39, In. Dan-Woniowei, F. D. &

Okeke-Ogbuafor, N. (2019). Emerging global offshore oil and gas industry in Nigeria: the paradox of legal regimes and survival of coastal communities in the

Niger Delta, 83-102 In. Ani, K. J. (ed.) (2019). *Environmental conflicts and Peace Building in Africa: A Festschrift for Victor Ojakorotu,* Academica Press, Washington-London.

Chapter 11
The Impact of Drought on Urban Agriculture: A Case Study of Urban Livestock Farmers in Bloemfontein, Free State Province

Ogundeji AA and Ojo TO

Introduction

Climate change, which is also referred to as "global warming", is a reality facing us today and is affecting the environment that we are currently living in. The term "climate change" refers to the rise in average surface temperatures on earth and the projected increase in temperature will affect water availability (Ogundeji et al, 2018). Scientific research attributes climate change to an increase in carbon dioxide and other greenhouse gases caused by human activities. As a result, there has been a mean rise in the global temperature by an average of two degrees Celsius, bringing about increasing risks, which cause catastrophes such as floods, tornados, and drought (Randalls, 2010). These problems usually affect the world's citizens, especially the poor and people in developing countries (Bryan et al., 2009; Raubenheimer, 2011).

One of the harms inflicted by climate change is drought, which often has a serious negative impact on agricultural production, the ecology, and the economy (Amusan & Olutola, 2017). Recurring drought is one of the biggest challenges for South African food security. This is due to insufficient knowledge and the low levels of resources available to farmers in vulnerable situations, thereby limiting coping and adaptation choices (Dakalo et al., 2019). Drought is a silent and pervasive disaster that creeps up for weeks and months, and often unexpectedly. Drought results from the deficit of water relative to normal conditions. With agriculture being one of the largest water-consuming sectors globally, the impact of the drought is devastating for agricultural production, with small-scale farmers being more vulnerable to the risk (Food and Agriculture

Organization ((FAO), 2013). With a need to improve agricultural output due to a growing population, drought makes it even more difficult for the adaptation and reduction of poverty and food security (Dagel, 1997; Wilhite, 2005; Sheffield & Wood, 2011; Holsten et al., 2009, 2009).

Agriculture is by far the largest water-consuming sector globally, as it largely depends on water for survival (FAO, 2011). Both plants and animals need water for their survival, and abiotic stresses, such as drought and extreme temperatures, affect them negatively. There has been an increase in livestock mortality caused by extreme drought conditions and deliberate human actions to reduce the impact of the drought. Although some interventions have been introduced to reduce the impact of drought on agriculture, there has not been much support for the poor urban households who participate in urban agriculture. The reason for this is that it is extremely difficult to predict drought, as it is a silent and pervasive disaster that creeps up without warning (Raubenheimer, 2011).

In recent years, South Africa and other parts of the African continent have been experiencing drought conditions that have had a seriously negative impact on agriculture in its entirety. In 2007/2008, the impact of the drought that occurred in South Africa caused serious mortality in livestock farming, which negatively affected the production and livelihood of livestock farmers, who had to find alternative strategies and support for survival (Ngaka, 2012). Although South Africa experienced drought in 2007/2008, the South African Weather Services (SAWS) confirmed that the 2015/2016 drought was the worst, with all nine provinces affected to different degrees (Davies et al., 2016). The SAWS reported that dams across the country were at their lowest levels in years. In 2015, national dam levels were estimated to be at 64.3%, which later dropped to 53% in September 2016. The drought increased the number of animals slaughtered as producers cull the animals due to poor or insufficient grazing and high cost of feed. For instance, commercial beef slaughters increased by 8 percent in 2015, rising almost 18 percent above the 5-year average (BFAP, 2016).

According to Gallaher et al., (2013), for the first time, the number of people living in urban areas outnumbered those in rural areas in the first decade of the twenty-first century. This marked a major shift in the distribution of the world population. The current estimates as revealed by Shah et al., (2019), show that by 2030, the world will be over 60 % urban, with most urbanization taking place in developing countries (UN Habitat 2003). The world is experiencing rapid urbanization, and it is estimated that the developing countries of Africa, Asia, and Latin America will be home to some 75% of all urban dwellers. Furthermore, it is expected that about 40% to 45% of the poor in Africa and Asia will be concentrated in towns and cities. Most cities in developing countries find it difficult to cope with the need for development, as they struggle to create sufficient formal employment opportunities for the poor, thereby increasing urban poverty and food insecurity. Urban agriculture can reduce poverty and enhance food security amongst the poor, who are vulnerable to the high cost of food in the urban areas (Haysom, 2007; RUAF Foundation, 2017).

Urban agriculture refers to the agricultural activity that is located within or on the fringe of a town, a city or a metropolis. The agricultural activity includes crop and livestock production, as well as the production of diverse other food products. Extant empirical studies on urban agriculture in Africa started with the notion that peasant farming methods could be a means of food provision and income generation for resource-poor urban households (Niñez, 1985, Olivier & Heinecken; Olivier, 2018). This idea became more popular with numerous authors arguing in support of urban agriculture's economic and food security benefits (FAO, 2012; Poulsen et al., 2015; Gallaher (2017). Despite this, some other authors criticized urban agriculture; such arguments were countered by the sheer volume of material promoting urban agriculture as the solution to African food insecurity (Webb, 2011).

Urban agriculture forms part of the livelihood strategies for many urban poor, who are unemployed and use it for food security, or also for the working class, who engage in it to support their income by selling the products (Haysom, 2007; RUAF Foundation 2017). Urban agriculture can reduce poverty and enhance food security amongst the poor, who are vulnerable to the high cost of food in the urban areas (Matteson and Langellotto, 2017). Therefore, this study sought to evaluate the impact of drought on urban agriculture and the coping strategies put in place to deal with drought by the urban livestock farmers. It also explored the conditions under which urban agriculture operates and the strategies utilized to mitigate the risk of drought and proposes policy options that will enhance its potential for improved food security and poverty alleviation in urban areas. Furthermore, the study looked at the key survival factors of urban livestock farms, adaptation strategies to drought and their effectiveness, and support structures for urban agriculture.

Study area

Bloemfontein is the sixth-largest city in South Africa and the capital of the Free State province and Mangaung Metropolitan Municipality (MMM). It is the main economic driver of the province, contributing about 25% of the gross domestic product (GDP) of the province. The population of the municipality has been growing steadily, with the city of Bloemfontein attracting more people as the world is urbanizing (Mangaung Metro Municipality Integrated Development Plan, 2012/2016).

The population of MMM increased from 645 438 in 2001 to 747 431 in 2011 according to the Community Survey and Statistics of 2011. According to the Integrated Development Plan (IDP) (2018/22), the current population is 828 270. This shows a population increase of approximately 13% for ten (10) years. According to the IDP of the MMM (2012/2016), the population growth of Mangaung is more due to migration than to an increase in fertility, with most migrants coming from adjacent municipalities such as Mantsopa, Naledi and Masilonyana, and other provinces and countries, including neighbouring Lesotho. The poverty levels of Mangaung are high, with more than 50% of the population earning less than R1 000 per month, and the majority of them are township and informal settlement dwellers.

Similar to all other parts of South Africa, Bloemfontein experienced less rain and serious drought conditions. According to the South African Weather Services, Bloemfontein receives approximately 407 mm of rain per year, with most rainfall in the summer period, especially in January (Davies et al., 2016). This has decreased due to the lack of rain, which culminated in drought conditions affecting all the residents and the environment of the city. Figure 1 shows the map of Mangaung, with Bloemfontein, which is the capital of the Free State province, is situated relatively in the centre.

Research design

Methodology and sampling technique

Both qualitative and quantitative research methods are used in this study to assess and analyse the impact of drought on urban agriculture, particularly livestock enterprises in Bloemfontein city within the Mangaung Metropolitan Municipality. The qualitative research method through focus group discussion with different stakeholders assisted in gathering relevant information about the opinions, perceptions, attitudes, and practices regarding the respondents' understanding of the concepts and challenges of urban agriculture and drought. This assisted in acquiring basic information, after which empirical evidence was obtained through the use of a structured questionnaire. This study employed the stratified random sampling technique, this is to ensure that specific groups are represented. A total of 120 urban livestock farmers were interviewed by making use of a structured questionnaire to collect information in Phase III, Bloemfontein. The data captured from the questionnaire were analysed for further inferences. Findings were presented through descriptive statistics (percentages, frequency distribution tables, histograms, and charts) and inferential statistics (cross-tabulation, correlation, and statistical reliability) for easy understanding.

Results and discussion

Profile of the respondents' socio-economic and livelihood attributes

According to Udmale et al., (2014); Ncube et al, (2016) and Belle et al., (2017) and), socio-demographic features of the respondents are important factors as a result of their influence on the economic behaviour of farmers and as well as their capability of coping with the effect of drought through their involvement in urban agriculture. In this study, some of the socioeconomic characteristics of the farmers practicing urban agriculture, such as age, gender, household size, and income were analysed. The livelihood of the urban farmers was evaluated on the basis of monthly income, water source, source of income, and type of farm activity.

Characteristics	Sub - characteristics	% Statistics (n=120)
Age group (years)	25 – 29	4
	30 – 34	10
	35 – 39	20
	40 – 44	22
	45 – 49	23
	> 50	21
Gender	Male	67
	Female	33
Livelihood attributes		
Monthly income (excluding Livestock)	R0 - R800	12.5
	R801 - R1500	25.8
	R1501 - R3500	24.2
	> R3501	37.5
Monthly income (Livestock)	< R999	20
	R1000 - R4999	3.3
	R5000 - R9999	5.8
	> R10000	70.8
Water Sources	Reclaimed water	2.5
	Harvested Water	75
	Stream or river	1.7
	Wetland	0.8
	Borehole	1.7
	Others	5
	Not applicable	13.3
Farm Characteristics	Subsistence	22.5
	Commercial	40.8
	Mix of commercial and subsistence	35.8

Table 1: *Socio-economic characteristics of the respondents (N= 120).*

As depicted in Table 1, the gender distribution of the household head shows that 33% of the household head were female while 67% were male. The role of being head of the household is predominantly played by the male gender. The result is following the national survey conducted in 2009, which showed that the total households headed by women in South Africa were 39.8%, comprising all races (Statistics South Africa, 2009). About the age group of the household heads, the largest groups were between 45 and 49 years of age (23% of the participants). Furthermore, age 50 and above, ages 40 to 44 and ages 35 to 39 comprised 21%, 22% and 20% of the respondents respectively. The age group from 25 to 29 and 30 to 34 together comprised 14% of the heads of the household; the majority of the respondents were older than 35 years (86%). This generally indicates that ownership and involvement of youth in urban agriculture is very low. It is vital to increase the participation of the youth to enhance the accessibility of affordable and nutritious food.

The income level of the respondents is explained in terms of four income categories, namely those who earn a monthly income of R800 or less, those who earn between R801 to R1 500 per month, between R1 501 and R3 500, and those who earn R3 501 or more per month. More than 37% of the respondents earned R3 501 or more, while those who earned between R801 and R1 500 and R1 501 and R3 500 per month comprised 26% and 24% respectively. The rest (12.5%) of the respondents earned R800 or less. This monthly income is income generated mainly from employment and other forms of economic activities, excluding livestock farming or related enterprises. Besides, Table 1 shows different incomes earned from livestock farming. Of the 120 respondents, 71% had a monthly income of R1 000 to R4 999 from livestock sales or livestock enterprises, while 20%, 6% and 3% had a monthly income of less than R999, R5 000 to R9 999, and R10 000 or more respectively. The monthly income from livestock does not include other income the household generates through activities other than livestock.

According to Waters (2009), subsistence farming refers to when a farmer is growing crops or rearing livestock only for household consumption; these farms comprised 22% of the participants in this study. On the other hand, commercial farming is farming for profit (Lai et al., 2018). According to Lai et al., (2018), mixed farming refers to the farming of both crops and livestock. In this study, however, mixed farming is not included, but rather the mix (combination) of commercial and subsistence farming. Table 1 refer to this as a mix of commercial and subsistence farming, not as mixed farming. The majority of the urban farmers who participated in this study were commercially driven or pursued a combination of commercial and subsistence farming. Farming for commercial purposes consisted of 41% and 36% for the local market and household consumption respectively. Identifying the water source is very crucial in analysing the impact of drought. Bloemfontein Phase III residents and participants in the study were provided some options to identify their water sources, as indicated in Table 1. Of the many water source options provided, 75% of the participants said they relied on harvested rainwater i.e., the community is highly susceptible to drought.

Although 13% of the participants did not identify their water sources, and only a fraction identified other options besides harvested rain, it is clear from Table 1 that the main source of water for Bloemfontein Phase III urban farmers is harvested rain. When drought hits this community, at least 75% of them are vulnerable to the impact of drought and the consequences thereof.

Farmers' perceptions of drought, climate change, and its impact

Farmers in general are vulnerable to different livelihood challenges. One of the most recent threats posed to farmers is climate change, and hence farmers' perceptions of climate change are imperative to determine and understand if their decision-making process includes climate risk factors. Therefore, in an attempt to understand the farmers' perceptions of the impact of drought and climate change, the following analyses were carried out.

Perception of the impact of drought

Perceptions of the impact of the drought that is listed in Table 2 were presented to the 120 Bloemfontein Phase III urban farmers in order for them to rank how severe the impacts are. This has been done by making use of a five-point Likert scale, with 1 being not severe, 2 slightly severe, 3 moderately severe, 4 severe, and 5 very severe.

Impact	Not severe (%)	A little severe (%)	Moderately severe (%)	Severe (%)	Very severe (%)
Drying of water resources	8	18	38	13	23
Makes surroundings drier	5	9	26	38	22
Crop failures	6	13	23	14	45
Loss of livestock	6	11	25	33	26
Poor health of livestock and people	6	13	42	20	20
Increase in food prices	6	13	30	29	22
Decline in livestock prices	7	13	40	15	26
Anxiety or depression about economic losses caused by drought	6	13	48	13	21
People may have to move from farms into cities, or from one city to another	4	13	40	25	18
Poor soil quality	5	13	44	19	18
Loss of human life	4	15	53	13	16
Other impacts on livelihood	5	13	52	14	16
Total average	**6**	**13**	**38**	**21**	**23**

Table 2: *Farmers' perceptions of impact of drought*

According to the responses, more than 90% of the farmers perceived the impacts listed in Table 2 to range from slightly severe to very severe. The total average of the entire response indicates that an average of 6% of the respondents perceived the impacts as not severe, while 13%, 38%, 21% and 23% of the respondent perceive the impacts as a little severe, moderately severe, severe and very severe respectively.

Lived experience of drought impacts

Having a perception of the impact of the drought is one aspect, but to have lived experience of it is quite different. From their experience, the

Bloemfontein Phase III urban farmers rated the list of drought-inflicted impact.

Experience	Very high (%)	High (%)	Medium (%)	Low (%)	Very low (%)
Drought has threatened household food security	33	58	8	2	0
Drought has caused food scarcity	26	64	8	3	0
Drought has caused no choice in food preference	18	70	9	1	2
Drought has caused malnutrition	14	69	13	3	0
Drought affects health	20	53	21	6	0
Drought has caused unemployment	22	63	13	3	0
Drought has caused a reduction in household income	18	67	13	3	0
Drought has caused a reduction in spending on festivals	16	62	19	3	0
Drought has caused population migration	13	55	28	3	0
Drought has affected school of children	18	40	38	4	0
Drought has caused homelessness and a sense of loss	15	45	35	4	0
Drought has caused conflict over water in the society	18	47	28	7	1
Drought has caused an increase in the rate of suicide by farmers	13	51	18	13	
Total average	**19**	**57**	**19**	**4**	**1**

Table 3: *Farmers' lived experience of drought*
cts in a range from very high to very low.

To measure the lived experiences, a list of experiences was laid out with a scale of very high to very low in Table 3. The provided Likert scale on the questionnaire used the following measures: 1 - very high, 2 - high, 3 - medium, 4 - low and 5 - very low. Considering the scale of measure from 'medium' to 'very high', a total average of 95% of the participants had been affected by drought-inflicted impacts. In the range of measurements of 'high' and 'very high' lived drought experience, variables such as threatened household food security, food scarcity, no choice in food preferences, unemployment and reduction of household income are perceived impact of drought as compared to other farmers' perceived impact of drought with 91%, 90%, 88%, 85%, and 85%, respectively.

Perceived impact of drought on environment

In this study, participants were asked which aspect of the impact of drought on the environment might require urgent attention. On the scale of 1 to 5 (1 - not significant, 2 - slightly significant, 3 - significant, 4 - fairly significant and 5 - very significant), the participants identified their perceptions of the impact of drought on the environment. From the list provided in Table 4, a total average of 93% of the participant identified all the impacts listed in the table as significant to very significant to be given urgent attention.

Perceived impact	Not significant (%)	Slightly significant (%)	Fairly significant (%)	Significant (%)	Very significant
Natural loss of vegetation	3	13	31	20	33
Drying of water pans for harvesting	3	3	34	19	40
Resource conflict	2	3	33	24	38
Migration of wildlife	2	3	38	22	36
Soil erosion	3	3	39	15	41
More wildlife	3	3	38	12	45
Lack of food and water for wildlife	3	1	27	8	61
Total average	**3**	**4**	**34**	**17**	**42**

Table 4: ***Perceived impact of drought on environment***

The participants also included deforestation, loss of wetlands and destruction of wildlife in their own words.

Perception of climate change

Climate change is arguably one of the most pressing global issues of the 21st century. According to Lee et al. (2015), 44% of adults globally have never heard of climate change, and these authors further stress the importance of climate change awareness and risk perception. Hence, it was crucial to know the perception of the farmers on the importance of the issue of climate change. Figure 2 captures the perceptions of the participants on the issue and importance of climate change.

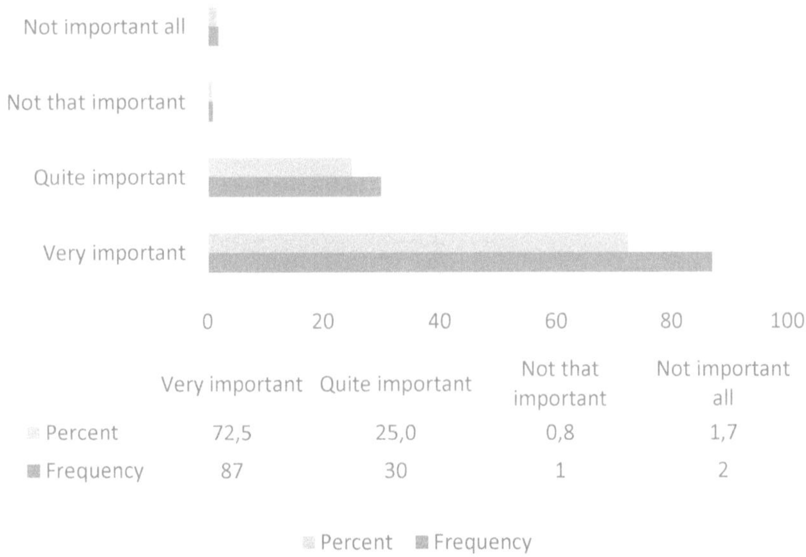

Figure 1: *Perceptions of importance of issue of climate change*

The farmers were asked how the issue of climate change was important to them personally, given the options of 1 being very important, 2 being quite important, 3 not that important and 4 not important at all.

The general response on the importance of climate change shows that the Bloemfontein Phase III farmers' perceptions were that it is 'very important'. Out of 120 respondents, 72.5% believed that issues of climate change are 'very important', while 25% believed it to be quite important. The general notion of the responses underlines the perception of farmers that they believe the issue of climate change is important. This implies that farmers have a considerable understanding of the impact of climate change on their farm operations.

Drought and vulnerability

Impact of drought on social and economic life

The Bloemfontein Phase III urban farmers have been affected by drought previously. They rated the socio-economic impact of the drought they have encountered in Table 5.

Impact	**Not severe (%)**	**Slightly severe (%)**	**Moderatel y severe (%)**	**Severe (%)**	**Very severe (%)**
Severity of drought on loss of employment	0	2	59	12	28
Severity of drought on reducing expenses on education/training	2	0	8	63	28
Severity of drought on psychological stress	0	0	53	16	31
Severity of drought on increasing stress and conflict in the family	0	3	60	8	28
Total average	**0.5**	**1.25**	**45**	**25**	**29**

Table 5: *Understanding of the severity of drought impact*

The impact of drought varies from a loss of employment, reduced expenses on education and training, psychological stress, and increased stress to conflict in the family, which the participants rated from moderate to very severe, at 98%, 98%, 100%, and 97% respectively. From this result, it is clear that the Bloemfontein Phase III farmers have encountered the harsh realities of the impact of drought on their social and economic lives.

Food consumption pattern during drought

Among the many impacts of drought, the rationing of food is very prominent. In Figure 3, the food consumption patterns of the participants during drought seasons have been captured based on their responses. Although 5% of the participants reported an increase in food consumption during the drought season, 92.5% of the farmers responded otherwise. A total of 92.5% of the respondents experienced a decreasing pattern of food consumption. The above result is not a surprise, considering that food shortages are one of the main impacts of drought.

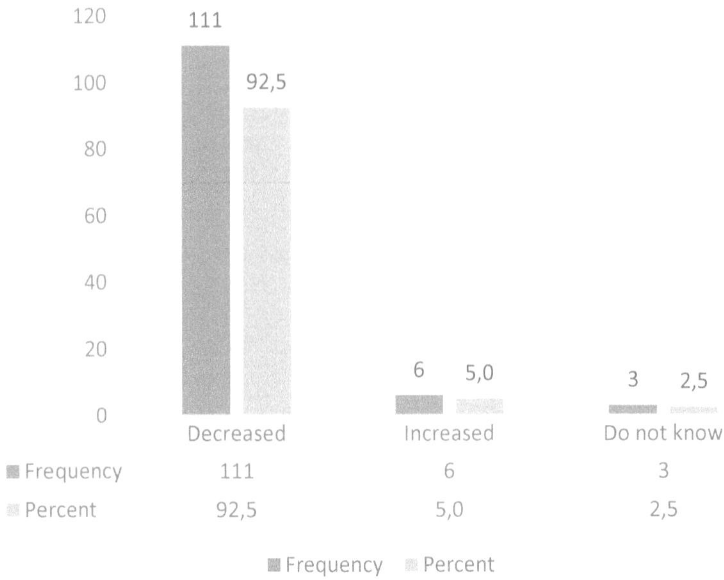

Figure 2: *Food consumption pattern during drought season*

Adaptation and coping mechanism

Adaptation and coping mechanisms are two essential concepts to overcome the challenges of drought or climate change. In the following sections, the main coping mechanisms used by the farmers, helpful drought-relief services they have identified and the section of the government that they receive support from are identified.

Main coping mechanisms

The majority of the participants (more than 70%) identified their coping mechanisms as follows:

- NGO interventions in the community – rely on goodwill

- Rainwater harvesting – susceptible to drought
- Maintaining flexibility in decision making that directly or indirectly influences the functionality of the farm

Generally, the above responses are not very assuring or dependable as coping mechanisms. NGOs function based on their goodwill, and also depending on rain as a coping mechanism makes them to be highly vulnerable to drought.

Governmental support

In this section, the participants were asked to choose from a list of government support options on the questionnaire. The list includes the drought relief assistance scheme, farm household allowance, rural financial counselling service, farm business concessional loans, drought community programme, managing farm risk programme, enhanced social support, and none of the above as options. Figure 4 shows that only 91 participants out of 120 answered this question and the remaining 29 participants left the space blank. Therefore, the 91 responses were considered as the total population in this section. Out of these total responses, 76% of the participant used rural financial counselling services to adapt and cope with drought, followed by 7% who used the drought relief assistance scheme and 8% who used a farm household allowance.

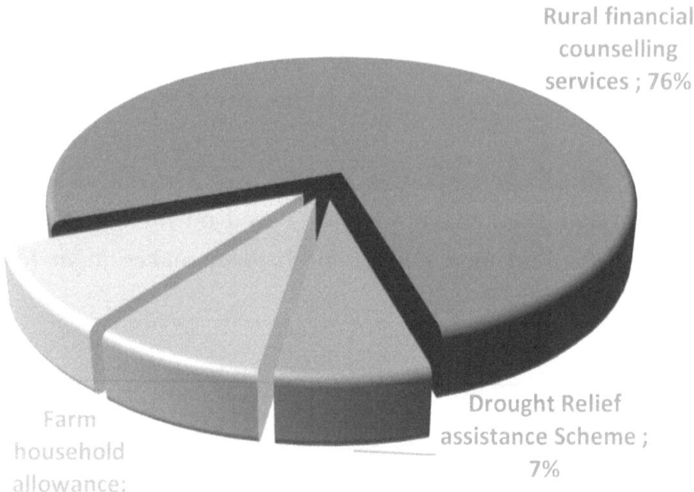

Figure 3: *Government support*

Urban livestock agriculture and drought impact

Urban agriculture is critical in supplying the local demand for different agricultural produce. Therefore, it is essential to evaluate the contribution of urban agriculture to enhancing livelihoods, the challenges it faces, and the level of coping therewith, as well as support, either received or currently needed.

The significance of the current level of farm activity

In this study, all the participants were asked to rate the significance of their current farm activity in improving their household income or food security. Figure 5 shows that the majority of the farmers identified their farm activity as poor. This implies a lack of support for, and less attention being given to urban agriculture.

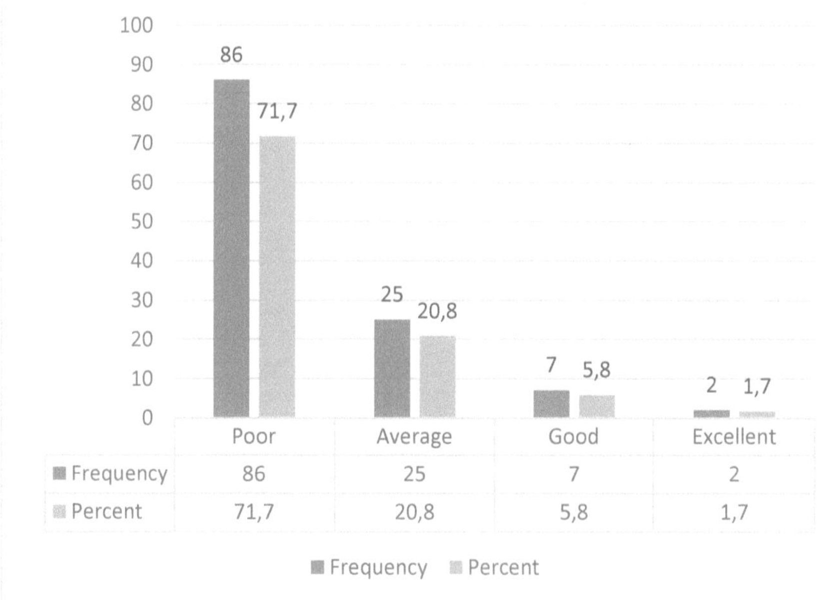

Figure 5: *Agricultural activity in improving income/food security*

According to Figure 4.12, 71.7%, or 86 out of 120 farmers, rated their agricultural activity as poor in terms of contributing to improving their household income and food security. Furthermore, 20.8% rated this as average, 5.8% as good, and 1.7% as excellent. Generally, the majority response being 'poor' or 'average' shows the stunted growth of urban agriculture.

Challenges of urban agriculture

As presented in Table 6, the main challenges of urban agriculture are listed, and the study participants identified their responses from not critical to very critical challenges.

Challenges	Very critical (%)	Critical (%)	Moderately critical (%)	Less critical (%)	Not critical (%)
Access to arable land	22	1	62	11	5
Restriction emanating from legislation and/policy	20	1	5	68	7
Access to financial and other supports	21	2	6	64	8
Lack of skills and knowledge	21	2	62	11	5
Lack of recognition of the sector	22	16	50	5	8

Table 6: *Challenges of urban agriculture*

The majority of the respondents identified access to arable land, lack of skills and knowledge, and the lack of recognition of the urban agriculture sector as moderately critical to very critical challenges. In the current state, Bloemfontein Phase III urban farmers believe that access to financial support and restrictions from policy and legislation are less critical challenges. From the general responses, it is clear that the Bloemfontein Phase III urban farmers are struggling with access to arable land and a lack of skills and knowledge about farming. Although access to financial support and restrictions emancipating from legislation and policy are also deemed as challenges, they are not on their priority list. Based on the responses in Table 4.15, the researcher asked the participants to rate their level of response from 'poor' to 'excellent' to circumvent or cope with the challenges. Figure 4.13 below shows that 71% of the respondents' level of coping with the challenges identified in the preceding section was average. The remaining 26% had a poor level of coping with the challenges, and only 3% had an 'excellent' level of coping with the challenges.

Support received

The most recent drought, in 2015/2016, has left many vulnerable, and the urban farmers in Bloemfontein Phase III are no different. Different programmes by the government and NGOs provided support in the response of the drought. Figure 6 shows that 95.8% of urban farmers (respondents) in Bloemfontein Phase III had received no support. Having almost no support for animal food supplies has precarious results. This situation leads to a loss of animal life, which leads to food and financial crises that eventually create a vicious cycle of poverty. Considering the vulnerability of the urban farmers, the researcher suggests the recognition and inclusion of urban farmers in the government support structure for farmers during times of drought as a first step.

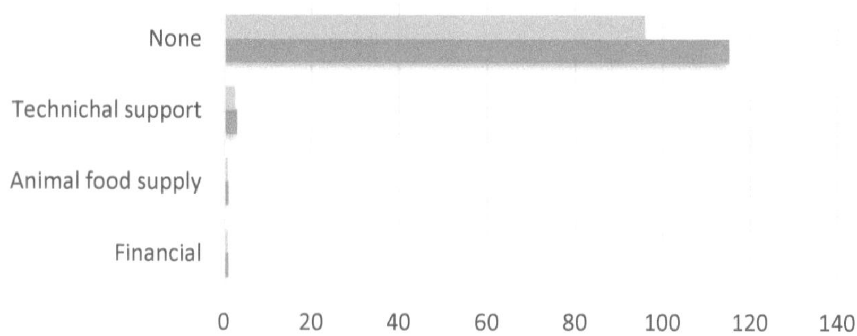

	Financial	Animal food supply	Technichal support	None
Percent	0,8	0,8	2,5	95,8
Frequency	1	1	3	115

Percent Frequency

Figure 5: *Support received in recent drought*

Correlation of major constructs

Correlation is a statistical procedure that defines the relationship between two variables. Correlation coefficients range from +1 to –1. If the result of two variables is closer to +1, this means that they have a strong positive correlation. However, if the result of the two variables is closer to –1, this implies that they have a strong negative correlation. On the other hand, if the result is closer to 0, this means that their relationship is weak or that they do not have a relationship (Coakes, 2005). Generally, to determine whether to analyse the relationship or not, we look at the significance, which is referred to in the table as Sig. (two-tailed) or, in other words, the *p*-value has to be less than or equal to 0.005 to consider the significance of the relationship. All the p-values in Table 4.16 are 0.000, which means that the relationships between the constructs are significant.

		Farmers' perceptions of drought	Drought and vulnerability	Urban livestock agriculture	Adaptation and coping mechanisms
Farmers' perceptions of drought	Pearson correlation	1			
	Sig. (2-tailed)				
	N	120			
Drought and vulnerability	Pearson correlation	.467**	1		
	Sig. (2-tailed)	.000			
	N	120	120		
Urban livestock agriculture	Pearson correlation	-.513**	-.550**	1	
	Sig. (2-tailed)	.000	.000		
	N	120	120	120	
Adaptation and coping mechanisms	Pearson correlation	.560**	.674**	-.599**	1
	Sig. (2-tailed)	.000	.000	.000	
	N	114	114	114	114

** Correlation is significant at the 0.01 level (two-tailed)

Table 4: *Correlation of major constructs*

The relationship between drought and vulnerability and farmers' perceptions of drought had a moderately strong positive relationship with the value of the Pearson correlation of 0.467 and a p-value of 0.000. Urban livestock agriculture had a moderately strong negative relationship with farmers' perceptions of drought and drought and vulnerability, with Pearson correlations of -0.513 and -0.550 respectively. Both relationships were significant, with a p-value of 0.000. Adaptation and coping mechanisms had a strong positive relationship with farmers' perceptions of drought and drought and vulnerability, with a Pearson correlation of 0.560 and 0.674 respectively.

Conclusion and policy recommendations

Urban agriculture can reduce poverty and enhance food security amongst the poor, who are vulnerable to the high cost of food in the urban areas. Therefore, this study evaluated the impact of drought on urban agriculture and the coping strategies put in place to deal with drought by the urban livestock farmers. Descriptive techniques and inferential statistics were employed to explore the impact of drought on urban agriculture among livestock farmers in Bloemfontein, Free State Province of South Africa. The result of the study shows that majority of the participants were male, at 67%, while the rest (33%) were female. Furthermore, 87% of the total participants were older than 37 years. Most of the respondents had a monthly income from the livestock of less than R4 999, and the highest qualification below matric. More than 69% of the respondents owned 11 or more livestock, and 75% depended on rain harvesting as a main source of water. The majority of the participants identified their farms as being affected seriously by drought. Furthermore, more than 90% of the participants were aware of climate change and believed that it was important to address the issue of climate change. Besides, 95% of the respondents did not receive early-warning information and 93% were not registered for a drought-relief programme. Urban agriculture training is the ideal vehicle for educating people to live healthy lifestyles and care for their natural environment. The Phase III Bloemfontein urban farmers are generally highly vulnerable to drought, with little government support during drought. With appropriate institutional support, much potential exists for building sustainable livelihoods by promoting urban agriculture on the Cape Flats, as well as in other African urban centres. Generally, the urban farmers are highly vulnerable to drought, with unreliable dependence on NGO interventions and rainwater storage as coping mechanisms. Also, urban farmers have extremely low access to information and early warning systems. From a policy point of view, urban farming, in general, has not been given much consideration, neither have the farmers received relief support during drought seasons. It is, therefore, recommended that improvement should be made towards access to grazing and arable land, adequate workshops, and training in various farming activities. In the same vein, provision of water supply by the municipality, veterinary services, and financial and technical support should be made available as a panacea for improved livelihood.

References

Amusan, L. & Olutola, O. (2017). Paris Agreement (PA) on Climate Change and South Africa's Coal-Energy Complex: Issues at Stake. *Africa Review,* 9(1), pp. 43-57.

Belle, J., Sithabile, M., & Ogundeji, A. A. (2017). Assessing communal farmers' preparedness to drought in the Umguza District, Zimbabwe. *International Journal of Disaster Risk Reduction, 22,* 194-203.

Bryan, E., Ringler, C., Okoba, B., Roncoli, C., Silvestri, S., & Herrero, M. (2013). Adapting agriculture to climate change in Kenya: Household strategies and determinants. *Journal of environmental management, 114,* 26-35.

BFAP. (2016). Policy Brief on the 2015/2016 drought. https://www.up.ac.za/media/shared/108/2016/2016%20Working%20Papers/policy-paper-1-bfap_policy-brief-on-2016-drought.zp102058.pdf.

Coakes, S. J. (2005). SPSS: Analysis without Anguish-version 12.0 for Windows, John Wiley & Sons Australia. Ltd, Queensland

Dakalo, M., Owusu-Sekyere, E., & Ogundeji, A. A. (2019). Smallholder Farmers' Adaptation to Drought: Identifying Effective Adaptive Strategies and Measures. *Water, 11*(10), 2069.

Davis, C. L., Timm Hoffman, M., & Roberts, W. (2016). Recent trends in the climate of Namaqualand, a megadiverse arid region of South Africa. *South African Journal of Science, 112*(3-4), 1-9.

Dagel, K. C. (1997). Defining drought in marginal areas: the role of perception. *The Professional Geographer, 49*(2), 192-202.

FAO. (2011). The state of the world's land and water resources for food and agriculture (SOLAW): managing systems at risk. Food and Agriculture Organization of the United Nations, Rome and Earthscan, London.

FAO, (2012). FAO's views on bioenergy. http://www.fao.org/bioenergy/47280/en/. Accessed 7 Nov 2012.

FAO, 2013. FAOSTAT. FAO, Rome, Italy.

Gallaher, C. M., Kerr, J. M., Njenga, M., Karanja, N. K., & WinklerPrins, A. M. (2013). Urban agriculture, social capital, and food security in the Kibera slums of Nairobi, Kenya. *Agriculture and human values, 30*(3), 389-404.

Deutsche Gesellschaft für Internationale Zusammenarbeit (GIZ); RUAF Foundation; Food & Agriculture Organization of the United Nations. City Region Food Systems and Food Waste Reduction—Linking Rural and Urban Areas for Sustainable and Resilient Development; Food & Agriculture Organization of the United Nations: Roma, Italy, 2016.

Habitat, U. N. (2003). The challenge of slums: global report on human settlements 2003. *London: Earthscan.*

Holsten, A., Vetter, T., Vohland, K., & Krysanova, V. (2009). Impact of climate change on soil moisture dynamics in Brandenburg with a focus on nature conservation areas. *Ecological Modelling, 220*(17), 2076-2087.

Matteson, K. C., & Langellotto, G. A. (2017). Bumble bee abundance in New York City community gardens: implications for urban agriculture. In *Urban Horticulture: Ecology, Landscape, and Agriculture* (p. 193). Taylor and Francis New York.

Haysom, G. (2015, September). Food and the city: Urban scale food system governance. In *Urban Forum* (Vol. 26, No. 3, pp. 263-281). Springer Netherlands.

Lai, J., Widmar, N. J. O., Gunderson, M. A., Widmar, D. A., & Ortega, D. L. (2018). Prioritization of farm success factors by commercial farm managers. *International Food and Agribusiness Management Review, 21*(6), 817-832.

Ngaka, M. J. (2012). Drought preparedness, impact and response: A case of the Eastern Cape and Free State provinces of South Africa. *Jàmbá: Journal of Disaster Risk Studies, 4*(1), 1-10.

Niñez, V. K. (1985). *Household gardens: theoretical considerations on an old survival strategy* (Vol. 1). International Potato Center.

Ncube, A., Mangwaya, P.T., & Ogundeji, A.A. (2016). Assessing vulnerability and coping capacities of rural women to drought: A case study of Zvishavane district, Zimbabwe. *International Journal of Disaster Risk Reduction, 28*, 69-79.

Olivier, D. W., & Heinecken, L. (2017). Beyond food security: women's experiences of urban agriculture in Cape Town. *Agriculture and human values, 34*(3), 743-755.

Olivier, D. W. (2018). Urban agriculture in Cape Town: Building sustainable livelihoods. In *Handbook of Sustainability Science and Research* (pp. 129-143). Springer, Cham.

Ogundeji, A.A., Jordaan, H and Gronewald, J. (2018). Economics of climate change adaptation: a case study of Ceres – South Africa, Climate and Development, 10:4, 377-384, DOI: 10.1080/17565529.2017.1301866

Poulsen, M. N., McNab, P. R., Clayton, M. L., & Neff, R. A. (2015). A systematic review of urban agriculture and food security impacts in low-income countries. *Food Policy, 55*, 131-146.

Randalls, S. (2010). History of the 2 C climate target. *Wiley Interdisciplinary Reviews: Climate Change, 1*(4), 598-605.

Raubenheimer, S. (2011). *Facing climate change: Building South Africa's strategy*. African Books Collective.

Shah, M., & Steinberg, B. M. (2019). Workfare and human capital investment: Evidence from India. *Journal of Human Resources*, 1117-9201R2.

Sheffield, J., Wood, E. F., & Roderick, M. L. (2012). Little change in global drought over the past 60 years. *Nature, 491*(7424), 435.

SAWS (2016) Weathersmart: Scientific meteorological and climatological news from the South Africa Weather Services. http://www.weathersa.co.za/Documents/Corporate/WeatherSmart%20August2016.pdf.

Udmale, P., Ichikawa, Y., Manandhar, S., Ishidaira, H., & Kiem, A. S. (2014). Farmers' perception of drought impacts, local adaptation and administrative mitigation measures in Maharashtra State, India. *International Journal of Disaster Risk Reduction, 10*, 250-269.

Waters, T. (2009). Social Organization and Social Status in Nineteenth and Twentieth Century Rukwa, Tanzania. *African Studies Quarterly, 11*(1).

Webb, N. L. (2011). When is enough, enough? Advocacy, evidence and criticism in the field of urban agriculture in South Africa. *Development Southern Africa, 28*(2), 195-208.

Wilhite, D. A., Sivakumar, M. V., & Pulwarty, R. (2014). Managing drought risk in a changing climate: The role of national drought policy. *Weather and Climate Extremes, 3*, 4-13.

Chapter 12
Indigenous Knowledge Contribution to Food Security in Bushbuckridge Local Municipality, South Africa: The case Study of Wild Fruits

Monicca Bhuda, Kutullo Nick Shai, Thabang Motswaledi, and Phemelo Marumo

Introduction

Rural African societies have been endowed with "unique" skills with which to carry out activities and make significant progress since the time of their forefathers. Despite this, people fail to recognize the value of indigenous knowledge as a source of "unique" knowledge for enhancing sustainable development. Indigenous knowledge has not been adequately incorporated into construction programs (Wole and Ayanbode, 2009). Poverty, epidemics, civil strife, economic turmoil, terrorism, and corruption, to name a few growth devourers, have all ravaged Africa (Dike, 2015). Indigenous knowledge is a valuable asset in terms of local people's social capital and is one of their key sources of income (Masango, 2010). For example, farmers in developing countries have used their IK to plan agricultural production to ensure food security and long-term agricultural production (Mascarenhas, 2003). IK will be used interchangeably with Indigenous Knowledge.

According to Van Wyk (2011), more than 100 different plant species are used as traditional fruits in South Africa alone. Traditional fruits such as Marula and Prickly pear are important because of their high nutritional value and ability to survive in harsh environments (Lephole, 2004; Modi & Bornman, 2004; Nesamvuni, 2000; Van Vuuren, 2006). Traditional fruits and crops thrive during droughts and in areas where rainfall is scarce or unpredictable, in the case of this chapter being the Bushbark ridge area in the Mpumalanga province. People's indigenous food security strategies have thus continued to maintain their livelihoods for decades.

However, hunger and food insecurity in South Africa is the product of centuries of colonial and apartheid policies that were intended to establish general conditions that were unfavorable to black people's overall well-being, specifically in their rural areas (Altman; Hart, & Jacobs, 2009). Even though hunger still exists in South Africa, the country has made strides in reducing extreme poverty, thanks in part to a progressive, pro-poor tax structure that promotes the provision of social assistance, health, education, and other free basic services (Motala *et al.*, 2015).

Defining indigenous knowledge and indigenous knowledge Systems

Indigenous knowledge and indigenous knowledge systems do not have a single meaning. As a result, indigenous knowledge is described in this chapter as what indigenous people know and do, and what they have known and done for centuries –methods that have developed through trial and error and have proven adaptable to change (Bhuda, 2019). African indigenous knowledge (AIK), according to Taremwa *et al.*, (2016), is an unenforced body of knowledge. It exists in a variety of minds, languages, and skills, as well as in as many classes, cultures, and environments as are currently accessible. Utilizing Uganda as a case chapter, Akullo *et al.*, (2007) have depicted how IK in agriculture has been used for the storage, processing, and protection of food.

Okoye and Oni (2017) further concur by noting that households maintain food security by storing and preserving food without jeopardizing potential food intake, resulting in access, entitlement, and security. The majority of agricultural produce is stored and processed using simple indigenous knowledge and practices in most parts of Africa such as Uganda (Akullo *et al.*, 2007). These strategies are mostly used by women, who are the primary contributors to food security, and they provide income and jobs (Amusan & Olutola, 2017). Cereals and legumes, for example, are essential components of the majority of people's diets, and issues related to their cultivation, storage, marketing, and processing are crucial (Tanyanyiwa & Chikwanha, 2011).

Indigenous knowledge system (IKS) is closely related to IK, according to Du Toit (2005), and is concerned with local communities' relationships with their environment, as well as their knowledge, stories, beliefs, rites, and rituals evolved over long periods and passed down through socialization from one generation to another. IKS is an emerging field of the chapter, according to Taremwa *et al.*, (2016), that focuses on ways of understanding, seeing, and thinking that are passed down orally from generation to generation. Indigenous awareness is culturally unique in the sense that different cultural groups have different structures that are specific to their way of life and the world in which they live.

Since IKS is diverse, new pearls of wisdom are introduced to the current body of information regularly. If the climate changes, so do people's values, beliefs, lifestyles, food security strategies, and knowledge systems. However, the change from one setting to another is incremental, and adaptation measures are important to sustain some impact (Du Toit 2005). Rural people value IKS, but it is not valued in the urban world, and this difference makes rural people more susceptible to food insecurity (Kamwendo & Kamwendo 2014).

Defining food security

Food security refers to a condition in which all people have access to nutritious food and healthy drinking water at all times (Maxwell, S. and Smith, M., 1992; Gregory, 2005; Pinstrup-Andersen, 2009; Gahukar, 2011; Walls, 2019). Food protection was viewed in the form of access to healthy and nutritious food at the 1996 World Food Summit (WFS) (Report of the World Food Summit, 1996). The World Forum on Food and Sovereignty in 2001, on the other hand, focused the idea of food security on personal freedom to establish their policies and strategies for sustainable food production, production, and utilization. However, it should be noted that whether or not food security is achieved is determined by several interrelated factors (Kamwendo & Kamwendo 2014).

Indigenous knowledge and food security

Four pillars that support food security are as follows: (i) Food availability: sufficient quantities of food available consistently as previously mentioned that IK methods are utilized to store and preserve food this ensures that there is sufficient availability of food; (ii) Food access: having sufficient resources to obtain appropriate foods for a nutritious diet, having access to wild fruits such as Marula and Prickly pear particularly they being in the wild ensure easy access to this food and in certain instances, no remuneration is needed. And (iii) Food use: appropriate use based on knowledge of basic nutrition and care.

Phasha *et al.*, (2020) has highlighted how culture influences food use and discourages food wasting and this provides an over food use in Africa and how several factors such as IK and culture work together to provide food security; (iv) Stability in food availability, access, and utilization (Capone *et al.*, 2014). Pawlak and Kołodziejczak (2020) stated that food security also includes food quality, supply continuity and regularity, and distribution among various population groups and areas, as well as within households. The majority of the population's access to sufficient and nutritious food is hampered by their low wages. As a result, many people now consider food access to be a luxury rather than a fundamental human right (Chitiga-Mabugu *et al.*, 2016). But culture and IK has provided a space to store, preserve and share food for better food security particularly in the Africa context (Phasha *et al.*, 2020)

Okoye and Oni (2017) argued that traditional food processing and storage methods such as milling and grinding date back thousands of years and unlike electronic and other modern high-tech industries, they existed long before any scientist understood their intrinsic existence and implications. Modern ingredients, as well as traditional food processing and storage methods, are rooted in the people's culture. These include grinding of mealie meal and drying of meat, they are an important body of indigenous knowledge that has been passed down through the generations and should be properly guided, registered, and promoted.

Study site

The research was carried out in the Hluvukani indigenous community, which is part of the Bushbuckridge Municipality in the Ehlanzeni district of Mpumalanga. Hluvukani is a Tsonga-speaking town in Mpumalanga's Bushbuckridge Local Municipality. It is west of the Manyeleti Game Reserve and south of the R531 highway. In 2011, it had a population of 9,631 (Statistics SA, 2011). With a population of 9,631 (1,255.47 per km^2) and households of 2,191 (285.61 per km^2), the village covers an area of 7.67 km^2. Tsonga is the most widely spoken language in the region, with 95% of people speaking it, Sotho 3%, and others 2%. According to census data from 2011, the population group is mostly made up of 100% Black/African people. The indigenous population of Hluvukani is made up of 55 % women and 45 % men. Farmers with experience of indigenous farming and techniques live in this village. For life, they depend on natural resources and food.

Methodology

Ethno-botanical survey

The ethnobotanical data on plant species were collected from January 2019 to March 2020. The information was collected employing face-to-face interview guides where details such as names, uses, and the availability of the plants was recorded. The knowledge holders were used as participated in the interviews in Hluvukani indigenous community. The identification and recruitment of participants were done with the assistance of a gatekeeper. The identification of the plants was conducted using a literature review (Mashile *et al.*, 2019; Shai *et al.*, 2020).

Data analysis

The chapter at hand has adopted a thematic descriptive method of content analysis, whereby a variety of themes were adopted to better suit the respondent's themes. The chapter looked at interviews and participant observation, they were able to describe their experiences with regards to food preservation and storage. this method of data collection is utilized to generate qualitative data (Gavin, 2008). The organization of the respondent's data was classified following their responses on the subject at hand and the chapter since clustered and made a theme in accordance to their responses as the participants of the chapter. Although many had made observations concerning harvesting, the data was organized with a theme to code the acquired data adequately.

Frequency of citation

The percentage of participants claiming the use of a certain plant species or plant organ for a particular purpose was calculated as follows:

$$FC = (Np / N) \times 100$$

Where Np is the number of participants that claim a particular use of plant species or plant organ as food, and N is the total number of participants. The frequency index was high when many informants mentioned a particular plant and low when there were few reports.

The current chapter applied the frequency of citations (FC), ethnobotanical indices to determine the importance of the indigenous fruits in the chapter area. Also, the ethnobotanical indices were adapted from different studies from the literature. The aforementioned ethnobotanical indices are calculated as follows:

$$FC = (Np / N) \times 100$$

Scientific Name & Family Name	Common Name/ Vernacular Name	Life Form	Plant Part Used	Usage	F.C
Annona senegalensis Annonacea	Motlhepo (N.S); muembe (V); wild custard-apple (E); wildesuikerappel (A)	Shrub	Fruit, root	Edible fruit, Snake repellent, Medicine	100
Carissa edulis Vahl. Apocynaceae	Dithokolo (N.S); mutogwemuhulwane (V); climbing num-num (E); ranknoemnoem (A)	Tree	Fruit, bark, roots	Edible fruit, firewood, medicine, social use	100
Diospyros mespiliformis Hochst. Ebenaceae	Ditshoma (N.S) musuma, mutsuma (V); jackal-berry, African ebony (E); jakkalsbessie (A)	Tree	Fruit, bark, root	Edible fruit, craftwork, medicine	100
Flueggea virosa (Roxb. Ex Willd.) *Royle subsp. Virosa* Phyllanthaceae	Ditlhalabo (N.S); muṱangauma, mavhelematshena (V); whiteberry-bush (E); witbessiebos (A	Shrub	Fruit, root, bark	Edible fruit, beverage, medicine, constructi on, and firewood	41.7
Mimusops zeyheri Sond. Sapotaceae	Mmupudu (N.S); mububulu, mutaladzi (V); red-milkwood (E); moepel (A	Tree	Fruit, root, bark	Edible fruit, medicine, firewood, and craftwork	100
Sclerocarya birrea (A.Rich.) Hochst. subsp. *caffra* (Sond.) Anacardiaceae	Morula (N.S) mufula (V); marula (E); maroela (A)	Tree	Fruit, root	Edible fruit, jam, beverage, medicine	100

Scientific Name & Family Name	Common Name/ Vernacular Name	Life Form	Plant Part Used	Usage	F.C
Syzygium cordatum Hochst. ex C.Krauss subsp. cordatum Myrtaceae	Motlho (N.S); muṱu (V); waterberry (E); waterbessie (A)	Tree	Fruit, root	Edible fruit, beverage, medicine	16.7
Vangueria infausta Burch. Rubiaceae	Mmilo (N.S); muzwilu (V); velvet wild-medlar (E); grootmispel, wildemispel (A)	Tree	Fruit, root	Edible fruit, beverage, medicine	100
Ximenia americana L. Olacaceae	Motsadi (N.S); tshiṱhanzwaṱhanzwan e, mutshilikhomu (V); blue sourplum (E); blousuurpruim (A)	Shrub	Fruit, root	Edible fruit, medicine	83.7
Ximenia caffra Sond Olacaceae	Mochidi (N.S); mutshili (V); large sourplum (E); grootsuurpruim (A)	Shrub	Fruit, root	Edible Fruit, jam, medicine	66.7

Results

Demographic overview of the participants in the study

Table 1 shows the age distribution shows that the majority (41.7) of the participants were 30-49 years old followed by 50-64-year-old (33.3 %) and 65- years and older (25%) individuals. Also, the current results show that knowledge holders show that women (58.3 %) are more dominant than males (41.7%) with the gender distribution (Figure 1). This indicates that more households were head by women were more than men because most of them were not available because they work at distant places in the urban areas. Moreover, the domination of female-headed households is becoming a common trend in South Africa and has been validated by existing research (Mashile *et al.*, 2019; Shai *et al.*, 2020). In terms of household size, the majority (66.7%) of households had 4-5 individuals.

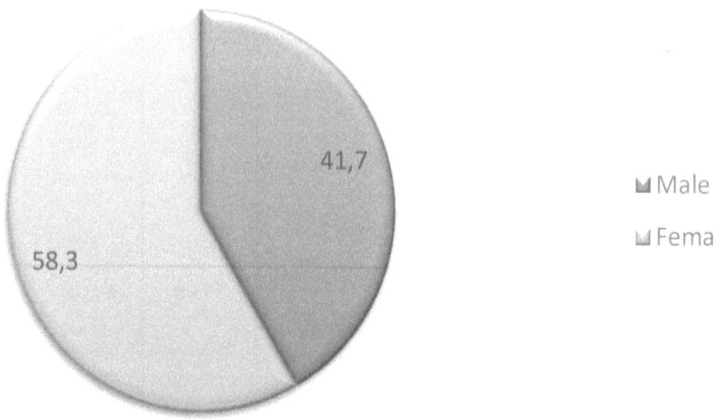

Figure 1: *Age distribution of participants*

Feature	Frequency	Percentage (%)
	Age groups	
20- 30	0	0
30-49	5	41.7
50-64	4	33.3
>64	3	25
Employment		
Full time	3	25
Part-time	2	16.7
Not employed	3	25
Retired	4	33.3
	Household size	
1-2	1	8.3
2-3	3	25
4-5	8	66.7
5-6	0	0
7+	0	0

Table 1: *Demographic characteristics of the participants in Bushbuckridge Local Municipality, Mpumalanga province, South Africa*

Ethno-botanical indices of 5 selected indigenous fruit species

The analysis of the current chapter indicated that 10 indigenous fruit species are popularly utilized in the chapter area (Table 2). The chapter has managed to identify the names of wild fruits used by the community. The participants managed to give out the common names of wild fruits in Northern Sotho. The table indicates the names of wild fruits and their frequency of citation. The Frequency Citation in this chapter revealed that *Annona senegalensis, Carissa edulis, Diospyros mespiliformis, Mimusops zeyheri, Sclerocarya birrea, Vangueria infausta* had the highest frequency citation 100%, followed by *Ximenia americana* (83.7%), and *Ximenia caffra* (66.7%). The least frequently cited plant species were *Flueggea virosa* (41.7%), *followed by* Syzygium cordatum (16.7%). For example, knowledge holders mentioned that there is a great potential contribution of wild fruits to their livelihoods. The chapter has managed to establish the importance of consuming wild fruits for food security in households. It has been mentioned that wild fruits are important for their health as they are part of our cultural diet. They help a lot because when one ate them they get the energy to go through the daily activities. They have multiple uses such as prevention from diseases, supplementary foods, cosmetics, and firewood. Also, similar studies conducted in the neighbouring villages documented the plant species with diverse uses same as the abovementioned (Shackleton *et al.*, 2000; Mashile *et al.*, 2019; Shai *et al.*, 2020). These aforementioned studies suggest that local communities strongly rely on plant species for diverse uses and livelihoods.

Life form and family distribution of selected plant species

A total of 8 families of fruit species were recorded with Olacaceae (n=2) being the most common one (Figure 2). The current results are similar to the chapter by, whereby Olacaceae had the common number of indigenous plant species in Bushbuckridge Local Municipality (Mashile *et al.*, 2019). On the other hand, reported families such as Anacardiaceae, Olacaceae common plant families of wild edible fruit tree species in the neighbouring villages in the Bushbuckridge Local Municipality (Shai *et al.*, 2020). Besides the current chapter, plant parts (fruit, leaves, roots, bark) had diverse uses among the participants (Figure 3).

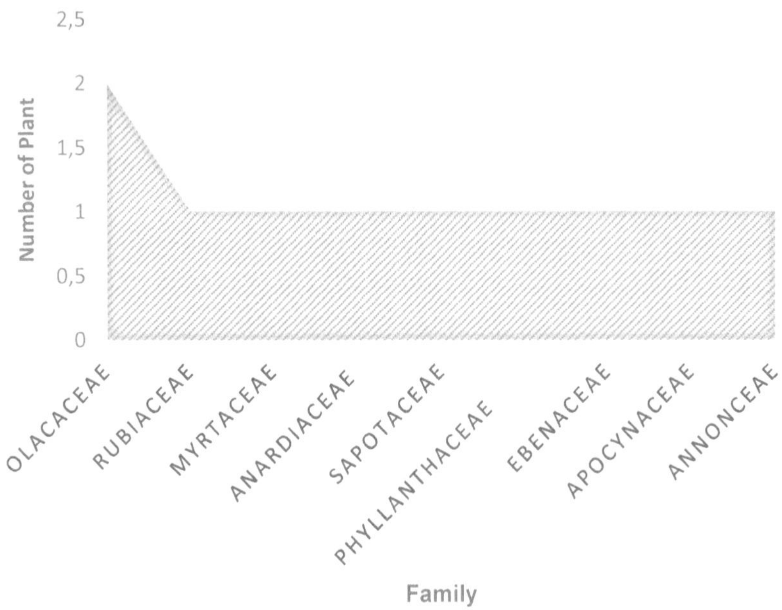

Figure 2: *Plant families of the selected plant species*

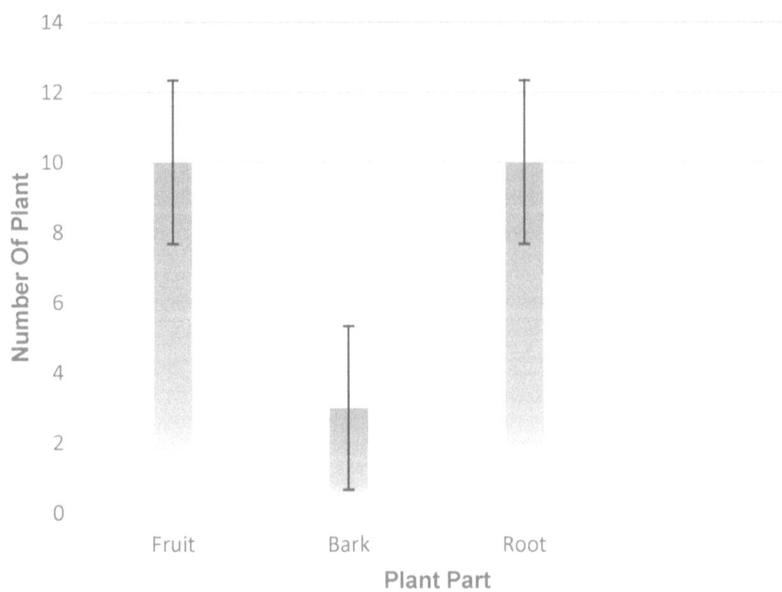

Figure 3: *Plant parts used of the selected plant species*

Table 2: Ethnobotanical information on indigenous plant species used in the Bushbuckridge Local Municipality, Mpumalanga province, South Africa. *Common/ Vernacular name (N.S) = Northern Sotho; (V) = Tshivenḓa; (E) = English; (A) = Afrikaans Sources of information from previous studies (Shackleton *et al.*, 2000; Mashile *et al.*, 2019; Shai *et al.*, 2020).

The role of indigenous knowledge systems in food preservation and storage

IK has always been a huge part of Africa, having limited resources and lack of access to well-advanced technology, Africans have always needed to depend on their knowledge to ensure the survival of their clan or generation. Through socialization, Africans have made sure that this information is passed down from generation to generation. As one of the oldest human species inhabitant areas, and has been under attack from drought and food security over the decades. South Africans have relied on the knowledge of forefathers to store, preserve and ensure food security for the clan.

These methods are passed down to include the grinding of mealie meal, which is done so that the food can be preserved for over a long period, and it will also be able to feed the entire clan or family. Furthermore, the drying of meat is also one of the most significant methods that has contributed to food security through preservation and storing this kind of food. The drying of meat allows it to be cooked in many different ways, creating food that can last over a long period.

The role of IK in harvesting, preserving and storing food

As the participants shared their cultural perspectives of how the methods have been used since time immemorial, the chapter was able to describe the Hluvukani community's harvesting methods. According to one of the participants, there are several different knowledge systems for harvesting and processing wild fruits. "Like the harvesting of *Marula* plants, we have information that as the summer season approaches, we will be able to enjoy pleasant marula (Sclerocarya birrea)," the participant continued.

Participant 2 affirms that harvesting is not a major issue because Mother Nature takes care of us without us having to do much work.

"Like the harvesting and storing of the *Marula* wine, we have information that as the summer season approaches, we will be able to enjoy pleasant marula (Sclerocarya birrea)," the participant continued. Participants 2 and 3 agree that harvesting is not a major issue because Mother Nature takes care of us without us having to do much work". Regardless of family origin, age, or gender, the philosophy teaches community members to share the shared wealth of their natural resources. According to participant 3, when the fruits are edible, they fall to the ground, they pick some to share with the whole family at home.

However, not all of the wild fruits are picked; others are stored and saved for other members of the group. The participants also shared their stories about how they learned about wild fruit harvesting and processing from indigenous experience. Their forefathers taught them how to pick and process these wild fruits. The methods for harvesting the wild fruits mentioned by participant 4 may vary depending on the season and the tree. Furthermore, a participant said, "Like Dithokolo (Carissa edulis), the trees are short and have thorns in the summer season, so when harvesting one must be careful not to be pricked." This will contribute significantly in ensure longer storage and preservation.

Participant 5 claims that certain wild fruits necessitate climbing trees and picking them from the upper branches. As a result, they know how to carefully climb trees without dropping or crushing the fruits that have been picked. Wild fruits naturally occur in forests, according to one of the experience holders, so they do not have to think about planting them. "We have many methods of harvesting and processing depending on the individual wild fruit," the participant said. About how to preserve and harvest the fruits, they use indigenous knowledge passed down from our elders, keeping into cognizance that they will have to store it for later summer use or family sharing.

Participants 7 claims that picking indigenous fruits necessitates learning from elders so that they can select fruits that are not harmful to their health. For example, when out in the wild, one must only select edible wild fruits and then bring them home to feed the entire family. "We first come into realization about the weather season, and then we can say if it is reaping time," the participant continued. The parents instilled in us an awareness of the various seasons. For example, the participants are aware that during the summer, they will consume the fruit of the Marula (Sclerocarya birrea) tree. The fruit's extracts can be used to produce juice and conventional beer.

Furthermore, participant 8 claims that "we go into the wild knowing that the Morula (Sclerocarya birrea) fruit has ripened." The participant also mentioned that processing wild fruits after they have been selected is not a difficult task since they are already fully grown.

Since some fruits require sun drying and storage in a cool location, the processing can vary depending on the fruit tree. "By storing in a cool spot, I mean either putting the wild fruits under a tree so they are cooled by the shade," said participant 9. Digging holes and placing clay pots to store the fruits are also options." The indigenous people explore the forest by observing and receiving vast information on how, where, and when to find wild fruits, according to the report. They venture deep into the wild bushes because they are difficult to reach the start of the wild. They learned how to pick and process wild fruits from their elders. As an example, sun drying fruits to keep them fresh and preserve their value. They also use the process of gathering wild fruits when they bloom. Other wild fruits, which are often found on the upper tree branches, may prefer one to climb the trees.'

Discussion

The Chapter has identified the names such as Marula and Prickly pear of the wild fruits used in the community. The current chapter has found that there is vast knowledge on the dependence of indigenous fruits in the Hluvukani indigenous community. The consumption of wild fruits acts as a cultural diet for the indigenous people as they are freely accessible and the knowledge has been used by knowledge holders (Kuhnlein and Receveur, 1996; Ahmad and Pieroni, 2016). Besides the indigenous fruit species have the highest utilization value in indigenous food resources have an important role in lifting those vulnerable to low diets and illness.

The wild fruits help a lot in enhancing the household food security of the indigenous people. According to Shackleton (2011), "the use of wild foods contributes to livelihoods as both a 'daily net' and as a 'safety net' during crises." For instance, they can help generate some income if sold in large quantities and will bring income to the households. Thus it will help reduce poverty in the family households. Food insecurity is a major concern so wild fruits can help in sustaining the livelihoods of people who are food insecure. Wild fruits play an important role in helping the community in reducing starvation (Kuhnlein and Receveur, 1996; Poulton and Poole, 2001).

Although there is vast knowledge on the contribution of indigenous fruits to household livelihoods, the wild fruits are not given any recognition. FAO (2015) stated that trees in the forests are not given recognition and there is limited documentation. The reason for fruit species to not be given any recognition is because of the introduction of foreign diets. So many indigenous people have lost their cultural diet and attained foreign cultural diets. Today many indigenous fruits were evaded by the European cultural food diet and most of the contribution of Indigenous wild fruits to household livelihoods has not been documented (Katz, 2016). This is why they are not given technical or research support. It therefore impossible for Indigenous people to function well as their diet has not been recognized. Moreover, people suffer from chronic malnutrition and illnesses.

The results have revealed that the consumption of wild fruits has helped in energizing and keeping them healthy. The participants reported that wild fruits are without any negative effects. It was observed by the participants that the body systems function well after they had eaten the fruits. The health benefits of fruit species have been found in the chapter conducted. Participants have revealed the role of wild fruits in community hardships of hunger. The chapter has revealed the role of wild fruits in curing diseases, whereby people have the advantage of preventing diseases by consuming these healthy foods. The findings of the present chapter show that there are many indigenous wild fruits are used depending on their time of availability. They are consumed when they are available in the community. Furthermore, the nutritional composition of wild fruits from this region reveals a positive possible contribution to the diet. Indigenous people in Bushbuckridge also use methods that have been developed locally to store and preserve wild fruits. This is to ensure that there is food security throughout all seasons of the year and for hunger not to be part of the challenges amongst people.

Conclusion

In conclusion, IK is vital in the preservation and storage of food which limits the discourse of food scarcity and ensures food security. African indigenous societies, having been filled with culture and customs over the years, the continents indigenous communities have used these advantages of food preservation to their advantage ensure that there is enough food for everyone, having the advantage of access to nutritious food. This is significant seeing that Africans have always believed in communal working or working together as a community to archive the spirit of humanity. With the use of methods such as grinding and drying of these fruits learned through IK, food security can be assured or limited.

References

Ahmad, K. and Pieroni, A., 2016. Folk knowledge of wild food plants among the tribal communities of Thakht-e-Sulaiman Hills, North-West Pakistan. *Journal of ethnobiology and ethnomedicine, 12*(1), pp.1-15.

Akullo, D., Kanzikwera, R., Birungi, P., Alum, W., Aliguma, L. and Barwogeza, M., 2007, August. Indigenous knowledge in agriculture: A case study of the challenges in sharing knowledge of past generations in a globalized context in Uganda. In *World Library and Information Congress: 73rd IFLA General Conference and Council* (pp. 19-23).

Altman, M., Hart, T. G., & Jacobs, P. T. (2009). Household food security status in South Africa. *Agrekon, 48*(4), 345-361.

Amusan, L. & Olutola, O. (2017). Contexualising African Women's Empowerment in Agriculture: Challenges from Climate Change and Mineral Extraction Perspectives. *Journal of International Women's Studies,* 18(4: 117-130. Available at: http://vc.bridgew.edu/jiws/vol18/iss4/9

Bhuda, M. T. (2019). *The role of ethnomathematics in the cultural life of AmaNdebele women at Ekosini village in Mpumalanga Province.* North-West University (Dissertation: MA)

Capone, R., Bilali, H. E., Debs, P., Cardone, G., & Driouech, N. (2014). Food system sustainability and food security: connecting the dots. *Journal of Food Security, 2*(1), 13-22.

Chitiga-Mabugu, M., Nhemachena, C., Karuaihe, S., Motala, S., Tsoanamatsie, N., Mashile, L., Ngwenya, T. and Magongo, B., 2016. Civil society organisations' participation in food security activities in South Africa.

Dike, S.C., 2015. Sustainable Environment, Economic Growth And Poverty Eradication Measures: The African Context: Why There Is No Meeting Point? *European Journal of Sustainable Development*, 4(2), pp.439-439.

Du Toit, C. W. (2005). The environmental integrity of African indigenous knowledge systems: probing the roots of African rationality. *Indilinga African Journal of Indigenous Knowledge Systems, 4*(1), 55-73.

Gahukar, R.T., 2011. Entomophagy and human food security. *International Journal of Tropical Insect Science, 31*(3), pp.129-144.

Gavin, H., 2008. Thematic analysis. *Understanding research methods and statistics in psychology*, pp.273-282.

Gregory, P.J., Ingram, J.S. and Brklacich, M., 2005. Climate change and food security. *Philosophical Transactions of the Royal Society B: Biological Sciences, 360*(1463), pp.2139-2148.

Kamwendo, G., & Kamwendo, J. (2014). Indigenous knowledge-systems and food security: Some examples from Malawi. *Journal of Human Ecology, 48*(1), 97-101.

Katz, S.E., 2016. *Wild fermentation: The flavor, nutrition, and craft of live-culture foods.* Chelsea Green Publishing.

Kuhnlein, H.V. and Receveur, O., 1996. Dietary change and traditional food systems of indigenous peoples. *Annual review of nutrition, 16*(1), pp.417-442.

Lephole, M. M. (2004). *Uses and nutritional value of indigenous vegetables consumed as traditional foods in Lesotho* (Doctoral dissertation, University of the Free State).

Masango, C.A., 2010. Indigenous traditional knowledge protection: prospects in South Africa's intellectual property framework? *South African Journal of Libraries and Information Science, 76*(1), pp.74-80.

Mascarenhas, A. (2003). *Indigenous Knowledge Livelihood and Development.* Non-Commissioned chapter presented at the Inaugural Tanzanian Biennial Development Forum April 2003, Dar es Salaam, Tanzania. http://www.tzonline.org/pdf/indigenousknowledgelivelihood.pdf Accessed 03 April 2021

Mashile, S.; Tshisikhawe, M.; Masevhe, N. Indigenous fruit plants species of the Mapulana of Ehlanzeni district in Mpumalanga province, South Africa. S. Afr. J. Bot. 2019, 122, 180–183.

Maxwell, S. and Smith, M., 1992. Household food security: a conceptual review. *Household food security: Concepts, indicators, measurements, 1,* pp.1-72.

Modi, A. T., & Bornman, C. H. (2004). Short-term preservation of maize landrace seed and taro propagules using indigenous storage methods. *South African Journal of Botany, 70*(1), 16-23.

Motala, S., Ngandu, S., Mti, S., Arends, F., Winnaar, L., Khalema, E., Makiwane, M., Ndinda, C., Moolman, B., Maluleke, T. and Chola, L., 2015. Millennium development goals: Country report 2015.

Nesamvuni, C. N. (2000). *The use and nutritional value of common edible indigenous green leafy vegetables in the diet of the Vhavenda* (Doctoral dissertation, University of the North).

Okoye, J. and Oni, K., 2017. Promotion of indigenous food preservation and processing knowledge and the challenge of food security in Africa. *Journal of food security, 5*(3), pp.75-87.

Okoye, J., & Oni, K. (2017). Promotion of indigenous food preservation and processing knowledge and the challenge of food security in Africa. *Journal of food security, 5*(3), 75-87.

Olatokun W. M., & Ayanbode, O. F. (2009). Use of indigenous knowledge by women in a Nigerian rural community. *Indian Journal of traditional knowledge, 8*(2), 287-295.

Pawlak, K., & Kołodziejczak, M. (2020). The role of agriculture in ensuring food security in developing countries: Considerations in the context of the problem of sustainable food production. *Sustainability, 12*(13), 5488.

Phasha, L., Molelekwa, G.F., Mokgobu, M.I., Morodi, T.J., Mokoena, M.M. and Mudau, L.S., 2020. Influence of cultural practices on food waste in South Africa—a review. *Journal of Ethnic Foods, 7*(1), pp.1-13.

Pinstrup-Andersen, P., 2009. Food security: definition and measurement. *Food security, 1*(1), pp.5-7.

Poulton, C. and Poole, N., 2001. Poverty and fruit tree research. *DFID Issues and Options Chapter*.

Report of the World Food Summit, 1996. Food and agriculture organization of the United Nations. http://www.fao.org/3/w3548e/w3548e00.htm. Date of access 28/04/2021.

Shackleton, C.M.; Dzerefos, C.M.; Shackleton, S.E.; Mathabela, F.R. The use of and trade in indigenous edible fruits in the Bushbuckridge savanna region, South Africa. Ecol. Food Nutrition. 2000, 39, 225–245.

Shai, K.N., Ncama, K., Ndhlovu, P.T., Struwig, M., Aremu, A.O., 2020. An Exploratory Study on the Diverse Uses and Benefits of Locally Sourced Fruit Species in Three Villages of Mpumalanga Province, South Africa. Foods 9, 1581.

Songok, C. K., Kipkorir, E. C., & Mugalavai, E. M. (2011). Integration of indigenous knowledge systems into climate change adaptation and enhancing food security in Nandi and Keiyo districts, Kenya. In *Experiences of climate change adaptation in Africa* (pp. 69-95). Springer, Berlin, Heidelberg.

Stats, S.A. Population, and Housing Census Indicators; National Statistics Agency: Pretoria, South Africa, 2011

Tanyanyiwa, V. I., & Chikwanha, M. (2011). The role of indigenous knowledge systems in the management of forest resources in Mugabe area, Masvingo, Zimbabwe. *Journal of Sustainable Development in Africa, 13*(3), 132-149.

Taremwa, N. K., Gashumba, D., Butera, A., & Ranganathan, T. (2016). Climate change adaptation in Rwanda through Indigenous knowledge practice. *Journal of Social Sciences, 46*(2), 165-175.

Van Vuuren, L. (2006). Wild vegetables tamed to decrease hunger: Emerging agriculture. *Water Wheel, 5*(6), 22-25.

Van Wyk, B.E., 2011. The potential of South African plants in the development of new food and beverage products. *South African Journal of Botany, 77*(4), pp.857-868.

Walls, H., Baker, P., Chirwa, E. and Hawkins, B., 2019. Food security, food safety & healthy nutrition: are they compatible? *Global Food Security, 21*, pp.69-71.

Chapter 13
Food Insecurity in sub-Saharan Africa: A Review of Agricultural Transformation Agenda (ATA) in Nigeria

Seun Bamidele

Introduction

The grazing conflict between herdsmen and farmers remains a persistent challenge to food production in Nigeria. Food production is one of the major tasks that a sovereign national state must undertake to ensure a decent life for its citizenry. Other institutions like the private sector, civil society, and informal social groups support the state and participate in this task. Governments, therefore, prioritize food production through budgetary allocations and the policy-making processes to ensure that the food supply at least matches the local demand. Even as governments strive towards these goals, the process is often subject to pressures leading to unexpected outcomes even from well-meaning attempts. Since independence, the Government of Nigeria through the Federal Ministry of Agriculture and Rural Development has over the years aspired to improve the well-being of its citizens through various Agricultural policies and programmes. Food production in Nigeria is not nearly as proportionate to the local demand. Farming in most states of Nigeria is still rain-fed and subsistent.

Unfortunately, the majority of farmers in Nigeria is poor and has little or no access to water supply for irrigation, fertilizers, and modern equipment required to sustain significant agricultural production (Abdullahi, 2015). For many years, Nigeria has depended on food imports from other countries to support local production and feed its local population (Aboluwaji and Aderibigbe, 2015). This system has been grossly unsuccessful in meeting local demands all year round (Ademuyiwa, 2013). Nigeria needs to be able to grow and depend on its food and raw materials production for food security and industrial growth (Adamu, 2016). This realization has created the federal government to introduce a policy known as Agricultural Transformation Agenda (ATA) that may be a strategy that focuses on finding the core problems at the guts of restricted food production and delivery of quality standards (Adewusi, 2016). As productivity improves domestically and standards are raised for all citizens' food production, export markets additionally create additional advantages, impacting completely on Nigeria's balance of payments. The major aim of the government initiative is to refocus and empower the agricultural sector (Akimono, 2017). It primarily is set to support local farmers' activities to increase production and feed the local population, especially since the majority of the citizens are low-income earners. This will allow farmers to sell more products and access more markets while also providing an opportunity to sustain the required standard.

Moreover, as violent conflicts between herdsmen and farmers also affect the farmlands required for food production, strategic decisions are required, especially in the agricultural sector as it is unarguably an important aspect of economic liberation. There is, thus, the need to engage traditional farmers to harness the rich agricultural potential of the Nigerian state (Alaba, 2016). ATA is a socio-economic strategy, which focuses on increased agricultural standards and quality as a solution to address starvation and food production. This initiative presents a blueprint to empower local farmers to move from a subsistence farming culture to a standard driven mode of farming which will provide a steady means of income for farmers and secure steady food supply to meet the ever-rising demand for food up to international standards. The innovations called ATA will give rise to other positive social and economic impacts such as the reduction in food prices, development of rural areas, improvement in healthcare, and an increase in production. With many citizens in engagement and involvement, ATA will aid in assisting to small-scale farmers. As evidenced in Nigerian states, the federal government provides support through a subsidy scheme which has helped various states avoid food crisis and has also increased production in the face of the violent clash between the herdsmen and farmers. Therefore, it can be assumed that the adoption of ATA by all state governments is the right step taken to address the food crisis.

Agricultural Transformation Agenda (ATA): An overview

Since 2011, the government of Nigeria at the federal level, after years of benign neglect, has begun to reform the nation's agriculture sector (Atitebi and Sikiru, 2013). To refocus the sector, the government at the federal level through the Ministry of Agriculture and Rural Development applied the Agricultural Transformation Agenda (ATA) on the precept that agriculture is an enterprise and therefore, needs to be supported with the aid of gorgeous programmes (Atoyebi, 2014). The foremost precedence of the programme used to be to restart the clock, reintroducing the Nigerian economic system to sustainable business-like agriculture, which is driven through the personal sector. That approach used to be cited in 2011, with the hope of coming to end in 2019.

The ATA was once commenced as a platform to re-engage farmers in Nigerian agriculture in the direction of a self-sustaining agribusiness targeted economy. The ATA focuses on how to make Nigeria's agriculture extra productive, environment friendly, and effective. Its goal has been to create 3.5 million jobs 2015; generate overseas exchange, and limit spending on meals imports (Audu and Abba, 2015). Among its key achievements is a restructuring of the federal fertilizer procurement device (Audu, 2017). The table below shows the achievement of ATA from 2011 to 2015:

Area	Illustrative Achievements from 2011 till 2015

Input Supply	• Set-up of the Growth Enhancement Scheme (GES) to register smallholder farmers and provide targeted input subsidies (E-Wallet)
	  o GES database contains 10.5 million farmers (data integrity not verifiable)
	  o Targeted means-based subsidies provided to 12 to 14 million farmers between 2011 – 2014
	• Farmers gained improved access to inputs i.e., access to fertilizer and of seeds

Financing	• In partnership with Central Bank and Bankers Committee, set up of Nirsal credit guarantees • Revival and partial N15 billion recapitalization of the Bank of Agriculture • Engagement with commercial banks to finance GES and boost lending to agriculture from ~1% to 6% of all formal credit by 2015 • Creation of special funds to support farmers, for example, N10B Cassava Fund and FAFIN/KfW Facility of $35M
Infrastructure & Logistics	• Designation of staple crop processing zones; 1st site in Kogi for cassava production remains under development • Concession of Federal warehouses and storage assets
Production	• Introduction of new higher-yielding crop varieties e.g., Cocoa, Rice (Faro 42 and 44) • Domestic food production rose by 20.1M tons (claims not evidence-based) o Rice paddy production rose by an estimated 2.0 – 2.5 million tons • Creation of a Federal Dept. of Agricultural Extension
Market Access	• Re-establishment of select commodity marketing boards, for example, Cocoa Marketing Corporation
Others	• Reform of the Agricultural Research Network (ARCN)

Sources: Table 1: *Select ATA Achievements (2011 – 2015) by Value Chain Stage*

The Agricultural Transformation Agenda (ATA) refers to the general development of conventional and quality farming approaches to tackle restricted food production and the implementation of quality products such as genetically modified crops and fertilizers to boost crop growth (Babagana, 2016). The word was coined in 2011, during the administration of former President Goodluck Ebele Jonathan in 2011 and later re-introduced by Audu Ogbeh, the Minister of the Federal Ministry for Agriculture and Rural Development in 2015 under President Muhammadu Buhari as the new government believed in a significant socio-economic involvement. This federal government funding initiative aims to counter the country's policy uncertainty caused by a high initiative turnover of the agricultural programme and workers, which in effect made the implemented of policy instruments highly unpredictable (Bakare, 2016). During the outset of ATA in the immediate past administration, however, the aim was to protect against unequal growth pathways for agriculture, lack of democratic responsibility, integrity, and due process of law relating to deliberate violations of the constitution and subordinate rules dominating Agricultural sector (Bukar, 2017).

Again, another purpose of ATA was to reduce poverty by expanding and building up farming in Nigerian states through the use of several agricultural research methods and science-based technologies (Cindo, 2016). This includes modern, genetically improved seeds and farming equipment. One main objective was to combat the issue of poverty and hunger in the country by vigorously training local agriculturalists on the practices of farming systems (Dahiru, 2016).

As the adoption of ATA began to increase in several states in Nigeria, the Federal Ministry of Agriculture and Rural Development invented more ATA strategies to cater for other popular food crops widely consumed across the nation such as yam, beans, cassava, maize, millet, and sorghum. The policies of ATA combined with the adoption of irrigation schemes have taken agriculture to another dimension as it has led to rapid growth in food production and served as a basis for economic development, especially in the northern region of Nigeria. Climate change and famine were prevented in this country and the fraction of malnourished people declined from 41 percent in 2011 to 37 percent in the year 2015 (Damina, 2017).

Although ATA played a vital role in improving economic growth and food production in Nigeria, much disapproval has been expressed against the scheme. Some have implied that the mechanizations of ATA have led farmers to run into debt as they are too expensive for small-scale farmers to afford (Dilolo, 2014). As a result of the inability to pay debts incurred, many farmers have been forced to give up their land, their source of income (Efome, 2013). This, in turn, has led to a further rise in the level of unemployment and suicide rates among farmers (Amusan & Setlalentao, 2017; , Mohammed, 2017). Also, claims have been made that the ATA has led to "interstate disparities," especially in the northern, western and southern states of Nigeria because its positive impacts have been felt in places where agricultural inputs such as fertilizers are easily accessible (Gambo, 2016). This disparity has brought about a wider gap between poor and rich farmers across the nation.

However, what many critics fail to recognize is that the adoption of these farming inputs has considerably improved weak farmlands in the country. Agricultural Transformation Agenda (ATA) is responsible for Nigeria's economic takeoff, as it has brought about development in many of the rural areas in the northern, western, and southern regions of Nigeria. The agricultural agenda is also accountable for significantly alleviating poverty and hunger in the country since its inception. Production of cereals has drastically increased from 20 to 25.8 million metric tons in 2015 (Hassan, 2015). Another indirect impact of the policy in the country is the reduction of food prices. This has made food more affordable for low-income earners, especially those with high nutritional value (Jamiu 2016).

For these reasons, suggestions have been made that for the complete success of ATA in Nigerian states, it should concentrate more on strengthening farming technologies for the sustenance of small-scale farmers, with support from both the private and governmental sectors. Nevertheless, to promote sustainability, both federal and state governments need to be committed to implementing policy reforms in support of small-scale farmers. Some state governments in Nigeria, for example, Adamawa, Benue, Nasarawa, Oyo, Benue, Ogun, Ekiti, Ondo and Kwara state are beginning to recognize the growing need to invest in the agricultural sector of their states, through dedicating large percentages of their national budget to agriculture and food security (Kande, 2017).

Nigeria and the issue of food insecurity

Food insecurity has been a persistent issue in Nigeria for several years. According to the Jamiu (2010), the word 'food protection' means' that all people have access to adequate, clean and nutritious food at all times to sustain a balanced and active life'. Although food insecurity as described by Kauna (2016), quoting the United States Development of Agriculture (USDA) is a situation where 'consistent access to adequate food is restricted at times during the year by a lack of money and other resources'.

Nigeria is one of the extremely food-insecure countries in Africa and it has remained susceptible to food crisis for several years, as a result of climate change, corruption (on the part of the government), drought, and very importantly, farmers and herdsmen clashes (Akinfenwa, 2015). The majority of the population suffers from chronic malnutrition and starvation (Kanu, 2015), and as a consequence, the citizenry, especially children in the northern region are grossly exposed to deadly vitamin-deficiency diseases.

Over 20 million people in Nigeria are at the risk of dying from hunger and starvation (Kingsley, 2016). Of all the states in the country, hunger seems to be most severe in the north-eastern region (Kolo, 2014). With an approximate population of 23.5 million, 90, 000 children are underweight in the north-eastern region and are expected to die in the next 12 months (Ladokun and Paul, 2017). Displaced people have been unable to farm in the worst-affected areas of Borno, Yobe, and Adamawa provinces, and are now suffering from serious food and insurgency crisis. One of Nigeria's geographical zones is the Northeastern region, composed of the following states: Adamawa, Bauchi, Borno, Gombe, Taraba, and Yobe. It occupies slightly less than one-third of Nigeria's total area and had a projected population in 2011 of 23,558,674, which was about13.5% of the country's population (UNICEF 2017).

In this region, more than half of an average person's income is spent on food alone, leaving them vulnerable to inflation of food prices. Inadequate food production is another reason for the rise in the hunger crisis. Due to the overall poor nature and perception of the country, this will only get worse in areas where there are major disparities between the demand for food and supply as predicted by the Magaji (2017) because of the country's general poor agricultural. There are several limitations to food security in Nigeria as most of its states are faced with numerous problems such as high levels of illiteracy, droughts, inadequate infrastructure, farmers-and-herdsmen crisis, and even overpopulation (Amusan, Abegunde & Akinyemi, 2017). These limitations reduce the competent agricultural labor, thus causing a drastically low production outcome.

However, the major hunger-causing problem in many rural areas, especially in the north-eastern and middle-belt region of Nigeria is poverty, which can be linked to the over-reliance on small-scale farming, the most common occupation among the rural population. Interestingly, many, of the subsistence and small-scale farmers, who produce 90 percent of the food in the country, are sad, the very people crippled with hunger and poverty (Magajiya, 2016). This is because of the high illiteracy level and limited alternatives to the source of livelihoods in those rural areas. Also, the majority, of the population, in this region are farmers who have little or no contact with appropriate farming materials needed for increased production. This limits the path to which farmers can access newly liberalized markets.

For this reason, the development of the agricultural sector through ATA will play a significant role in resolving issues about food insecurity. One of the major setbacks of agricultural growth in Nigeria is the lack of proper farming mechanization such as the use of fertilizers to replenish the degrading soil, modern farming inputs to produce food, and poor facilities for water control and irrigation. This is because farmers do not have access to the three basic farming inputs for beneficial agriculture, which are: fertilizers for soil nutrients, irrigation systems, and comprehensive advice on agriculture (Mallam and Musa, 2017).

The food security challenge in Nigeria has become a national issue. Efforts to tackle poverty and hunger-related challenges that are affecting millions have been stated as a priority of the Millennium Developmental Goals

(MDGs) to be achieved by the end of 2015 (Mohamed, 2016). It is also a major priority under the Sustainable Development Goals (SDGs) to be achieved in 2020 (Micheal, 2013). Many emergency food-assisted programmes from the Federal Ministry of Agriculture and Rural Development have been supporting state governments but this approach has not been successful in putting a stop to food insecurity. Nigerian states cannot keep depending on food support from the Federal Ministry of Agriculture and Rural Development (Mohammed, 2016). The nation is a net importer of food, has the potential to produce its food, and become a net exporter of food. This, however, can only be possible with a combination of both the federal and state government's will and investments to support farmers with modern farming technologies. Nigeria, indeed, needs to be able to grow and depend on its food for development to take place.

Currently, in Nigeria, agricultural yields are relatively lower in some parts than in others, as many lack access to necessary agricultural inputs (Momoh, 2015). Investments in the agricultural sector need to be made to reduce hunger and starvation and promote sustenance. To achieve this, recommendations have been provided for federal governments to put in place, policies and initiatives to support small-scale farmers by developing degraded environments, through the provision of soil fertilizers and seeds, necessary infrastructure, as well as risk management and credit initiatives for crop yields and access to land. However, since state governments are not strong enough to achieve these on their own, there has been a call for the federal government to assist in averting hunger and starvation related problems. This is where ATA comes in, an Agricultural agenda that primarily provides "modern scientific techniques for managing soils, water, and seed varieties" (Muhammad and Kasaore, 2017). It is obvious that Nigeria needs ATA, Nigeria needs a change and until those actions are taken, the country will continue to be estranged from the benefits of the national and regional markets.

Appropriate actions need to be taken urgently as appeals have been made to implement efficient mechanisms, including public-private partnerships to provide farmers with critical tools and support for ATA in Nigeria. Besides, the federal and state governments have a major role to play in supporting these small-scale farmers through policy reforms that provide subsidies on farming inputs if ATA is to be more successful.

Agricultural Transformation Agenda in the Nigerian State

The impression that ATA has never made any positive attempt at improving agriculture across the various states may not be completely true as an attempt was initially made by the pioneers of ATA though they failed. Efforts to implement ATA were initially not successful since farmers in Nigeria were not educated in the use of modern seeds, fertilizers, and other chemicals proposed by the federal government, and also, the majority of state governments were not fully devoted to developing their respective Agricultural sectors. In addition to providing farmers with the modern method of farming, ATA has been designed to promote the national agricultural participation by training agricultural scientists for crop development and also by modifying agricultural policies towards a greater impact.

Small-scale farmers are currently participating significantly in the research and analysis of ATA to provide sustainable agricultural measures. The farmers have been placed as the central concern since they make up the major proportion of poor people in the country. There is a crucial need to adopt the use of a modern way of identifying quality seeds for agricultural development to take place. As the best qualities of seeds are made available, farmers can grow and produce more food, thereby, allowing them to participate in markets and earn more money. As seen in many Nigerian states, the rate of adoption of these seeds is increasing (Muideen and Kareem, 2016). For instance, the rate of adoption in Nigeria is 88 percent, through the help of ATA. This has brought about higher yields with relatively fewer farming inputs (Muili and Paul, 2016). This has proven to have positive indirect social influence in the rural areas where children are now more available to attend schools as less labour is required in the fields.

Concerning the use of modernized seeds, many questions have been raised about how such crops will grow considering that most lands are highly infertile. This situation, however, is caused by the little or no access of farmers to essential fertilizers. The subsistence farming system usually ignores cropping activities that conserve good soil formation. An essential tool for increased food production is the use of fertilizer. Fertilizers are very critical to crop growth as many farmlands in Nigeria lack vital soil nutrients such as nitrogen and phosphorus. Farmlands are also being overused with no provisions for replacing soil nutrients. This has been a huge problem for over 30 years in the nation's agricultural history, causing a relatively less than average production of crops of about 1 ton per hectare (Oladejo, 2017). The federal government, state governments, international institutions, and scientists are now recognizing the need to enrich soils for increased food production. This is very important because due to the high cost of these fertilizers and the poor condition of the transport system, many Nigerian farmers are unable to afford and access them.

Nigeria-Benue State experience

In Benue state, the farmers and herdsmen crisis continues to limit food availability and access for households, particularly in Agatu, Buruku, Gowen, Tiv-Guma, Guma, Tse Abatse and Tse Yoo, Tarok Wase and Gwer-West, for several consecutive years (Olakunle, 2016). Impacts of farmers and herdsmen violence in Benue state, Nigeria continues to limit access to food, water, and health services as the clashes persist in the state. Even, the information from recently liberated populations confirms that acute food insecurity could be occurring in the worst affected and less accessible pockets of the state (Olonisakin, 2016). Populations in several recently accessible Local Government Areas (LGAs) centers in Borno state remain in emergency acute food insecurity; recent information from these areas show larger gaps in basic food needs and suggest high levels of acute malnutrition. While there has been some improvement in food assistance delivery and government services in these Local Government Areas (LGAs), there are still security risks and limited opportunities for Internally Displaced Persons (IDPs) and returnees (Oluwasesanmi, 2017).

Development is bound to take place with the increase in agricultural production is serving, as agriculture is the bedrock for economic and social advancements in any state. During the 1980s and early 1990s, many Nigerian leaders in Benue, both of the military and civilians, saw the need to introduce the use of fertilizers on farmlands to increase production. Due to the challenge of a violent crisis in the state, Benue state government under Governor Samuel Ortom introduced the adoption of direct subsidies on fertilizers to enable small-scale farmers to afford them. With the help of the subsidy programmes, it was recorded that the Benue state also had a notable increase in food production (Rani, 2017). However, the program was short-lived as many federal government policies began to go against the policies of the state towards the effective distribution of these inputs, because of the fragility of the state as a result of farmers and herdsmen violence. This negative development brought about a rise in food prices, following series of food crises, which left small-scale farmers vulnerable to other negative social impacts such as theft of crops.

Benue state, one of the major food-producing states in Nigeria, suddenly being faced with the chronic food crisis, shows significantly how food insecurity can be attained through the destabilization of small-scale farmers. With a population of over 4.2 million, according to the 2006 population census, Benue state has a large dependency on agriculture where about 90% of its labor force is in the agricultural sector (Salim, 2015). After many years of farming and little access to the use of fertilizers, Benue state began to face the low production of food, with a rise in the food crisis in 2015 (Solomon, 2017). From the Benue state government report, about 4.2 millions of Benue inhabitants were in dire need of food support with an average population density of 99 persons per km2 (Tanko, 2017). The then Governor, Samuel Ortom, decided to abstain from dependence on food importation but rather take action by re-introducing the farm input subsidy programmes through ATA, for the subsidies on fertilizers, and to modify crops for small-scale farmers. The use of fertilizers almost doubled between 2010 and 2017 (Tajudeen and Mudashiru, 2015). This support programme, from the federal government has accounted for an increase in the production of maize, Benue's staple food with a price drop of 57% in 2016, allowing average households to afford and consume more food (Wojuade, 2017).

In addition to the subsidy programme, the Benue state government set up rural food projects to provide support for farmers in rural villages. These projects were set up in rural communities with extremely poor farmers where 20kg of maize seeds and a significant amount of fertilizers were distributed to different households (Yacuba, 2017). Food production in 2017 nearly tripled and as the food crisis began to reduce, food production increased, with the excess production of food being distributed to other states (Yahaya, 2017). This drew much attention, even from the federal government. Contrary to the negative criticisms of the Benue state government subsidy programmes, it has been able to substantially raise food security in households in rural communities within the state. According to the Benue state government report of 2016, the subsidy programme has contributed immensely to eliminating severe hunger and poverty from 60 to 40 percent only between the years 2015 and 2016 (Yusufu, 2017).

Considering the success of the subsidy programme to avert food crisis, it is clear that it has been beneficial to Benue as well as other state governments such as Adamawa, Sokoto, and Kastina state have watched Benue grow, many are now looking into adopting such schemes. However, for such a scheme to work effectively, the Benue state government needs to fully commit to supporting small-scale farmers through investments in farming inputs. Nonetheless, concerns are being raised as to whether this form of agricultural reform is a sustainable approach in dealing with the food crisis with the ongoing effects of climate change. The Benue state government is aware of the consequences and has made provisions for farmers to adjust with these inevitable effects, through crop insurance programmes, the extension of irrigation schemes and water sources from rural areas, and also the planting of seed varieties with higher climate tolerance.

Concerning Benue's fertilizer subsidy programme, Federal and state governments, however, being aware of these challenges to sustainability have introduced a soil protection program that has been making improvements in dealing with these environmental effects. With the introduction of soil management, small-scale farmers have observed the need for fertilizers. Over 723,000 farmers have now greatly benefited from this program (Yusufu, 2017). Recognizing the high costs of fertilizers, the programme has also sought ways to assist needy farmers through funds from farmers associations and cooperatives and also credits from banks. One of such associations is the Agricultural Development Bank.

About Benue's subsidy programme, ATA intends to improve the productivity of the soil with the provision of fertilizers in smaller more affordable packages and also the subsidies on fertilizers through vouchers which can be obtained in local areas. The federal government supporting Benue state government in Nigeria, have pledged to support small-scale farmers. As seen in the Nigeria fertilizers programme in Abuja, a pledge by the Benue state government was made to financially support agro-dealers (the village traders who deal on fertilizers, farm equipment) through the Nigerian Agricultural Cooperative Bank and Nigerian Agricultural Insurance Bank, having understood that these fertilizers are crucial for achieving Nigeria's ATA (Oluwasesanmi, 2017). With the sustainability of these programmes in question, ATA promises a better solution. The establishment of 170 million naira aims to drastically expand food production through state governments in Nigeria.

Conclusion

In this article, the importance of federal government policies, alongside the use of modern farming technologies, has been projected as an effective approach to feed Nigerians. Looking at how ATA was able to avert poverty in Nigerian states, many state governments have been showing interest in being able to grow and maintain food production for the benefit of its people. It has been argued how states in Nigeria have been food insecure for decades due to the high poverty rate. The majority of people in Nigeria live below the poverty line where many earn as low as a dollar per day, or even less. It is obvious Nigerians need help, and with agriculture being a great potential source of wealth, there is an intense need for ATA to support Nigerians in exploiting such potential effects. This article agrees with the aims of ATA to solve Nigeria's food insecurity by concentrating on small-scale farmers since they hold the key to agricultural development. Since they also contribute immensely to the population of Nigerians living in poverty, there is a strong need to empower these farmers as a way of tackling the ever-increasing poverty rate.

Many state governments in Nigeria are aware of their incapacity to feed their members due to the challenging economy and political structure, and have called for an increased ATA effort, in addition to federal government supports to help the state governments in building up their agricultural sectors with the help of farming inputs. This development will also be beneficial across other social sectors. For example, with the adoption of these modern farming inputs, less labor, especially of children will be needed on farmlands, and this would encourage more children to attend schools.

Though many claims that ATA only offers short-term solutions to feed Nigerians, this article has shown that Nigeria needs an urgent response to its food crisis. As opposed to evaluating the situation without concrete solutions, ATA has been able to substantially tackle the ongoing situation. In general, provisions of ATA have had more beneficial than negative effects. With many Nigerian leaders in support of the scheme, the interests of small-scale farmers are bound to be prioritised.

References

Abdullahi, Buba. (2015). "Agricultural Transformation in Nigeria: Trends, Complexities and Implications for Food Security Africa." *Agricultural Review,* vol.7, 2015. p.5

Aboluwaji, Olawale and Aderibigbe, John (2015) *Agriculture and Food Production in Modern Age,* Ibadan: Arowosegbe Publishers

Adamu, Kauda (2016) *Agricultural Transformation Agenda: Development and Practice,* Dutse: Hadijah Publishers

Ademuyiwa, Yahya. (2013) *Food Supply in Nigerian Communities,* Kaduna: Al-Salaam Publishers

Adewusi, Paul (2016) *Agricultural Policies and Food Security in Nigeria,* Zaria: Lallia Publishers

Akimono, Railwon. (2017) *Reforms in Agricultural Sectors in the Nigerian States,* Lagos: Liman K. K. Nigeria Limited

Akinfenwa, Otunba (2015) Challenges of Food Security in Nigeria, *Ekiti State Journal of Agriculture,* vol.1, no. 1, pp.34-45

Alaba, Olowu (2016) The Future of Nigeria Lie with Food Security, *Apex Journal of Agricultural Science,* vol.1, no. 2, pp. 35-77.

Amusan, Lere, Abegunde, Ola and Akinyemi, Temitope E. (2017). Climate Change, Pastoral Migration, Resource Governance and Security: The Grazing Bill Solution to Framer-Herder Conflict in Nigeria. *Environmental Economics,* 8(3), 35-45.

Amusan, Lere and Setlalentoa, Marilyn. (2017). An Assessment of Socio-Cultural Aspect of Large Scale Food Production Policies and Politics in Africa. *Transylvanian Review,* XXV(17), pp. 4347-4356.

Atitebi, Muideen and Sikiru, Muritala (2013) Agricultural Transformation Agenda in Nigeria: An Overview, *Apex Journal of Agricultural Studies,* vol.2, no. 1, pp. 1-23

Atoyebi, Isaiah (2014) Business and Agricultural Policies in Nigeria, *Briefing Paper* No. 1, Private Agricultural Business Centre.

Audu, Patrick and Abba, Muhammed (2015) *Agricultural Transformation Agenda (ATA): What is wrong with the policy?* Jigawa: Hadahia Publishers

Audu, Samson (2017) *Food Security in Nigeria: Policies and Issues,* Monograph No. 1, Department of Agriculture and Aquatic Management, Sokoto State University, Nigeria

Babagana, Nathaniel (2016) *Agricultural Transformation Agenda (ATA): New Strategies in Food Production in Nigeria,* Unpublished Seminar Paper, presented at the Department of Agriculture and Rural Development, Bayero University, Kano

Bakare, Cicilia. (2016) *Policy Instability in Agricultural Sector: What is Agricultural Transformation Agenda (ATA)*? Lagos: Daily News Publication

Bukar, Awadi (2017) *The Dynamics of Agricultural Transformation Agenda (ATA) and Food Security: Nigerian Experience*, Zamfara: Zamsibad Publishers

Cindo, Faula (2016) *Agricultural Transformation Agenda (ATA) and the Cost and Finance of Food Security in Nigeria*, Monograph No. 4, Department of Agriculture and Fishery Management, Bayero University, Nigeria

Dahiru, Umaru (2016) The Subject Matter of Agricultural Transformation Agenda (ATA) and Food Security, *Working Paper* 1, Department of Agriculture, Madibbo University of Science and Technology, Adamawa State

Damina, Tijani (2017) Climate Change, Food Security and Famine in Northern Nigeria, Unpublished Ph.D. Seminar paper, Department of Agriculture, Taraba State University, Nigeria

Dilolo, Nana (2014) The Benefits of Agricultural Transformation Agenda (ATA) Intervention in Nigeria, *Agricultural Report*, No. 13, Brass Agricultural Centre, Lagos

Efome, Umaru (2013) Agricultural Transformation Agenda (ATA) and Mechanised Farming in Nigeria, *Journal of Agricultural Studies*, vol. 1, no. 2, pp. 78-89

Gambo, Wasiu (2016) Agricultural Transformation Agenda (ATA) Campaign in Nigeria, Unpublished Ph.D. Thesis, Department of Agriculture, Tafawa Balewa University, Nigeria

Hassan, Isaiah. (2015). Food Security and Production of Cereal in North-East Nigeria, *Agricultural Insight*, 12 April 2015

Jamiu, Ahmed (2016) *Agricultural Transformation Agenda (ATA) in Nigeria: An Analytical Interpretation of Agricultural Policies*, Ilorin: Danfra Publishers

Jamiu, Hamed (2010) *What is Food Security?* Ilorin: Danfra Publishers

Kande, Mohammed (2017) *Agricultural Transformation Agenda (ATA) and the Nigerian States*, Handbook of Agricultural Policy, Benue State University Press

Kanu, Lawal (2015) Planning against chronic malnutrition and starvation in Nigeria, *Journal of Agricultural Management*, vol. 4, no.1, pp.67-78

Kauna, Patrick (2016) Food Security and Food Insecurity in Africa, Unpublished Ph.D. Seminar, Department of Agronomy, Ekiti State University, Ekiti State, Nigeria

Kingsley, Garba (2016) *Given Strength to People with chronic malnutrition and starvation'*, Benue: Evelon Publishers

Kolo, Buba (2014). Chronic malnutrition and starvation in the north-eastern region of Nigeria, *International Journal of Agricultural Studies*, vol. 1, issue 2, pp. 1-7

Ladokun, Dayo and Paul, Kehinde (2017) *Insecure Community in north-eastern Nigeria*, Ila-Orangun: Gold Publishers

Magaji, Ruaf. (2017) Perceptions of Food Security: An Introduction, Monograph, Department of Agricultural Science, Benue State University, Nigeria

Magajiya, Sulaimon. (2016) Poverty and Food Security in Nigeria, Department of Agriculture, Osun State College of Education, Ilesha, Nigeria

Mallam, Umaru and Musa, Titus. (2017) Shortage of Fertilizer Supply in Nigeria, *Kano Journal of Agricultural Science*, vol. 3, no. 2, pp. 14-34

Micheal, John. (2013) *Food Security and Agricultural Development in Nigeria: Issues and Prospects*, Enugu: Wiscar Publishers

Mohamed, Marwa (2016) Millennium Developmental Goals (MDGs) and Sustainable Development Goals (SDGs) in Nigerian Agricultural Sector, *Jemix Journal of Agricultural Management Studies*, vol.1, no. 2, pp. 34-48

Mohammed, Abdullahi (2016) New Challenges for Federal Ministry of Agriculture and Rural Development, *Sokoto Journal of Agricultural Studies*, vol. 2, no, 2, pp. 1-27

Mohammed, Mohammed. (2017) Agricultural Transformation Agenda (ATA): The Rise and Success of Nigeria Unpublished Academic paper, Department of Agriculture, Madibbo University of Science and Technology, Adamawa State

Momoh, Ganiyu (2015) *Managing Agricultural Sector in Nigeria: Issues and Options*, Unpublished Ph.D. Seminar paper at the Department of Agriculture, Bauchi State University, Bauchi, Nigeria

Muhammad Kauna and Kasaore, Tarwa (2017) *Introduction to Agricultural Development in Nigeria*, Hadijah: Dutse Gunmi Publishers

Muideen, Quyuim and Kareem, Wahab (2016) Agricultural Regulations and the Food Marketing in Nigeria, *Biu Journal of Agricultural Science*, vol.1, no. 2, pp. 21-31

Muili, Ebenezar and Paul Crush. (2016) N*igeria and African Transformation Agenda (ATA): Way Forward*, Zamfara: John King Publishers

Oladejo, Peace (2017). *Issues in Agricultural Sector in Nigeria*, Ibadan: Badjoko Publishers

Olakunle, Isaiah. (2016) *Agriculture Transformation in Benue State*, Abeokuta: Adeagbo Publishers

Olonisakin, Akinwale (2016) Food Insecurity in Benue State, A paper presented in the Conference of Nigerian Agricultural Association, Abuja

Oluwasesanmi, Funke (2017) *Farmers and Herdsmen Violence: Food insecurity in Benue State*, Unpublished Paper presented at the Taraba College of Education, Taraba state

Rani, Wahab (2017) Contemporary Issues in Benue State, *Journal of Agricultural Science*, vol. 1, no. 1, pp. 11-26

Salim, Kaka (2015) *Evaluation of Food Insecurity in Benue State, Nigeria*, Handbook on Food Security, Ilorin: Haliazad Publishers

Solomon, Garba (2017) *The Selected Opinion of the Expert Opinion on Benue Food Security*, Lagos: Paul Flowers Publishers

Tajudeen, Rilwan and Mudashiru, Bbuba (2015) Agricultural Subsidy Programmes in Benue State, Offa: Abdusalm Publishers

Tanko, Haliu (2017) Field Research on Food Support in Benue State: Issues of New form of Food Security, Unpublished Diploma Thesis, Department of Agriculture Science, Osun State College of Education, Ilesha, Osun State

UNICEF (2017) 90,000 children are expected to die in Nigeria over the next 12 months, Unicef warns http://www.independent.co.uk/news/world/africa/ nigerian-children-starve-to-death-2017-nigeria-africa-help-unicef -international-community-aid-a7546176.html (accessed 02 February, 2018)

Wojuade, Awoniyi (2017) *Production of Cereal Crops in Benue State, Nigeria,* Lagos: Alfred Copt Publishers

Yacuba, John (2017) Reflections on Food Security and Fertilizer Distribution in Benue State, *Journal of Agricultural Science,* vol. 2, no. 1, pp. 90-110

Yahaya, Karba (2017) *Food Production and Food Crisis in Benue State,* Abia: Zainab Publishers

Yusufu, Halima (2017) *Mapping Strategies against Food Security in Benue State,* Lagos: University of Lagos Press

Chapter 14
Food Security and Boko Haram Insurgency in Nigeria: The Northeast Experience

Utibe Monday TITUS and Justin IJUPTIL

Introduction

Historically, Nigeria has been described as the fastest-growing economy in Africa and a country with strong growth potential in agricultural produce (Idachaba 2009; Eme, Onyishi, Uche & Uche, 2014; Modupe, 2019). The sector has been transformed by commercial activities from the small to medium and large-scale enterprises. Before the discovery of crude oil in Nigeria, food production (cash crops mainly) used to be the centrepiece of Nigerian's economy. It serves not only as a source of foreign exchange earnings but also a strong source of employment and poverty reduction. However, with the emerging problem of the various insurgent activities, there is massive destruction of human and natural resources that would have contributed to the sustainable growth and development of the nation including constituting a potent threat to the nation's food security (Osagie, 2013; Titus, 2016). Besides, with the recent (incessant and deadly) attacks by Boko Haram insurgency in north-eastern Nigeria, farmers and marketers lost many lives and properties worth billions of naira with their lands destroyed and confiscated by the insurgents. This incidence has denied farmers and marketers in the area access to their usual economic activities due to the continued threat created by Boko Haram.

This violent conflict in the northeast of Nigeria is growing worse. Almost five million people in the region (8.5 million across the wider Lake Chad basin) are facing severe food insecurity. This primarily is a result of insurgency by Boko Haram, which provoked forced displacement as well as massive infrastructure destruction. The food crisis in the northeast of Nigeria (and across neighbouring Lake Chad basin countries, Cameroon, Chad, and Niger), currently Africa's largest humanitarian emergency, has its roots in the conflict with Boko Haram that began in 2009 (Amusan & Ejoke, 2017; Amusan & Oyewole, 2015). Over the last seven years, fighting has caused the deaths of more than 20,000 people and displaced almost two million, with another 200,000 fleeing to neighbouring countries (ICG, 2017). At present, Nigeria is facing huge food security challenges both in terms of food availability, access, utilization, and sustainability owing to pervasive insurgent activities in different parts of the country. For example, in the northeast, the Boko Haram insurgency has forced some of the crop farmers and pastoralists to abandon their lands and relocate to the neighbouring countries of Niger, Chad, and Cameroun, while those left behind could no longer go to the farm for fear of attacks (Walker 2013; World Bank, 2012; Modupe, 2019). The consequences of these to the region concerned are low agricultural production, low income, and increased inflation such as high prices of food and farm products leading to food insecurity and widespread famine (FAO, 2008). It is against this background this study attempts to examine the nexus between food security and Boko Haram insurgency in the northeast of Nigeria.

Statement of the problem

It should be noted that the impacts of the Boko Haram insurgency are so numerous and cut across all aspects of life especially in the north-eastern part of Nigeria. Some of these conflicts have sadly led to a massive loss of lives and property and to environmental destruction with dire consequences for agricultural production and food shortages. The protracted violence in the affected zone has forced large scale farmers to abandon their farming activities in search for their dear lives (Beatrice, 2015). Babagana, Ismail, Mohammed, Dilala, Hussaini & Zangoma (2018) argued that the Boko Haram insurgency has to some extent crippled economic activities and hence led to a reduction in internally generated revenue of some states in the region. For example, the mass displacement of people has resulted to a poor harvest in the northern and some central part of Adamawa state; mainly Mubi North, Mubi South, Michika, Madagali, Maiha, Hong, and Gombi Local Government Areas of the State. The impact of the crisis is multidimensional among which is food, shelter, livelihoods, health, security, and education. The extremely high price of food and its limited availability has been the major challenge to food security since the start of insurgency. It was argued that insecurity at the markets, the inability of farmers to cultivate, and high cost of transportation to affected areas are some factors that account for the high prices of food and their limited availability (Gylych, *et al.,* 2018). For example, prices of cereals in north-eastern markets were between 74% and 120% higher in January 2017, compared with the past two years average price level (FEWS-NET, 2017).

It is obvious that as a result of Boko Haram insurgency, large hectares of farmland were destroyed, markets were burnt down, the emigration of people from affected area meant the cultivation of farmland, animal rearing as well as fishing was abandoned, the imposition of curfew for days meant the restriction of business activities and the closing of international frontiers within the region limited cross-border trade. Many are farmers, as nearly 80 percent of Nigeria's northern population works in the agriculture industry. With an increase in Boko Haram attacks and the displacement of nearly two million Nigerians, agricultural production has plummeted, and staple food prices have sky-rocketed. Northeast Nigeria now faces one of the world's worst food security crises, with around 3.8 million people who face critical food insecurity and around 7.7 million in need of life-saving humanitarian assistance this year (Babagana, Ismail, Mohammed, Dilala, Hussaini & Zangoma, 2018).

The UN Office for the Coordination of Humanitarian Affairs UNOCHA (2017) reported that 4.7 million Nigerians in the northeast now urgently need food assistance, including 1.4 million facing "emergency" and 38,000 famine-like conditions. Over 2.3 million people were internally displaced from their homes and communities. More than 15 million people were reported to be food insecure at the height of the insurgency, among which 5.1 million people were experiencing severe food insecurity (FAO, 2017). The Northeastern states of Adamawa, Borno, and Yobe alone had an estimated 450,000 children under the age of five suffering from severe acute malnutrition (WFP, 2017).

As farmers, herders and fishermen fled or were forcefully uprooted from their communities, agriculture became a major casualty of the violence. The situation was aggravated as thousands of young and able-bodied men, crucial for farm labour, were either killed by Boko Haram or fled both the insurgents and the military. In Borno state, for example, the insurgency's epicentre, staple cereal production plummeted between 2010 to 2015 – sorghum by 82 per cent, rice by 67 percent and millet by 55 per cent (WEP, 2017).

Today, the state, which used to produce about a quarter of Nigeria's wheat, grows none. Oluwashina Olabanji, the Lake Chad Research Institute executive director, revealed that wheat production across the entire Northeast Zone (comprising Borno and five other states) "has declined to just 20 percent of what it used to be due to the insurgency and livestock production also is ruined (ICG, 2017). The Meyati Allah Cattle Breeders Association of Nigeria reported that as of February 2016, 1,637 members were killed, and over 200,000 cattle, sheep and goats, as well as 395,609 sacks of food items, lost in insurgents' attacks in Borno state. Beginning in December 2014, the fishing industry suffered a similar fate as Boko Haram stepped up attacks on communities around Lake Chad.

George, Weatherspoon & Adelaja (2019) revealed that Boko Haram was involved in a total of 2002 conflict incidents in Nigeria, with the north-eastern states of Borno, Yobe, and Adamawa accounting for 80% of those incidents (see also ACLED, 2017). It was also stressed at the height of the insurgency, 26 of the 27 LGAs of Borno State were either fully or partially occupied by Boko Haram (Cooke & Sanderson, 2016). Most of such territories were rural areas where agriculture is the dominant industry. In Borno state for example, at the height of the insurgency, annual grain flow to and from other states was reduced from 300,000 tons in the fourth quarter of 2010 to 100,000 tons in the second quarter of 2014 (Sidney, Hayatudeen & Kwajafa, 2017). With respect to specific crops, in 2016, the production of sorghum, millet, and rice in the state was estimated to have dropped by 82 percent, 55 percent and 67 percent, respectively, compared to the five-year average (Kimenyi, Adibe, Djiré, Jirgi, Kergna, Deressa, Pugliese, & Westbury 2014). The decline of agricultural production in the region is attributed to the restriction of physical access to farms by Boko Haram, regional paramilitary, or the state military (Van Den Hoek, 2017); delays in planting and harvesting due to lack of availability of physical and human capital; abandonment of fields due to huge population displacement (Awodola & Oboshi, 2015; Adelaja & George, 2019); and disruptions in input markets, storage, transportation and sales of harvested crops (Kimenyi *et al.*, 2014; Van Den Hoek, 2017).

Also, food prices also took a significant hike at the onset of the conflict. The USAID's Famine Early Warning Systems Network (FEWS NET) reports that, in January 2017, corn prices in Adamawa were up 31 percent, compared to the previous year, and in Maiduguri, the capital of Borno, prices had increased by 25 percent. The prices of millet were also around 20 percent higher in Maiduguri and in Yobe state. In January 2017, the prices of cereals in northeastern markets were 70%–124% higher than the year before (FEWS NET, 2018). However, from the foregoing facts presented, scholars have presented their views (explanation) concerning this threat and its implication to food insecurity in Nigeria, however, there is no extensive data that explain and compares food security before Boko Haram uprising and its aftermath in Northeastern Nigeria. This is because most of the research conducted were desk research, because no researcher wants to risk a visit to the volatile area to collect data. It is against this premise that the study extrapolates into respondents' perception of the implications of Boko Haram insurgency on food security in the northeast of Nigeria.

Methodology

This study used Adamawa, Borno, and Yobe states as a study area. This is because the three selected states were major food producers in the region and the most affected area by the Boko Haram insurgency. Adamawa, Borno, and Yobe states are located in the north-eastern part of Nigeria; they share virtually the same relief features and political lineage. The major economic activities of the people of the area include farming, fishing, trading, and pastoralist. Four Local Government Areas (Gwoza, Baga, Chibok and Bama) of Borno state, four Local Governments Potiskum, Gujeba, Jakusku and Dapchi of Yobe state and two local government areas (Madagali and Michika) of Adamawa state were contacted, making Ten (10) local governments in all. These farming communities are well known for cash crop production, fish farming, and business activities. The study used a purposive sample technique to collect primary data using structured interviews. Returnees (Farmers, Fishermen, Businessmen/women, Traditional rulers) were contacted for quality data. The data collected include respondent's farming experience, total hectares of land, previous and current output, challenges faced, initial business capital-based, and current capital based as well as a documentary from the national bureau of statistics. Since the study is qualitative data collected were analysed using a simple descriptive technique to illustrate how the Boko Haram insurgency affects food security in the northeast.

Conceptual clarifications

Food security

Lack of food security is food insecurity, while food insecurity means lack of, not having enough food (Richard, 2002). This could be used vice versa. Food insecurity has persisted in Nigeria as a result of a confluence of factors, ranging from inefficient policies of the government for agriculture i.e., failure to properly administer policies and initiatives which has a connection to food. The insecurity of food occurs when people, have no access to means of sustenance, i.e., Safe and nutritious food to meet their dietary needs and food preferences for an active and healthy life. It is a situation where food is not available to an individual; it could affect the behaviour of such individuals, and output towards national development (World Food Summit, 2003). Food insecurity includes hungry or malnourished people, underweight children, and people suffering from malnutrition or micronutrient deficiency. The importance of food to individuals and households is very essential. Nations are said to be partly protected when food is available to its growing population especially when issues of social security are being discussed. But the lives of people come under threat when the privilege to have food is absent (Idachaba, 2004).

There are four sides to food security: Availability of food, Accessibility to food, Utilization of food, and Stability of food supplies at all times. Availability or abundance of food makes a nation partly secured; most especially when issues of social security are being discussed. However, the lives and livelihoods of people come under threat when this privilege is absent or not within one's reach. In this study, food security is best understood in terms of agricultural production, because agriculture maintains an intricate dominance in the region's economy (Wolfe & Frongillo, 2001). Local food production and animal husbandry account for much of the daily food and nutritional needs of Nigerians; this also is a major employment and income-generating activity for both the urban and rural dwellers (Food and Agriculture Organization-FAO, 2013).

Insurgency

According to Powell & Abraham (2006), insurgency refers to a violent move by a person or group of persons (as Boko Haram group) to resist or oppose the enforcement of the law or running of government or revolt against the constituted authority of the state or of taking part in the insurrection. As Imasuen, (2015) argued insurgency as defined above violates the constitution's criminal law and the international treaty obligations of a nation in the following circumstance, when it is:

> An attack on defenseless citizens and other property resulting in injuries, loss of lives and properties as well as forced or massive internal displacement of people out of their habitual places of residence. When it drives business/investors away from an insecure area and also when it constitutes domestic and international crimes punishable by law such as treasonable felony, terrorism, murder, crimes against humanity, and genocide (Powell & Abraham, 2006:34).

Traditionally, however insurgencies seek to overthrow an existing order with one that is commensurate with their political, economic, ideological, or religious goals (Gompert & Gordon 2008). According to Kilcullen, "Insurgency is a struggle to control a contested political space, between a state (or a group of states or occupying powers), and one or more popularly based, non-state challengers". He further draws a line between classical and contemporary insurgencies indicating that the latter seeks to replace the existing order, while the former sometimes strive for the expulsion of foreign invaders from their territory or seeks to fill an existing power vacuum (Kilcullen, 2006; Titus, 2016).

Theoretical underpinning

This study adopted the State fragility theory as a guide to explain the nature of conflict in the region. According to Imasuen (2015), the state fragility theory stresses the fundamental failure of a state to perform functions necessary to meet citizen's basic needs and expectations. It also shows the incapability of government in assuring basic security, maintaining rule of law and justice, or providing basic services and economic opportunities for their citizens. The centrality of state fragility theory posits weak and ineffective central government with little practical control over much of its territory; non-provision of public services widespread corruption and criminality; refugees and involuntary movement of populations (Organisation for Economic Co-operation and Development, 2008).

Rotberg (2003) argued that in a fragile state, there is a tendency for increased criminal violence which further weakens the states' authority. He further stressed that fragile states are usually associated with tensed, deeply conflicted and dangerous warring factions leading to a breakdown of law and order increased humanitarian disaster, which concerns not only the people directly affected but also others in the country as well as people in neighbouring states. As Gros (1996) gives a typical example, that ethnic genocide in Rwanda and the Balkans or flight of Haitians to Florida could hardly be ignored by the international community. Conflicts, humanitarian crises, human rights violations, constitute global and local impacts on fragile states.

Collier, Elliot, Hegre, Hoeffler, Reynal-Querol, & Sambanis (2003) identify three ripple effects that emerge from armed conflict: they are the internal effects (as a result of the burdens of internally displaced persons), the regional effects (as a result of the burden of refugee's influx) and the global effect (as a result of foreign interventionists). According to him, these three ripple effects generate unique challenges. While the internal effects constitute a problem of food insecurity, loss of means of livelihood, rise in the displacement of people, the regional effect constitute spread of contagious diseases across borders from the inflow of refugees and the global effect constitute the growth in narcotics trade across borders sponsored by foreign non- state actors. As Hentz (2004) notes that such spillover has occurred in both West Africa (from Liberia) and East Africa (from the Democratic Republic of Congo).

In this study State, fragility theory is useful in explaining the phenomena, Boko Haram, and food crises in North-East Nigeria. It shows the failure and weakness of the Nigerian state in ensuring security and practical control over her vast territories in the North East region which has been threatened by the Boko Haram insurgency (see Imasuen, 2015). The activities of the Boko Haram sect have increased humanitarian crises in North-East Nigeria especially in the form of food insecurity, leading to a rise in prices of staple foods within the nation and dairy products in neighbouring nations of Chad, Niger, and Cameroon. This continues to increase the rate of refugee influx and adverse economic and security implications.

Insurgency and food security nexus: A review of literature

On the international scale, recent studies have found an adverse effects of terrorism and insurgency on agricultural (food security) and economic development of nations including Burundi, Colombia, India and Iraq. Singh (2012) focuses on Punjabi farmers' labour-related decisions in the face of insurgent violence. This insurgency emanated out of the demand for a Sikh-dominated Punjabi-speaking independent state, to be called Khalistan, which the government of India refused to grant hence resulting in violence since which is focused on India's government and its representative.

Using micro-level farmer expenditure surveys for the period 1981 to 1993 to focus on the monetary amount spent by farmers on two types of hired labour, permanent and casual labour and how it relates to insurgency-related violence. It is found that insurgency-related violence adversely affected farmstead spending on permanent, but not temporary hiring basically because workers wanted short-duration contracts. Although this effect was not generalized for the entire households surveyed as it was found only for the richer half of the surveyed households. In a related study in Singh (2011), argued that the presence of major terrorist incidents in the district of Punjab is found to reduce long term fixed investment in agriculture by as much as 17% in a year. Grun (2008) examine the impact of 2 kinds of violence endemic in Colombia, guerrilla warfare and common delinquency households' portfolio to invest in fixed assets or mobile assets. Using a survey of 11,500 households it finds that fixed asset investment in fixed-assets would go down to the benefit of its mobile counterparts in the presence of guerrilla and paramilitary because they cannot be carried away in case of displacements. However, the reverse was the case in the presence of common delinquency.

Guerrero-Serdan (2009), stressed that the wave of violence and turmoil that started in Iraq since 2003 is seen to have profound effects on the nutritional outcomes of children, as children born in areas with high levels of violence are shorter than children born in low violence areas. In Peru, Leon (2009) finds a negative impact of Peruvian civil conflict on human capital accumulation for children exposed to the conflict. The Peruvian conflict is internal between the government and several terrorist groups starting in 1980 and still ongoing. The negative impact observed exists both in the short run and long run. A similar conclusion was reached by Chamarbagwala & Moran (2011), who finds a strong negative impact of the civil war in Guatemala on female education for girls exposed to the war than for those not exposed. Bundervoet, Verwimp & Akresh (2009) examined the impact of Burundi's civil war on the health status of children exposed to the war and finds that children exposed to war during early childhood are negatively affected. This effect is seen to grow stronger the longer the child is exposed to the war.

According to Le Roch, Pons, Squire, Anthoine-Milhomme & Colliou (2010), the insurgency and sectarian violence in Iraq led to a deepening humanitarian crisis which created about two million Iraqi IDPs within and over two million Iraqi refugee's influx into Jordan, Syria and other neighbouring states in the year 2007. He further indicates how in subsequent years, the Iraqi government ministries have helped in assisting the IDPs through the Ministry of Displacement and Migration (MODM), the Ministry of Education in charge of registering school children who have been displaced. Similarly, the sectarian crisis in Mali has increased humanitarian crisis since 2012, where thousands of IDPs compete for scarce resources. The food insecurity constitutes a major challenge to the Malian government inadequately responding to the humanitarian crisis (Collins, Myatt & Golden, 1998). According to Collins (1993), over one million Somalis have become internally displaced as a result of armed conflicts, this has increased food insecurity, limited access to clean water, sanitation and hygiene (WASH), limited access to medical facilities, outbreaks of diseases and sexual violence among women at various IDP camps (Collins,1993).

It was argued that the armed conflict in the Central African Republic since 2013 has brought about severe humanitarian consequences. The total population in need of assistance is about two million, including 533,000 IDPs. The CAR government responses have been in the provision of integrated life-saving assistance particularly to internally displaced persons'(IDPs), to reinforce the protection of civilians, rebuild affected communities' resilience, and to provide reconciliation and rehabilitation of CAR refugees (see Gonzaga, 2012). Pinstrup-Andersen & Shimokawa (2008) found that poor health and nutrition are associated with a greater probability of civil conflict, though their findings were based on small sample sizes. Countries with lower per capita caloric intake are more prone to experience civil conflict, even accounting for their levels of economic development (Sobek & Boehmer, 2009; Henk-Jan & Cullen, 2011). This relationship is stronger in those states where primary commodities make up a large proportion of their export profile. Some of the countries most plagued by conflict in the past 20 years are commodity-rich countries characterized by widespread hunger, such as Angola, DRC, Papua New Guinea, and Sierra Leone. The mixture of hunger which creates grievances and the availability of valuable commodities – which can provide opportunities for rebel funding is a volatile combination (Henk-Jan & Cullen, 2011).

World commodity prices could also trigger conflict, as higher prices, especially for food, increase affected groups' willingness to fight. In line with this, Timothy & Torsten (2008) found that as a country's import prices increase, thereby eroding real incomes, the risk of conflict increases. Oeindrila, Dube & Juan (2008) arrived at similar conclusions when looking at Colombia, where higher export prices for coffee (which is labour intensive and a source of rural income) reduced violence in coffee-producing areas while higher export prices for oil (which is capital intensive and a source of income for rebels and paramilitary groups) increased violence in regions with oil reserves and pipelines.

Other research links transitory weather shocks to civil conflict. In these studies, Henk-Jan & Cullen (2011) argued that weather shocks like drought and excess rainfall are thought to trigger conflict by causing crops to fail and reducing agricultural employment opportunities, thus increasing food insecurity both in terms of food availability and food access (ability to pay). The people most likely to participate in armed conflict young men from rural areas with limited education and economic prospects are likely to seek work in the agricultural sector. As that work dries up, fighting looks more attractive. However, the empirical link between transitory weather shocks and civil conflict is still ambiguous. Some studies find that civil conflict is more likely to begin following years of negative growth in rainfall (Miguel, Satyanath & Sergenti, 2004; Hendrix & Glaser, 2007), suggesting that drought and decreased agricultural productivity expand the pool of potential combatants and give rise to more broadly held grievances. However, approaches that look at levels of rainfall, rather than growth in rainfall from year to year, find tenuous, or positive relationships, between rainfall abundance and the onset of conflict (Burke, Miguel, Satyanath, Dykema & Lobell, 2009; Buhaug, 2010; Hendrix & Salehyan, 2010).

Some case-based research, however, links drought to conflict though mediated by the government's response to the crisis. For example, during the Tuareg rebellion in northern Mali, drought – aggravated by the government's embezzlement of drought relief supplies and food aid was a significant source of grievance that motivated young men and women to take up arms (Benjaminsen, 2008; Henk-Jan & Cullen, 2011).

Recently, warmer temperatures have been linked to an increase in civil conflict, though this finding has been challenged (Buhaug, 2010). Civil war is also more likely in the aftermath of quick-onset natural disasters, such as earthquakes, major volcanic eruptions, floods, and cyclonic storms (Brancati, 2007; Nel & Righarts, 2008). The relationship between disaster and conflict is strongest in countries with high levels of inequality and slow economic growth; food insecurity and resource scarcity are among the more plausible explanations for this correlation.

At the national level, there are various studies on the impact of Boko Haram activities in Nigeria and the effect of the insurgency on food security basically due to the challenges of the affected individuals to meet their basic food needs.

Insurgencies have been associated with food insecurity in Nigeria. FAO (2002), for example, insurgency, and poor agricultural policies were the major causes of exceptional food insecurity in 2015 and early 2016. The Boko Haram attacks affect food security due to its detrimental effects on the agricultural sector and the economy as a whole. Several studies have been conducted to determine factors affecting food security in Nigeria (Mustapha, 2015) Also, in the North-Eastern zone; the insurgency has led to the declaration of a state of emergency in three states namely; Yobe, Adamawa and Bornu states. Such incessant killings often hinder the day to day activities of local farmers in carrying out agricultural activities. Many farmers have become targets with a number of them were killed while some are abducted (Davies, 2009).

The National Emergency Management Agency (NEMA) revealed that about 65 percent of farmers in the northeast had migrated to the South because of the insecurity they faced. These effects of insurgency have affected sustainable food production and consequently raised prices of foods such as pepper, tomatoes, onions, cowpea, millet, etc., that are majorly cultivated in these regions. George, Weatherspoon & Adelaja (2019) conducted an empirical study on then nexus between conflict and food security. The authors argued that conflict could negatively on food security conditions by destroying agricultural production, distribution, and markets, hindering economic growth, and increasing unemployment levels. In this article, they quantify the causal effects of the Boko Haram insurgency on the food security conditions of Nigerian households, especially their dietary diversity and access to adequate quantity and quality of food during the 2010 to 2016 period.

They used the General Household Survey (GHS) panel dataset for Nigeria, which provides information on various food security measures for a panel of nearly 5000 households across three different periods. Specifically, they examine whether a household's exposure to conflict significantly affects its Food Consumption Score (FCS) and the number of days for which it had to (a) rely on less preferred foods, (b) limit the variety of food eaten, (c) limit the portion size at mealtimes and (d) spend a whole day and night without eating anything. Their time-varying conflict measures, which are constructed at the Local Government Area (LGA) level, include the number of fatalities and the number of attacks perpetrated by Boko Haram. They found that an increase in conflict intensity, measured by the number of fatalities, increases the number of days where the household had to (1) rely on less preferred foods, (2) limit the variety of foods eaten, and (3) limit the portion size of meals consumed. However, the number of days that households went without eating anything, a more severe measure of food insecurity, was not affected. The Food Consumption Score is also negatively affected by conflict. They also found that conflict-driven food insecurity is mainly materialized through agricultural input and income shocks.

In Awodola & Oboshi (2015), the impact of the activities of Boko Haram on food security in Maiduguri, the capital of Borno state is examined. Using fieldwork from 2012 to 2013 from 222 respondents, they found that foreign business individuals deserted their businesses, virtually all businesses and markets in Borno state has collapsed completely; the most affected sector is the agricultural sector with high a cost of farm produce. In a similar study by Mohammed and Ahmed (2015), the impact of the Boko Haram insurgency in Borno state is examined using both primary and secondary data. Primary data were generated from 300 respondents. The study reveals that before the insurgency, the annual grain flow between Borno and her trade partners was 294940 tons; however, the flow of grain decreases to 94,500 tons by the 2nd quarters of 2014. Besides, all traditional trade routes were no longer available.

The report by AGI (2014), the impact of conflict in Northern Nigeria on Agricultural Value chains is examined for Borno state. 4 value chains are concentrated upon with 4 respondents who are all farmers and experienced the conflict in its entirety. For the crop value chain, a substantial decline is observed in the average production of major crops like rice, millet, maize, and cowpea. Also, the amount of fish harvested during the period dropped drastically by almost 80%. For livestock production, the inability to access markets led to the high cost of livestock. Lastly, the agriculture-related value chain experienced a negative impact as investors' confidence dropped and less investment in the agricultural projects is observed for areas most affected by Boko Haram activities (Gylych, Ramat, Selman, Bilal & Natalia, 2018). In general, the studies reviewed show that civil conflict, like insurgency and terrorist-related violence do have an impact in income level, health outcomes, educational attainment, agricultural development and, food security generally among others. The more commonly studied causality in the academic literature on development looks at the role of conflict on in explaining food insecurity. In comparison, the role of food insecurity (and especially severe forms such as hunger or famine) as a driver of violent conflict, i.e., the reverse causality, has not been explored in as much detail (Martin-Shields & Stojetz, 2018).

This study tries to analyse the causal relationships between food security and (insurgency) violent conflict. Recognizing the large qualitative literature on this topic, this study would draw on complementary quantitative case studies to expand one's understanding of the interdependencies between these issues at the micro-level. This paper does not intend to "resolve" the issue of causality or endogeneity in one direction or another, but rather intends to shed light on the complexities of this two-way relationship of the two research field. While identifying causality would be important in this undertaking, the main focus is on demonstrating how varying circumstances could shape the nature of food security and insurgency nexus.

To this end, study directs its concerns on the implications of the Boko Haram insurgency include a negative impact on food availability through the destruction of agriculture, roads, bridges, and border crossing; limited access to markets; and disruptions in the food distribution systems, all of which could have also driven up food prices and reduced food accessibility. The loss of community water supply systems and other rural amenities also suggest adverse effects on aspects of food utilization in the conflict zones. However, empirical evidence of the causal effects of Boko Haram insurgency on food security is non-existent, despite the virulence of the attacks.

Discussions of Findings

How Boko Haram insurgency influences food security in the northeast of Nigeria

This section discusses respondents' perceptions on the nature of the Boko Haram insurgency and how its effects on food security in the region. In doing so, reference was made to data from interviews conducted (primary data) and some literature reviewed by the researchers. In the course of interviewing respondents, priority was given to people (farmers and businessmen) with large hectares of lands as well as prominent businessmen and women in the study areas. Furthermore, the experience of the respondents in a particular line of endeavor was put into proper consideration.

The escalating Boko Haram insurgency has disrupted the lives and livelihood of millions of people in north-eastern Nigeria and caused a deep humanitarian crisis. Despite the recapture of most Local Government Areas (LGAs) in Adamawa, Yobe, and Borno in 2016, several LGAs in the region remain inaccessible either due to the presence of Boko Haram fighters or as a result of the ongoing operations by the Nigerian security operatives to overcome the insurgency. With limited humanitarian assistance and little or no agricultural production during the past three years, livelihoods and food security conditions remain highly constrained in the worst affected localities.

This argument confirms with the recent report which remarked that:

> The majority of the farmers and fishermen are now in internally displaced (persons) camps. Men and women who once produced food fed their families sometimes including numerous dependents have now been reduced to beggars, depending on others to provide for them (ICG, 2017).

The lives and livelihoods of people come under threat when that privilege is absent. Over years, farmers in the north-eastern part of Nigeria, particularly Adamawa, Yobe, and Borno states are no longer able to farm for security reasons especially for fear of attacks by the dreaded Boko Haram insurgents who continued to unleash untold havoc in the part country. This insurgent activity has in turn affected food production and consequently raised prices of foods that are majorly cultivated in these places like pepper, tomatoes and onions, cowpea as well as the production of fish (Amuwa, 2019). This region has been known for the mass rearing of cattle, which made meat available to other parts of the nation but today, the story is not the same (Interviews, 2020).

A raining season farmer in Madagali Local Government Area of Adamawa State lamented on how the Boko Haram insurgence has negatively affected the economy (especially crop production) activities in the area. Thus he remarked that:

> If not for the emergence of this insurgence in our area, I can boldly tell you that today I am a millionaire… (sic). I used to produce ton of beans (Brown and White) but today is a pity that I could not produce even one tons due to the damages created by Boko Haram in our lands (Interview, 2020).

Related to the above, another farmer in Gwoza complained bitterly about how the scarcity of inorganic fertilizer (Urea) has reduced food production in his area. He stated that:

> Unfortunately the fertilizers that we use to have access to in the past have now become not only the hot cake but a criminal offence… (sic). This is because security operatives believed that the Boko Haram uses the fertilizers in making Improvised Explosive Device (IED). According to the farmer lack of access to fertilizer like before has reduced food production drastically especially maize farming that depends much on fertilizer for higher yield (Interview, 2020).

For years, farmers have been unable to sow their crops as the security situation remains too uncertain for them to return to their farms. Landmines and improvised explosive devices also make it dangerous for them to return to their fields. As a result, food security has diminished across the region. Over years, farmers in Yobe state and many parts of the North-Eastern parts of Nigeria, particularly Adamawa and Borno states were no longer able to farm for security reasons especially for fear of attacks by the dreaded Boko Haram sect who continued to unleash untold havoc in the part country. This insurgent activity has in turn affected food production and consequently raised prices of foods that are majorly cultivated in these places like maize, sorghum, corn, beans, peanut, pepper, tomatoes, and onions. Besides, it is noteworthy that this same part of the country has been known for the mass rearing of cattle, which made meat available to other parts of the nation but today, the story is not the same. The gravity of the crisis has brought about a decline in productivity which in turn led to the escalation in the prices of Agricultural output and reduced the per capita income of thousands of farmers.

Also, it was stressed that rising prices of food and other services in Adamawa for example, have always been linked to a high rate of insurgency in the region. There are challenges to low productivity, mass displacement, and a decrease in internally generated revenue of the state. Consequently, farming activities in many parts of these states were seriously hampered by the insurgency leading to a very significant drop in crop production which in turn led to food security.

Another respondent (farmer) remarked that fear of insurgence has stopped many farmers from going to (bush) farms. He stated that "unlike before that we used to walk kilometers and even slept in the (bush) farms. But today we only concentrate only on subsistence farming; this is due to the incessant kidnapping of our wives and children" (Interview, 2020).

Similarly, a Village Head and also a seasonal farmer in the Dapchi community lamented on the hardship created by the insurgency in his district. This captured his position:

> To be candid our people have suffered and still suffering, it even takes a strong mind to survive this trauma. A farmer that uses to produce 50 to 60 bags in the past is now competing for measures of rice in the IDP camps. He further stated that the most annoying thing

> is that even though we (farmers) produced our crops, Boko Haram frequently attack and burn our houses and sometimes lot of our food. This has discouraged many farmers to produce large crops like before due to the fear of uncertainty (Interview, 2020).

On his part, a renowned rural farmer and a businessman express his mind on the effects of the insurgency on farming and business activities in his area. He stated thus:

> Though as a person I am seriously against Boko Haram ideology. But when one looks at the situation critically, we can say that it is a blessing in disguise for a few people like me. The hectares of land that I used to produce 60 bags of Bean seed between 2000-2007 can now produce 73 bags. This is because the land was left uncultivated (fallowed) since Boko Haram captured our town in 2013. I think the land might have naturally regained its fertility (Interview, 2020).

Other respondents lamented that another major criminal activity greatly affecting food security in the region is cattle rustling (which is the act of stealing herds of cattle ranging from 50 to 200, 300). Before the crisis, Potiskum (in Yobe State) used to be the largest cattle market in West Africa. But now, it is deserted. Recently, the Bauchi State police command reported an arrest of ten rustlers, who stole about 32 cows from a herdsman. The issue of cattle rustling became noticeable in 2009. The crime goes with huge economic losses and hikes in the price of meat considering that most cattle headsmen lose huge sums to these coordinated attacks so they in-turn hike the price of the commodity (Interviews, 2020).

Consequently, socio-economic activities dropped drastically, as most of the states in the regions were under the control of the insurgents, the educational system was grounded with public schools burnt down. The health sector was not left out with primary health care centres burnt down and physicians recruited by the insurgents for their personal use.

According to Babagana, *et al.* (2018) assessments in late 2014 alone in Gombe, Yobe and Adamawa states revealed that vast areas of southern Yobe and Borno, and northern Adamawa were under-cultivated and/or not harvested during the May to December main farming season as a result of attacks and conflict-related fears orchestrated by the Boko Haram insurgency in the area. Many of the internally displaced persons in north-eastern Nigeria can only secure a single meal a day. They have abandoned their farms, agricultural activities, and homes due to insecurity (Henry, 2017).

In Nigeria, 50 percent of crops and 47 percent of livestock consumed by the Southerners were produced in northern States (Jessica, 2014). Borno, Yobe and Adamawa States which are the epicentre of the Boko Haram insurgency in Nigeria also happen to contain the largest farmlands in the country dominated by different kinds of farmers. These States produce staple foods such as corn, cowpeas, rice, millet, tomatoes, yams, onion, fish, and livestock. The fear of Boko Haram has prevented farmers from cultivating their farmland and the few that did, have lost their farm products to the terrorists who set them ablaze, killing the farmers and destroying their products. These States are closer to Niger, Chad, and Cameroon where agricultural business activities were booming especially in the area of export of groundnuts and groundnut oil (Mustapha, 2015). These activities are now becoming history due to the Boko Haram attacks.

In another dimension, a farmer (returnee) stated thus:

With the incessant and subsequent capturing of our houses and lands by Boko Haram, cash crops production especially millet and groundnuts have reduced drastically in our area. This is due to the fact that most of the active labour force was either killed or recruited by Boko Haram, thereby reduced crop production (Interview, 2020).

Other respondents believed that the reason why there is a setback in food production in the northeast is that money meant for the rehabilitation and reconstruction of the region especially revamping of agricultural activities were siphon by corrupt government officials. In line with this, a farmer argued that the money and other agro-inputs supplied by the government to boost food production in the north-east are commonly diverted for personal gains. This has left food production to remain a mirage (Interview, 2020).

Boko Haram insurgency led to massive displacements of many hundred thousands of rural farmers and resulted in high levels of food insecurity in northeast Nigeria. Already poor and vulnerable host communities have absorbed large numbers of people fleeing violence, placing considerable pressure on fragile agricultural and pastoral livelihoods, while the insecurity has severely disrupted markets and food availability. Staple food crop prices are extremely high due to inflation and its pressure on the national economy. Food consumption level across the many Boko Haram stricken communities in the region is in a crisis.

In some areas, many households are facing extreme food deficits, resulting in high acute malnutrition. Besides, the agricultural sector which is the backbone of the economies of Northeast has been crippled by the 7 year-long insurgency by the Boko Haram group and food insecurity is still at extremely high levels especially in Yobe state as well as in Borno and Adamawa states due to decreased land cultivation, lack of access to seeds, farming tools land among other factors.

From business perspectives, the respondents express their sadness on how insurgency in the area has affected their source of income. A driver complains about how things reduced all of a sudden. He stated that:

> Unlike in the past where I used to transport three trucks of cotton or beans in a month from Maiduguri to Lagos or Port Harcourt, the story has now changed. I could only manage to travel once in a month due to no goods on ground and the roads are no longer safe (Interview, 2020).

A famous fisherman and a major supplier of fish in the Nigerian Lake Chad axis (Baga) remarked that:

> The fish business which used to be a lucrative business in the area now became Boko Haram occupation … (sic). They now recruit and captured most of our members to be fishing for them. That is why there is a shortage of smoked fish in the entire north-east. Most of Nigeria depends on our sweet and natural fish, but now finds it difficult to fish any longer. This has made some people shift their

attention to the neighbouring country, though it is illegally imported (Interview, 2020).

In a similar vein, another fisherman stated that the Boko Haram insurgency virtually affects every sector of the Nigeria's economy, but that fishing sector is the most affected one, this is because everybody consumes fish. According to him shortage in fish supply from the Baga area has affected many people balanced diets and made the government lost huge tax (Interview, 2020).

According to the Food and Agricultural Organization of the United Nations (FAO) (2016), more than 80 percent of the rural population in northeast Nigeria depends on crop or livestock farming. Because of its distinct vegetation cover favourable for agricultural activities, Gujba Local Government Area happens to be an agricultural stronghold in Yobe state and considered as one of the food baskets of the state with over 60% of its population being farmers (see Babagana, *et al.*, 2018).

However, it was argued that consistent attacks on many towns by the dreaded Boko Haram group have led to the displacement of many rural farmers from these places thereby leading to significant drawbacks in agricultural activities affecting both crop and livestock productions. Many major towns in Gujba Local Government Area for example, which were well known for agricultural activities including Gujba, Katarko, Mutai, Wagir, Goniri, and Buni Yadi were at one time or the other completely deserted for more than 2 years. Certainly, such an unprecedented displacement of people who were mainly peasant farmers could have a significant impact on agricultural activities not only on the affected areas but on the state and the nation at large.

Consequently, crop production was seriously affected due to reduced land cultivation resulting in a shortage of staple food crops such as maize, sorghum, corns and beans as well as an increase in the prices of these crops. Moreover, livestock farming was more or less affected by the insurgency as many animal rearers who were mainly nomadic herdsmen have relocated to remote places considered to be safer. Thus, many returnees to these towns after two years of exile now survive on food Aids from some international Non- Governmental Organisations such as the Action Contre la Faime popularly known as Action against Hunger (ACF), the World Food Programme (WFP), Catholic Relieve Service (CRS) and the Red Cross Society among others.

According to the World Bank report (2016), an estimate of about 20,000 citizens have been killed in Borno state during the violence, more than 2.0 million people were displaced, 956,453 (nearly 30 percent) out of 3,232,308 private houses were destroyed, 5,335 classrooms damaged across primary, secondary and tertiary institutions. Besides, 1,205 municipal, local government or ministry buildings, 76 police stations, 35 electricity offices, 14 prison buildings, 201 health centres, 1,630 water sources, 726 power sub-stations and distribution lines (World Bank, 2016). It is also estimated that parks, game, forest and grazing reserves, orchards, river basins, and lakes have been poisoned in 16 of the 27 areas, and 470,000 livestock killed or stolen (World Bank, 2016). The total cost of damage was put at $5.9 billion.

Conclusion

The continued increase in the spread of the nefarious activities of the Boko Haram insurgency since 2009 has created adverse humanitarian consequences to the Northeast region. Life in the various communities of Borno, Yobe, and Adamawa states has been characteristically nasty, brutish, and most times short. The region has ceased to know civil normalcy as a result of the dire humanitarian situation as evident in human casualties, human rights abuses, population displacement, and refugee debacle, loss of means of livelihood, food insecurity, limited medical facilities, and other social amenities.

In addition, the Boko Haram insurgency in the North-Eastern Nigeria has significantly affected the food security and livelihoods of populations. High proportion of households within the three northeast states (Borno, Adamawa, and Yobe) remain food insecure despite ongoing intervention by humanitarian groups. The level of food insecurity is underpinned by the insurgency. The dire food security situation is also driven by the loss of livelihoods and a substantial decline in agricultural production which has left the majority of the population largely dependent on purchased grains to meet their food needs. Food insecurity has a gender dimension with female-headed households worst affected than their male counterparts. In addition to the low level of own-produced grains underscored by the impact of the insurgency on local agricultural production, the substantial dependence of households on purchased grain (over 70 percent in all three states) and increased prices is worrisome, especially among displaced households that already reliant on asset depleting coping strategies to secure food access. Also, many markets in several local government areas remain disrupted due to insecurity and inaccessibility, thus posing an additional threat to food security in some parts of Borno State (Ngala, Bama, Chibok, Mafa, Gambaru-Ngala, Kala-Balge, and Askira Uba), Adamawa (Hong, Mubi, Michika, Maiha, and Madagali) Yobe (Potiskum, Nguru, Jakusku, and Gujeba).

To this end, it was recommended that there is a need for the Nigerian government and other international intervention agencies to urgently crush Boko Haram in the northeastern Nigeria, to enable people in the area to pursue their economic interest without any fear or threat. Also, farmers in the area need to be empowered with soft loans and other modern (high breed agro-inputs) to revamp food production in the area and ensure adequate food supply within the country and beyond.

References

ACLED. (2017). Armed Conflict Location and Event Data Project (ACLED), Version8. Available at https://www.acleddata.com/data/.

Adelaja, A., and J. George. (2019). Effects of Conflict on Agriculture: Evidence from the Boko Haram Insurgency, *World Development*, 117: 184-195.

Africa Growth Initiatives, AGI (2014). The impact of conflict and political instability on agricultural investments in Mali and Nigeria. Global Economy and Development Program, AGI Working Paper 17.

Amusan, L and Ejoke, U. P. (2017). The psychological trauma inflicted by Boko Haram insurgency in the North Eastern Nigeria, *Aggression and Violent Behavior.* 36, pp. 52-59.

Amusan, L and Oyewole, S. (2014). Boko Haram Terrorism in Nigeria: A Reflection on the Failure of Democratic Containment. Politeia: Journal for Political Science and Public Administration, 33(1), pp. 35-49.

Amuwa, S. (2019). Boko Haram And Food Security In Nigeria, Boko Haram And Food Security In Nigeria — Economic Confidential

Awodola, B., and A. Oboshi. (2015). "Terrorism in Northern Nigeria: A Threat to Food Security in Maiduguri", *Mediterranean Journal of Social Sciences* 6 (3): 11-17.

Babagana, M., Ismail, M. Mohammed, B.G., Dilala, M. A. Hussaini, I, Zangoma, I M (2018). "Impacts of Boko Haram Insurgency on Agricultural Activities in Gujba Local Government Area, Yobe State, Nigeria", *International Journal of Contemporary Research and Review*, 9 (12), 20269-20282.

Beatrice, E. A. (2015). "Boko Haram Insurgency and the Underdevelopment of Nigeria", *Research on Humanities and Social Sciences*, 5 (6).

Benjaminsen, T. A (2008). 'Does Supply- Induced Scarcity Drive Violent Conflicts in the African Sahel? The Case of the Tuareg Rebellion in Northern Mali'. In *Journal of Peace Research* 45 (6): 819–836.

Brancati, D. (2007). "Political Aftershocks: The Impact of Earthquakes on Intrastate Conflict". *Journal of Conflict Resolution*, 51(5): 715-743.

Buhaug, H. (2010). Climate not to blame for African Civil Wars, *Proceedings of the National Academy of Sciences*, 107(38): 16477–16482.

Bundervoet, T., Verwimp, P., & Akresh, R. (2009). "Health and Civil War in Rural Burundi". *Journal of Human Resources*, 44(2), 536–563. https://doi.org/10.3368/jhr.44.2.536.

Burke, M.B., Miguel, E., Satyanath, S., Dykema, J.A. & Lobell, D.B.(2009). "Warming Increases the Risk of Civil War in Africa". *Proceedings of the National Academy of Sciences*, 106 (49): 20670–20674.

Chamarbagwala R, & Morán H. (2011): The Human Capital Consequences of Civil War: Evidence from Guatemala", *Journal of Development Economics*, 94(1), 41-61.

Collier P, Elliot V, Hegre H, Hoeffler A, Reynal-Querol M, & Sambanis N (2003). *Breaking the Conflict Trap: Civil War and Development Policy*. Washington, DC: World Bank.

Collins S (1993). "The Need for Adult Therapecitic Care in Emergency Feeding Programmes: Lessons from Somalia", *Journal of the American Medical Association*, 270 (5): 637-638.

Collins S, Myatt M, & Golden, B. (1998). "Daily Treatment of Severe Malnutrition in Adults", *Am. J. Clinical Nutrition*, 68 (1):193-199.

Cooke, J.G., and T.M. Sanderson. (2016). Militancy and the Arc of Instability: Violent Extremism in the Sahel. Washington DC: Rowman & Littlefield.

Davies A.E. (2009), "Food Security Initiatives in Nigeria: Prospects and Challenges," Journal of Sustainable Development in Africa, 11 (1), .186-202.

Dube, O. & Vargas. J. F. (2008). Commodity Price Shocks and Civil Conflict: Evidence from Colombia, Harvard University Center for International Development Graduate Student and Postdoctoral Fellow Working Paper, 14. Cambridge.

Eme, O, Onyishi, A.O., Uche, O. A. & Uche, I. B., (2014). "Food Insecurity in Nigeria: A Thematic Exposition", *Arabian Journal of Business and Management Review* (OMAN Chapter), 4 (1) August. 20141

Famine Early Warning Systems Network FEWS NET (2017). Nigeria food security outlook. February – September 2017.

FAO (Food and Agriculture Organization). (2013). "Key Indicators." Mali Country STAT. http://www.coun-trystat.org/home.aspx?c=MLI&p=ke

FAO. (2017). Northeastern Nigeria: Situation Report-January 2017. Rome: FAO. Available at http://www.fao.org/3/a-bs154e.pdf.

FAO/WFP. (2008). The State of Food Insecurity in the World 2008: High food Prices and Food Security Threats and Opportunities, Rome: FAO/WFP.

Food and Agricultural Organisation (FAO) (2016). Northeast Nigeria Situation Report October/November 2016.

George, J., Weartherspoon, D. D. & Adelaja, A. (2019). Armed Conflict and Food Insecurity: Evidence from Boko Haram's Attacks, Department of Agricultural, Food and Resource Economics Michigan State University.

Gompert, D. C, Gordon, J. (2008). "War by Other Means: Building complete and balanced Capabilities for Counterinsurgency," Rand Corporation, California. As of February 1, 2013:http://www.rand.org/content/dam/rand/pubs/monographs/2008/RAND_MG595.2.pdf.

Gonzaga, S. (2012). "Enhanced medical assessment strategy for Central African Republic", Morbidity and Mortality Weekly Report, 46(52), 1250-1254.

Gros, J. (1996). "Towards Taxonomy of Failed States in the New World Order: Decaying Somalia, Liberia, Rwanda and Haiti." *Third World Q*. 17(3):455–472.

Gylych, J., Ramat, A., Selman, T., Bilal, C., & Natalia, O. (2018). "Impact of Terrorism on Agricultural Business in Borno State, Nigeria", *Applied Studies in Agribusiness and Commerce,* 4 (3).

Hank-Jan, B. & Cullen, S. H. (2011). Food Security and Violent Conflict : Causes, Consequences, and Addressing the Challenges, World Food Programme, Occasion Paper, no 34.

Hendrix, C. S., & Salehyan, I. (2012). "Climate Change, Rainfall, and Social Conflict in Africa". *Journal of Peace Research,* 49(1), 35–50 https://doi.org/10.1177%2F0022343311426165.

Hendrix, C.S. & Glaser, S.M. (2007). Trends and Triggers: Climate, Climate Change, and Civil Conflict in Sub-Saharan Africa, *Political Geography,* 26(6): 695–715.

Hendrix, C.S. & Salehyan, I. (2010). Climate Change, Rainfall Triggers, and Social Conflict in Africa, Working paper, University of North Texas.

Henry, K. K. (2017). "Boko Haram is Losing, But so is Food Production: Conflict and Food Insecurity in Nigeria and Cameroon". Council for the Development of Social Science Research in Africa. *Africa Development,* XLII (3), 177- 196.

Hentz, J. J. (2004). "State Collapse and Regional Contagion in Sub-Saharan Africa: Lessons for Zimbabwe." *Scientia Militaria,* 32 (1): 143–56.

Idachaba, F. S. (2004). Strategies and policies for food security and economic development in Nigeria, Lagos: CBN.

Idachaba, F.S. (2009). "The Looming Food Crisis", Newswatch, Lagos, (August 3), Special Colloquium Edition

Imasuen, E. (2015). Insurgency and humanitarian crises in Northern Nigeria: The case of Boko Haram, *African Journal of Political Science and International Relations,* 9 (7), 284-296.

International Crisis Group – ICG (2017). Instruments of Pain (IV): The Food Crisis in North East Nigeria, Crisis Group Africa Briefing N°126, Abuja/Dakar/Brussels, 18 May 2017.

Jessica, P. (2014). *The Impact of Conflict and Instability on Agriculture in Mali and Nigeria.* Brookings: Africa in focus.

Kilcullen, D. (2006). "Counter-Insurgency Redux in Survival": United Kingdom. IISS Q. 48(4).

Kimenyi, M., J. Adibe, M. Djiré, A.J. Jirgi, A. Kergna, T.T. Deressa, J.E. Pugliese, &. Westbury, A (2014). The Impact of Conflict and Political Instability on Agricultural Investments in Mali and Nigeria. Africa Growth Initiative Working Paper 17. Washington, DC: Brookings.

Le Roch K, Pons E, Squire J, Anthoine-Milhomme J, & Colliou Y. (2010). "Two Psychosocial Assistance Approaches for Iraqi Urban Refugees in Jordan and Lebanon: Center-based Services Compared to Community Outreach Services". *J. Muslim Mental Health,* 5(1):99-119.

León G. (2009). Civil Conflict and Human Capital Accumulation: The Long Term Effects of Political Violence in Peru. BREAD Working Paper No. 245. Berkeley, CA: University of California, Berkeley.

Miguel, E., Satyanath, S. & Sergenti, E. (2004). "Economic Shocks and Civil Conflict: An Instrumental Variables Approach", *Journal of Political Economy*, 112(4): 725–753.

Modupe, B. A. (2019). "The Relativity of Insurgency to the Achievement of Food Security in Nigeria", in Aloysus, O, Hassan, S. & Gerald, E. *State, Governance and Regional Integration in Africa*, (eds), Published by the Nigerian Political Science Association, July 2019.

Mohammed, D. T, Ahmed, F. F. (2015). The Effect of Insurgency on Borno State Economy (2008 – Oct. 2014), *Journal of Economics and Sustainable Development*, 6, (16), 94 – 102.

Mustapha, M. (2015). Boko Haram insurgency gnawing at Nigeria's food supply. Bloomberg business. Retrieved from http://www.bloomberg.com.

Nel, P. & Righarts, M. (2008). "Natural Disasters and the Risk of Violent Civil Conflict", *International Studies Quarterly*, 52(1): 159–185.

Organisation for Economic Co-operation and Development (OECD) (2008). "Measuring Fragility: Indicators and Methods for Rating State Performance". Produced for review by the United States Agency for International Development by ARD, Inc. June. http://pdf.dec.org/pdf_docs/PNADD462.pdf

Osagie, C. (2013), "Fear of Food Insecurity Grips Nigeria," Saturday This Day, November 8, P.24.

Pinstrup-Andersen, P. & Shimokawa, S. (2008). "Do Poverty and Poor Health and Nutrition Increase the Risk of Armed Conflict Onset"? *Food Policy*, 33(6): 513–520.

Powell, C. H, Abraham, (2006).'Terrorism and International Humanitarian Law',1st African Yearbook of International Humanitarian Law 118:127.

Richard M (2002). Food Security Strategies Poverty Eradication in Africa. In: S. A. Breth (ed) From Subsistence to Sustainable Agriculture in Africa. Papers from the Workshop from Subsistence to Sustainable Agriculture: Policies, Strategies, and Implementation, Held in Johannesburg South Africa, 18th -19th November 2002.

Rotberg, R. I. (2003). Failed States Collapsed States, Weak States: Causes and Indicators. In State Failure and State Weakness in a Time of Terror, Washington, DC: Brookings Institution Press.

Singh P. (2012). Insurgency, Crime, and Agricultural Labor Expenditure: Evidence from Punjab, 1978-1990, *The Economics of Peace and Security Journal*, 7 (2), 33 – 40.

Sobek, D. & Boehmer, C. (2009). If They Only Had Cake: The Effect of Food Supply on Civil War Onset, 1960–1999, Unpublished manuscript.

The World Bank (2016). North-East Nigeria. Recovery and Peace Building Assessment, Synthesis Report, Volume 1.

Titus, U. M. (2016). "Domestic Terrorism and its Impacts on Nigerian State: An Analysis of Boko Haram Insurgency". *International Journal of Innovative Research and Studies*, 5 (1), 164-194

UNHCR (2017). Global trends – Forced displacement in 2017. Geneva: UNHCR. UNHCR. (2018). Syria emergency. Retrieved from http://www.unhcr.org/ syriaemergency. html, Accessed on March 23, 2020.

United Nations Office for the Coordination of Humanitarian Affairs (OCHA) (2017). Nigeria North-East: Humanitarian Emergency. Situation Report No. 6 (as of 24 February 2017).

Van Den Hoek, J. (2017). Agricultural Market Activity and Boko Haram Attacks in Northeastern Nigeria, West African Papers, No. 09, Paris: OECD Publishing. Available at http://dx.doi.org/10.1787/13ba9f2e-en.

Walker, A (2013). What is Boko Haram? United State Institute of Peace. Special Report. Washington, DC

WFP. (2017). WFP Nigeria Situation Report #13. WFP: Rome. Available at https:// documents.wfp.org/stellent/groups/Public/documents/ep/WFP292051.pdf.

Wolfe S, Frongillo, E. A (2001). Building Household Food Security Measurement Tools from the Ground Up. Food and Nutrition Bulletin, 22: 5-12.

World Bank, (2012). Agriculture for Development: World Development Report 2008, Washington DC: The World Bank.

Chapter 15
Incessant Oil Spills and their Impact on Food Production in the Niger Delta: An appraisal of the Legal Framework

Oladiran Akinsola Ayodele

Introduction

Oil and gas have been exploited indiscriminately in the Niger Delta since 1956 when crude oil was discovered in commercial quantity at Oloibiri now in the Bayelsa State of Nigeria. This is more worrisome because oil and gas are non-renewable resources; once exploited cannot be regained. Even though the exploitation of the resources is important for the enhancement of socio-economic development of the state, it is also important that these resources are exploited sustainably. The question then is how much of the resources should be exploited in a lifetime? This question has been a source of international discourse and serious concerns to environmental activists and organisations under the auspices of the United Nations. However, there has been a consensus that mineral resources ought to be exploited in such a way as to guarantee development and at the same time not jeopardising the needs of future generations (Stockholm Declaration, 1972 and Rio Declaration, 1992). Although Nigeria bought the idea of sustainable development, from all indications the extraction of the resources is not sustainably done.

Although, the spill is unavoidable during the processes of oil exploitation, however, international best practices demand that necessary precautions are put in place to reduce the incessant spills from oil installations. Environmental impact assessment is to be carried out to determine the anticipated environmental effect of the project. The likely negative effect is weighed against the social benefit derivable from the project. However, the exploration and corrupt mining of crude oil in Niger Delta are done with less emphasis on the environmental implications but rather on the economic gains. The extraction of oil has led to several uncontrolled oil spills which have resulted in water and land pollution. It has disrupted the biodiversity of the Niger Delta; aquatic life is the worst hit; farmlands are destroyed by fire resulting from oil spills. It is against this background, that this paper gives a brief historical background of the Niger Delta, which bears the brunt of oil exploitation and examines its excruciating effects on the environment. It also examines the effectiveness of the legal and regulatory frameworks on the extraction of crude oil in Nigeria. A brief historical background of the Niger Delta is discussed hereunder.

The Niger Delta

The Niger Delta is the major oil and gas producing area of Nigeria, described as a major wetland in the world, and certainly Africa's largest (Sagay, 2001). It covers approximately 70,000 square kilometres and this makes the Niger Delta the largest delta in Africa (UNEP, 2011: 20). Its development has been traced to the times of high rainfall when the Atlantic Ocean exceeded its usual boundaries and encroached on land (Peek and Keith, 2002). It withdrew in successive periods of persistent dryness, leaving deposits of sediments. The Delta came into existence through this process over time (Peek and Keith, 2002). The region has some unique characteristics that tend to make economic development difficult (Nwilo and Badejo, 2005: 567). The Niger Delta comprises distinct ecological zones that are typical of a large river delta in a tropical region; coastal ridge barriers, mangroves, and freshwater swamp forests (UNEP, 2011: 20).

The name 'Niger Delta' is identical to the Riverine people of Nigeria (Abila, 2009: 175). The Niger Delta Mangrove Forest is 6000 square kilometres in area and its freshwater swamplands are 11,700 square kilometres. It has many rivers, streams, brooks, and canals as over 60% of the region is traversed by creeks and dotted islands while the rest is a lowland rainforest (Abibe and Essaugh, 1999: 45). Because of this, the Niger Delta is relatively strategic for development being the economic nerve centre of Nigeria. It is also endowed with enormous water resources, with major rivers connecting the region to the Atlantic Ocean, which is a water highway that opens coastal Nigeria to all parts of the world. However, the extraction of crude oil in the region has led to environmental degradation and has impoverished the inhabitants of the Niger Delta. By extension, impacts on farming and fishing with deleterious effects on food security and nutrition, which continue to perpetuate women as an object of poverty (Amusan, 2014).

Oil spillage

As pointed out earlier, crude oil exploration and exploitation carry along with it some unavoidable consequences like oil spills, pipeline explosions, flaring of gas leading to air pollution; they have long term effects on the people and the ecosystem (Etikerentse, 2004: 44). However, this paper shall be limited to oil spills with emphasis on its negative consequences on a major wetland in the world and certainly Africa's largest. There are oil pollution problems wherever oil has been exploited, but the control measures vary between countries and with the availability of economic means and technology, as well as with environmental concerns and government policies (Amusan, 2014; Ogri, 2001: 11). In developing countries, the emphasis is usually on increasing crude oil production levels at the expense of the people and the environment (Ogri, 2001: 15). Nigeria is not an exception to this; Nigeria has been planning to increase her daily production from an average 2.2 million barrels to 2.8 million barrels per day despite the outcry from the Niger Delta inhabitants for neglect and environmental degradation. The devastating effects of oil extraction are glaring in the Niger Delta despite claims by oil companies that they adhere strictly to the "environmental standards that are to be maintained to reduce oil spill impact on the environment to the barest minimum in the Delta" (Orubu, 2004: 203). Since 1956, when oil and gas were first discovered in commercial quantity in Nigeria, the Niger Delta has been suffering from the devastating effects of oil and gas production ((Nwilo and Badejo, 2007: 8). Ogri has rightly observed that the deposit of crude oil and natural gas is in large quantity hence, its exploitation in large quantity has improved Nigeria's economy substantially with an indelible environmental cost. Serious environmental damages have happened in the Niger-Delta being the base of most oil industries. Environmental protection bye-laws applicable to the oil industry in Nigeria seem to be inadequate and invariably ineffective. Wherefore pollution such as air and oil spillage are yet to be addressed properly. The legal measures for air pollution with respect to the operation of compressed natural gas (CNG) and liquified natural gas (LNG) projects are encouraged with measures for environmental quality, control, and resource conservation. (Ogri, 2001: 11).

While describing the negative effects of oil and gas exploration and exploitation on the environment in the Niger Delta region, Inokoba and Imbua have opined that multi-dimensional environmental oil-related issues have made life intolerable for the residents of Niger-Delta, these include air pollution- acid rain from gas and oil processing plant; industrial solid waste disposal; water pollution due to oil spillage; deforestation, farmlands destruction, human settlement demolition loss of biodiversity such as fauna and flora habitat; destruction of mangrove swamps and salt marsh and several others. This was in a bid to locate and install pipelines that will convey crude oil, and gas across Niger-Delta communities (Inokoba and Imbua, 2010: 104). Amnesty International in its report titled "Nigeria: Petroleum Pollution and Poverty in the Niger Delta" describes the deplorable standard of living of the people of Niger Delta because of oil pollution. It states further that the people living in the Niger Delta region of Nigeria need water for basic things such as drinking, cooking and washing but the unfortunate situation is that the water is polluted. The fishes are also contaminated with oil and other toxins. The land used for agriculture is being destroyed due to lack of regard for the ecosystem needed for survival; they are also besieged by lack of quality air to breath because the air is polluted as a result of oil and gas and other pollutants that reeks in the air; skin lesions and other health problems, meanwhile, their agitations are not taken seriously and they are not well informed on the impacts of pollution (Amnesty International, 2009). The causes of oil spillage are multifarious and multi-dimensional, ranging from equipment failure, human error, sabotage to acts of God (Ogri, 2001: 11). Oyekunle has identified some causes of oil spillage as failure to check the old pipeline for periodic maintenance, the pipeline bursting accidentally when work is on around the pipeline, drilling activity at the new site, and vandalisation of pipelines by aggrieved youth and members of the oil-producing communities.

Oyekunle has further asserted that the Federal Government and its collaborators in joint ventures always blame oil spillage on the people of Niger Delta which, according to him, is misconstrued. For instance, Shell Petroleum Development Company (SPDC) owned up to the fact that her infrastructure requires being fixed and that corrosion was the reason for about 50% of the oil that spills that its infrastructure needed to be fixed and that corrosion was responsible for 50 percent of oil spills (Amnesty International, 2009: 15). An example was the explosion of Jesse pipeline in October 1998 in Delta State which claimed the lives of over 1000 people (Sahhed, 2012: 179). It was reported that the Government did not come to the aid of those affected, as it would have been done in the developed world (Oyekunle, 2019). The incidences of oil spills are hereunder discussed.

The oil spill at Bodo 2008

In 2008, a fault of the Trans-Niger pipeline was reported which led to Bodo Creek, Ogoniland oil spillage (Amnesty International, 2009: 7). The oil flowed into the swamp and cove for weeks, unchecked either by the regulatory authorities or the Shell Petroleum Development Company (SPDC) even though the spill was reported to them (Amnesty International, 2009: 7). The oil spill covered the area, killing several species of fish and destroyed the trees that grow in or near the river which are an important fish breeding ground (UNEP, 2011: 3). The killing of fish resources resulted in protein deficiency in the community of Bodo (Amnesty International, 2009: 7). The destruction caused by the spill led to food shortages in the community without any relief from either the Federal Government or SPDC. The spill started on 28 August 2008 and was only stopped by the 7 November 2008 (Amnesty International, 2009: 7). In an interview conducted by an NGO, the Centre for Environment, Human Rights and Development (CEHRD), a local fisherman said that Whenever they want to go fishing, they will have to paddle their canoe for four hours to catch fishes where the effect of the oil spillage is lesser, yet fishes in such waters still smell the crude oil when the stomach is opened (CEHRD's, Report, 2009: 157).

The Nigerian oil industry regulations require clean-up of oil spills immediately, but this is not done until the spill has destroyed the aquatic life in the area (Amnesty International, 2009: 8). The state of affairs was confirmed by the UNEP Environmental Assessment of Ogoniland (UNEP, 2011: 3). This is an example of a non-implementation of the regulation or a typical weak regulator (UNEP, 2014). What happened in Bodo is also an example of how multinational oil companies exploit the weak systems that typify the most vulnerable countries, which often end with the poor being the most susceptible been taking advantage of by corporate actors (Amnesty International, 2009: 10). The mishap in Bodo raised fundamental human rights abuses like:

1. violations of the right to an adequate standard of living, including the right to food as a consequence of the impact of oil-related pollution and environmental damage on agriculture and fisheries, which are the main sources of food for many people in the Niger Delta.
2. violations of the right to gain a living through work – also as a consequence of widespread damage to agriculture and fisheries, because these are also the main sources of livelihood for many people in the Niger Delta.
3. violations of the right to water – which occur when oil spills and waste materials pollute water used for drinking and other domestic purposes.
4. violations of the right to health – which arise from failure to secure the underlying determinants of health, including a healthy environment, and failure to enforce laws to protect the environment and prevent pollution.
5. the absence of any adequate monitoring of the human impacts of oil-related pollution –although the oil industry in the Niger Delta is operating in a relatively densely populated area characterized by high levels of poverty and vulnerability.
6. failure to provide affected communities with adequate information or ensure consultation on the impacts of oil operations on their human rights.
7. failure to ensure access to an effective remedy for people whose human rights have been violated (Amnesty International, 2009: 10).

The Bodo oil spills were later to be taken up against Shell in the UK court, but Shell decided to settle before the case began. Shell agreed to compensate 15,600 fishermen and farmers who were to collect about £2,000 each for compensation as part of the £55m pay-out by Shell for pollution caused by the two oil spills in 2008 and 2009. The settlement is to be split as £35m for individuals and £20m for the Bodo community. While this is major in the circumstance of poverty in the Niger Delta, it won't reverse the dreadful conditions of the environment which the community depends on for water, livelihood, and food (Guardian News, 2015: Jan. 07). It is important to note that Nigeria on 2 June 2016 set in motion a $1 billion clean up and restoration programme of the Ogoniland region in the Niger Delta and in July 2016 flagged off the implementation of the UNEP Environmental Assessment of Ogoniland report (UNEP, 2016). The Federal Government inaugurated a 13-person Governing Council and a 10-person Board of Trustees for the implementation of the UNEP Report on Ogoniland (UNEP, 2016). If the Nigerian government follows the recommendations of UNEP the clean-up may not take more than thirty years to complete (Oil watch, 2016). This is a step in the right direction; however, the Federal Government still needs to establish a clean-up fund; coordinate multi-stakeholder efforts; carry out emergency measures to reduce community exposure, and initiate institutional and regulatory reforms as recommended by UNEP (This Day Newspaper, 2017: June 22).

Ibeno shoreline oil spill 2016

There was a massive oil spill in some communities situated on the Ibeno shoreline in Akwa Ibom State (Vanguard News, 2016: 21 December). The spill has been traced to Exxon Mobil installations located at Okposo, Atia, Western end, and Eastern end of Ibeno communities. It was allegedly caused by the Niger Delta Avengers, and it has impacted the ecosystem of the communities negatively.

Other examples

On 25 June 2001 a major oil spill was reported in Ogbodo in Rivers State which continued for several days before the spill was contained (Amnesty International, 2009: 21). Rukpokwu in Rivers State experienced an oil pipeline spill on the 3 December 2003 (Amnesty International, 2009: 32). On 27th March 2007, Amnesty International also recounted an oil spill incidence in Kira Tai in Ogoniland (Amnesty International, 2009: 31). On 2nd September 2016, there was an oil spillage in Ologama, in Bayelsa State, and as of 8 February 2017, the oil spills were yet to be cleared, and no relief materials had been supplied (Personal communication interview, 2017: 07 February). On the challenge of the oil spill and the lackadaisical attitude of the oil companies to clear the spillage and pay compensation to assuage the suffering of the victims and restore the environment to the state it was before the spill, a Senator in the National Assembly of the Federal Republic of Nigeria observed as follows:

> The laws are there to regulate the activities of the oil companies and the regulators are there to ensure compliance with best practices in the industry but the problem is one lack of competent personnel and equipment to work with. Again, another problem is the Nigerian factor of not doing things professionally. I think one area we need to look at seriously is this because overseas when there is a spill, the company responsible for the spill does clean up and pay compensation; I do not think this is happening in Nigeria. So, I believe this is an area the National Assembly should look at and amend the law and let oil producers pay for their negligence. This is called the "polluters pay" principle widely adopted in the petroleum industry globally (Personal communication interview, 2017: 02 March).

The peoples of Bodo, Ogbodo, Rukpokwu, and Kira Tai and recently Ologama in Bayelsa State witnessed their human rights trampled by oil companies and their government cannot or will not hold the companies responsible (Ologama spills, 2016).

Three different oil spills were reported in August and September 2016. These spills had destructive impacts on environments, agriculture, and overall well-being of the communities (Stakesholersdemocracy.Org, 2016). The first one was in Delta State which affects ten communities of Ijaw along Escravos River, Warri Southwest LGA, Delta State. Three oil spills were reported in the press in August and September 2016. These spills have had devastating impacts on the agriculture, environments, and general well-being of the local communities (Stakesholersdemocracy.Org, 2016). The first one was in Delta State affecting ten Ijaw communities along the Escravos River in Warri South West Local Government Area of Delta State, namely: Tebujor/Okpele-Ama, Ikpokpo, Okerenkoko-Gbene, Opuedebubor, Opuede, Opuendezion, Atanba, Oto-Gbene, and Meke-Ama Communities in the Gbaramatu Kingdom, along the Escravos. The oil spill was said to be from one of the trunk line facilities of Pipelines and Products Marketing Company (PPMC) - the products marketing and distribution subsidiary of the Nigerian National Petroleum Corporation (NNPC) (Stakesholersdemocracy.Org, 2016). The host communities blamed PPMC for not carrying out a proper investigation of the incident by the stakeholders' representatives - community, NNPC, National Oil Spill Detection and Response Agency, (NOSDRA), and the Department of Petroleum Resources (DPR). The people also accused the PPMC of drafting in the military men to ward off attacks.

The second oil spill took place in the Kalaba community of Bayelsa State which has been in recent times plagued by gas leaks. A spill was discovered in August 2016, which continues to spill crude oil into the forests and swamps, threatening local ecosystems, and agriculture capacity (Stakesholersdemocracy.Org, 2016). The oil field from which the reported spill came is operated by Nigerian Agip Oil Company. In respect to the third oil spill in Ahoada East, Rivers State, Nigeria in August 2016, resident of the community reported a fight between military officers watching over Total petroleum staff and youth of the host community as the management of the oil company was denied access to investigate the cause of the spill by the youth of the host community, (Stakesholersdemocracy.Org, 2016). The Niger Delta provides a plain case study of the lack of accountability of a government to its people and multinational companies' lack of accountability when it comes to the impact of their operations on human rights. It is important to reiterate the provisions of the 1999 Constitution regarding the protection of the environment and responsive governance in the exploration and exploitation of natural resources. For example, Section 20 of the 1999 Constitution provides that "the state shall protect and improve the environment and safeguard the water, air and land, forest and wildlife of Nigeria". And Section 16 (2) provides that the State shall direct its policy towards ensuring that the nations material resources are distributed to serve the citizen by providing suitable and adequate food, shelter, old age care and pension, a minimum living wage, cater for the welfare of the sick and disabled and not leaving out the unemployed youth (Amnesty International, 2009: 12).

According to Section 17 (2) (d) "exploitation of human or natural resources in any form whatsoever for reasons, other than the good of the community, shall be prevented." Apart from this municipal law, the African Charter in Article 24 recognizes people's right to a "satisfactory environment which aids their growth and development". Also, the Economic, Social and Cultural Rights Committee to the United Nations explained that the right to health under article 12 of the International Covenant on Economic, Social, and Cultural Rights covers the underlying determinants of health, including "a healthy environment". As stated earlier, Nigeria is a signatory and has domesticated these agreements and thus she is obliged to implement them.

Nevertheless, the government's failure in taking necessary steps to prevent third parties from polluting the air, food, water including the failure to enforce laws for the right of health (Section 17 (3) (d), 1999 CFRN). In a way, the Nigerian government supports and provides security using its military to shield oil companies against attacks from the aggrieved local communities. Most of the local people believed that there is hardly any distinction between the oil industry and the state. The two are perceived as the same entity. This view was expressed in the statement of one of the Frontline Niger Delta civil society activists that there exists an agreement between the government and the oil company on oil extraction without involving the host community in the agreement. Whenever there is a misunderstanding between the host community and the oil company, the oil company usually brings in soldiers to defend themselves and not the residents. Situations like this are unlikely in the developed countries where agreements are between the host community and the oil companies (Omeje, 2005).

Company	Number of Spills	Percentage of Occurrences	Volume	Percentage by Volume
SPDC	2,191	40%	44,945.25	25.1%
NAOC	1833	33.5%	76,902.03	43%
EXXON MOBIL	973	17.7%	6,889.098	3.9%
CHEVRON	442	8.1%	6,195.49	3.5%
SNEPCO	3	0.1%	40,050.144	22.4%
TOTAL	5,475	100%	178,677.592	100

Table 1: ***Oil Spill Incidents and Volume (2006-2012)***
Source: Oyegun (2012b, 2018).

Effects of oil spillage

Environmental degradation

The Niger Delta is the worst hit in terms of environmental degradation due to constant oil spills. The eco-system has been changed; the natural habitats of fishes and other aquatic lives are destroyed because of the pollution of the streams and other water sources. The weather condition has changed- people experience more heat, more than ever before. When it rains the rainwater is acidic and this is dangerous for human consumption. The natural vegetation is affected by oil spillages; when such spills are mismanaged, they result in fire consuming acres of farmlands.

Effects on water supply

Water is a source of life; especially fresh or unpolluted water. Therefore, water is a public good that ought to be provided for by the government. Nigerians have the right of access to portable water and streams and other water bodies, and the sources of water should remain unpolluted for their uses. The international human rights instruments like the Convention on the Elimination of all Forms of Discrimination against Women (CEDAW, Article 14 (2)), the United Nations Convention on the Rights of the Child (Nigeria's Child's Right Act No.26 of 2003) and the African Charter on the Rights and Welfare of Children provide for the right to clean water. Nigeria is also a signatory to the International Covenant on Economic, Social, and

Cultural Rights (the Covenant) which, among other things enjoined member states to ensure adequate, safe, and suitable water for personal and household uses (CESCR, Arts. 11 and 12). With the domestication of these international engagements, they are applicable as part of Nigerian law (Section 12 (1), 1999 CFRN).

The right for a good standard of living is assured in Article 11 of the covenant, which is linked directly to the right of health (Article 12) and food (Article 11 (1)). Water is declared as indispensable to human survival and to achieve an adequate standard of living (E/C. 12/2002/ 11 of 26/ Jl /2002). The inhabitants of Niger Delta depend on water systems for drinking, harvesting, fishing, and fermenting cassava. However, the water body is polluted as a result of the works carried out by the oil companies and by the incessant spills into the water streams and rivers (Yusuf, 2007: 78). Available statistics revealed that 6,817 oil spills took place between the years 1976 and 2001 with loss of about three million barrels of oil, almost 25% spilled in swamps, and 69% offshore in the region (UNDP Report, 2006).

Farming and Fishing are the major occupations of the residents of the Niger Delta with ample natural resources and rich water bodies that usually characterize the region. In popular opinion, mangrove forests are a nursery bed for countless sea fish. The Niger Delta is engulfed by mangrove forests, which serve as protection for the majority of the freshwater swampland in the interior Delta. Flora and fauna thrive well in such area. The region is a breeding ground for marine life which a lot of people depend on for their daily living. Approximately, 60% of the fish in the Gulf of Guinea breed in the Niger Delta mangrove forests. Oil spillage, no doubt has negatively affected the aquatic resources (Akpofure et al, 2000).

A study conducted by Aworawo (2000), posited that Niger Delta economy condition reflects unequivocally that poverty is prevalent in the region meanwhile, it is getting worse as a result of oil spill on the coastal water that breeds fish consumed by the people. Members of communities interviewed said there has been a reduction in number of fishes caught in recent years. In course of this study, we also observed that in rivers polluted by oil spillage, fishes were coated with crude oil, which makes it not fit to eat, while some others were found floating dead on the surface. In another study conducted by Osuagwu and Olaifa (2015), there was said to be an adverse effect on fish production in the Niger Delta as a result of oil spills. Osuagwu and Olaifa (2015) in their study of the impacts of oil spills on fish production in the Niger Delta confirm the adverse effect of an increase in oil spills on fish production in the region. Their findings confirm the finding of Akpokodje and Salau (2015) that oil pollution reduces agricultural output in the Niger Delta of Nigeria. They found that oil activity depresses fish production in the long run because of the unpleasant environmental degradation that accompanies the exploration of crude oil in the region.

Effects on farmlands and food production

Apart from the harm to fisheries, oil pollution has damaged farms and natural resources (both living and non-living things in the eco-system). The oil companies construct their pipelines, other oil installations like wellheads and flow stations on the farmlands or close by. Oil pipelines run close by or sometimes right through farmland, and other oil infrastructure, such as well heads and flow stations, is often close to agricultural land (Bribena, 2011: 230). It has been discovered that the location of these pipelines on farmlands makes farming extremely difficult and when there is an outburst of oil, the spill destroys the crops and renders the site useless for farming purposes. At times, oil spills result in large scale fire outbreaks leading not only to the destruction of plants, but valuable properties and lives are lost in the process. The following examples will hopefully put the problem into a proper perspective.

On the visit of this researcher to parts of Delta, Bayelsa, and Rivers in February 2017, some of the farmers interviewed complained that staple foods, mostly cassava, now yield very tiny tubers at harvest time. Cassava is a local tuber planted by the local farmers and is usually fermented and processed into *garri* (fried cassava flour). In Effurum, Delta, Ologama, and Otueoke in Bayelsa State, foods produced from cassava, including *garri* and other forms of the carbohydrates taken with palm kernel soup or fish pepper soup are very scarce and costly, out of the reach of poor people. The chairman of the oil-producing communities in Delta interviewed also maintained that cassava tubers were usually contaminated by oil spills, to the extent that there used to be traces of crude oil in the fermented cassava when processed by local farmers. Other staple crops consumed in the local communities—such as plantains, yam tubers, and coco-yams are equally affected leading to the high cost of yam seedlings. When oil spills occur many farmers usually harvest their crops prematurely, to salvage the crops left because of the risk of losing them.

Economic impacts

As a result of the degradation of the environment, unemployment has increased in an alarming proportion in the Niger Delta (Okon and Egbon, 1999). As discussed above, most of the farmlands are destroyed and the rivers are polluted leading to the death of fishes, most of the farmers and fishermen as a result became jobless. The Federal Office of Statistics confirmed the unemployment claims in the delta through its official news published in 2001 (Federal Office of Statistical News, 2001). Poverty pervades the entire region of the Niger Delta due to pollution of sources of livelihood like farmlands, fishponds, streams, rivers. The effects on farmlands have been discussed above. It is important to note that local communities in the Niger Delta are predominantly fishermen, hunters, and farmers. Therefore, oil spillage has adversely affected people's sources of livelihood.

Legal framework to control and compensate victims of oil spills

The legal and regulatory framework on the environment in Nigeria can be found in a couple of laws. These range from international to national laws. Environmental related provision is contained in the Constitution, other relevant national and state laws. There are other relevant case laws and customary laws that are applicable as well.

International laws

The world through the agencies of the United Nations has come to the realisation that socioeconomic development of states and environmental protection must go on hand in hand in order to sustain the universe. This concept was affirmed by Article 15 of the Rio Declaration on Environment and Development explains that in order to safeguard the environment, the preventive approach shall be extensively applied by States according to their abilities. In case of threats of severe or irrevocable damage, unsure scientific certainty won't be used as a reason for postponing cost-effective measures to stop environmental degradation. It is trite that, pursuant to the environmental and developmental policies of each state, all states possess the right to manage its natural resources, and saddled with the responsibility to ensure that activities within her jurisdiction do not cause great damage to the environment of neighbouring states or of areas beyond the limits of national jurisdiction. However, the states that are to manage their natural resources are to do so in a rational, sustainable, and safe way to conserve and sustain the use of such natural resources and protect the environment, including ecosystems.

The UN Commission on sustainable development of mineral resources has said that precautionary approach is vital to sustainable development in that it enjoins states, international organizations and civil society, particularly the scientific and business communities, to avoid human activities which may cause substantial harm to human health, natural resources or ecosystems. The approach includes accountability (or what is referred to as the "polluter pays" principle) for harm caused. Nigeria bought into the idea of a precautionary approach to environmental protection and that was why she enacted the Environmental Impact Assessment (EIA) Act.

The Convention on Civil Liabilities for Oil Pollution Damage (CLC), 1969

There are international instruments on pollution due to oil, such as the Convention on Civil Liabilities for Oil Pollution Damage (CLC, 1969) and the Convention on the Establishment of International Fund for Oil Pollution Damage (FUND Convention 1971). These Conventions cover compensation for all seagoing vessels carrying oil in bulk as cargo and they apply to pollution damage within the waters of countries that are party to them; they are applicable to oil spillage caused by ships while on the high seas (HNS by sea, 1996). The occurrence of oil spillage under the international regime is a strict liability offence and therefore, there is no need to prove that the shipowner is negligent or not. More importantly, the plaintiff has the opportunity of claiming from shipowners whose ships caused the oil pollution harm where the sum from the shipowner is limited or is insufficient to compensate the victims because of the enormity of the damage; the victims can also recover from the FUND. The FUND is raised by levies from all persons who have received in the calendar year, more than 150,000 tons of crude oil and heavy fuel oil from a state party to the FUND and from the contributions received from state contributors. Although there are no uniform compensation schemes under international law, there are few principles they have in common, which are:

1. damage to property tends to be calculated by reference to the actual cost of repairing or replacing the property, or the difference between the value before and after the spill;
2. compensation for damage to natural resources (where this is provided for) tends to be calculated by reference to the cost of remediating or replacing the lost or damaged natural resources. The compensation schemes do not generally provide for additional, independent compensation for damage to natural resources;
3. damages for loss of subsistence use of natural resources can be included;
4. compensation for consequential losses and pure economic losses (such as loss of income) are generally provided;
5. it can include the cost of bringing a claim, including the use of advisers where appropriate;
6. the heads of loss identified in the compensation schemes are generally not exhaustive or exclusive: for example, the French court awarded damages for non- pecuniary losses in addition to those provided for by the International Convention on Civil Liability for Oil Pollution Damage 1992 similarly, the American Oil Pollution Act does not contain damages for personal injury, but these can be claimed under state or admiralty law;
7. non-pecuniary losses (save to the extent that these might be recoverable as damage to natural resources or loss of subsistence use) and punitive damages are generally not expressly recoverable under the compensation schemes (NOSDRA, 2004: 6).

It should be noted, however, that the Conventions do not apply to inland waters, but it is expected that member nations should take care of such similar occurrences in their domains. The convention is easy to apply to the Nigerian context in relation to offshore oil production; however, it is difficult to apply the provisions of the convention to the frequent spills from onshore pipelines, affecting farms and villages in the Niger Delta and other regions of Nigeria. It seems that Nigeria has a particular context in which global systems do not contemplate like the losses that arise from the pollution of communal water supplies that are not easy to measure and therefore difficult to calculate the monetary value. The same applies to nature endowed resources like mangrove swamps and the natural vegetation, which are of great importance to the people.

National laws

Constitution of Federal Republic of Nigeria, 1999

It is a constitutional requirement that an environmental impact assessment of the potential impacts of a proposed project on the environment is carried out before the commencement of such a project. Section 20 of the Constitution of 1999 empowers the state to protect and improve the environment and safeguard the water, air and land, forest and wildlife of Nigeria. The construction of oil and gas facilities is listed in the schedule of Mandatory Study Activities under item 12 (c) and (e) of the EIA Act and this provision reinforces section 20 of the 1999 Constitution (Usman, 2010: 6). However, section 6(6)(c) of the Constitution renders the environmental right non-justiciable. Section 6(6)(c) states that:

> The judicial powers vested by the foregoing provisions of this section -(c) shall not except as otherwise provided by this Constitution, extend to any issue or question as to whether any act of omission by any authority or person or as to whether any law or any judicial decision conforms with the Fundamental Objectives and Directive Principles of State Policy set out in Chapter II of this Constitution.

In *A. G. Ondo v. A. G. Federation*, ((2002) 9 NWLR (Pt 772), 222) the Supreme Court held, inter alia, that courts cannot enforce any of the provisions of

Chapter II of the Constitution. According to the Supreme Court, the principles and objectives used as the governance constitutional policy remain ordinary declarations that can't be enforced by the legal process but would be as a failure of responsibility and duty of state organs if they acted in outright disregard of them. The court further maintained that the Directive Principles (or some of them) can be made justiciable by legislation.

The above provision of the law implies the infringement of environmental rights by the Nigerian government cannot be adjudicated upon by the Nigerian courts. However, the victim can sue for damages against polluters. The compensation for oil spills is however not adequate. To worsen the situation, the Land Use Act is made to govern the award of compensation. The Land Use Act is inadequate in the award of compensation to the farmer and owners of the land taken over by the oil companies. The issue of compensation remains a volatile issue in the exploration and exploitation of oil and gas in Nigeria. The compensation paid is usually neither fair nor adequate in comparison with the volume of oil extracted daily from the communities of the Niger Delta region. To make the matter worse, the compensation paid is calculated in line with the provisions of the Land Use Act in terms of the number of economic trees and other physical developments found on the land (Sections 29 and 35, Land Use Act 1978). The Land Use Act is incorporated into the 1999 Constitution thereby making amendments to its provisions difficult because of the onerous provision for a constitutional amendment.

Environmental Impact Assessment Act, 2004

The EIA Act makes conducting an EIA study compulsory before an oil and gas project can be started (Section 22 (a), EIA, 2004). Environmental Impact Assessment is to be carried out to determine the nature of the project and the impact the project will have on the environment (Section 2, EIA, 2004). EIA studies are to be carried out on private projects and projects being carried out by public organisations (Section 2 (1), EIA, 2004). The EIA Act failed to stipulate whether an assessment is to be conducted internally or through an external body (Section 58). To address this gap in the law, it is imperative that an independent body (an external body) must be established and entrusted with the responsibility for the EIA study of projects in the petroleum industry. The Environmental Guidelines and Standards for the Petroleum Industry (hereinafter referred to as 'EGASPIN') also make EIA studies mandatory. The projects that do not require EIA are those that the President of the Federal Environmental Protection Council thinks that they are likely to cause negligible environmental impact or projects executed during emergencies or are for public benefits. It was recommended that the EIA study must be prepared by the project promoter or originator, jointly with consultants authorized by the Department of Petroleum Resources (DPR) (sometimes) and in conjunction with the DPR (EGASPIN, 2004).

The EIA Act like many other Nigerian laws has suffered from poor implementation due to the weak regulatory framework; governments at all levels violate the principles of EIA (Nwoko: 27). They approve projects within the mandatory list even before any impact assessment is carried out, which runs contrary to Section 12 of the Act (Nwoko: 27). For example, the Niger Delta Development Commission decided in a press release to dredge the Ayetoro canal before carrying out any EIA (Anago, 2002: 11). In most cases, projects involving government agencies are carried out without resort to EIA; where the EIA is done, it is after the project has taken off to forestall resistance from any quarters. Where the EIA is done, it is usually with insufficient or lack of consultations with the communities likely to be affected directly by the project (Nwoko: 27).

It is because of the need to access information, enable public participation in decision-making and access to justice in environmental matters that the Convention on Access to Information, Public Participation in Decision-Making and Access to Justice in Environmental Matters was signed in Aarhus, Denmark on 25 June 1998 (Convention to Access to Information, Chapter XXVII). The European Union has expressed its satisfaction with the present Convention as an essential step forward in further encouraging and supporting public awareness in the field of environment and better implementation of environmental legislation in the UN/EU region, by the principle of sustainable development (Convention to Access to Information, Chapter XXVII). It is important to note that this Convention incorporates the language of Principle 1 of the Declaration of the United

Nations Conference on the Human Environment (Stockholm Declaration). This Convention for Nigeria implies that it imposes governmental accountability, as it grants the public rights of access to information and imposes obligations on public authorities to provide this information. This is expected to lead to more environmental decision-making and greater potential for environmental justice (Jeffery, www.paclii.org/journals). Nigeria is a signatory to Stockholm Declaration; it is therefore expected of it to implement its principles (Ishaya, 2016).

In Nigeria however, when access to information and accountability in environmental decision-making concerns multinational companies, especially the oil companies, the government waives the provisions of the law to accommodate investment in the petroleum sector to the detriment of the people and the environment. To aggravate the sufferings of the victims, the government most of the time refuses to commence litigation on behalf of the victims of violations of environmental statutes and there is no provision of private law remedies for victims of the environmental harm in the form of common law remedies of damages and injunction (Yusuf, 2007: 78). The Bodo spill is a typical example of how the people of the Niger Delta have been deprived of access to information about how oil extraction will affect them and are continually denied access to justice. It should be noted that private individuals, communities and Non-government Organisations are now allowed to sue oil companies for oil spills, and claim damages (*SERAC*'s case, 2001 *AHRLR* 60).

Judicial decisions

The Social and Economic Rights Action Centre (SERAC) documented the degradation of the Niger Delta environment. In the *SERAC* case, the Social and Economic Rights Action Centre (SERAC) and Centre for Economic and Social Rights (CESR) took the case against Nigeria to the African Commission for breach of human rights and environmental degradation (*SERAC*'s case). SERAC accused that the Military Government of Nigeria among other things was guilty of a violation of the right to health, a clean environment, dispose of wealth and natural resources, family rights since it facilitates the operation of oil corporations in Ogoniland. Nigeria pleads guilty of violating the economic and environmental right of the people of

Niger Delta and on that basis, the African Commission founded the Federal Republic of Nigeria In violation of Articles 2, 4, 14, 16, 18 (1), 21 and 24 of the African Charter on Human and Peoples' Rights. The commission appealed to the Nigerian state to guarantee safeguard of the environment, health, and sustenance of the people of Ogoniland by:

1. Making sure to stop all assaults on Ogoni residents and leaders by the Rivers State Internal Securities Task Force and giving their citizens entry and independent investigators unrestricted admittance to the region;
2. Enquiring the human rights violations mentioned above and institute proceedings against the authorities of the security forces, NNPC, and appropriate agencies implicated in human rights violations;
3. Ensuring sufficient reparation to victims of the human rights violations, as well as support and relocation backing to victims of government-backed incursions, and undertaking a wide-ranging tidying of lands and rivers destroyed by oil operations;
4. Ensuring that suitable environmental and socio-economic effect evaluation are equipped for any future oil growth and to facilitate the safe operation of any more oil development is definite through efficient and self-regulating oversight bodies for the petroleum industry; and
5. Providing detailed reports on health and environmental dangers and consequential reach to regulatory and administrative bodies to communities liable to be affected by oil operations.

The Nigerian Government promised that remedial actions will be taken by the new government authority, which added the creation of a Federal Ministry of Environment with sufficient wherewithal to tackle environment-related difficulties common in the Niger Delta region and to set up the Niger Delta Development Commission (NDDC) with satisfactory financial support to handle the environmental, social and economy affiliated problems of the region and other oil generating areas in Nigeria. The government also promised to set up a Judicial Commission of Inquiry to investigate the alleged human rights violations (*SERAC*'s case, para 30

(3)). Nevertheless, the story of woes did not abate because of environmental degradation and human rights violations persist in the Niger Delta.

The *case of Shell v Farah* ((1995) 3 WLR (Pt. 382) 148) points out the problems that Niger Delta encounter in obtaining a just and sufficient benefit. Such that, numerous families were incapable of carrying out their farming activities for years but did not get any reparation for income loss and were unable to secure adequate restoration before instituting court actions. In 1970, a bust at Shell's Bomu Well II in Ogoniland caused severe destruction to adjoin lands, where the host community farm and hunt. Shell compensated the members of the community whose crops and economic trees got destroyed. They did not furnish reparation for damage to the land, but assured the indigenes on their intention to restore the land which the affected families could not farm on it again. Almost two decades later, when the land had not been decontaminated, residents of the area commenced a lawsuit in 1989.

In 1991, the High Court in Rivers State – Bori High Court granted the sum of 4.6 million Naira (US$210,000 at the official exchange rate) in damages to the Plaintiffs. The court found that the compensation formerly paid by Shell wasn't reasonable and sufficient. While Shell had paid for destruction to crops and trees, the court held that the victims should be paid for the loss of income because the residents still feel the impact of the disaster even after twenty years hence their inability to farm. The court also held that the victims should be remunerated for the blow, trepidation, and general difficulty they had experienced.

In December 1994, Shell appealed the judgement the Appeal Court dismissed by maintaining the judgment of the lower court. The Court held that compensation for only the crops and economic trees destroyed at the time of the occurrence "unquestionably could not equal a fair and satisfactory compensation as the damage went well away from scant damages to crops and economic trees, [and] the tillable land was greatly soiled and made infertile for many years." The case of *Farrah* is an illustration of how a redress could be deferred in Nigeria. The case was only resolved after twenty-five years.

Common law causes of action

Apart from statutory provisions, the common law causes of action, such as negligence, nuisance, trespass and the doctrine in Rylands v Fletcher ((1868) LR 3 HL 330) are also available to an injured party in cases involving trespass to land and environmental pollution. In the case of Rylands v Fletcher, Fletcher hired a skilled engineer, and contractor to construct a reservoir, playing no active role in its construction. The contractors discovered several coal shafts improperly filled with debris, but they chose to continue working rather than properly blocking them. They filled the reservoir constructed with water, but due to the pressure of the water, it broke through the filled-in shaft of an abandoned coal mine and flooded connecting passageways in the plaintiff's active mine nearby.

Two points were canvassed. First, whether the defendants were liable regardless of the proof of negligence on their part, or on the part of any person employed by them to put up the reservoir. Second, whether they, while personally blameless of any negligence, were liable for the negligence of the contractor engaged by them to build the reservoir, the Court of Exchequer found in favour of the defendants on the second point, and was not argued upon in the succeeding appeals, because it was held irrelevant given the decision that the defendants were liable upon the first point. On the first point argued in the Court of Exchequer, Pollock, C. B., Martin and Channell, B. B., held that the defendants, not being guilty of negligence, were not liable for the harm done by the bursting of the reservoir. However, Bramwell, B., held a dissenting opinion because he was of the view that the plaintiff had the right to enjoy his land free from the flood. On appeal, Mr. Justice Blackburn, who delivered the opinion of the court, found in favour of the Plaintiff thereby reversing the decision of the lower court.

The case was further appealed to the Privy Council. The Council affirmed the judgment of the appellate court and adopted the *ratio* determined by Mr. Justice Blackburn. Likewise, the laying of oil and gas pipelines is an unnatural use of the land by the licensee or lessee concerned and in the event of oil spillage leading to fire incidence the licensee or lessee should be held responsible for the damage caused as a result of the spill. Despite the laws that are meant to regulate environmental hazards caused by the extraction of oil, oil spills have continued unabated in the Niger Delta region (Raji and Abejide, 2014: 40).

The institutional framework of the oil industry

The Federal government established some institutions for the smooth running of the petroleum industry. Two of these institutions are discussed below: the Department of Petroleum Resources (DPR) and the National Oil Spill Detection and Response Agency (NOSDRA).

Department of Petroleum Resources (DPR)

DPR is a department in the Ministry of Petroleum Resources. It is charged with the responsibility of regulation and supervision of all the operations being carried out under licenses and leases in the Oil and Gas. The discharge of these responsibilities for all the chains in petroleum production involves supervision of operations at drilling sites, production wells, crude oil export terminals, production platforms and flow stations, storage depots, refineries, pump stations, retail outlets, and other sites where petroleum is either sold or stored, and all pipelines carrying crude oil, natural gas, and petroleum products. However, in the history of oil and gas, regulation seems to be consigned to the background in favour of NNPC and Multinational Oil companies (Subai, 2014: 75). DPR's activities are also hampered by human and financial incapacities (Gboyega et al, 2011: 28). The staff of DPR moved to the NNPC; due to relatively poor civil service compensation, the DPR could not attract to it the right calibre of personnel. So, DPR is dependent on the NNPC for staffing. The arrangement in place allows DPR to tap into the human resources available in the NNPC and to allow for the fluid movement of personnel and for ease of sharing experience (Nwokeji, 2007: 26).

DPR has been treated just like another arm of the NNPC subject to its directives, those of the Ministry, and the presidency (Usman, 2017: 6). In 2006 the government admitted failure to enforce the rule that production companies must relinquish 50% ownership of oil blocs not developed over ten years under the Deep Offshore and Inland Basin Production Sharing Contract Decree 1999 (Nwokeji, 2007: 18). This is an indication of DPR's low capacity to regulate (Nwokeji, 2007: 19). Because of the inadequacies of the DPR, the new PIGB seeks to establish a regulatory Commission to be known as the Nigeria Petroleum Regulatory Commission. The Commission is expected to assume all the rights, interests, obligations and liabilities of the Petroleum Inspectorate, the DPR, and the Petroleum Products Pricing Regulatory Agency (PPPRA) when the PIGB is passed into law.

National Oil Spill Detection and Response Agency (NOSDRA)

NOSDRA was established in 2006 by an Act of National Assembly of the Federal Republic of Nigeria to coordinate the implementation of the National Oil Spill Contingency Plan (NOSCP) for Nigeria by the International Convention on Oil Pollution Preparedness, Response and Cooperation (OPRC 90) to which Nigeria is a signatory. The Agency is also to perform the following functions *inter alia*:

a) to be responsible for surveillance and ensure compliance with all existing environmental legislation and the detection of oil spills in the petroleum sector;
b) to organize the execution of the preparation for the elimination of toxic substances as may be promulgated by the Federal Government; and
c) to execute such other responsibilities that may be needed to accomplish the aims and objectives of the Agency under this Act or any arrangement as may be put together by the Federal Government under to this Act (Section 6, NOSDRA).

The agency is also to perform other special functions such as:

a) make certain to harmonize and execute the Plan within Nigeria including within 200 nautical miles from the foundation for which the breath of the territorial waters of Nigeria is measured;
b) carry out supervision, coverage, warning, and other response operations 'as they relate to oil spillages;
c) support regional collaboration among member States of West African

sub-region and in the Gulf of Guinea for fighting oil spillage and pollution in our contiguous waters;

d) reinforce the national capability and regional feat to foil, manage, fight, and alleviate the effects of marine pollution (Section 7, NOSDRA).

In case of spills, an oil spiller is by the Act expected to report to the Agency in writing not later than 24 hours after the occurrence of an oil spill, in default of which the failure to report shall attract a penalty for five hundred thousand naira (N5OO, OOO.OO) for each day of failure to report the occurrence (Section 6 (2), NOSDRA). The failure to clean up the impacted site, to all practical extent, including remediation, shall attract a further fine of one million naira (Section 6 (3), NOSDRA). However, if the notice is delivered at the nearest zonal office of the agency closer to the impacted site, within the stipulated time such notice is deemed to have been made (Section 6 (4), NOSDRA). These penalties are insufficient to guarantee observance with the law and to avert destructive practices. The fine for refusal to purge and ameliorate oil infected sites is a source of concern, as it is a given that such refusal protracts severe human rights infractions. The sum of money paid by oil companies in fines is indefinite, but many civil society organizations in the Niger Delta are worried that low fines are a sign of the fact that the government is the most important collaborator in the joint undertaking and so responsible for the majority of any fines levied (Amnesty International, 2009: 52).

Conclusion

From the foregoing, it could be observed that Nigeria's environmental challenges are not limited to the inadequate legal framework for oil and gas, but includes lack of political will on part of the Nigerian government to implement environmental related laws. The government places a premium on increasing the daily production of crude oil to the detriment of the environment and the people. More importantly, the exploitation of mineral resources in Nigeria does not translate to a good life, infrastructural facilities are still largely un-provided for, and people still wallow in abject poverty. Most of the cases against Multinational Oil companies MOCs are compromised by the Nigerian government because petroleum is seen as the backbone of the economy. The government is not ready to tolerate any disturbance of crude oil production in the form of injunctions or final judgments restraining the activities of the oil companies. This paper, therefore, recommends that Nigeria should seek to promote good governance, credible elections, democratic culture and respect for the rule of law. Without developing these virtues, the instrument of law and legal reform in the petroleum sector will have limited impact.

Recommendations

Where environmental pollution is inevitable, the government and oil companies ought to take proactive steps to provide adequate compensation and ameliorate or remediate the environment when it occurs. Apart from the provision of adequate compensation to assuage the environmental devastation government in collaboration with oil companies should provide infrastructural facilities such as schools, water supply, power supply, create employment opportunities, scholarships, vocational skills programmes, agricultural support programmes and other examples of corporate social responsibility. The government should implement the "polluter pays" principle in which the oil company responsible for oil spills is made to pay for damages caused.

The government should establish the "Petroleum Trust Fund" to ameliorate the environment and compensate the victim of oil pollution for losses they might have suffered. Most of the time the damages are done to the environment by oil spills are more than what the polluter can fix in this wise the "Trust Fund" can be made use of. National Oil Spill Detection and Response Agency (NOSDRA) which is saddled with the responsibility for enforcing environmental regulations in the oil and gas sector should be well equipped to carry out its functions. As an alternative to the destruction of the natural habitat of aquatic animals, the government should create and maintain nursery and feeding grounds for numerous species of finfish and prawns and habitat for crabs and molluscs. If this could be done, it will boost food security in the Niger Delta. All stakeholders must collaborate to sustain mangrove forests and coastal ecosystems by introducing adjustments to industrial processes, oil spill prevention, response preparedness; restoration framework, and implementation plan. Corporate Social Responsibility (CSR) and Environmental Stewardship should be required of the oil exploitation industries, and this should be enforced by the Federal Government.

References

Abibe, E and Essaugh, A, (1999) *Environmental Impact Assessment.* Enugu: Immaculate Publication: 45-50.

Abila, SE (2009) "Historic Philosophical Foundation of Minority Rights Movements in the Niger Delta" in Emiri F and Deinduomo G (eds) *Law and Petroleum industry in Nigeria: Current Challenges* (Malthouse Lagos) 175-210.

American Society of International Environmental Law (2019) www.asil.org/eisil/convention-access-information-public-participation-decision-making-and-access-justice accessed 11 June 2019.

Amnesty International (2009) "Nigeria: Petroleum, Pollution and Poverty in the Niger Delta" *Amnesty International* 21 <www.es.amnesty.org/uploads/media> accessed 02 June 2019.

Amusan, L. (2014). Evaluating the Gender Content of the Amnesty Programme in the Niger Delta of Nigeria: A Concern for the Socio-economic Development of Women? *Gender & Behaviour*, 12(3), pp. 5924-5935.

Anago, I (2002) "Environmental Impact Assessment as a Tool for Sustainable Development: The Nigerian Experience" *FIG XXII International Congress Washington, D.C. USA,* 11 https://www.fig.net/resources/proceedings/fig_proceedings/fig_2002/Ts10-3/TS10_3_anago.pdf accessed 11 June 2019.

Bribena EK (2011) "Nigeria, oil and gas exploration and the Niger Delta question: A study in corporate social responsibility" being a thesis submitted for the degree of Doctor of Laws in the School of Post Graduate Studies and Research, Faculty of Law North-West University Mafikeng Campus, South Africa, 230.

CEHRD's, (2009) *Report on the state of human rights abuses and violence in the Niger Delta region of Nigeria,* 157 <www.cehrd.org> accessed 02 June 2019.

Committee on Economic, Social and Cultural Rights (CESCR), General Comment No. I S: The Right to Water (Arts. II and 12 of the International Covenant on Economic, Social and Cultural Rights), UN Doc E./C. I2/2002/ 1I, 20 January 2003. Nigeria has domesticated the agreement and as such, it has the force of law like any other Nigerian law.

Environmental Guidelines and Standards for the Petroleum Industry in Nigeria (EGASPIN), 1991. It was revised in 2002, The Guidelines were issued by the Department of Petroleum Resources (DPR).

Etikerentse, G *Nigerian Petroleum Law,* (2nd edn, Dredew publisher, Lagos 2004) 144.

Gboyega, A *et al* (2011) "Political Economy of the Petroleum Sector in Nigeria" World Bank Policy Research, Working Paper 5779 p 28.

Inokoba, PK and Imbua, DL (2010) "Vexation and Militancy in the Niger Delta: The Way Forward" *29(2) Journal of Human Ecology* 101-120 at 104.

Omeje, K (2005) "Oil conflict in Nigeria: Contending issues and perspectives of the local Niger Delta people" *10 (3) Journal New Political Economy* <www.tandfonline.com> accessed 20 June 2019.

Ishaya, DA (2016) *et al* "Challenges in the delivery of environmental sustainability in housing development in Abuja, Nigeria" in *Emerging trends in construction organizational practices and project management knowledge area,* the 9th cidb Postgraduate Conference February 2-4, 2016, Cape Town, South Africa.

Jeffery, MI "Environmental governance: a comparative analysis of public participation and access to justice" *Journal of South Pacific Law* http://www.paclii.org/journals/fJSPL/vol09no2/2.shtml accessed 11 June 2019.

NOSDRA (2004) "Towards a new Oil Spill Compensation System in Nigeria" 6

Nwilo, PC and Badejo OT (2005) "Oil Spill Problems and Management in the Niger Delta" *International Oil Spill Conference* 567 <http://ioscproceedings.org> accessed 22 June 2019.

Nwokeji, GU (2007) "The Nigerian National Petroleum Corporation and the Development of the Nigerian oil and gas Industry: History, Strategies and Current Directions" *The James A Baker II Institute for Public Policy and Japan Petro0leum Energy Centre* 17 – 30.

Nwoko, CO "Evaluation of Environmental Impact Assessment System in Nigeria" *2(1) Greener Journal of Environmental Management and Public Safety* 27 <www.gjournals.org> accessed 1 June 2019.

Ogri OR (2001) "A Review of the Nigerian Petroleum Industry and the Associated Environmental Problems" *21 The Environmentalist* 11 at 1

Oil spills in Delta and Bayelsa States, Nigeria unknown page <www.stakeholdersdemocracay.org> accessed 19 June 2019.

Oil watch http://oilwatchafrica.org/content/ogoni-clean-up-set-to-commence-after-years-of-popular-campaigns/ accessed 22 June 2019.

Orubu, CO *et al* (2004) "The Nigerian Oil industry: Environmental Diseconomies, Management Strategies and the Need for Community Involvement" 16(3) *Journal of Human Ecology* 203.

Peek, P and Keith, N (2002) "Lower Niger Bronze Industries and the Archaeology of the Niger" page unknown.

Raji, AOY and Abejide TS (2014) "Compliance with oil & gas regulations in the Niger Delta Region, Nigeria C. 1960s-2000: An assessment" *3(8) Arabian Journal of Business and Management Review (OMAN Chapter)* 40 <www.arabianjbmr.com> accessed 11 May 2019.

Sagay, IE "The Niger Delta and the case for resource control" <www.profitsesagay.com/pdf> accessed 16 June 2019.

Sahhed, ZS and Egwaikhide, CI (2012) "Impact of Social Crises on Economic Development: Theoretical Evidence from Nigeria" 2 (6) *American International Journal of Contemporary Research,* 179 http://www.aijcrnet.com/journals/

Vol_2_No_6_June_2012/21.pdf accessed 11 June 2019; AllAfrica "Nigeria: Pipeline Vandalism and Culpability of Security Agents" (2014) unknown page http://allafrica.com/stories/201410140258.html accessed 11 October 2019.

Subai, P *Towards a Functional Petroleum Industry in Nigeria: A Critical Analysis of Nigeria's Petroleum Industry Reform* (PhD-dissertation Newcastle University 2014) 75.

This Day newspaper of Thursday, 22 June 2017

UN environment, UN Environment's Ogoniland Assessment Back in Spotlight <http://www.unep.org/newscentre/un-environments-ogoniland-assessment-back-spotlight> accessed 22 June 2019.

UNEP, Environmental Assessment of Ogoniland (2011) 20 <www.unep.org/nigeria accessed 20 June 2019>; Akpabio, EM and Akpan, NS "governance and Oil Politics in Nigeria's Niger Delta: The Question of Distributive Equity" *30(2) J Hum Ecol,* 111-121 at 111

United Nations Environment Programme (UNEP), Environmental Assessment of Ogoniland, Executive Summary (2011) 3 www.unep.org accessed 22 June 2019.

United Nations Treaty Collection Chapter XXVII Environment titled Convention on Access to Information, Public Participation in Decision-Making and Access to Justice in Environmental Matters <https://treaties.un.org/Pages/ViewDetails.aspx?> accessed 11 June 2019.

Usman, AK *Environmental protection Law and Practice* (1st edn. Ababa Press Ltd, Ibadan, Nigeria 2010) 6.

Vanguard News 21 December 2016 "Fresh oil spill hits Ibeno communities in Akwa Ibom" <www.vanguardngr.com/2016/12/fresh-oil-spill-hits-ibeno-communities-akwa-ibom> accessed 21 June 2019.

Yusuf RO *et al* (2007) "Environmental Impact Assessment Challenge in Nigeria" *2(2) Journal of The Environmentalist* 11-21 at 11 Kluwer Academic Publishers http://link.springer.com/content/pdf> accessed 31 May 2019.

Statutes

Article 14, the Charter entered force on 29/ 1/99.

Article 11(1).

Article 12.

Article 14(2). CEDA W entered force on 3/9/81 and was ratified by Nigeria on 13/7/85.

Article 24, The Convention entered force on 2/9/90 and the Bill of Rights, which it established for children, has been incorporated into Nigeria's Child's Right Act No.26 of 2003.

Constitution of Federal Republic of Nigeria, 1999.

Convention on Civil Liability for Oil Pollution Damage (CLC),1969 < www.admiraltylawguide.com> accessed 5 June 2019.
Environmental Impact Assessment Act, 2004.

General Comment 15 (2002) and the United Nations Economic and Social Council, "Substantive Issues Arising in the Implementation of the International Covenant on Economic, Social and Cultural Rights" E/C. 12/2002/ 11 of 26/ Jl /2002.

Land Use Act, 1978.

NOSDRA (Establishment) Act, 2006.

Oil Pollution Damage (FUND Convention) 1971

Section 17 (3) (d) of the 1999 Constitution of Nigeria.

Section 2 (1) of the EIA Act, Section 2 of the Act Section 22 (a)

Section 58 only stipulates that the Agency can facilitate environmental assessment.

Section 6 (2), Section 6 (3), Section 6 (4), Section 6 of the Act and Section 7 of the Act.

Sections 29 and 35 of the Land Use Act 1978, Cap 202 Laws of Federation of Nigeria 1990.

Section 12 (1) of the 1999 Constitution of Federal Republic of Nigeria.

Stockholm Declaration by the United Nations Conference on the Human Environment of June 1972 and Rio Declaration on Environment and Development of June 1992.

Cases

A. G. Ondo v. A. G. Federation, ((2002) 9 NWLR (Pt 772), 222)

Rylands v *Fletcher* ((1868) LR 3 HL 330).
Shell v Farah ((1995) 3 WLR (Pt. 382) 148).

Social and Economic Rights Action Centre (SERAC) and Another v Nigeria (200I) AHRLR 60 <www.achpr.org/files/sessions/30th/comunications/155.96/achpr30_155_96_eng.pdf> (para 1) 1 accessed on 13 June 2019.

Chapter 16
Traditional Farm Settlements as a Veritable Strategy for Resuscitating Sustainable Development in Underdeveloped and Misaligned Economy

Elijah Babasola Afolabi AGBAJE and Olumide OMODUNBI

Introduction

Problems associated with socioeconomic disempowerment (Buheji 2018) arising from youth unemployment (Karim and Surajo 2016) rising urban idleness and joblessness, socially-induced crimes and violence as well as pervasive communal insecurity are on the increase in Nigeria, just as the unpleasant effects of starvation-induced ailments and its associated social costs and pitfalls are widening (Action Against Hunger 2020). This study, adopting field observation, provides understanding to the problem of youth unemployment, rising inflation, increasing threat of food insecurity (International Committee of the Red Cross 2017), dependence on imported food, and the threat to meaningful industrial take-off as a result of decline in agricultural production, poor and inadequate deployment of productive factors and resulting mass unemployment in Nigeria. This attempt, therefore, represents a modest effort at going beyond the rhetoric to properly situate agriculture within the frameworks for the attainment of sustainable development in Nigeria. The study focused on the possibility of combining the existing traditional farm settlement system and techniques with the modern production factors for the empowerment of youths and idling productive populace in Nigerian southwest supposed agrarian communities. Arising from the discussion above, this article will seek to provide answers to the following research objectives and questions;

Research objectives

Focusing on traditional farm settlements in the Odo-Otin Local Government Area of Osun state, to use it as a pilot study for re-engineering improvement in agro-industrial synergy in Western Nigeria, the study unveiled measures to counter the factors responsible for the decline in agricultural practices among the indigenous farming communities in Nigeria. Specifically, the study:

1. Account for the factors responsible for the decline in the agricultural engagement of Nigerian farmers.
2. Identify the potentials of encouraging youth to re-embrace agriculture as a means of living.
3. Documents for attention different crop specialization of each community and identify areas of possible official assistance.
4. Explore the possibility of effecting, through policy measures, backward reintegration of rural-urban migration.
5. Sensitize and explore the possibility of securing official assistance to bring about an improvement in practice, production, and marketing of agricultural produce.
6. Identify areas in which traditional authorities can create necessary synergies to improve agro-allied local employment opportunities of the school-leavers as a way of improving local expertise and promoting the local investment of critically needed human and other productive factors.

Research questions

The research attempted to answer the following questions:

1. What has been the trend in agricultural preoccupation in average Nigerian rural communities over the last five decades?
2. What are the critical factors still presently available for meaningful engagement in agricultural practices and what are the missing-gaps and challenges faced by the remaining farming communities?

3. What is the rate of idleness and joblessness among the urban lower class, and what percentage of urban loafers and school leaving youth could be interested in embracing agriculture if encouraged?
4. What assistance has been provided by official institutions to encourage the practice of agriculture among the idling youth and productive group of the rural populace, and what are the areas in which further encouragement is needed?
5. Is the marketing of farm products as a major sector promoting national development?
6. How substantially could agro-based rural-urban reintegration help in reducing unemployment as a way of promoting sustainable development in Nigeria?

Review of literature

Towards addressing the problem of underdevelopment and mass poverty, Nigeria has embarked on a series of programmes (Ibietan and Ekhosuehi 2013). Among such programmes known in Nigerian history are: Operation Feed the Nation (OFN), Green Revolution (GR), Austerity Measure (AM), Structural Adjustment Programme (SAP), Better Life (BL), Poverty Alleviation (PA) just to mention but a few. But regrettably, the adoption of these programmes in Nigeria have not addressed the persistent problem of poor per-capita income (PPCI), poor standard of living (PSL), poor health and high mortality rate (PHHMR), low life expectancy (LLE) and a high index of systemic instability (HSI). This situation is better reflected in the rationalization by the National Planning Commission (NPC 2004). This is largely because many of these programmes failed to take advantage of the existing national comparative factors and opportunities for accelerated development, but are merely conceived and pursued as opportunistic political agenda of the political gladiators in neglect of critical mass of national resources across urban and rural settings and in many instances, without consideration for inter-sectoral linkage.

Lane and Ersson (1997:25) have noted that development is a major goal for most if not all third world nations. It is believed to be the key to solving social problems and a necessary condition for not having to face greater difficulties, to usher in not only affluence and economic growth but also improved quality of life and democracy. Myrdal (1957, 1968) identified the following as critical factors of development: production output and incomes, conditions of production, levels of living, attitudes towards life and work and, the quality of institutions and policies. According to Olopoenia (1983:13) solving the problem of 'not developing' in the UDCs, require the correct articulation of the meaning of development as the foundation on which the solutions to the problem of 'not developing' can be built. Inanga (1983:76), viewing development from an economic point of view agreed with Aboyade (1976), that development is "a process of transformation which combines economic growth with social and economic change, to generate an improvement in social welfare (and) a rise in the standard of living of the people".

Canvassing inclusive development via agriculture, Maoist ideology clearly states that if we want to develop rapidly, we must make everybody happy and enthusiastic in his work. Stolper (1963:13-14) has emphasized momentary self-denial by all to save for investment and not, where the ruled exclusively suffered for the exclusive comfort of the rich. The time has come for the rich occupants of government to begin to pay close attention to the needs of the downtrodden. Without this happening, Nigeria should brace up for increased manifestation of negative vices than it is currently witnessing.

And if we want this to happen, we must promote agriculture and light and heavy industries simultaneously (Paine 1976:278). The success of the Chinese economy testifies to the efficacy of the Maoist principles (Paine 1976:296). To paraphrase, Aspe and Gurra (1993:12-14), both the old and new literature on development, point to the primacy of government efforts to bridge missing markets and open opportunities for the people. Very useful for our analysis, howbeit, is the Lewis thesis (1988) that development calls for the existence of three major conditions: the ability to avoid wastage, the ability to develop and apply new technologies (see also Bamikole 2009). While the focus of this paper is not downplaying the need for the introduction of modern technology, it canvasses that while making effort to invent and adopt new technologies, it would be a monumental loss and a drag on development if the existing ones are allowed to continue to waste away. No doubt, combining the already existent and viable factors of production with the newly invented technologies can only lead to unimaginable rapid growth in Nigeria. Stone has argued that, to adapt an economy from one rate of growth to another, require the capacity to make decisions with knowledge of the subject (Stone 1966:555) that is, having a full grasp of the issues involved towards a renewed effort to re-awaken the declined interest in agricultural preoccupation. Examining Hungarian development, Belassa (1982:29) in his exposition on what he termed 'second economy' noted the establishment of an economic system, which combines the large-scale socialist sector, cooperatives, and small-scale private activities such as agro-allied activities in a flexible manner as the engine of growth. For this to be, however, requires the enthronement of enlightened government committed to the welfare of all (See also Kasper (1994, Herberger 1984 and Johnson 1982) that will be ready to tap and develop factors of production wherever and in whatever magnitude they may be found.

The hint is drawn from Bhagwati (1966), that there is no passive path to development. Resources must be raised, invested, framework planned, timing element agreed, proper phasing scheduled, and perspectives made clear. For this analyst, agriculture and industrialization must complement each other, just as appropriate education and manpower development should be considered as a priority. However, for Nigeria, contrary to the experience in other climes, the drive towards inclusive development, in particular, has been lukewarm as all well-advised solutions have either been neglected or shoddily implemented (Onimode 1987). Igbuzor (2005: 281-282) chronicled not less than fourteen initiatives aimed at addressing the problem of poverty in Africa over the last four decades with the result, just as indicated above, that poverty is waxing stronger in its attack on African masses. One thing remains very clear, Nigeria, or any nation for that matter cannot attain development without first finding a way out of unending wastage of her productive factors and potentials (Nwajiuba 2012).

In line with the goal of this research, one area that has been neglected for so long, despite its high utility in era of multidimensional developmental challenges as Nigeria faces, is re-tapping the hitherto neglected existing development factors like traditional farm settlements. There is so much fertile land, so much manpower, so much domestic needs, and so vast commercial and industrial market for products. But, as revealed in the last four decades, not so much can be done with the apparent mismatch of reconcilable opportunities and challenges that abounds in several sectors of the Nigerian disarticulated and misaligned economy. Of great importance and pointedly too, development requires gradual reintegration of the rural-urban synergies; this means linking the agro-based population with the commerce-infused urban dwellers. To achieve sustainable development, going forward, this remains the most appropriate strategy that must be adopted to take care of all advantages and disadvantages of the urban-rural nexus. In this case, harnessing the critical factors of production currently lying waste in the extensive traditional farm settlement system in Nigeria will represent a critical move for meeting the unmet urban cum industrial food and production demands, and create backward reintegration of the idling urban population into the more expansively abounding agro-allied sector in the rural communities.

The imperatives for and challenges of sustainable development in Nigeria

Nigeria is a country with a good climate and a large traditional agrarian populace. Even in this modern era, farming and agro-allied preoccupations are estimated to constitute about 70 percent of the Nigerian population engaged in the non-oil sector. Regrettably, compared with South Korea which at a time had only 8 percent of her population in farming, and against the late 60s prediction of a notable Africa development scholar, Stolper, Nigeria is unable to feed her population not to talk of supplying critical agricultural inputs to her declining or now almost non-existent secondary and tertiary manufacturing industries.

An economy once sustained on the export of agricultural products –cocoa, groundnut, and palm oil, presently, has agricultural export accounting for less than 10 percent of Nigerian foreign earnings. The lamentation by analysts, which started close to four decades ago (Olatunbosun 1975), has for a long time remained loud as the much expected dramatic change is yet to be witnessed. This declined contribution of the agricultural sector to the national macroeconomic-mix could have been commendable if the decline in agricultural contribution to the national gross domestic product (GDP) results from an increased level of industrialization and export of tertiary products. Far from this, Nigeria runs an oil-dependent pensile economy. Due to internal contradictions relating to some systemic delinkage in rural-urban synergy, the nation in the first decade of the 21st century, from all indicators of development has taken a downturn recording real development index that is unimaginably lower and poorer than what obtained in the 70s. Thus:

> Poverty reduction… [has become] the most difficult challenge facing Nigeria and its people and the greatest obstacle to the pursuit of sustainable socio-economic growth…The challenge is not only to reform the economy in order to boost economic growth but also to empower the people as a means of revitalizing the weakened social pillar (National Planning Commission 2004).

Almost all critical factors of development are in abundant supply in Nigeria, but as the African boss of the World Bank sometimes in recent past indicated, there is so much idleness in Nigeria. In his expression, the level of production in Nigeria, as in the rest of most African countries, is ridiculously low. Whereas Nigeria is a natural agrarian society blessed with great and incomparably high prospects for full employment and food security, yet the country today, against prediction, is one of the starving nations of the world with a mass of despondently idling and jobless manpower. The reality of the increasing spate of gentrification resulting from urban renewal and consequent displacement of people at the lower rungs of the society from their menial means of livelihood: motorbike/okada riding, road-side petty shop-holding and selling, and street-corridor-crafts (bike and motor mechanic, vulcanizing, furniture-making; and outright on-road traffic/congestion-aided trading), reveals the stark outcome that many of the Nigerian potential productive populations are becoming far less-engaged, more starved beyond what Abacha described in the eighties (Abacha cited in Onovo 1997 see also Akinsanmi 2005), cripplingly idle, and increasingly hopeless. Comparing the contemporary experience with those of the 70s when agriculture provided food and other basic requirements of life, generating somewhat full employment of old and young, and providing some essential raw materials

–cotton, cocoa, palm and groundnut oils- inputs for industries, the reverse has become the case over the recent decades. Nigeria, at the birth of the fourth republic and inception of the 21st century, was in a pervasive crisis of underdevelopment (Zehender 1990).

As an important factor of sustainable development, this research sets out to examine the nexus between the negative effect of a generational shift in agro-allied preoccupation and neglected opportunities of abandoned traditional farm settlements in some of the existing traditional farm in Odo-Otin Local Government Area of Osun State in Nigeria. This is with a view to determining whether or not the resuscitation of traditional farm settlements as a component of readily available developmental factors, could count as one relevant means by which the problems associated with rural-depopulation, urban poverty, and social despondency, critical human underdevelopment and pauperization among the youth particularly, and urban poor generally, can be mitigated. The goal is to see how agro-enabled rural-urban reintegration could become one of the credible paths to Nigerian agricultural reawakening for sustainable development. Just as Ishikawa opined, it is here conjectured that resuscitation of traditional farm settlements in Nigeria, apart from reversing the tendencies towards food insecurity, could address the challenges of unemployment, facilitate the development of cottage industries and further boost national production through crops and livestock farming specialization and efficiency (see Ishikawa 1966). If found plausible, this will well serve as a trigger to promoting an aggressive revival of agriculture and positive reintegration of rural-urban synergies to stem the tide of unending life-wasting rural-urban migration, and its attendant growing disablement of national manpower and continued wastage of national resources.

Methodology

The research deployed both historical, field observation, and interview techniques. This includes field trips to the six traditional farm settlements in the area of study to determine the trend in farming population, farming techniques, farming production, general standard of living of the remaining farming communities, and the challenge they face. This method became necessary because these farm settlements have the history of being well established in the pre-60s and 70s providing means of employment and sustenance to several thousand people from far and near. Many of the traditional farm settlements, if the situation of the 60s and 70s had continued, was capable of developing to moderately-sized modern communities with necessary modern facilities, just as witnessed in the present Opete Village. During the study, particular notice was taken of the farming populace, ages of farmers, social facilities, socioeconomic and infrastructural challenges, and the worrying trend in occupational preferences of the children. An effort was made to determine the percentage of the farming family which has the tradition of bequeathing their farmlands and practice to their upcoming children. Where there are children of school age on and around the farms, an effort was made to determine the easiness of combining education with assisting parents on the farm, and to know whether if given necessary encouragement they could stay back in farming. COVID-19 lockdown did not make it possible to observe the vitality of the schools and public health centers, where available (Amusan & Agunyai, 2021). An effort was made to determine whether youths would like to stay back after school to get engaged in agricultural practice. The response was poor, but the interview revealed that youth will be willing to stay-back if given needed assistance and encouragement by the government.

Specific observation

There was a visit to the local government council where not less than five ploughing tractors were rusting away in the open air, while the entire local government does not have a single one working to serve the ploughing need of farmers in the local government, thereby relying on few privately owned ones and sometimes having to wait unendingly, in turn, to be served after making booking many of which never come through before the rain ceases.

As a pilot study, the research could not meet some of the stakeholders (traditional rulers and government officials) in the community to ascertain the certainty of land tenure, traditional security arrangements, and possible communal efforts relating to agro-allied development.

In future studies, efforts will be made to find out possible avenues and modalities for official intervention from different government agencies (local, state, and federal governments) responsible for the development of agriculture as a means to employment generation, food security, and national development.

To determine the rate of urban idleness among the productive age bracket, all that is needed is to undertake an unobtrusive survey (observational) across major cities in Nigeria. One will be stunned by the extent at which abled-bodied men of productive age sit idly at motor parks and popular centers such as markets, major event centers, under bridges and similar places, begging for alms or pleading by-passers for token financial assistance to meet daily food ration. A careful x-ray of this increasing social malady of idleness will show a significant proportion of the idling population to be the most needed productive population whose labour can be better deployed to farming if encouraged. Some sit in this manner at different locations particularly in major cities for as much as eight or more hours, from around 8 am till 6 pm or later hours each day. A descriptive presentation of the research findings is presented in the composite analytic table below.

Observational term/ Factors of production	Traditional farm settlements visited during field trip					
	Alapata Village	**Igbotele Village**	**Reke Village**	**Oponda Village**	**Imuleke Village**	**Opete Village**
Farmland availability						
Nature of land available	Extensive good fertile land	Extensive good fertile land	Extensive good fertile land	Extensive good fertile land	Extensive good fertile land	Extensive good fertile land
Housing (All Houses are roofed with Zinc roofing sheets)	**Alapata Village**	**Igbotele Village**	**Reke Village**	**Oponda Village**	**Imuleke Village**	**Opete Village**
Village Size (In terms of Households)	About 30	About 10	About 6	About 8	More than 30	Above 100
Modern Cement plastered Brick Houses	Few	None	None	One	Many	Many
Modern un-plastered Brick Houses	Some	Some	One	One	Few	Many
Cement plastered Mud Houses	Many	Most	Two	Two	Few	Many
Unplastered Mud Houses	Few	Few	Three	Four	Few	Few
Plank Made Houses	None	None	None	None	None	None
Most Important Cash/Food Crop Grown	**Alapata Village**	**Igbotele Village**	**Reke Village**	**Oponda Village**	**Imuleke Village**	**Opete Village**
Cocoa	Used to exists but mostly now Disused	Used to exists but mostly now Disused	Used to exists but mostly now Disused	Used to exists but mostly now Disused	Used to exists but mostly now Disused	Used to exists but mostly now Disused
Kolanut	No longer produced	Used to exists but now Disused	Produced	Produced	Produced	Produced
Walnut	No longer produced	Produced	Produced	Produced	Produced	Produced
Palm fruits/Oil	Domestic	Domestic	Produced	Produced	Produced	Produced

Plantain	Produced	Produced	Produced	Produced	Produced	Produced
Banana	Produced	Produced	Produced	Produced	Produced	Produced
Groundnut	Not produced	Produced	Produced	Produced	Produced	Produced
Sheal nuts	Not produced	Not produced		Not produced	Not produced	Not produced
Cashew nuts	Not produced	Produced	Produced	Produced	Produced	Produced
Pineapple	Produced in abundance	Produced in abundance	Produced in abundance	Produced in abundance	Produced in abundance	Produced in abundance
Yam	In abundance	Produced in abundance	Produced in abundance	Produced in abundance	Produced in abundance	Produced in abundance
Cocoyam	Not in abundance	Produced in abundance	Produced in abundance	Produced in abundance	Produced in abundance	Produced in abundance
Cassava	Produced in abundance	Produced in abundance	Produced in abundance	Produced in abundance	Produced in abundance	Produced in abundance
Tomatoes	Produced in abundance	Produced in abundance	Produced in abundance	Produced in abundance	Produced in abundance	Produced in abundance
Maize	Produced	Produced in abundance	Produced in abundance	Produced in abundance	Produced in abundance	Produced
Millet	Produced		Not produced	Produced	Produced	
Orange	Not in abundant	In abundance	Produced	Produced in abundance	Produced in abundance	Produced in abundance
Mango	Produced	Produced	Produced	Produced in abundance	Produced in abundance	Produced in abundance
Potato	Produced	Produced in abundance	Not produced	Produced	Produced	Produced in abundance
Vegetables	Produced	Produced in abundance	Produced in abundance	Produced in abundance	Produced in abundance	Produced in abundance
Pepper	Produced in abundance	Produced in abundance	Produced in abundance	Produced in abundance	Produced in abundance	Produced in abundance

Other Production Activities	**Alapata Village**	**Igbotele Village**	**Reke Village**	**Oponda Village**	**Imuleke Village**	**Opete Village**
Animals	Yes (Domestic)	Yes (Cattle rearing)	Yes (Domestic)	Yes (Cattle rearing)		Yes (Cattle rearing)
Fish	No		No	Yes (Stream Ponds)		Fishing stream
Poultry	Yes (Domestic)	Yes (Domestic)	Yes (Domestic)	Yes (Commercial)		Yes (Commercial)
Agricultural processing facilities						
Local Small scale processing	Lacking	Lacking	Lacking	Lacking	Lacking	Lacking
Medium scale processing	Lacking	Lacking	Lacking	Lacking	Lacking	Lacking
Large scale processing	Lacking	Lacking	Lacking	Lacking	Lacking	Lacking

Means of transportation	**Alapata Village**	**Igbotele Village**	**Reke Village**	**Oponda Village**	**Imuleke Village**	**Opete Village**
Lorries	Available when needed	Available when needed	No	Available when needed	Available when needed	Available when needed
Buses	Available when needed	Available when needed	No	Available when needed	Available when needed	Available when needed
Motor cars	Available when needed	Available when needed	No	Available when needed	Available when needed	Available when needed
Motorbikes	Available when needed	Available when needed	Available when needed	Available when needed	Available when needed	Available when needed
Animal carriage	No	No	No	No	No	No
Modern farming amenities						
Field Plowing Tractors	None from Govern-ment but Occasion-ally hired from private owners	None from Govern-ment but Occasion-ally hired from private owners	None	None from Govern-ment but Occasion-ally hired from private owners	None from Govern-ment but Occasion-ally hired from private owners	None from Govern-ment but Occasion-ally hired from private owners

Motorised Sprayers	None	None	None	None	None	None
Harvesters	None	None	None	None	None	None
Modern Preservation Facilities	None	None	None	None	None	None
Age Categories of farmers	**Alapata Village**	**Igbotele Village**	**Reke Village**	**Oponda Village**	**Imuleke Village**	**Opete Village**
Old Adults Above 50s	More	More	Few	Few	Some	Many
Middle: Age 30s-40s	Few	Few	More	Few	Some	Some
Adolescent 10 - 20	Rare	Rare	Some	Some	More	More
Children: Below 10	More	Many	More	More	More	More
Social amenities available	**Alapata Village**	**Igbotele Village**	**Reke Village**	**Oponda Village**	**Imuleke Village**	**Opete Village**
Market Outlet						
Local Market	Available but not functional in recent times	None	None	None	None	Available
Nearby Bigger Town Markets	Available	Available	Available	Available	Available	Available
Education facilities						
Primary Sch	Available in the immediate proximity	Available in the immediate proximity	Available in the immediate proximity	Available in the immediate proximity	Available in the immediate proximity	Available in the immediate proximity
Secondary Sch	About 3-4 kilometers away	About 3-4 kilometers away	About 1 hour walk away	Available about 1 kilometer away	Available about 1 kilometer away	About 3-4 kilometers away
Tertiary Sch	4 Kilometers away	4 Kilometers away	4 Kilometers away	4 Kilometers away	4 Kilometers away	4 Kilometers away
Local health facility	Available	Available	Not available	Available	Available	Available
Water supply	Hand Pump Well	Hand Pump Well	Hand Pump Well	Hand Pump Well	Hand Pump Well	Hand Pump Well
Electricity	Connect-ion to National Grid Available	Connect-ion to National Grid Available	Not available	Connect-ion to National Grid Available	Connect-ion to National Grid Available	Connection to National Grid Available

Security Institution	About 3-4 kilometers away	About 3-4 kilometers away	About 3-4 kilometers away	Available within 1 kilometer away	Available within 1 kilometer away	Available 1 hour walk away
Telecommunication	GSM Network available	GSM Network available	GSM Network available	GSM Network available	GSM Network available	GSM Network available
Road	2 Kilometers of Yearly Graded Non-Asphalt	2 Kilometers of Yearly Graded Non-Asphalt	3 Kilometers of Foot Path rarely main-tained Motorable Non-Asphalt	2 Kilometers of Yearly Graded Non-Asphalt	2 Kilometers of Yearly Graded Non-Asphalt	Asphalt covered Motorable road with Many non-Asphalt Graded Road to neighbour-ing farms

Table 1: *Observational table for descriptive analysis of neglect of traditional farm system of agriculture as a component of sustainable development effort in Nigeria*
Source: Researchers' Field Trip Observation 2020

*KEY TO THE ABOVE TABLE

Abundance:
Means at a time in the past when manpower was available to farming, the area was and still capable of producing beyond the domestic consumption of farmers if aided with equipment and have access to guaranteed market.

Produced:
Produced for consumption and petty sales demand but can be cultivated in large quantity is aided.

Local/Neighbouring Markets:
The usual local 5-day markets rotated among the neighbouring towns and communities.

Findings and discussion
Using a qualitative descriptive analysis method with a special effort to provide a reflective illustration of issues and findings, we make the following submissions.

Availability of farming land

Generally, the entire Southwest of Nigeria has a good climate and vegetation suitable for agricultural practices and production. Though, these lands are not as extensive as it is available in the northern part of the country, yet, given the almost all-year-round agriculture friendly climate, the available land, much of which is either not cultivated or not maximally profitably utilized now can be a veritable asset for national development. Respondents interviewed across these farm settlements are willing to allow the use of their land by even non-members of the community. Only that while some communities are willing to sell land to outsiders, a few are opposed to an outright sale of land to outsiders, in the hope that when the government gets its acts right, agriculture will still witness a good turnout.

Housing for farmers

These are settlements that have existed for a long time. Some of them have fairly modern buildings built and plastered with modern cement bricks. In most places, such as Opete, Imuleke, Alapata, and Igbotele several modern houses are much more decent than what some people rent in major towns lying fallow and unoccupied by anyone. The fact that electricity and water supply (Hand Pump Boreholes) are available in all of these communities except Reke which is a border town between Erinle Kwara state and Ila-Odo and Ijabe Osun state. We need to note the presence of the Federal Government and the United Nations Programme in the facilitation of Education, Water Supply, and Health facilities across all the settlements. So also, is the effort of the Osun State Government in maintaining the non-asphalt road paths yearly. By all standards, observations from our field trips show that there are housing and other modern facilities (electricity, radio and television, telephone -GSM- and in some cases internet signals) available for anyone who may choose to take to farming in majority those traditional farm settlements, except Reke, which lies at the Kwara state end of the farming communities. The case of this community is worst compared to the rest. Respondents here complained that while the Kwara state government will bring polling booths to them during the election, there is nothing the state government has contributed to the welfare of the community beside the United Nations assisted education, health, and water facilities. Rather than develop, the community is on its path to extinction as a farm settlement. The major reason for this is the lack of access road. The only passable road from the Osun state end, which is the access road for now for the settlement, is not passable during the raining season.

Presence of social amenities in farming communities

Without doubt, giving the presence of social amenities around the proximity of the farm settlements, the Nigerian government has provided basic amenities that can sustain a farming living community. In all the farming communities visited, there are educational and a health institution within or very close to the communities as well as a constant supply of electricity than it is even enjoyed in most urban centres. But the fault lies in not recognizing the peculiar needs of the farming communities as different from the needs of the town or urban dwellers. Most importantly, they need government assistance in the provision of heavy equipment such as tractors and bush clearing machines. Also, fear of insecurity, because of the rising tension within the nation arising from the activities of kidnappers and herdsmen, is a big issue for the working populace who might want to adopt farming as an additional venture. Kidnapping, herdsmen attacks, grazing on farmers' crops and outright setting ablaze of farmers' farms have discouraged individuals that have the means to self-sponsor themselves for greater agricultural exploit. On this note, the governments of the Nigerian Southwest States have set up a security outfit to further assist the Nigerian Police to improve on the neighbourhood security in the Southwest. All that is needed is for the government to help provide tractors and other equipment for the kick-off mass agricultural production enterprise across the Nigerian rural setting. When this becomes part of the national plan, concern for the security of lives and properties will follow and be extended to the farm settlements.

Lack of farming machinery/equipment

There is the stark reality of lack of modern assistance to agriculture despite the presence of modern social amenities in most of these farm settlements. It is this lack of essential agricultural assistance that has driven youth away from the farm. In the immediate, they need machinery to open up and plough, and if possible, assist in the planting of the opened fields. Very well needed is machinery for opening up the fields and tractors for ploughing. The rest can be handled using labour and manual efforts. In all the settlement, farmers complained of lack of heavy equipment assistance from the government. Even when the pay to hire tractors from individual owners, they are rarely attended to in good time during the raining season. This is one area where local governments should come in to play a critical role. A visit to the Local Government Headquarters revealed that more than 5 ploughing tractors of various models, Massey Ferguson, John Deere, and others are parked and rusting away as scraps within the local government. Efforts could have been directed to at least scrapping few to repair some if purchasing new ones is not feasible. The outcome is that these essential farming equipment and machinery that could best be provided by local governments are just not available for the use of these vast farming communities, even when the farmers are ready to pay rentals for hire.

Age category of the farming population

From our field observation, the result of a lack of modern farming facilities is that Nigerian farmlands and settlements are populated by aged and physically out-used men and women. It seems a paradox that while Nigeria is blessed with a youthful but idling productive population endlessly roaming the urban centres for non-available jobs, the farming population is aged and weak. In all the settlements visited, it is confirmed that the bulk of the farming populace is above sixty years. Rarely are middle-aged and secondary school leaving age groups found. Even, when they lack the skills to be meaningfully engaged in urban centres, they will rather choose to travel to cities irrespective of the poor fate that awaits them. Middle productive age groups are mostly non-existent in most of the farm settlements, except some few civil or public servants who choose to combine small-scale self-maintained farms to cushion family needs with their secular job. Commercial or large-scale farming is non-existent. While, in the previous Survey, (Agbaje, Adeyeye, Omodunbi 2020), many youths signified interest to engage in agriculture if aided with modern facilities, the continued absence of these facilities has been the major factor that makes farming an unattractive endeavour to the teeming youthful populace in Nigeria.

Agro-allied processing facilities

Agriculture is one key sector that is capable of generating chains of economic activities as a precursor to manufacturing and industrial development. To depict, the extent of neglect in Nigeria of this crucial synergy, despite the presence of basic industrial requirements like water and electricity, most communities lack the presence of even small-scale farm product processing and preservative facilities. There were few instances of cassava and palm-oil manual labour processing activities as few pieces of evidence that value addition to farm products could be a gainful endeavour. It would be surprising that a medium-sized flour processing factory, referred to as TJ Mills is located in the local government; but no mention was made of its farm product demand and processing impact by any of the farmers. It shows, the siting of the firm did not take into consideration the need to encourage local farmers as an immediate source of farm produce supply for processing. Besides electricity supply challenges, which is comparatively better in the study area judging from the national average, encouraging local farmers' input could have made a better impact on the sustenance of the firm's operation. But this was not done, the factory demanded more on other sources, mostly foreign, no wonder the Milling firm has been less functional since established.

The impact of declining moral values and negative orientation

Nigeria is a nation on a fast slide into anarchy. Because of the public examples of quick and unexplained wealth among public political and economic gladiators, the youth of nowadays in Nigeria have delved into the wrong value of making wealth without work. It is not uncommon to see jobless youth, students, and idling youths in the present-day Nigeria driving SUVs cars and Jeeps, building or living in posh houses without any question from the authority or community members. There have been examples of parents helping their children with rituals, as there are cases of parents killing theirs or other peoples' children for the sake of money rituals. The phenomenal rise in unexplained wealth and the easiness with which it is enjoyed without question has made anything that will involve brain tasking or hard-labour such as farming a no-go area for the Nigerian youths and even middle-aged and older productive population. The slang is, if the sweetness of wealth can be easily secured, why sweat to become rich. Money rituals, kidnapping, and outright armed robbery have become the path and pastime of the average Nigerian youth dream for wealth. Agricultural preoccupation is never in the list of wealth-creating attractions.

Insights and lessons from the case study

As a pilot case study, the study examined the rate of the national decline in agricultural undertakings using some of the traditional farm settlement communities in Odo-Otin Local Government. Okuku town which is the local government headquarters has a measurable presence of most modern socioeconomic, educational and technological facilities. It has a General Hospital, Federal Fire Station, Post Office, full-fledged Commercial Bank Branch and Community Bank, Railway Station (has not been operational for years due to national collapse of infrastructure), and a major Campus of the Osun State University, a Health Outlet of the University of Ibadan, and a Divisional Police Station, and two Secondary Schools. Other medium-sized towns within the Local Government Area include Inisa, Oyan, Igbaye, while there are several other small size towns like: Konta-Ijabe, Ashi, Asaba, Ila-Odo, Faji, Ekusa and rapidly modernizing Opete considered as the sixth farm settlement in this work.

The entire six traditional farm settlements visited during the field trip had a conducive climate and used to engage in the production of the following crops: cocoa, kola nut, walnut, plantain and banana, yam, cassava, cocoyam, pineapple, orange, mango, spices and other vegetables. However, with increasing urban migration of youths and ageing of the adult farmers, farming is becoming an obsolete practice in these farm settlements and the entire Odo Otin communities as it seems in all other Southwest states that yet have no other means of survival than engagement with the land and nature.

Unfortunately, on the one hand, much of the critical factors needed to advance the contribution of the agrarian rural communities to sustainable development in Nigeria are now urban-based, **manpower** (idling youths and other middle-aged productive populace sitting or roaming idly, most time all-day-long at motor parks, airports, seaports, railway stations, garages, workshops, etc), **technologies** (tractors, abandoned but re-usable motor vehicles, motorbikes, tricycles that are considered no longer suitable for main cities but that can still be used to move goods from the farms, which regrettably queues up for days at motor parks before getting to their turn to embark on a trip), **market** (a large market that is now dominated with the influx of foreign products that could be locally produced if Nigerian farms and industries are properly synergized and working).

On the other hand, much of the poverty in the urban settings are created by lack of essential factors that are in abundant supply in the rural areas-land, food, cheap housing, etc. Until these loosely-tied ends of complementary opportunities and challenges of the rural and urban system are more pragmatically reintegrated with one another, there cannot be but increasing unemployment and self-disablement of the productive populace. At a glance, a theoretical comparison of the contrasting and yet complementary mismatched matrix of challenges and opportunities of rural-urban realities in Nigeria is further presented below:

Productive factors	**What is available in the rural communities**	**What is lacking in the urban communities**
Land	Extensively available	Land rarely available
Climate	Good climate and weather	Congested atmosphere
Housing	Cheap Housing available	Cheap housing rarely available
Food and Crops	Cash/Food Crop Productive opportunities massive	While the urban centers starve to death
Means of Transportation	Means of transportation available if roads are well maintained	Available but stressful, hectic and costly
Travel time/Easiness of movement	Travel time short and less stressful	Travel time hectic and costly
Productive manpower	Productive manpower: Aged, weak mostly poorly educated but over-laboured	Productive manpower: Youthful, strong, well-educated but idle
Market outlets	Market outlet and demand limited	Market outlet massive and poorly served
Social amenities	Social amenities available	Scarcely sufficient in reasonable distance proximity
Road network	Road network is fair	Scarcely adequate with serious congestion
Security of lives and properties	Security: Worrisome as it is nationwide	Security: Worrisome
Government concern for productive development	Government concern for rural socioeconomic productive development fairly encouraging	Government concerns for urban socioeconomic productive development is encouraging, however, it is important to note that these developmental strides cannot get to all the teeming population in the urban centers.
Location of processing facilities	Rarely are these found in rural areas	Whereas the source of input materials needs of most agro-processing farms should be the rural setting, but in the case of Nigeria, where they exist at all, they are all urban based.

Table 2: *Rural-urban mismatched matrix of productive opportunities and challenges in Nigeria*

Source: Researchers' Field Trip Observation 2020

Conclusion

The presence of government, state, and federal as well as the assistance of international agencies such as the United Nations is not missing in most of the so-called rural communities. If anything, there are instances they enjoy better electricity, proximate social services, and a better living environment than the urban-trapped poor. What is further needed to make notable socioeconomic sustainable development a feasible feature of Nigeria, is that decision-makers must move out of their comfort zones to encourage and improve the investment of needed manpower, equipment and finance in developing grassroots agriculture starting with some of the existing wasting productive factors, resources, and capacities in traditional farm settlements scattered all over the Nigerian southwest states. Rather than concentrate on building aesthetic landmarks and mansions, in the name of city beautification and housing, that workers can seldom afford, directing investment to the farming needs of the populace will result in no less than needed substantial and rapid transformation of the socioeconomic, processing, manufacturing and bottom-up industrial development of the nation and better life for Nigerians and revenue for the Nigerian economy.

References

Aboyade, O. (1976) *Issues in the Development of Tropical Africa,* Ibadan: Ibadan University Press

Action Against Hunger 2020, *Nigeria.* www.actionagainsthunger.org/countries/Africa/Nigeria

Agbaje, E.B.A., Adeyeye. A.I and O. Omodunbi (forthcoming) Communal tracking approach to insecurity in Nigeria: A prognostic contemplation on *Amotekun*, the Nigerian southwest security outfit, a paper submitted for the 2020 Conference of Nigerian Political Science Association.

Akinsanmi, A. (2005). Gender Relations and Food Security of Rural Families in Imo State, Southeast Nigeria, Farming and Rural Systems Economics, Vol. 68. Margraf Verlag, Weikersheim, Germany.

Amusan, L and Agunyai, S.C. (2021). Nigeria's Ministry of Humanitarian Affairs, Disaster Management and Social Development, COVIC-19 Palliatives and the School Feeding Programme: Insights from Iyanfoworogi Community, Ile-Ife, Nigeria. Victor Ojakorotu and Bamidele Olajide (Eds.), Proceedings on the Conference on the Implications of COVID-19 on Gender and Behaviour in Africa, pp. 250-270. ISBN: 978-0-620-91446-8

Aspe, and Gurra, J. A. (1993) The State and Economic Development: A Mexican Perspective, *Proceedings of the World Bank Annual Conference on Development Economics,* In: L. H. Summers and S. Shah (eds), Washington: The International Bank for Reconstruction and Development/World Bank. 12-14.

Bamikole O.O. (2009) The Lewis theory of development: Is the theory applicable to Nigeria as a country? www.papers.ssrn.com/sol3/papers.cfm?abstract_id =1895006

Belassa, B. (1982) The Hungarian Economic Reform, 1968-81 World Bank Staff Working Paper No. 506, February, The World Bank, Washington D.C. 29.

Bhagwati, J. ((1966) *The Economics of Underdeveloped Countries,* London: World University Library. 113.

Buheji M. (2018) Empowering young people in disempowering times, *Advances in Social Science Research Journal,* United Kingdom: International Institute of Inspiration economy, 5(5): 290-291. DOI: 10.14738/assrj.55.4587.Herberger, A. C. (ed.) (1984) *World Economic Growth,* San Francisco: ICS Press,

Ibietan J. and O. Ekhosuehi (2013) "Trends in development planning in Nigeria: 1962-2012", *Journal of sustainable development in Africa,* USA: Clarion University of Pennsylvania, 15(4): 297-311. www.eprint.covenantuniversity.edu.ng /3761/1/ibietan%2526oghator.pdf&ved

Igbuzor, O. (2005) *Perspectives on Democracy and Development,* Lagos: Joe Tolalu & Associates. 294.

Inanga, E. L. (1983) Accounting and Economic Growth and Development in Nigeria, In: I. Osayimwese (ed) (1983) Op cit. 76.

International Committee of the Red Cross (2017) Massive scaling up urgently needed to tackle hunger crisis, ICRC. www.icrc.org/en/document/massive-scaling-urgently-needed-tackle-hunger-crisis-says-icrcs-director-operations

Ishikawa, S. (1966) The Chinese Economy: A General Framework for Long Term Projection, *The China Mainland Review, Vol. 2, No. 2,* September. 78-82.

Jan-Erik, L. and Ersson, S. (1997) *Comparative Political economy: a developmental approach,* Pinter, Second Edition

Karim, Z. Z and A.Z. Surajo (2016) Youth unemployment and poverty in Nigeria: A threat to sustainable growth and development, *International Journal of Scientific Research and Management Studies,* Malaysia: International Islamic University. 4(11): DOI: 10.18535/ijsrm/v4i12.02

Kasper and Johnson (1982) *The Japanese Miracle,* Stanford: Stanford University Press.

Kasper, W. (1994) Global Competition, Institutions and the East Asian Ascendancy, International Centre for Economic Growth, ICS Press, Institute for Contemporary Studies, San Francisco, California, Paper Number 50, March.

Lewis, W.A, (1988) The Roots of development theory, *Handbook of Development Economics, Vol I* In: H. Chenery and T.N. Srinivasan (eds) and Lewis, W.A. (1955) *The Theory of Economic Growth,* London, Allen & Unwin, cited in Lane and Ersson p6, 15,

Lewis J.D. (1987) Stimulating Alternative Development Strategies: Some suggestion from Koreas Experience, Harvard Institute for International Development, World Bank, University of California, June.

Renaud, B. (1976) Economic Growth and Income Inequality In Korea, World Bank Staff Working Paper. No 240, The World Bank: Development Economic Department, February.

Mao, Tse-tung ssu-hsiang wan-sui (Long live Mao Tse-tung's thought), translated by the US Joint Publication Research Service, and published under the title 'Miscellany of Mao Tse-tung thought. 277. Cited in Paine, S. (1976) Balanced Development: Maoist Conception and Chinese Practice, Economic Reprint No. 8, reprinted from World Development, Vol. 4, No. 4, University of Cambridge. 278.

Mrydal, G. (1957) *Economic theory and underdeveloped regions,* New York: Harper Torchbooks

National Planning Commission (2004) *National Economic Empowerment and Development Strategy (NEEDS),* Abuja: National Planning Commission. 28

Nwajiuba, C. (2012). Does agriculture have a future in southeast Nigeria? Inaugural lecture, No. 5, Imo State University Owerri, Nigeria

Olatunbosun, O. 1975. *Nigeria's Neglected Rural Majority,* Ibadan: Oxford University Press.

Olopoenia, R. A. (1983) On the Meaning of Economic Development, *Development Economics and Planning: Essays in honour of Ojetunji Aboyade,* In: I. Osayimwese (ed), Ibadan: Unibadan Publishing Consultants. 13.

Onimode, B. (1987) Technology and Political Economy, *Structural Adjustment Programme in a Developing Economy: The Case of Nigeria,* In: A. O. Phillips and E. C. Ndekwu (eds), Ibadan: Nigerian Institute of Social and Economic Research. 128.

Onovo, N. J. (1997) *To Hell With Democracy,* Enugu: Fourth Dimension Publishing Co. Ltd

Paine, S. (1976) Balanced development: Maoist conception and Chinese practice, Economic Reprint No. 8, reprinted from *World Development, Vol. 4, No. 4,* University of Cambridge 296

Stolper, W.F. (1963) Politics and Economics in Economic Development, Rivista Di, Politica Economica, Estratto dal fasc. VI, giu, anno LIII, III serie. 3-4 being a planned final chapter to- his book on Planning without Facts. An abbreviated version was presented in Professor G. Ugo Papi's Seminar at the University of Rome on April 2

__________ (n.d.) Limitations of Comprehensive Planning in the Face of Comprehensive Uncertainty: Crisis of Planning or Crisis of Planners, Michigan: Center for Research on Economic Development, University of Michigan, October. 23-24.

Stone, R. (1966) Transitional Planning: The Adaptation of the Economy to a Higher Rate of Growth, Great Britain. 555.

Zehender, W. (1990) Indebtedness and Adjustments- The Malaise of Sub-Sahara Africa, Economics- A Biannual Collection of Recent German Contribution to the Field of Economic Science, Tubingen: Institute for Scientific Co-operation, Vol. 41. 62-76

Chapter 17
From Brown to Green Economy: An Analytical Study of Willingness to Act Pro-Environmentally Among Farm Youths in Edo State, Nigeria

Victor. O. Okorie and Lere Amusan

Introduction

Sustainable production and consumption are increasingly discussed at both academic and policy levels as a panacea for global warming and the rising sea level (Seyfang, 2006; Barbier, 2010; Bauhardt, 2014). They are also envisioned by pundits as the key to the emergence of a green economy (Meadows et.al., 1992; Jacobs, 1993; Hopwood *et.al.*,2005; Ciocoiu, 2011; Okorie, 2019). Narratives of sustainable production unfold in multiple spaces and sectors, and seem to converge around the concept of green production. The term 'green production' has sympathetic concepts such as green growth, green economy, and sustainability. These concepts, collectively, command scholarly attention in many sectors, including but not are limited to manufacturing, mining, construction, and agriculture.

In the agricultural sector, the narrative of green production co-exists with the discourse of brown production. Both narratives collectively constitute the two sides of the same coin. The latter indicates that some agricultural practices contribute significantly to global warming and climate change (Cerri, *et.al.,* 2007; Scheper *et.al.*, 2013), whereas the former suggests that certain farming practices are capable of stemming the rise of ocean level and healing the warmed Planet Earth. Brown production practices threaten the global ecosystem through greenhouse gas emissions while green production practices provide sinks and filters for sequestration of carbon dioxide as well as offers other ecosystem services (Tilman *et. al.*, 2002; Tscharntke *et.al.*, 2005).

How to transit global food systems from contributing a high percentage of greenhouse gas (GHG) emissions to sequestrating carbon dioxide are highly desirable but hotly debated among professionals, practitioners, and civil society. Epistemic communities across the globe are busy searching for the way to the 'green world'- where more healthy foods would be produced for, distributed to and consumed by over 9.6 billion people without any energy loss. The quest to feed the world with healthier food in a circular economy or green economy has led many scholars into examining various features of both brown and green food production systems (Okorie *et.al.* 2013). Others have analysed institutional characteristics (Nhamo, 2013; Death, 2014) as well as the pro-environmental behaviours of both producers and consumers. Yet, less is still known about crucial factors driving pro-environmental behaviours of both producers and consumers. The determinants of pro-environmental behaviours at either the supply or demand side of the global food systems are very dynamic and complex; as such, they cannot be visualised through some synchronic frameworks or diagrams (Price and Leviston, 2014; Kollmuss and Agyeman, 2002). Drivers of pro-environmental behaviours vary in time and space, necessitating a continuous search for better understanding in a changing world.

Searching for this form of behaviour amongst youths is quite strategic as young people have been characterised as having innovative capacity, quick reaction time, and preference for boldness and adventure (Okorie *et. al.*, 2013). These characteristics are known in the literature to drive positive changes, including the adoption of agricultural innovations (Jibowo and Sotomi, 1996). Morris (2000) suggests that youths have a role to play in addressing environmental and sustainability issues. With their knowledge of these issues and their passion, enthusiasm, and constructive naivety, youths can offer a fresh perspective on the implementation of sustainable change. Farm youths are better favoured as successors in various farm succession plans (Ball and Wiley, 2005). Therefore, their willingness to act pro-environmentally, although brown production practices are still dominant in many farms, is an indicator that a better future awaits global food systems. Farm youths are the bridge between today and tomorrow of global food systems (Farinde *et al*, 2008). As such, their willingness to transit from their inherited brown to innovative green practices holds the key to the emergence of a green economy in the agricultural sector and by extension the emergence of a green economy across other sectors of the global economy.

To this end, this paper, using empirical evidence from farm youths in Nigeria, seeks to contribute to a growing body of literature articulating the drivers of producers' environmental behaviours. A clearer understanding of the drivers will certainly enhance the uptake of green agricultural practices which has remained abysmally low despite an upsurge in the number of profitable environment-friendly farming practices (Price and Leviston, 2014). The paper would also complement recent scholarships which seemed to have privileged farming practices' characteristics over farmers' (Price and Leviston, 2014). The focus of the paper is, therefore, on the willingness of rural farm youths to act pro-environmentally by changing from brown to a green production. A pro-environmental behaviour' is a "behaviour that consciously seeks to minimize the negative impact of one's actions on the natural and built world" (Kollmuss and Agyeman, 2002). The paper constructs farm youths' willingness to act pro-environmentally with respect to some soil management and agronomic practices, identifies correlates of their willingness and draws out the implications for transition from brown to a green economy.

Conceptual framework

This paper draws from concepts of brown and green productions and economies (Vetter *et al.*, 2017) as well as from the concept of environmental behaviour (Hine *et al.*, 1986) to interrogate the readiness of farm youths to act pro-environmentally in Nigeria. Farm youth is contextually conceptualised as an individual within the age bracket of 13 and 30 years who manages a farm either as a tenant farmer or a landlord. This age criterion aligns with the extant youth programs and some labour laws in the study area (Torimiro and Okorie, 2009; Okorie, 2018). The focus on individuals who manage farms is because management as a factor of production makes decisions including those that make the production process either a brown or green economy activity (Notarnicola, 2017). Brown and green productions as concepts are widely used in manufacturing (Milani, 2000), mining (Bekbassarov *et. al.*, 2015), construction (Careri *et.al.*, 2011) and agriculture sectors (Brand, 2012). The meanings of green and brown productions are very similar in these fields. In agriculture, brown production is associated with a high input production system or conventional agriculture. It is increasingly viewed by experts as a great threat to the ecosystem as well as a powerful driver of global warming. Green production, on the other hand, is associated with sustainability and environmental friendliness. It includes agricultural practices that simultaneously address issues of climate change mitigation and adaptation along with productivity (MAP).

Green production sustainably increases agricultural productivity without any significant negative impacts on the environment (Jacobs, 1993). In doing so, it contributes significantly to the satiation of the food and nutritional security needs in the present generation without necessarily compromising future generations. Concerning adaptation, green production focuses on reducing farmers' exposure to short-term risks, while also building their capacity to adapt and prosper in the face of shocks and longer-term stresses through the protection of ecosystem services. For mitigation, green production aims at reducing greenhouse gas (GHG) emissions and preventing deforestation (Weber & Cabras, 2017; Pearce, et.al., 1989). The willingness of farm youths to abandon brown for green production practices is the readiness of the youths to embrace or adopt farm practices that support the emergence of a green economy at the expense of those that support a brown economy or conventional agriculture. This form of environmental behaviour is conceptualised following Hines *et al*'s classification, which divides environmental-related variables into cognitive, affective, and situational factors (Hines *et al.*, 1986). The authors argue that cognitive factors include awareness and knowledge levels of individuals about environmental issues. Awareness and knowledge are often correlated. They also posit that affective factors concern with feelings and perceptions while situational factors deal with economic constraints, social pressures, and opportunities to choose different actions, either counteract or strengthen the cognitive and affective factors (Hines *et al.*1986).

Consistent with this view, farm youths' level of awareness of some negative effects of brown production practices was conceptualised as a cognitive variable while their willingness to act pro-environmentally and the prevailing environmental policies were conceptualised as affective and situational variables, respectively.

Methodology

The study area

The research site was the Edo state of Nigeria. Its geographical coordinates are 7° 17' 0" North of the Equator and 6° 6' 0" East of the Greenwich Meridian. The state has a landmass of about 17,802km^2 and lies at an elevation level of about 500 feet in the South and up to 1800 feet in the North. It is mainly in the tropical rain forest region of Nigeria, but northern portions are located in the derived savannah zone of the country; and some communities in the southern area fall within the mangrove swamp vegetation. The state undergoes two seasons: the rainy and dry seasons. The rainy season starts from April to October while the dry season commences from November to March with a cold harmattan spell between December and January. Farming is a dominant occupation in the state. The adolescents and young adults (10-24 years of age) account for 32% of the population, making Edo state one of the states in Nigeria with a very high concentration of young people (National Population Commission, 2006).

Sample size and sampling procedure

Edo state has three (3) Federal Senatorial Districts, namely, Edo North, Edo Central, and Edo South. A multi-stage sampling procedure was used to select respondents. Given that agriculture is predominant in each of the districts, Edo North was randomly selected through balloting at the first stage of the procedure. Edo North comprises six of the eighteen Local Government Areas in Edo State. At the second stage, four of the six Local Government Areas were randomly selected through balloting. At the third stage, three communities each were purposively selected from each of the four selected Local Government Areas to choose agrarian communities. Thus, a total of twelve agrarian communities were selected. At the final stage, one hundred and forty (140) self-identified farm youths were randomly selected from all the communities chosen. A structured protocol was used to elicit information from the 140 youths.

Measurement of variables

Willingness to act pro-environmentally is the dependent variable. It was measured on a five- point Likert scale of very unwilling to very willing, drawing from the work of Brundin, *et.al.* (2008) titled *Managers' emotional displays and employees' willingness to act entrepreneurially* and from Fortner *et. al*'s (2000) titled *Public understanding of climate change: Certainty and willingness to act.* About nine farming practices strongly associated with environmental degradation (brown production) were presented to the farm youths on a five-point Likert scale. Responses generated were used to rank the willingness of the youths to abandon particular brown agronomic and soil practices. To measure their brown practice involvement index, the respondents were also asked to indicate the frequency of involvement in particular brown practices on a five-point Likert scale that ranged from never to always.

Following Hines *et al.* (1986) the independent variables were divided into situational, cognitive and, affective. Some of the situational variables such as ownership of factors of production were measured by asking the youths to indicate their access to and sources of farm inputs (fertilizer, seed, labour, land). They were also asked to indicate the likely impact of the subsidy on green production inputs and taxation imposition on brown production practices. Cognitive variables like awareness of environmental issues were measured on a four-point Likert scale, which ranged from never to experience. The youths were asked to indicate their level of awareness of nine selected negative effects of brown soil and agronomic practices on the scale of never, heard, seen and, experience. Previous studies indicate that direct experience of environmental issues has a greater impact on behaviour than indirect like hearing/learning about it in school (Whitmarsh, 2008). Therefore in generating awareness score for each of the nine negative effects, 'experience' was scored as the highest level, followed by seen, and then heard. 'Never' was scored zero. For affective variables, respondents' perceptions of brown agronomic and soil practices were measured with a set of twelve statements each indicating consequences of brown production on a five point-Likert scale which ranged from strongly agree (5) to strongly disagree (1).

Results

Socio-demographic characteristics of respondents

The mean age of the respondents was 20.31 years with a standard deviation of 2.74. Some (17.14%) of the respondents were within the age range of 14 and 17 years, while 46.43 percentage and 36.43 percentage were in the ranges between 18 and 21 and between 22 and 25 years, respectively. Over half (58.6 %) of the respondents were male while 41.4 percentage were female. The majority (90.7%) of the respondents were single while 8.6 percentages and 0.7 percentages were married and divorced, respectively. This finding agrees with the population census of the country putting the population of the male slightly higher than the female counterpart (National Population Census, 1991).

Many (65%) of the respondents were indigene just as 35 percentage were non-indigene. Also, many (69.9%) of the respondents indicated that they got access to land through inheritance and gift. Only about 22.1 percentages claimed to be tenant farmers. All the respondents claimed ownership of seeds and fertilizers. Some (30.1%) of the respondents had between 16 and 20 years of farming experience, one-quarter (25.0%) of the respondents had spent between 1 and 5 years in the farm. Only less than one-fifth (19.2%) of the respondents had farm experience within the range of 21 to 24 years. Almost one-tenth (12.9%) had spent between 11 and 15 years in the farm just as 12.8 percentage had spent between 6 and 10 years. The mean of the household size was 5.96 (SD = ±2.97). Half (50.7%) of the respondents indicated that they were in the household size that ranged from 1 to 5 while some (42.1%) were in the household size of 6 and 10 and 7.1 percentage of the respondents were in the household of above 10.

The mean income of the respondents was (NG) 25,123[2] with while its standard deviation was 18890. Some (38.60%) of the respondents earned income between NGN 1000 and NGN 10000, 24.45 percentage earned income between NGN 11000 and NGN 20000. Some (21.08%) of the respondents earned income in the range of NGN 21000 and N30000 while

[2] $1USD is equal to N 319

8.77 percentage had income between NGN 31000 and NGN 40000. Only 7.02 percentage earned an income between NGN 41000 and NGN 50000. A majority (88.6%) of the respondents had formal education while 11.4 percentage had no formal education. Many (88.57%) attended primary school while 11.43 percentage did not attend primary school. Many (78.57%) of the respondents completed secondary school, 4.29 percentage did not complete secondary school, and 5.71 percentage are still ongoing while 11.43 percentage did not attend secondary school. Some (32.9%) of the respondents were still in tertiary institutions just as 21.4 percentage had completed tertiary institutions, 14.3 percentage did not complete tertiary institutions and 31.4 percentage of the respondents did not attend a tertiary institution.

Many (78.6%) of the respondents were members of social organizations while few (21.4%) had no membership of any organization. About 70.10 percentage were in a cooperative society, 3.27 percentage each was in producing firm, school alumni, model group, farmers association, and 16.32 percentage are in credit organisation. About three-quarter (71.0%) of the respondents practiced arable crop, 4.3 percentage practised fishery, 1.4 percentage practised poultry and 0.7 percentage were into oil palm plantation.

Some (34.3%) of the respondents often had access to the radio while 31.4 percentage rarely had access. Only 26.4 percentage always had access to the radio just as 7.9 percentage of the respondents often had the access. However, over half (55.7%) of the respondents always had access to the television while some (33.6%) often had the access. Only 7.1 percentage and 3.6% of the respondents rarely and never had access to television, respectively. A majority (71.4%) of the respondents never had access to the agricultural newsletter. Only 2.9 percentage of the respondents always had access to the agricultural newsletter. Some (36.4%) and 33.6 percentage of the respondents often and rarely had access to newspapers, respectively. While 22.9 percentage of the respondents claimed to have always had access to newspapers, 7.2 percentage said they never had access.

Respondents' level of awareness of the negative effects of brown production

While only about one-fifth of the respondents never heard, seen, or experienced infrequent rainfall as a consequence of brown production, over 80 percentage claimed to have heard, seen, or experienced it. Those who claimed to have heard were about 27.9 percentage just as 25.0 percentage and 27.1 percentage said that they had seen and experienced it, respectively. Some (34.3%) of the respondents claimed they had heard that air and water pollutions were associated with brown production just as 33.6 percentage and 23.6 percentage claimed to have seen and experienced it , respectively. Thus, only a few (8.6%) of the respondents, had never heard, seen, or experienced, air and water pollutions as consequences of brown production. Although 8.6 percentage of the respondents claimed not to have heard, seen, or experienced erosion as a consequence of brown production, a higher percentage had heard, seen or experienced it as followed: few (7.1%) claimed to have heard while 39.3 percentage 45.0 percentage said they have seen and experienced it, respectively. Some (32.1%) of the respondents had experienced land pollution, 30.7 percentage had heard of it, 22.1 percentage had seen it, and only about 15 percentage never heard, seen, or experienced land pollution as a consequence of brown production.

About 35.0 percentage of the respondents claimed to have experienced extreme cold and heat as consequences of brown production, 22.9 percentage and 19.3 percentage claimed to have heard and seen it, respectively. Some (37.1%) of the respondents had experienced flooding as a consequence of brown production while 29.3 percentage and 14.3 percentage said they had heard and seen it, respectively. Only 19.3 percentage of the respondents said they had never heard, seen or experienced flooding as a consequence of the brown practices. However, many (61.4%) of the respondents said that they had never heard, seen, or experienced desertification as a result of brown production. Some (25%) of the respondents claimed to have heard that desertification is caused by brown production while 8.6 percentage and 5.0 percentage claimed to have seen and experienced it, respectively. Half (50%) of the respondents said they never heard, seen, or experienced loss of biodiversity as a consequence of brown production. Some (35.7%) of the respondents said that they had heard that loss of biodiversity as a consequence of brown production while 6.4 percentage and 7.9 percentage claimed to have seen and experienced it, respectively.

Respondents' willingness to act index versus their brown practice involvement index

About 39.3 percentage of the respondents indicated their unwillingness to change from mono-cropping, 33.6 percentage of the respondents were indifferent about mono-cropping, 23.6 percentage of the respondents were willing to change mono-cropping and 2.3 percentage of the respondents were ever willing to change mono-cropping. The respondents' Willingness to Act Pro-environmentally (WTAP), that is, to abandon mono-cropping for a green alternative, was 2.9 while their Brown Practice Involvement Index (BPII) was 2.5. More than half (52.1%) of the respondents were unwilling to abandon clean clearing, few (22.1%) were very unwilling while 21.4 and 4.3 percentages were willing and very willing, respectively, to change from engaging in a clean clearing to green production alternative. The WTAP and BPII were thus ranked 3.1 and 2.4 of 5, respectively. While some (39.3%) and 7.1 percentage of the respondents were willing and very willing to change from their excessive application of inorganic fertilizers to green alternative, about 29.3 and 24.3 percentages indicated their unwillingness and very unwillingness, respectively, to make the change. The WTAP was 2.4 whereas BPII was 3.1. Some (41.4%) and 11.4 percentage of the respondents, respectively, were willing and very willing to abandon bush burning while 26.4 and 20.7 percentages were unwilling and very unwilling to do so. The WTAP and BPII were 3.3 and 2.4, respectively.

About half (51.4%) of the respondents were unwilling about changing the practice of continuous tillage just as 21.4 percentage were very unwilling to abandon it for its green alternative. Only about 21.4 percentage and 5.7 percentage of the respondents, respectively, were willing and very willing to abandon continuous tillage for green alternatives. The WTAP and BPII were 3.1 and 2.3 respectively. Many (43.6%) and few (9.3%) of the respondents were willing and very willing to change from excessive application of herbicides and pesticides. Only about 26.4 percentage and

20.7 percentage of the respondents were unwilling and very unwilling to change from the practice. The WTAP and BPII were 3.4 and 2.4, respectively. The use of Gamalin20 for fishing and cropping had WTAP and BPII of 3.3 and 2.1, respectively. The deforestation, overfishing, and dumping of farm waste into near stream canals had the following WTAPs 3.3, 3.1, and 3.5 respectively. Their corresponding BPII were 2.2, 2.1, and 2.8. These findings indicate that the WTAP of each practice was greater than its corresponding BPII. The farm youths' willingness to act index (WTAP) for each of the brown practices is greater than their corresponding involvement in brown practices index (BPII).

Correlates of willingness to act pro-environmentally

Correlates of willingness to act pro-environmentally are as follow: Perception of negative effects of brown practices($r = 0.204$); input support pay ($r = 0.213$); imposing taxation on brown practices($r = 0.115$); level of environmental awareness($r = 0.484$); educational status ($r = 0.380$); perceived degree of input ownership ($r = 0.275$); and perceived ability to make change ($r = 0.114$) had positive and significant relationships with youths' willingness to act pro-environmentally at 0.05 probability level.

Discussion and implications for the green economy

Harnessing the opportunity that farm youths represent requires translating the youths' willingness to act pro-environmentally to actual environmental behaviour. This transition could be achieved through influencing the cognitive, affective, and social situation dynamics within the environment in which the farm youths are situated. The correlates of farm youths' willingness to act pro-environmentally indicate pathways through which the youths could be moved into action. Levels of environmental awareness and education are important correlates of willingness. These correlates are critical to moving the youth into actual behaviour. They affirm the growing evidence that education is crucial to environmentally friendly behaviour (Fien and Guevara, 2013). Moving from brown to green production requires well planned environmental education. While general education is important, Sauvé (1996) shows that environmental education for sustainable development and climate change education, in particular, is highly important. The youth farmers can be reached through in-school and out-schools' fora given that a majority belongs to social organizations. This view aligns with Leeuwis's (2013) findings which show that group method enhances the adoption of innovations. In addition to this, there is growing evidence that environmental education shapes perception (Ham and Sewing, 1988). The positive correlations between affective variables; the perception of brown production, perceived degree of input ownership, and ability to make a change- and farm youths' willingness to act pro-environmentally emphasise the importance of environmental education in changing behaviour. The content of such education must address real-life situations such as mono-cropping, inorganic fertilizer, herbicides application, amongst others. The content must also be structured to influence not only the affective but also the psychomotor domains.

Although the promotion of environmental concerns through education runs counter to the claims of political liberalists, who maintain that the state should not intentionally promote any comprehensive religious, philosophical or ethical doctrines (Bell, 2004), such a claim is invalid in the context of deteriorating ecosystem. It is like forbidding instructions that could assist the sick with medications. Inculcating behaviours that stem the rise of the ocean and cool the warmed Planet through environmental education is timely.

Similarly, social situation variables- tenure security, input pay support, and imposing taxation on brown practices- had positive correlations with youths' willingness to act pro-environmentally. These findings suggest the importance of given attention to the personal characteristics of various stakeholders as well as the policy environment in which they are situated in the context of the transition of the economy from brown to green production. The findings indicate that input pay support policy represents a fertile ground in which governments should invest resources to address the key challenges of the brown economy (Tilman, *et. al.*, 2002; Vetter, *et al*, 2017).

The positive relationship between taxation on brown practices and willingness to act pro-environmentally raises a critical question about the possibility that polluters-must-pay principles might work in certain income brackets. This is because the farm youths were relatively within low-income bracket. Therefore there is a need for further investigations on the feasibility of using taxation as instrumental policy in the transition of the global economy to green production (Dewees, 1983; Barde, and Centre de développement de l'OCDE, 1994). Given that such a policy like carbon credit system has been proved to be fatally flawed in many contexts (Ghouri, 2009), it may be useful to ascertain the income bracket that would respond more positively to the polluters-should-pay principle.

That said, it clear that the prevailing policy environment and youths' awareness of the negative effects of brown production correlate with youths' willingness to act pro-environmentally and that youths' willingness to act pro-environmentally somewhat mirrors their actual behaviour.

This position is buttressed by the findings of Hines, Hungerford and Tomera in their published Model of Responsible Environmental Behaviour, which was based on Ajzen and Fishbein's theory of planned behaviour (Hines *et. al.*, 1986; Hungerford and Volk, 1990; Sia et. al. 1985; Hwang *et. al.*, 2000; Braun and Dierkes, 2017). These authors demonstrated that "knowledge of issues, knowledge of action strategies, locus of control, attitudes, verbal commitment, and an individual's sense of responsibility" have a strong influence on actual environmental behaviour.

As the debate for the emergence of a green economy (Amaruzaman, *et al.*, 2017) - an economy that is not only efficient but also fair as well as based on low-carbon- continues to rage, it is crystal clear that smallholder farmers, especially farm youths, have critical roles to play. Their roles could become highly significant and beneficial if appropriate policy environment and farmers' characteristics such as awareness, knowledge, and ownership of factors of productions are adequately harnessed. Given that green economy requires the contribution of every stakeholder, the greatest challenge to its emergence in the context of farm youths is not necessarily an inherent tension between economic and natural systems, but the political will to address the environmental consequences of their current economic development patterns as well as articulate the alternative.

Conclusion

This paper demonstrates the relevance of appropriate policy environment and farmers' characteristics such as awareness, knowledge, and ownership of factors of productions in the context of transition of global economy from brown to green- "that to be green, an economy that is not only efficient, but also fair. Fairness implies recognising global and country level equity dimensions, particularly in assuring a just transition to an economy that is low-carbon, resource efficient, and socially inclusive. It shows that farm youths, who are mainly smallholder farmers, are highly willing to act pro-environmentally. The paper recommends that environmental education and appropriate policy environment such as input pay support and tenure security be put in place by the government, civil society, and other stakeholders to ensure that farm youths' pro-environmentally behaviour is metamorphosed into actual environmental behaviour. Inculcating such behaviour in youths holds the key to the future green world.

Reference

Ajzen, I., & Fishbein, M. (1980). Understanding attitudes and predicting social behaviour. Englewood Cliffs, NJ: Prentice- Hall.

Amaruzaman, S., Leimona, B., van Noordwijk, M., & Lusiana, B. (2017). Discourses on the performance gap of agriculture in a green economy: a Q-methodology study in Indonesia. *International Journal of Biodiversity Science, Ecosystem Services & Management*, *13*(1), 233-247.

Amusan, L. (2018). Development from the Bottom: Small and Medium Farm Holders Empowerment and Challenges of Food Security in Zimbabwe. *Ubuntu: Journal of Conflict and Social Transformation*, 7(1): 157-176.

Barbier, E. B. (2010). A global green new deal: rethinking the economic recovery. Cambridge University Press.

Barbier, E. (2010). How is the global green new deal going? Nature, 464(7290), 832-833.

Barde, J. P., & Centre de développement de l'OCDE (Paris). (1994). *Economic instruments in environmental policy: Lessons from the OECD experience and their relevance to developing economies*. Development Centre of the Organisation for Economic Co-operation and Development.

Bauhardt, C. (2014). Solutions to the crisis? The Green New Deal, De-growth, and the Solidarity Economy: Alternatives to the capitalist growth economy from an ecofeminist economics perspective. Ecological Economics, 102, 60-68.

Bell, D. R. (2004). Creating green citizens? Political liberalism and environmental education. *Journal of Philosophy of Education*, *38*(1), 37-54.

Bowers, K., & Norris, J. H. (2017). A growing part of the green economy. *Routledge Handbook of Ecological and Environmental Restoration*, 440.

Braun, T., & Dierkes, P. (2017). Evaluating Three Dimensions of Environmental Knowledge and Their Impact on Behaviour. *Research in Science Education*, 1-19.

Brundin, E., Patzelt, H., & Shepherd, D. A. (2008). Managers' emotional displays and employees' willingness to act entrepreneurially. *Journal of Business Venturing*, *23*(2), 221-243.

Cerri, C. E. P., Sparovek, G., Bernoux, M., Easterling, W. E., Melillo, J. M., & Cerri, C. C. (2007). Tropical agriculture and global warming: impacts and mitigation options. *Scientia Agricola*, *64*(1), 83-99.

Ciocoiu, C. N. (2011). Integrating digital economy and green economy: opportunities for sustainable development. *Theoretical and Empirical Researches in Urban Management*, *6*(1), 33.

Dewees, D. N. (1983). Instrument choice in environmental policy. *Economic Inquiry*, *21*(1), 53-71.

Fien, J., & Guevara, J. R. (2013). Skills for a green economy: Practice, possibilities, and prospects. In *Skills Development for Inclusive and Sustainable Growth in Developing Asia-Pacific* (pp. 255-263). Springer Netherlands.

Fortner, R. W., Lee, J. Y., Corney, J. R., Romanello, S., Bonnell, J., Luthy, B., ... & Ntsiko, N. (2000). Public understanding of climate change: Certainty and willingness to act. *Environmental Education Research, 6*(2), 127-141.

Ghouri, N. (2009). The great carbon credit con: Why are we paying the Third World to poison its environment? *Daily Mail, 1*(06), 2009.

Ham, S. H., & Sewing, D. R. (1988). Barriers to environmental education. *The Journal of Environmental Education, 19*(2), 17-24.

Hopwood, B., Mellor, M., & O'Brien, G. (2005). Sustainable development: mapping different approaches. *Sustainable development, 13*(1), 38-52.

Jacobs, M. (1993). *The green economy: Environment, sustainable development and the politics of the future*. UBC press.

Jibowo, A. A., & Sotomi, A. O. (1996, September). The youth in sustainable rural development: A study of youth programmes in Odeda local government area of Ogun State, Nigeria. In *Sustainable Development in Rural Nigeria. Proceedings of the 8th Annual Conference of the Nigerian Rural Sociological Association* (pp. 35-40).

Meadows, D. H., Meadows, D. L., & Randers, J. (1992). Beyond the limits: confronting global collapse envisioning a sustainable future.

Notarnicola, B., Sala, S., Anton, A., McLaren, S. J., Saouter, E., & Sonesson, U. (2017). The role of life cycle assessment in supporting sustainable agri-food systems: A review of the challenges. *Journal of Cleaner Production, 140*, 399-409.

Okorie V. O., Torimiro D. O. & Mankinde **(2013).** Whither youths' involvement in climate smart-agriculture? Exploring environmental responsibility and economic prosperity among farm youths in Osun State. *Annals of youth Studies* (4) 111-123. Nigeria

Price, J. C., & Leviston, Z. (2014). Predicting pro-environmental agricultural practices: the social, psychological and contextual influences on land management. *Journal of Rural Studies, 34*, 65-78.

Sauvé, L. (1996). Environmental education and sustainable development: A further appraisal. *Canadian Journal of Environmental Education, 1*, 7-34.

Tilman, D., Cassman, K. G., Matson, P. A., Naylor, R., & Polasky, S. (2002). Agricultural sustainability and intensive production practices. *Nature, 418*(6898), 671-677.

Tomaselli, M., Hajjar, R., Ramon-Hidalgo, A. E., & Vasqez-Fernandez, A. M. (2017). The problematic old roots of the new green economy narrative: How far can it take us in re-imagining sustainability in forestry? *International Forestry Review, 19*(S1), 1.

Programme des Nations Unies pour l'environnement. (2011). *Towards a green economy: pathways to sustainable development and poverty eradication*. United Nations Environment Programme.

Vetter, S. H., Sapkota, T. B., Hillier, J., Stirling, C. M., Macdiarmid, J. I., Aleksandrowicz, L., ... & Smith, P. (2017). Greenhouse gas emissions from agricultural food production to supply Indian diets: Implications for climate change mitigation. *Agriculture, ecosystems & environment, 237*, 234-241.

Weber, G., & Cabras, I. (2017). The transition of Germany's energy production, green economy, low-carbon economy, socio-environmental conflicts, and equitable society. *Journal of Cleaner Production*.

Whitmarsh, L. (2008). Are flood victims more concerned about climate change than other people? The role of direct experience in risk perception and behavioural response. *Journal of risk research, 11*(3), 351-374.

Notes on Contributors

Adeyeye, Olajumoke, PhD is a Research Fellow I at the Centre for Gender and Social Policy Studies (CGSPS), Obafemi Awolowo University, Ile-Ife, Nigeria where she teaches, undertakes research and advocacy issues on development and social policy. Her research focus is on micro-level analysis of multidimensional empowerment, gender, youth empowerment, poverty, and inequality, especially in agriculture and rural livelihoods. Olajumoke holds a doctoral degree in Agricultural Extension and Rural Development, Federal University of Agriculture, Abeokuta, Nigeria. She has over 10 years' experience working with local and international organizations in areas such as market engagement activities, monitoring, evaluation and learning of programmes and policies, transformational leadership, collectives learning agenda, formulation and mainstreaming of HIV/AIDS and gender workplace policies, youth engagement and capacity building. Olajumoke has worked with different teams including the CARE US (Pathways program), OXFAM-Novib Gender Mainstreaming and Leadership Trajectory (GMLT), and the Bill and Melinda Gates Foundation funded Nigeria Country Plan Baseline and Varietal Monitoring Survey (NIBAS) projects on monitoring and evaluating the outcomes of different programmes. Olajumoke is a 2011 Fellow of the African Women in Agriculture Research and Development (AWARD) and a member of several organizations including Development Studies Association, Agricultural and Applied Economics Association among others. jumoke.adeyeye@gmail.com

Adewumi, A. A. PhD. is a Senior Lecturer in the Department of Wildlife and Ecotourism Management, Osun State University, Nigeria He obtained PhD in Wildlife Management from the University of Ibadan, Nigeria. He is the Acting Head of Department of Wildlife and Ecotourism Management. His area of research is Wildlife Conservation and Management with a focus on Wildlife Domestication and Ranching. He was the Principal Researcher of TETFund Institutional Based Research in 2014. Dr Adewumi has published both locally and internationally on wildlife conservation and management. He is a member of the Wildlife Society of Nigeria (WISON) and one of the Zonal Coordinators of the Society.

Agbaje, Elijah Babasola Afolabi PhD and Professor, Department of Political Sciences/Centre for Human Resource Development and Lifelong Learning Osun State University, Osogbo, Nigeria. He is a thorough-bred Political Scientist who holds BSc, MSc, and PhD in Political Science with a political economy orientation. Agbaje's research activity centres on development challenges in transiting societies. Comparatively studying state-economy relations in Nigeria and South Korea away from neoliberal pretences, he convincingly advocates strong reprofiled and continuing state-economy mutual reinforcements as the primary condition for sustainable development in the LDCs. He is a past laurel and member of the 2006 APISA-CLACSO-CODESRIA South-South Development Institute. He has several publications in reputable local and international outlets. Professor Agbaje's experiences within the university system is quite versatile. He is currently teaching at Osun State University, Nigeria.

Agunyai, Samuel Chukwudi, PhD, is a postdoctoral fellow in the Department of Political Studies and International Relations, North West University, Mafikeng South Africa. His primary areas of research interests include food and human security, political theory, migration studies, and governance in comparative sub-Saharan Africa contexts. Specifically, he specializes on how food insecurity engenders crises in Sub-Saharan Africa.

Akinwale, Yusuf Opeyemi is an Associate Professor of Economics at the College of Business Administration, Imam Abdulrahman Bin Faisal University, Saudi Arabia. He is a first-class economics graduate and faculty award prize winner of Obafemi Awolowo University, Nigeria where he also had his MBA. He further had his MSc in Economics from the University of Aberdeen in UK and earned his PhD from African Institute for Science Policy and Innovation in Obafemi Awolowo University. He was at North West University in South Africa as Postdoctoral Fellow and Extraordinary Research Fellow where he participated in various research and received excellent awards in research. His research interests include economics of innovation and entrepreneurship, energy, and developmental studies.

Aluko, Opeyemi Idowu, PhD, is a Lecturer in the Department of Political Science, Ajayi Crowther University, Oyo, Oyo State Nigeria. He has over 85 publications in both national and international credible outlet. Dr. Aluko specialises in Comparative Politics with focus on urban violence studies and election studies. He also published on other areas in political science. He has participated in several conferences and research methodology workshops.

Amusan, Lere, PhD, is a Professor and Subject Chair, Department of Political Studies and International Relations, North West University, South Africa. Lere is also a member of Food Security and Safety Niche Area of the same university. He has published widely on issues of development and underdevelopment with special focus on Africa. His academic career takes him to the five continents (Asia, Africa, North America, South America, and Europe) of the world where he presented papers on politics in developing areas with interest in climate change, and food politics and policies with some flavours of gender and development. He is a member of International Political Science Association, South Africa Association of Political Science, South African Association of Public Administration and Management, Nigerian Society of International Affairs among others. Amusan has over 120 publications in internationally recognised journals, chapters in books, edited books, and monographs. In 2019, he was one of the globally selected members by the Department of State's United States Institute for Scholars (SUSI) that went to The University of Delaware on the study of the American Foreign Policy.

Atijosan, Ayobami Basirat, PhD holds a Doctoral degree in Biochemistry, Obafemi Awolowo University, Ile-Ife. She also has various certificates in gender studies. She is a Research Fellow I at the Centre for Gender and Social Policy Studies, Obafemi Awolowo University, where she teaches and researches on diverse issues in gender and social policy. Her research focus is on women's health, women entrepreneurship/ empowerment, Gender, and Health, specifically on the intersection of health and socio-cultural issues on the well-being of male and female. She is a gender expert with various publications in both local and international reputable journals in the field of Gender Studies. Ayobami is a grant winning researcher and as a result, she has facilitated various gender sensitive trainings and capacity building works. She is a member of various organizations such as Society of Gender Professionals (SGP), Development Studies Association, among others.

Ayodele, Oladiran Akinsola, PhD is a Senior Lecturer and an Acting Dean, Faculty of Law, Osun State University, Nigeria. He attended the University of Ibadan, Ibadan, Nigeria where he studied education and was awarded a Bachelor of Education (B.Ed.) with Second Class Hons (Upper Division) in 1991. He also attended Obafemi Awolowo University, Ile-Ife, Nigeria, where he received a Post Graduate Diploma degree in Public Administration in 1995. Thereafter, he enrolled for law programme at the same university where he was awarded Bachelor of Laws (LL.B) with Second Class Hons (Upper Division) in 2001 and Master of Laws (LL.M) in 2006. He was called to the Nigerian Bar in 2003. He also attended North-West University, South Africa, where he was awarded Doctor of Laws (LL.D) in 2018. He has attended local and international conferences. He has also published in reputable journals both in Nigeria and abroad. His areas of research are Petroleum Development and Environmental law.

Bamidele, Seun, PhD is a lecturer in the Department of Peace and Conflict Studies, Federal University Oye-Ekiti, Nigeria. He is a recipient of many international awards and fellowships, notably the Next Generation Social Sciences in Africa Program, Social Science Research Council and Carnegie Corporation of New York; CODESRIA College of Academic Mentors Institute, Council for the Development of Social Science Research in Africa (CODESRIA), Dakar, Senegal and Carnegie Corporation of New York, USA; Women in International Security (WIIS), Washington, USA; Trust Africa Illicit Financial Flow; and Equator Peace Academy, Uganda Martyrs University, Uganda. His scholarly work has been published in top-notched peer-reviewed international journals including GeoJournal; Social Change; African Conflict and Peacebuilding Review; India Quarterly: A Journal of International Affairs; International Journal on World Peace; International Journal on Minority and Group Rights; Jadavpur Journal of International Relations; and African Journal of Legal Studies.

Monicca, Thulisile Bhuda is a culture activist, an indigenous scholar, and a lecturer at the University of Mpumalanga. She holds a Bachelor's degree (hons) in Indigenous Knowledge Systems, a Master's degree in Indigenous Knowledge Systems, both from the North-West University. Currently, she is busy with her PhD in indigenous Knowledge Systems at the North-West University. Ms Bhuda specialises in African Ethnomathematics and African Indigenous Cosmology. Ms Bhuda has been featured on numerous media platforms such as TV, Radio, Magazines, and Newspapers that were based on her interests as an indigenous scholar and on Indigenous Knowledge Systems. Her interests include decolonization of education, indigenous knowledge preservation, protection, management, and dissemination.

Dan-Woniowei, Fie David, PhD, is a seasoned university administrator and a promising scholar of Politics and International Relations in the Department of Political Science, Niger Delta University, Wilberforce Island, Bayelsa State, Nigeria. He was a Deputy Registrar with over 19 years' experience in university administration. Dan-Woniowei recently converted to academic research, and showing great interest in teaching and research in the wider field of Political Science. His work in the academic world is quite recent; however, he has published in a number of reputable national and international publishing houses/journals on issues concerning the Nigeria's Niger Delta and the African continent. His research interests include the environment, international political economy, politics of international law/institutions, security/conflict/peace, and/or strategic studies among others.

Ijuptil, Justin holds PhD in Political Science from Usmanu Danfodiyo University, Sokoto, Nigeria. His areas of interest include Political Economy, International Relations, Comparative Politics as well as Conflicts and Developmental Studies. His research works are: The role of Social Media in Influencing Political Participation in Nigeria and Egypt, Impact of Globalization on Nigeria's Economy, Foreign Direct Investment and Agricultural Development in Nigeria.

Marumo, Phemelo Olifile, PhD is a Senior Lecturer/Deputy Director in the Faculty of Humanities, School of Philosophy. Pursuing Philosophy Perspectives in Teaching and Learning at Northwest University. He serves in various committees in the academic community. Besides that, he has worked with NWU's Centre for Teaching and Learning (CTL) in the

Scholarship of Teaching and Learning (SoTL) projects and has contributed to several book chapters and published in different accredited local and international journals.

Motswaledi, Thabang Richard is an emerging scholar at the North West University. Recently graduated at the North West University, his junior degree (Bachelor of Social Sciences in Psychology) he is currently pursuing a Bachelors (Hon) degree in political studies in the school of governance at the North West University Mafikeng campus. He is actively involved in academia with specific attention given to both political science and African philosophy related research.

Oduntan, Oladapo Olukoya PhD is an Associate Professor of Wildlife Extension and Human Dimension in the Department of Forestry and Wildlife Management, Federal University of Agriculture, Abeokuta. He holds a PhD in Wildlife Management from the University of Ibadan. Dr Oduntan teaches wildlife conservation and extension related courses at both undergraduate and postgraduate levels. He is the principal consultant to Arcane Global Limited on Wildlife Hazard Assessments of International Airports in Nigeria. Dr Oduntan is a member of Wildlife Society of Nigeria (WISON).

Ogundeji, Abiodun Akintunde, PhD is a Professor of Applied Economics. He obtained his PhD in Agricultural Economics from the University of the Free State, Bloemfontein, South Africa. He is currently an Associate Professor and Senior Researcher at the same University. He presents classes and supervises master's, PhD, and Postdoctoral candidates. He is also a guest lecturer at the Disaster Management Training and Education Centre (DiMTEC), where he presents classes on the economic impact assessment of disasters. As a researcher, he works with international and local organizations as a project leader and principal investigator. He was a research fellow at the social protection department of the Food and Agriculture Organization of the United Nations (FAO). He has published 37 articles in peer-reviewed journals, made several conference presentations, supervised 14 Masters candidates, and promoted 5 PhD candidates in Agricultural Economics and Disaster Risk Management. Professor Abiodun Ogundeji's current research focuses on climate change and adaptation in the agricultural sector, focusing on small-scale farmers. He is currently working on a project titled 'Development of Scenarios for Future Agricultural Water Use in South Africa', a project sponsored by the Water Research Commission of South Africa.

Ogunjinmi, A. A. PhD. is an Associate Professor in the Department of Ecotourism and Wildlife Management of the Federal University of Technology, Akure, Nigeria. He is a Wildlife and Ecotourism Management specialist with about two decades of successful experience in wildlife and ecotourism research and extension. He holds PhD degree in Wildlife Management from the University of Agriculture, Abeokuta, Nigeria. Dr Ogunjinmi's research is centred on public attitudes and behaviours towards wildlife conservation, protected area management, particularly, national parks and game reserves, community participation in conservation, human wildlife conflicts, wildlife hazards assessment, and sustainability of wildlife and other natural resources. He teaches wildlife and ecotourism management related courses at undergraduate and postgraduate levels including wildlife policy, conflict resolutions in wildlife management, wildlife and ecotourism extension, park planning and interpretation among others. He is involved with others in collaboration on capacity building and research with Nigeria National Park Service and currently serves as one of the consultants to Arcane Global Limited on Wildlife Hazard Assessments of International Airports in Nigeria. Dr Ogunjinmi is a member of Wildlife Society of Nigeria (WISON) and serves as the pioneer Editor in Chief of the Nigerian Journal of Wildlife Management, a Journal published by Wildlife Society of Nigeria.

Ojakorotu, Victor PhD and Professor is currently Deputy Director, School of Government Studies, Mafikeng at North West University, Mafikeng, South Africa. His research interests are African Politics, Nigeria, Conflict and Peace, Environmental Politics and Security. He is widely published in internationally accredited academic journals on the vexing subject of the Niger Delta. Some of the books he has published on the Niger Delta are Contending Issues in the Niger Delta of Nigeria, Fresh Dimensions on the Niger Delta Crisis of Nigeria, Checkmating the Resurgence of Oil Violence in the Niger Delta of Nigeria, and Anatomy of the Niger Delta Crisis: Causes, Consequences and Opportunities for Peace.

Ojibara, Isa Ishaq is currently a PhD student at the Federal University of Lafia, Nassarawa State, Nigeria. He obtained his first and Master's degrees in Political Science at the University of Ilorin, Ilorin, Nigeria - in 2012 and 2017 respectively. His research interests include Electoral Studies, Legislative and Executive Relations, Comparative Analysis, and Intergovernmental Relations.

Ojo, Temitope Oluwaseun, PhD. He is a Post-Doctoral Fellow at the Disaster Management Training and Education Centre for Africa at the University of the Free State, Bloemfontein, South Africa. He received his PhD in Agricultural Economics from the University of KwaZulu-Natal, South Africa. His areas of interest are climate change and adaptation with bias in smallholder farmers in Africa. He has published widely on Food Security and Urban Farming in highly reputed journals globally. He is a lecturer in the Department of Agricultural Economics, Obafemi Awolowo University, Ile-Ife, Nigeria.

Okorie, Victor O. PhD, is a Post-Doc Fellow, Food Security and Safety Niche Area, Department of Political Studies and International Relations, North West University, South Africa. Okorie is an Associate Professor of Agriculture Extension and Rural Studies at the Obafemi Awolowo University, Ile-Ife, Nigeria. He has published extensively in the area of food security and Food Sovereignty. He won many international grants on food security and travelled widely on academic engagement. He is currently working on the impacts of Covid-19 on food availability in selected states in Africa.

Olaopa, Olawale Rafiu, PhD is an Assistant Professor of Economics at the College of Business Administration, Imam Abdulrahman Bin Faisal University, Saudi Arabia. He is a multidisciplinary scholar and an astute administrator. He earned a BSc in Politics, Philosophy and Economics (PPE) and an MSc in Political Science from the prestigious Obafemi Awolowo University, Nigeria. He holds a Doctoral degree in Public Policy from the University of KwaZulu-Natal (UKZN), Howard College, South Africa. He was also at North West University in South Africa as Postdoctoral Research Fellow. His research fields include Public Policy, Research Methods, Gender Issues, Political Economy, Public

Administration & Finance, Indigenous Knowledge, Democratic Governance and Sustainable Development.

Olatunji, Olabimpe Ajoke, PhD is a lecturer at the Federal University, Oye-Ekiti, Ekiti State, Nigeria. She holds a PhD degree in Developmental Psychology. She served as the Head of Department of Psychology between year 2016 and 2018. Her research interest spans the developmental period of adolescents (teenagers, youth, and emerging adults) emphasizing on the biological and socio–emotional processes that interacts with adolescents' development. Her research also focuses on some collaborative research in the area of adulthood (early, mid, and late adult life) development. The importance of gender issues, particularly women and the psychosocial factors surrounding them is of utmost concern in her research.

Oloba, Olusola, PhD, is currently the Agriculture and Agribusiness Coordinator of the National Action Committee on African Continental Free Trade Area (AfCFTA) in Nigeria. Before this time, Oloba was a Post-Doc Fellow with the Department of Political Studies and International relations, North West University, South Africa where he specialised in the Political Economy of Food Politics and Policies. He has published in many recognised academic journals and contributed to chapters in edited books. He is a graduate of the Obafemi Awolowo University where he received his PhD in Economics.

Oluwatoyin, Olajide Christina is a Junior Research Fellow at the Centre for Gender and Social Policy Studies (CGSPS), Obafemi Awolowo University, Ile-Ife, Nigeria. In this role, she supports and contributes to the research and teaching mandate of the institution. Oluwatoyin holds an LLM in International Human Rights Law from the University of Essex, United Kingdom and has built a global career in international development by working with international organizations focused on gender equality in the UK, Senegal, and Nigeria. Oluwatoyin's research interests are geared towards the exploration of how women's human rights can deliver tangible benefits. This has led her to publish on the torture dimension of certain gender-based practices within the framework of international human rights law, women's right to work, and sexual harassment as well as its interconnectedness with the Sustainable Development Goals. She has also researched on a myriad of topics within the gender and development domain including feminist organising, adolescent girls' agency, women's leadership, and patriarchal bargains. Oluwatoyin sits on the board of an NGO working in Lagos slums to reduce inequalities among vulnerable groups. She has also developed organizational gender and sexual harassment policies. She is a member of the British Red Cross, Development Studies Association, and a volunteer with the Women at Risk Foundation.

Omodunbi, Olumide is a Graduate of Political Science and International Relations of Osun State University Osogbo, Osun State. He also holds a Master of Science degree in Political Science from Obafemi Awolowo University Ile-Ife, Osun State, Nigeria. Olumide Omodunbi is currently affiliated with the Department of Political Sciences, Osun State University as lecturer. His research interest includes Conflict, Terrorism, Insurgency and Nigeria government and Politics.

Orisadare, Monica Adele, PhD is a Senior Lecturer in the Department of Economics, Obafemi Awolowo University, Ile-Ife, Nigeria where she obtained a PhD, MSc, and BSc in Economics. She also holds a Certificate in e-Learning Design and Facilitation from the Open Polytechnic, New Zealand. She is the current Acting Director at the Centre for Gender and Social Policy Studies, Obafemi Awolowo University, Ile-Ife, Nigeria. She is also the current Editor in Chief of the African Journal of Gender and Development. Her research area is in Gender, Development Economics and Public Finance, where she has published widely in reputable international journals. She is a member of both national and international associations, among which are Nigerian Economics Society (NES), Organisation for Women in Science for Developing World (OWSDW), African Econometrics Society (AES). International Association of Feminist Economics (IAFFE), Association for the Advancement of African Women Economists (AAAWE), International Political Science Association (IPSA), International Sociological Association (ISA) and Development Studies Association.

Osunsina, I.O.O. PhD is an Associate Professor in the Department of Forestry and Wildlife Management, Federal University of Agriculture, Abeokuta. He obtained a Bachelor's degree in Forestry and Wildlife

Management, Master of Wildlife Ecology and Management and Doctor of Philosophy (Ph.D) Wildlife Management. He also obtained Postgraduate Diploma, Urban Management Tool in Climate Change, Erasmus University, Rotterdam, The Netherlands. He is involved in teaching and Supervision of both undergraduate and postgraduate students. His research focus is in the area of Wildlife Extension and Management, Natural Resources Management, Biodiversity Conservation and Climate Change. He is currently the Deputy Director of the World Bank Centre of Excellence in Agricultural Development and Sustainable Environment (CEADESE). He is a member of Wildlife Society of Nigeria (WISON).

Oyeleke, O. O., PhD is an Associate Professor in the Department of Ecotourism and Wildlife Management of the Federal University of Technology, Akure, Nigeria. She holds a PhD degree in Wildlife Management from the Federal University of Technology, Akure, Nigeria. She has been involved in research projects on protected area and habitat management in Nigeria National Parks. Her research interests are currently focused on protected area management, animal ecology, ecological tourism, and sustainable management of wildlife resources. She previously worked in the Federal College of Wildlife Management, New Bussa (under Forestry Research Institute of Nigeria) where she was involved in training middle-level manpower in sustainable management of wildlife resources. She is a member of the Wildlife Society of Nigeria (WISON) where she serves as the pioneer National Treasurer of the Society. She is also the National Public Relations Officer of the Organization for Women in Science for the Developing World (OWSD). She currently serves as one of the consultants to Arcane Global Limited on Wildlife Hazard Assessments of International Airports in Nigeria.

Shai, Kutullo Nick is an emerging scholar of indigenous knowledge systems, at the faculty of Natural and Agricultural Sciences at North West University. He has a bachelor's degree and Master's degree of Indigenous Knowledge Systems. The researcher conducted an ethno-botanical survey of wild fruits collected and eaten in three villages in Mpumalanga Province, South Africa, and examined how these locally sourced ingredients continue to play an important role in the Mapulana people's daily lives. The described fruit species, according to the scholar, have the potential to be a significant alternative food source to help meet the dietary requirements and health needs of communities, especially those in remote rural areas. His favourite place to do research is his home village which has an abundance of plant species. A manuscript was published with Foods 2020, 9, 1581.The researcher presented at the following conferences; 45th Annual SAAB, AMA & SASSB Joint Congress, 8 -11 January 2019, University of Johannesburg, Gauteng Province, South Africa; Indigenous Plant Use Forum 22nd Annual Conference, 7-10 July 2019, Tshipise, Limpopo Province, South Africa; 46th SAAB Annual Conference, 7-10 January 2020, University of Free State (UFS) QwaQwa campus, Free State Province, South Africa.

Titus, Utibe Monday is a PhD candidate with the Department of Political Science, Usmanu Danfodiyo University, Sokoto, Nigeria. His area of interest includes International Relations, Political Theory, Research Methods, Conflicts and Development Studies. He has published with local and international journals. His recent publications include Causes of Violent Agitations in the Niger Delta Region, Political Parties, Politicians and Political Mobilization in Nigeria, Domestic Terrorism in Nigeria, Insurgency and State Response in Nigeria. He is currently working on Corruption and Infrastructural Development in Nigeria's Niger Delta Region.

www.ingramcontent.com/pod-product-compliance
Ingram Content Group UK Ltd.
Pitfield, Milton Keynes, MK11 3LW, UK
UKHW041133071026
15587UKWH00009B/457

9 781804 410509